HARMONISATION IN EU ENVIRONMENTAL AND ENERGY LAW

HARMONISATION IN EU ENVIRONMENTAL AND ENERGY LAW

Edited by
Bernard Vanheusden
Theodoros Iliopoulos
Anna Vanhellemont

INTERSENTIA
Cambridge – Antwerp – Chicago

Intersentia Ltd
8 Wellington Mews
Wellington Street | Cambridge
CB1 1HW | United Kingdom
Tel: +44 1223 736 170
Email: mail@intersentia.co.uk
www.intersentia.com | www.intersentia.co.uk

Distribution for the UK and
Rest of the World (incl. Eastern Europe)
NBN International
1 Deltic Avenue, Rooksley
Milton Keynes MK13 8LD
United Kingdom
Tel: +44 1752 202 301 | Fax: +44 1752 202 331
Email: orders@nbninternational.com

Distribution for Europe
Lefebvre Sarrut Belgium NV
Hoogstraat 139/6
1000 Brussels
Belgium
Tel: +32 (0)800 39 067
Email: mail@intersentia.be

Distribution for the USA and Canada
Independent Publishers Group
Order Department
814 North Franklin Street
Chicago, IL 60610
USA
Tel: +1 800 888 4741 (toll free) | Fax: +1 312 337 5985
Email: orders@ipgbook.com

Harmonisation in EU Environmental and Energy Law

Artwork on cover: Image licensed by Ingram Image

ISBN 978-1-83970-163-4
D/2022/7849/8
NUR 828

British Library Cataloguing in Publication Data. A catalogue record for this book is available from the British Library.

FOREWORD

1. INTRODUCTION

After nearly fifty years of EU environmental law-making, the discussion on codification and harmonization is not only more relevant than ever, but it is also unavoidable for at least three reasons:

1) The increase of legislation across very different thematic areas/sectors – water, nature, air, waste and chemicals; often leading to a certain dispersion of legal instruments.
2) The volume of legislation (in the order of 50 main legal instruments) which needs to be effectively enforced.
3) The use of very different kinds of instruments and approaches over time (directives, regulations, decisions).

The Commission is working hard in ensuring the overall coherence when *developing* and *evaluating* legislation.

Let me address these matters further.

2. DEVELOPING LEGISLATION

1) In the field of environmental policy, it is important to note the key role of Environmental Action Plans (EAPs) since 1973 in outlining the priorities of the EU legislative agenda for five-year periods.

   We are now on our 7th EAP and have tabled our proposal for an 8th EAP under Art. 192 (3) of the Treaty. Environmental Action Plans are adopted through the co-decision procedure by the Council and the European Parliament.
2) The Treaty, of course, plays a very significant role, in particular its Environment Chapter (Articles 191 and 192 TFEU) frames the level of ambition and steers EU action forward by means of certain basic principles.

   The Chapter, introduced in 1987, was in part a Treaty codification of what was endorsed in earlier action plans. The first action plan in 1973 already announced the polluter pays principle. The action plans themselves are mentioned in Article 192(3).
3) Significant initiatives developing new "concepts" have contributed to greater EU harmonization in this area. The Circular Economy or the recent

European Green Deal, are very good examples in moving forward our environmental policy.

3. EVALUATING AND REVIEWING LEGISLATION

Codification has already taken place at the level of most EU environmental individual instruments. This means integrating amendments and streamlining legal texts.

From the 1990s on, serious consolidation has occurred within several thematic areas. Let me mention some very concrete cases:

- In 2001, The adoption of the Water Framework Directive allowed the repealing of several earlier directives;
- In 2008, the Air Quality Directive created a comprehensive legal framework for controlling individual air pollutants;
- In 2011, with the Industrial Emissions Directive it was possible to codify and replace several more specific directives.

Over the past 10 years, the introduction of systematic evaluations (better known as fitness checks) of existing legislation under the Better Regulation initiative is also a very significant development. These look at the efficiency, effectiveness, relevance, coherence and EU added value of our legislation.

Environment has been a front-runner in this area, with 13% of legislation already evaluated by the end of 2013. The figure currently stands at around 60%. This has included very high-profile evaluations like the Nature Fitness Check, where more than 550,000 citizens participated in the public consultation. Evaluations do not necessarily mean re-writing legislation, but they steer the Commission in new directions. For example: the fitness check of reporting across our legislation is stimulating a much greater emphasis on transparency at national level.

4. IMPLEMENTATION

Implementation has often tended to be the "Cinderella" of the policy cycle.[1] However, here too the Commission seeks greater coherence:

1) Through the Environmental Implementation Review, we now provide a regular EU-wide "big picture" of implementation across all environmental legal instruments in all Member States.

---

[1] "Cinderella" was the poor daughter of the family and was badly treated. Implementation should not be neglected.

2) In 2018, the Commission created a new Environmental Compliance and Governance Forum to bring together top national administrators as well as heads of networks of environmental agencies, inspectors, police, prosecutors and judges.

   The initiative aims at achieving a more harmonized approach to tackling on the ground serious issues like environmental crime, enhancing coordination and developing effective responses.

Of course, this is without prejudice to the work of the Commission as a guardian of the Treaties. Environment is one of the areas with the highest number of complaints and cases brought forward by the Commission against the Member States for breach of EU law.

5. FUTURE PERSPECTIVES

On the basis of the above considerations, it can be concluded that a lot has been done in order to ensure that environmental legislation is not only fit for purpose, but also effectively enforced and implemented by Member States.

The question is: What more can be done?

In this context, it is important to have a global and not simply an EU perspective.

Environmental issues are global issues because the environment cannot be limited by administrative frontiers. Global warming will never be solved by Europe on its own, neither will the pollution problems of plastics in the oceans nor the collapse of nature. We therefore need to be outward-looking and outward-thinking. Europe has been leading multilateral negotiations in the field of climate biodiversity. The Treaty of Paris would not have been concluded without the active leadership of the EU.

Europe needs to support initiatives to create a more harmonized approach *globally*. This is also the philosophy behind the European Green Deal: the transformative agenda put forward by President von der Leyen to facilitate the ecological transition. The European Commission is currently also backing the idea of a *global pact* on the environment.[2] If adopted, this would codify the key principles of environmental law and put environmental protection on a better footing everywhere.

2 See https://globalpactenvironment.org/en/the-pact/.

Environmental issues are increasingly of great concern for both citizens and Member States. The need to act more effectively will not diminish in the coming years. Europe has the responsibility and the means to lead this action by projecting its internal policies globally.

Daniel Calleja Crespo
Director General, European Commission
Brussels, June 2021

CONTENTS

LIST OF CASES

SUPRANATIONAL

COURT OF JUSTICE OF THE EUROPEAN UNION

EUROPEAN COURT OF HUMAN RIGHTS

EUROPEAN OMBUDSMAN

NATIONAL

BELGIUM

GREECE

Decisions of Court of Cassation

THE NETHERLANDS

Council of State (the Netherlands)

UK

LIST OF CONTRIBUTORS

Daniel Benrath
Postdoctoral Assistant in Energy Law, Ruhr University Bochum, Germany

Nicolas de Sadeleer
Professor of EU law, Saint Louis University, United States

Costanza Di Francesco Maesa
Professor of Law and Biotechnology at the University of Siena, teaching assistant, under the direction of Professor Massimiliano Montini, in Advanced European Law and Sustainable Development Law at the University of Siena and post-doctoral researcher at the University of Florence

Michael Faure
Professor of Comparative and International Environmental Law, Maastricht University, and Professor of Comparative Private Law and Economics, Erasmus School of Law Rotterdam, the Netherlands

Matteo Fermeglia
Assistant Professor of International and European Environmental Law, University of Hasselt, Belgium

Susann Handke
Independent Researcher, specialised in energy and climate law and governance, the Netherlands

Alison Hough
Senior Lecturer, Faculty of Business and Hospitality, Midlands Campus, Technological University of the Shannon (TUS), Athlone, County Westmeath, Ireland

Theodoros G. Iliopoulos
Postdoctoral researcher in Energy and Environmental Law, Hasselt University, Belgium

Valentina Jacometti
Associate Professor of Comparative Private Law, University of Insubria, Italy

Georgios Kalogerakis
Doctoral Candidate in Civil Law, National and Kapodistrian University of Athens, Greece

Ludwig Krämer
Head of unit of the Environmental Department of the European Commission (retired)

Anna Vanhellemont
Doctoral researcher in Environmental Law at Hasselt University, Belgium

Elien Verniers
Doctoral Candidate in Environmental Law, specialising in Animal Law, Ghent University, Belgium

INTRODUCTION

Anna VANHELLEMONT*

Following the 2019 conference titled 'Harmonisation in environmental and energy law', 13 contributors offer a unique perspective on the topic of harmonisation from their fields of expertise. With a critical mindset, the authors discuss a variety of issues reaching from more general harmonisation concepts and processes to harmonising specific pieces of environmental and energy law. Throughout the book, an overview of the current state of the law is supplemented with a look into the future, proposing ways forward and presenting different harmonising solutions for the problems raised.

1. THE 2019 CONFERENCE

Within the context of celebrating its 10th anniversary, the Law Faculty of Hasselt University, together with several other Belgian universities and the European Environmental Law Forum, organised an international conference on harmonisation in environmental and energy law, which took place on 28 and 29 March 2019. The conference was chaired by Professor Bernard Vanheusden. During two very rewarding days, the Environmental Law Unit of the Research Centre for Government and Law (CORe) was pleased to host around 70 academics, practitioners and policy-makers from all over Europe. This book contains the written account of several of the thought-provoking presentations of the 2019 conference. However, current developments that have emerged since then were also incorporated into the contributions.[1]

---

* Doctoral researcher in Environmental Law at Hasselt University, Belgium.

1 The contributions were finalised in March 2021.

Environmental legislation is often incoherent and fragmented, causing hurdles to its application and enforcement. In this regard, rule-makers resort to harmonisation. Harmonisation is seen as referring to a number of techniques and instruments that all aim to clarify rules and create a more coherent and solid legal framework. The main aim of the conference was to examine the merits of harmonisation – without overlooking potential problems – and ask critical questions to spur fundamental discussions. The rather broad topic of harmonisation in environmental and energy law was selected because it fits with research currently being conducted in the Environmental Law Unit on internal harmonisation of environmental law, considering, for example, the possibility of an EU Environmental Code.

Besides five keynote speeches from renowned academics and the Director-General of the Directorate-General (DG) for the Environment of the European Commission, 33 other researchers in the field of environmental and energy law shared their findings during five parallel sessions. These sessions were organised in four tracks, covering the topics of harmonisation theory, harmonisation techniques, harmonisation in environmental law and harmonisation in energy law. Presenters were first invited to elaborate on their selected topic, while afterwards other participants had the opportunity to ask questions and give remarks during a short panel debate.

The book before you includes 13 contributions, tackling topics that were discussed during the conference. However, it also stands alone as a reference book on harmonisation in environmental and energy law, covering recent evolutions, general questions and future perspectives.

2. PART I: HARMONISATION THEORY AND TECHNIQUES

In the first section of the book, several authors reflect on harmonisation theory and techniques. Considering legislative developments and best practices, the opportunities and obstacles for further harmonisation of environmental and energy law at the EU level are examined.

In the first chapter, titled 'To codify or not to codify EU environmental law: That is not the question', Michael Faure approaches the topic of codification from a law and economics standpoint. He proclaims that although an environmental code may lower search costs for the public and stakeholders, it will not necessarily entail lower transaction costs as a whole. Harmonisation of legislation may not be costless, and (environmental) lawyers may have an interest in keeping the law non-transparent and complex in order to increase job security and their market value. Furthermore, Faure investigates how many EU Member States actually codified their environmental legislation and whether this has improved environmental quality. Although most Member States have an Environmental Protection Act in place, which is supplemented by sectoral legislation, and five Member States even have a comprehensive Environmental Code, it is impossible to measure if these 'codified' Member States are in fact 'better'. This poses a reversed causality problem: did the Member States with high levels of environmental protection introduce a code? Or did the codification of environmental law in these Member States lead to a higher level of environmental protection? Furthermore, the absence of an environmental code does not entail bad environmental quality per se. Looking at the EU level, Faure considers that an Environmental Code undoubtedly offers benefits on paper. However, there are far more fundamental problems in environmental law that cannot be countered solely with textual changes. Faure thus concludes that without any fundamental changes, there is a danger that a codification of EU environmental law remains yet another paper operation without proven potential to improve environmental quality in the EU.

Ludwig Krämer takes a more detailed view on the topic in his chapter titled 'Possibilities of and limits to codification of EU environmental law'. Illustrating the existing discrepancies between environmental legislation, Krämer looks into the different reporting obligations for Member States, which range from one to six years. He considers several possibilities for codifying environmental law, concluding that codification may be possible for procedures, but not for substantial environmental law. Furthermore, the question of subsidiarity is posed: is codification of environmental law at the EU level necessary? Other hurdles are the absence of political will to codify environmental law, both from Member States and EU institutions, and the problem of lacking transparency. Concluding his chapter, Krämer puts forth the introduction of an EU Environmental Agency with enforcement powers as a 'maximum scenario'. Another option is to turn the 2019 Reporting Regulation into a useful instrument to achieve transparency. Moreover, the need for EU enforcement in environmental cases is stressed, but again a lack of political will from the Member States is expected.

A more general overview of harmonisation in environmental policy is provided by Nicolas de Sadeleer. He explores several key issues arising in the harmonisation process of environmental rules, focusing on different topics throughout the discussion. This comprehensive contribution looks at drivers of EU environmental policy, legal bases upon which environmental measures can be adopted and the remaining challenges and hurdles to overcome in seeking out common ground between the Member States. Finally, a number of EU harmonisation measures are discussed, offering a more practical perspective on the matter.

Valentina Jacometti also takes a practical approach to the matter of harmonisation and its relation to European multilingualism. The multilingual character of EU law inevitably leads to terminology issues, which especially affects effective harmonisation of environmental legislation in the Member States.

Due to terminological inconsistencies, contradictions and lacking definitions, much discretion is left to national law-makers, which leads to divergent outcomes in the national legal practices. This evidently hinders the process of harmonisation of environmental law. Jacometti illustrates these problems with several clear case studies.

Adopting a different point of view, Anna Vanhellemont looks into the concept of internal harmonisation of environmental law, asking the question whether lessons can be learned from the Member States when harmonising the body of EU environmental law. Internal harmonisation does not concern the approximation of laws between different legal systems, but focuses on one legal system or one branch of law. In this case, it entails resolving incoherencies within the body of environmental law in a coordinated and integrated manner. The development of environmental legislation in three Member States is scrutinised, ultimately questioning whether these processes may be transposed to the supranational level. Potential ways forward are discussed, including necessary future steps in the research of internal harmonisation in EU environmental law.

In her contribution, Alison Hough discusses the doctrine of consistent interpretation as an important tool for harmonising environmental law across the different bodies and institutions of the EU and its Member States. She focuses on access to justice before the Court of Justice of the EU under article 9(3) of the Aarhus Convention, extensively considering and citing relevant case law. This discussion brings up an evident threat to the harmonious application of the Aarhus principles, undermining the integrity of EU law, as well as the Aarhus Convention and its compliance mechanism.

In the last chapter in this general part, Costanza Di Francesco Maesa looks into the actual merits of harmonising environmental laws. She asks the important question of whether harmonisation can in fact resolve current shortcomings of the environmental enforcement system, or whether it merely has symbolic value. In a look forward, additional measures are suggested that may supplement the current practice of adopting harmonised rules.

3. PART II: HARMONISATION IN ENVIRONMENTAL LAW

The second part of the book contains three contributions tackling several environmental topics. Going more into specifics, these chapters look at harmonisation in the field of soil and climate change, treatment of wild animals and the possibility to adopt civil law tools to harmonise environmental civil liability law.

Sustainable soil and land management has an important function in tackling climate change, due to soil playing a crucial role both as a source and sink of greenhouse gases. In his contribution, Matteo Fermeglia discusses the EU regime on soil organic carbon. He uncovers a highly inconsistent patchwork of policy and regulation that is not up to par in terms of ensuring effective protection of soils. Fermeglia presents other available methodologies for addressing soils' climate change functions and proposes solutions to reach an adequate level of coordination and integration between the different levels of soil and law policy from a climate change mitigation perspective.

Elien Verniers dives into the topic of EU species protection law, analysing the legal regimes and case law to illustrate the great differences in treatment of wild animals. She reflects on the underlying motivations and the impact of this difference in treatment from several points of view. Finally, she poses the question of whether more harmonisation could be a solution, both within the domain of species protection and between animal welfare law and species protection law. Practical solutions are put forth, and further harmonisation is overall encouraged.

In the last chapter of the section, Georgios Kalogerakis stresses the importance of civil law for the protection of the environment. Scrutinising the general duty of care and the right to personality, he examines whether environmental civil liability law can be harmonised through the tools of civil law. In this discussion, he considers both case law from the European Court of Human Rights and a national perspective from Greece. Kalogerakis concludes that the value of civil law should not be underestimated in the legal protection of the environment, deeming it even more effective in some cases than specific provisions of environmental law.

4. PART III: HARMONISATION IN ENERGY LAW

In the third section of the book, three very concrete topics in the field of energy law are discussed. From a harmonisation viewpoint, the EU low-carbon power transition; Europeanisation and harmonisation of renewable energy support law; and hydrogen and carbon capture and storage (H_2-CCS) chains are explored.

Susann Handke proposes that the low-carbon transition requires harmonisation across several fields of law because of its multifaceted nature. To achieve this, she argues that oversight mechanisms have to be put into place. Handke goes deeper into the State Grid to illustrate the harmonising efforts of governance structures that guide the EU low-carbon power transition. Central to her argument is the notion that oversight of sustainability, energy justice and third-party investment is vital in this evolution.

Theodoros Iliopoulos calls attention to the recent developments in renewable energy support law. He analyses the novelties in the field brought about by the recast Renewable Energy Directive 2018/2001 and assesses them against the concepts of Europeanisation and harmonisation. Iliopoulos argues that

Europeanisation and harmonisation are not poles apart. Instead, the latest phases of the process of Europeanisation have already resulted in an embryonic harmonisation and have paved the way for further harmonisation in the future.

In the final chapter, Daniel Benrath goes into the relevant legislation governing H_2-CCS chains. Although there is currently no specific EU law addressing this topic, it can be situated in the fields of the natural gas market and renewable energy harmonisation, trans-European networks and emission trading. In his contribution, Benrath focusses on lacunae and blind spots in EU energy law with regards to the cross-border transport of CO_2, hydrogen in networks and existing schemes of guarantees of origin and emission trading. Finally, reflections on how EU law can be further developed to fill in these gaps are presented.

PART I

HARMONISATION THEORY AND TECHNIQUE

TO CODIFY OR NOT TO CODIFY EU ENVIRONMENTAL LAW

That is not the Question

Michael FAURE*

1. INTRODUCTION

It is striking that this book puts harmonisation and codification in environmental and energy law again on the agenda. At first blush that may seem surprising. Looking at the literature one can easily see that the codification of environmental law was an issue that was high on the agenda in the last decade of the previous century. A team around the famous Ghent Professor Hubert Bocken devoted an entire conference to the codification of environmental law and dedicated a book to that topic.[1] But that conference took place on 21–22 February 1995, more than 25 years ago.

---

* Michael Faure is Professor of comparative and international environmental law at Maastricht University and Professor of comparative private law and economics at Erasmus School of Law Rotterdam. I am grateful to Belén Bernal Ordóñez (Maastricht University) for assistance with research.

1 *Bocken, H. & Ryckbost, D.* (eds.), Codification of Environmental Law, Proceedings of the International Conference, The Hague, Kluwer Law International, 1996.

The popularity of a codification of environmental law in that period can partially be explained by the fact that environmental law had emerged as a rather scattered body of various sectoral laws that in many countries was spread over a wide variety of different statutes and regulations. It can therefore be understood that codification, in the sense of bringing together all existing environmental legislation in one legislative document, was popular in that period. It was popular in academia,[2] but the concept of codification was also popular at the policy level; in many European Member States some harmonised environmental law had been introduced[3] or was at least discussed.[4] Already in that period the objectives of codification were discussed whereby a distinction was made between, on the one hand, a simple bringing together of existing environmental laws into one legislative document and, on the other hand, a more substantive operation whereby, for example, procedures and enforcement would also become harmonised. The first type of operation is more a coordination of existing environmental law and could be qualified as a restatement, which mostly provides esthetical benefits and the benefit of easier access to the contents of environmental law. This type of coordination was described by Gilhuis as a middle point between the totally segregated sectoral environmental legislation, which still existed in many Member States at that time, and fully integrated harmonised environmental law.[5] Codification was considered also a more substantive exercise, assuming that it would go beyond a restatement of existing laws, but would also harmonise (and thereby improve) permitting, standard-setting and enforcement procedures.[6] Interestingly, the current wave of interest in harmonisation and codification is not so much related to the codification within the EU Member States, but is rather addressed at the EU level itself. Indeed, whereas the harmonisation and codification operations which took place in Member State law approximately 25 years ago have to a large extent led to more streamlined legislation within the Member States, European environmental law has not yet gone through a similar process. And the fact that EU environmental law has to a large extent been developed in a rather haphazard, ad hoc manner justifies the question of whether a similar operation might be useful at the EU level, as well.

---

2 See for example the many contributions to the book by Bocken & Ryckbost cited in the previous footnote, but also *Lavrijsen, L.*, 'The Cofidication of Flemish Environmental Law', *European Environmental Law Review*, 1999, 230–233 as well as *Faure, M.G.*, 'The Harmonisation, Codification and Integration of Environmental Law: A Search for Definitions', *European Environmental Law Review*, 2000, 174–182.

3 Such as, for example, in Sweden, the Flemish Region in Belgium, Denmark, the United Kingdom.

4 Such as, for example, in Germany.

5 *Gilhuis, P.C.*, 'De integratie van de milieuwetgeving in de WABM: een zinvolle onderneming?', in *Eijlander, Ph. et al.* (eds.), *Milieu als wetgevingsvraagstuk*, Zwolle, Tjeenk Willink, 1991, 57.

6 Faure, *supra* n. 2, 176.

This chapter aims to contribute to this debate by focusing on some of the history of the codification at the Member State level, thereby examining whether there is some scope for learning as far as a potential codification at the EU level is concerned. The second section will therefore examine the original reasons behind the codification operations that took place at the Member State level, by examining the arguments advanced in favour of codification in legal doctrine. That may shed some light on the expectations concerning the beneficial effects of codification. In addition to this legal analysis it is equally interesting to search for economic arguments that may support the codification operation as it took place within the Member States (section 3). The question equally arises to what extent Member States did indeed follow the advice of either codifying or at least harmonising their environmental legislation (section 4). Obviously the question can also be asked as to what extent the codification of environmental law has any relationship with the improvement of environmental legislation or even environmental quality (section 5). After this focus on the developments at the Member State level, we turn to the EU level showing the wild development of EU environmental law (section 6) and the attempts undertaken so far in EU environmental law towards coordination (section 7). The question then arises as to whether the arguments that justified the codification of environmental law within the Member States at that time could also support a similar codification exercise at the EU level (section 8), turning again to an economic perspective arguing that more EU environmental law may be urgently needed (section 9). However, the chapter will conclude by arguing that, as the title suggests, the crucial question is not whether we should codify EU environmental law, as there are more urgent and pressing issues that need to be tackled in order to improve the quality of EU environmental law (section 10).

This chapter therefore does not aim to provide final answers concerning the questions of whether and – if so – which domains of EU environmental law should be further coordinated or even codified; it rather aims to contribute towards agenda-setting concerning this fascinating topic by providing a historical sketch of the codification of environmental law within Member States, as well as an economic perspective concerning the role of EU environmental law.

2. WHY CODIFY?

As already mentioned in the introduction, in the heat of the debate concerning codification, 25 years ago, there were high expectations, at least in environmental legal doctrine, concerning the potential benefits of that codification. A few quotations can illustrate that optimism, as well as the objectives that codification aimed to accomplish.

Rehbinder, for example, sees substantial ecological benefits from codification. He holds:

> A codification is not only a legal technical process, but rather the expression of a political will towards better environmental protection. Codification, through its rationalisation effect, would, or at least could, improve voluntary compliance, public access to environmental law, environmental awareness as well as public enforcement.[7]

Another well-known German scholar, Kloepfer, points at four aims of codification, being:

1. ecological progress;
2. harmonisation and clarification;
3. improvement of implementation;
4. more consistency in environmental legislation.[8]

These arguments underscore the fact that codification was at the time especially considered as an important reaction against the (then) strongly sectoral environmental legislation. This can also be noticed from another quotation from Rehbinder:

> Codification could to a certain degree also overcome the traditional, but – at least partly – dysfunctional, sectoral approach by adopting a new transsectoral concept of environmental regulation. Most environmental laws do not apply to the environment as a whole, but rather to specific environmental sectors, specific sources of pollution of specific substances; in particular, they do not normally adequately consider a transfer of pollution from one sector to another, nor do they consider total pollution burdens. An ecological development of environmental law through codification using stronger holistic elements could improve the steering capacity of environmental law. Although it does not appear to be possible to entirely renounce sectoral regulation, codification could at least overcome the traditional fragmentation of environmental law and reconcile transsectoral and sectoral approaches to environmental regulation.[9]

It is striking that the idea of codification of environmental law receives so much support from German scholars, but that various attempts towards codification in Germany (the most recent being in 2009) all failed. The so-called

[7] *Rehbinder, E.*, 'Points of Reference for a Codification of National Environmental Law', in *Bocken, H. & Ryckbost, D.* (eds.), Codification of Environmental Law, Proceedings of the International Conference, The Hague, Kluwer Law International, 1996, 159.

[8] *Kloepfer, M.*, 'On the Codification of German Environmental Law', in *Bocken, H. & Ryckbost, D.* (eds.), Codification of Environmental Law, Proceedings of the International Conference, The Hague, Kluwer Law International, 1996, 91.

[9] Rehbinder, *supra* n. 7, 159–160.

Umweltgesetzbuch never saw the light. Various reasons are advanced to explain the failure of these codification attempts in Germany. Most of these arguments relate to constitutional barriers linked to the powers of the federal government in the fields of nature protection and water and the lack of an agreement among the federal government, the *Länder* and the stakeholders.[10] Moreover, it was argued that German industry might have lobbied against the environmental code as fragmented legislation may make it easier for industry to keep environmental standards low.[11] The idea of codification also received support from legal doctrine in other legal systems, such as, for example, from the well-known French environmental lawyer Martin. In his chapter to the book on *Codification of Environmental Law*, he presents several arguments in favour of an environmental code:

1. Higher quality and effectiveness of the environmental provisions in this form, giving shape to environmental principles.
2. More accuracy, certainty and coherence of environmental law: the code would put together rules with different origins and different periods, resolving contradictions, removing repetitions, ambiguities and dissipation.
3. Codification as a way to limit the effects of the 'contemporary flurry of legislation' and providing stability. In words of the author 'codification could initially discourage the uncontrolled production of rules which rapidly become pointless except for keeping civil servants busy'.
4. Codification can be an opportunity to make law understandable by practitioners and improve the democratic debate.[12]

In sum, one can notice that the legal literature at the time was quite optimistic concerning the potential benefits of codification. On the one hand it was argued that bringing together all acts within one document would simplify the accessibility and implementation of environmental law by providing more consistency than the traditional sectoral approach. But at the same time it was also expected that codification would have an important symbolic function and could lead to ecological progress.

---

10 See in that respect, *inter alia*, *Gabriel, S.*, 'The Failure of the Environmental Code – A Retrospective', *Environmental Policy and Law*, 2009, Vol. 39(3), 174–176.

11 This is suggested in contributions in *Federal Environmental Agency*, Article from the Federal Environmental Agency (2018), https://www.umweltbundesamt.de/en/environmental-code-0#textpart-1; *German Environment Agency*, An Environmental Code: Unifying German environmental law (2019), https://www.oeko.de/en/research-consultancy/issues/environmental-policy-and-environmental-law/an-environmental-code-unifying-german-environmental-law/.

12 *Martin, G.J.*, 'French Experiences of the Codification of Environmental Law', in *Bocken, H. & Ryckbost, D.* (eds.), Codification of Environmental Law, Proceedings of the International Conference, The Hague, Kluwer Law International, 1996, 117–118.

3. ECONOMIC ARGUMENTS IN FAVOUR OF CODIFICATION

Potential benefits of codification can be addressed not only from a legal perspective, but equally from an economic perspective. To some extent the legal arguments in favour of codification could be 'translated' as economic arguments as well. For example, the expectations that codification could create more accuracy and provide the opportunity to make the law more understandable and accessible in practice would amount to the economic argument that bringing law together in one document would lower search costs for the public at large and for the stakeholders involved, and therefore might lower information costs concerning the applicable rules. The arguments concerning the lowering of information costs can, moreover, also be combined with an argument concerning better compliance. In other words, if codification leads to the contents of legal rules being more accessible for stakeholders (those who would have to apply the law), then this could also guarantee a better compliance with the rule. From an economic perspective, this means that it would contribute to the law realising its economic objective of correcting the market failure related to the negative externalities from environmental pollution.

It is equally tempting to argue that bringing all documents together into one would lower administrative or transaction costs. In that respect, one must, however, be careful. After all, that argument would assume too easily that codification as such would be a costless exercise. In reality the costs of bringing all types of different legal rules that have emerged over a long period of time in different contexts together into one document may not be a costless exercise at all. It should therefore be clear that the benefits of codification outweigh the potential costs of codification itself. Moreover, a potential danger of codification is that a code would too easily be considered as 'the bible' of environmental law, which would, in other words, jeopardise any changes to a document that has come together after so many efforts. If that were the case, codification would have the disadvantage that it would become a static document, insufficiently able to dynamically adapt to changing circumstances.

Finally, Anthony Ogus argues that (environmental) lawyers and other professionals may have an interest in keeping a particular complexity in regulation, as this will guarantee a demand for their services.[13] Lawyers generally may strive to keep the law complex and not transparent. Those barriers to accessing legal rules may be in the interest of the legal profession. Fully transparent and simple legal rules would reduce the demand for legal services. That argument could

[13] *Ogus, A.*, 'Competition between National Legal Systems: A Contribution of Economic Analysis to Comparative Law', *International & Comparative Law Quarterly*, 1999, Vol. 48(2), 405–418.

theoretically explain why among some circles there could be opposition against codification to the extent that it would lead to simplification and a reduced demand for legal services. Whether this type of lobbying against simplification of legal rules via codification has effectively taken place within particular legal systems is, of course, an empirical issue.

4. HAS THE PATIENT FOLLOWED THE DOCTOR'S ORDERS?[14]

In the following, we provide an overview of the attempts at codification in the various EU Member States. For each Member State, we will indicate whether, to the best of our knowledge, an attempt has been made at codification or harmonisation, or whether that is not the case. The date of the harmonising efforts will be mentioned, and a distinction will be made between a true environmental code, on the one hand, and coordination via an environmental protection act, on the other. Even though the name may differ, both usually aim for the same goal. Codification is in some cases more comprehensive in that it at least aims to bring together all available environmental legislation in one document, whereas an environmental protection act may lay down unified procedures concerning, for example, licensing, instruments and enforcement, in addition to sectoral legislation.[15]

Table 1. Codification of environmental law in EU Member States

Country	Codification or other harmonising act	Date
Austria	No	
Belgium	*Flanders* Decree on general environmental policy	1995
	Wallonia Environmental code	2004
	Brussels Code on inspection (…) environmental offences	1999
Bulgaria	EPA + sectoral	
Croatia	EPA + sectoral	2013
Cyprus	No	
Czech Republic	No	

(continued)

14 Paraphrasing the title of the article by *Hahn, R.W.*, 'Economic Prescriptions for Environmental Problems: How the Patient Followed the Doctor's Orders', *Journal of Economic Perspectives*, 1989, Vol. 3(2), 95–114.

15 This table was created through the appreciated research assistance by Belén Bernal Ordóñez (Maastricht).

Table 1 *continued*

Country	Codification or other harmonising act	Date
Denmark	EPA + implementation orders	2016
Estonia	Env. Code	2014
Finland	EPA + sectoral	2014
France	Env. Code	2006
Germany	No	
Greece	No	
Hungary	No	
Ireland	EPA + sectoral	1992, 2003
Italy	Env. Code + sectoral	2006
Latvia	EPA	1991, 2006
Lithuania	EPA + sectoral	1992
Luxembourg	Env. Code	2018
Malta	EPA + sectoral	2016
Netherlands	Environmental Management Act	1990s
Poland	EPA + sectoral	2001
Portugal	Environmental policy law	2014
Romania	EPA + sectoral	1995
Slovakia	EPA + sectoral	1992
Slovenia	EPA + sectoral	2004
Spain	No	
Sweden	Env. Code	1999
UK	No	

As this table shows, Member States did indeed to a large extent move to some form of, at the very least, coordination. If one counts the Member States with an environmental protection act and sectoral legislation, there is a total of 17. Only five (Estonia, France, Italy, Luxembourg and Sweden) have explicitly adopted an environmental code. Six Member States have no or little integration, and at least no formal environmental protection act or code.

This table needs to be taken with a grain of salt, as there are often blurry boundaries between those categorisations. Additionally, the countries that do have a formal environmental code do not always have all environmental legislation integrated in a comprehensive manner in the code. And as already mentioned, in some cases an environmental protection or environmental management act can serve the same goal as a code. Moreover, measurement may be complicated for some Member States where competences in environmental matters have been allocated to *Länder* (Germany), regions (Belgium) or autonomous regions (Spain).

But the most important conclusion from this rough overview is that the tendency towards codification has indeed affected the environmental law of Member States. If the combination environmental protection act plus sectoral is taken together with the environmental code, then there is a total of 22 Member States that have either an environmental protection act or an environmental code. The least one can therefore say is that the arguments advanced in the 1990s and summarised in the previous sections were apparently considered convincing by policy-makers. Nevertheless, there is a remarkable difference between the timing of the codification. Some Member States – like Belgium, the Netherlands, Latvia, Romania, Slovakia and Sweden – were relatively early, whereas for others codification came much later. But there again measurement is complicated by the fact that in some Member States codification took place in different phases.

5. DOES CODIFICATION MATTER?

When one discusses relatively formal operations like codification of environmental law, the question always arises of whether it merely brings about a better structure of environmental legislation or whether it can actually increase the quality of environmental law. That was at least what some of the scholars in the 1990s hoped for: that codification would engender ecological progress.

Esty and Porter undertook a magnificent exercise measuring the relationship between the intensity of environmental regulation on the one hand and environmental quality and gross domestic product (GDP), on the other.[16] They found that there is a correlation between environmental regulation, GDP and environmental quality. In other words, those states that had more stringent environmental regulation also had better environmental quality and higher GDP levels. The research fits into the so-called environmental Kuznets curve (EKC) doctrine, examining the relationship between economic development and environmental quality.[17] Esty and Porter articulated the fact that an increase in GDP is correlated with higher environmental quality (as the EKC predicts), but only on the condition that the increase in GDP is accompanied with more stringent regulation. There is, in other words, no 'automatic' relationship between an increase in GDP and better environmental quality.

16 *Esty, D. & Porter, M.E.*, 'Industrial Ecology and Comparativeness', *Journal of Industrial Ecology*, 1998, 35–43 and *Esty, D.C. & Porter, M.E.*, 'National Environmental Performance: An Empirical Analysis of Policy Results and Determinants', *Environmental and Development Economics*, 2005, 391–434.

17 *Faure, M.G.*, 'Does Environmental Law Matter?', in *Faure, M.G. & Smits, J.* (eds.), Does Law Matter? On Law and Economic Growth, Antwerp, Intersentia, 2011, 385–416.

Theoretically, it would be possible to undertake a similar exercise for codification. The empirical strategy would then focus on the question of whether the environmental quality in the 'codified' Member States is higher. However, it may be clear that much of the criticism that has been brought against the EKC literature[18] could to an even stronger extent also apply to this type of empirical research. The main reason for this is that the direction of the causality is unclear. It is very possible that the Member States that were already having a decent environmental legal framework in place (and therefore good environmental quality) are also the ones moving towards codification. In other words, introduction of a code as such cannot be a proxy for good environmental quality. And the contrary can equally be true: a Member State may well have a decent environmental legal framework (and a corresponding environmental quality), but no codification. Germany could undoubtedly be an example of such a case.

This therefore should lead to some warnings: it may be impossible to show empirically that codification as such would lead to increased environmental quality. Cynically, one could argue that it may be the 'green' Member States (but certainly not all, like Germany) that moved to codification. It is simply impossible to suggest any relationship between codification and environmental quality. Moreover, it should also be recalled that codification could be a very costly exercise (see section 4), especially for Member States where the variation in previously existing rules is large.

6. ENVIRONMENTAL LAW AT THE EU LEVEL

Numerically, EU environmental law has become one of the most important domains of environmental law. In 35 years, the EU has developed over 200 secondary legislative instruments covering a wide range of environmental issues.[19] Morgera therefore qualifies EU environmental law as 'abundant and pervasive'.[20] It has become one of the policy domains in which numerically the EU has been most active. Krämer also notes that there is a wide range of environmental instruments used at the EU level, varying from regulations to the setting-up of administrative structures, transposition of international environmental conventions, directives, recommendations, action programmes and communications.[21] Environmental law is not only a numerically important

18 *Stern, D.L.*, 'Progress on the Environmental Kuznets-Curve?', *Environment and Development Economics*, 1998, 173–196 and *Stern, D.L., Common, M.S. & Barbier, E.B.*, 'Economic Growth and Environmental Degradation: The Environmental Kuznets-Curve and Sustainable Development', *World Development*, 1996, 1151–1160.

19 *Morgera, E.*, 'EU Environmental Law', in *Barnard, C. & Peers, S.* (eds.), *European Union Law*, Oxford, Oxford University Press, 2014, 651–679.

20 Ibid.

21 *Krämer, L.*, EC Environmental Law, 6th edn., London, Sweet & Maxwell, 2007, Chapter 2.

part of EU law, but the wide variety of instruments, as explored by Krämer, also underscores the fact that there are many different instruments for the various aspects and areas of the environment, as a result of which it may become difficult to maintain the overview.

Not only is environmental law an important part of EU law, but EU environmental law has had a substantial influence on the domestic law of the Member States. Douma and colleagues examined the impact of EU law on Dutch environmental law and found that 66% of Dutch environmental law was of EU origin.[22] For other policy domains, like education law, this was only 6%.

7. EXISTING COORDINATION IN EU ENVIRONMENTAL LAW

Even though EU environmental law now consists of more than 200 documents and a wide variety of different legal instruments that were developed over a longer period of time, attempts have of course already been undertaken within EU law towards some coordination.

In the first place, one can point to various cross-sectional issues regulated by EU environmental law of a more horizontal nature, such as, for example, access to information, environmental impact assessment, the Environmental Liability Directive and the Environmental Crime Directive, to mention just a few.[23] Those are not limited in their application to particular sectors; they have a cross-sectional nature instead. Moreover, as directives in particular areas such as waste and water had developed in such a way that many different directives applied, a coordination was undertaken by creating so-called framework directives. However, Krämer indicates that differentiations such as whether something is a 'framework directive' or a 'daughter directive' are not that relevant. It only signals that the specific directive is placed in a close context with other directives; however, the specific directive is to be interpreted by itself including, of course, possible references to other directives, so Krämer holds.[24] Framework directives do therefore not constitute a true coordination or codification.

As a result of the rather haphazard legislative process, directives were created at many different points in time and often as a reaction to a particular

---

22 *Douma, W., Pieters, K., Feenstra, K. & Koch, R., Pilote-Monitor.* EU invloed. Een onderzoek naar de realiseerbaarheid van een permanente monitor voor het meten van invloed van Europese regelgeving op in Nederland geldende wet- en regelgeving, The Hague, T.M.C. Asser Instituut, 2007 in *Douma, W.*, 'Europese invloed op regelgeving meetbaar?', *Nederlands Juristenblad*, 2007, Vol. 29, 1828–1834.

23 For a more in-depth discussion of these cross-sectoral instruments in European environmental law, see *Jans, J.H. & Vedder, H.B.*, European Environmental Law after Lisbon, 4th edn., Groningen, Europa Law Publishing, 2012, 339–390.

24 Krämer, *supra* n. 21, 57–58.

political need. The result is that between the different directives and various sectors of the environment, differences can be observed not only in the structure of the particular regulations, but also in the terminology, the instruments used and the enforcement. There is therefore undoubtedly room for coordination (and potentially codification) within EU environmental law as well.

8. CAN ENVIRONMENTAL CODIFICATION SAVE THE EU?

Anyone reading the newspapers today will notice that the EU is undergoing an existential crisis.[25] For the first time in history, Member States are not lining up to become new members, but one Member State has left the EU (Brexit). There is increasing doubt on the legitimacy of EU decision-making,[26] *inter alia* related to the lacking democratic deficit, and populist anti-EU parties seem, at least in some countries, to be able to convince the electorate.

One of the goals Napoleon Bonaparte had with the creation of the French Civil Code of 21 March 1804 was to bring a divided France together.[27] Napoleon was (because he had the possibility to use force to an extent that the EU lacks) successful in harmonising France. The Civil Code may have played a role in that process, but was surely not the only instrument employed by Napoleon. It is, however, not very likely that an EU (environmental) code would have a similar success.

Codification could undoubtedly have many benefits on paper. The EU is already actively involved in a critical analysis of its own legislative framework through the so-called REFIT exercise.[28] Codification might therefore fit into the better regulation and good governance rhetoric. If that were able to achieve more coherence and simplification, it could be welcomed. However, we have to warn again (see section 3) that such a codification process in itself is not a cost-free exercise; the costs of codification may even be substantial, and it should therefore be clear that the potential benefits outweigh the costs.

Moreover, some of the arguments advanced in the 1990s (*inter alia* by Rehbinder and Kloepfer) in favour of codification of domestic environmental law may not to the same extent apply to the EU level. Those arguments relate

---

25 For an analysis of the crisis from a law and economics perspective, see, *inter alia*, *Van den Bergh, R.*, 'Farewell Utopia?: Why the European Union Should Take the Economics of Federalism Seriously', *Maastricht Journal of European and Comparative Law*, 2016, Vol. 23(6), 937–964.

26 See the contributions in *Bovens, M., Curtin, D. & Hart, P.* (eds.), The Real World of EU Accountability. What Deficit?, Oxford, Oxford University Press, 2010.

27 See in that respect *inter alia* the contributions in *Parise, A. & Van Vliet, L.* (eds.), Re-De-Co-dification? New Insights on the Codification of Private Law, The Hague, Eleven, 2018.

28 REFIT is a plan to make EU legislation simpler and cheaper. It is part of the Better Regulation Agenda of the EU. For details see: https://ec.europa.eu/info/law/law-making-process/evaluating-and-improving-existing-laws/refit-making-eu-law-simpler-and-less-costly_en.

to making environmental law more understandable to practitioners, to achieve ecological progress and to obtain better compliance. But the problem is that EU environmental law is, in contrast to domestic law, not directly addressed at the citizens and stakeholders (who have to comply with the rules), but at the legislators within the Member States. The stakeholders within the Member States that have to comply with EU environmental law are (except for the case of directly applicable regulations) not directly confronted with EU environmental law, but only know the domestic law implementing EU environmental law. Stakeholders may often not even be aware of the fact that the domestic rules with which they have to comply have an EU origin.

This brings us also back to the fundamental question, why we need European environmental law in the first place.

9. THE NEED FOR EU ENVIRONMENTAL LAW FROM AN ECONOMIC PERSPECTIVE

Setting the question of the necessity or desirability of an EU environmental code aside for the moment, let us go back once more to economics to recall the fundamental reasons why EU environmental law – in other words, centralisation of environmental norms – was needed in the first place. Two reasons can be distinguished from an economic perspective. The first and most important justification for centralisation of legislative competences within a federal system is the existence of so-called transboundary (cross-border) externalities.[29] If one state were to have the possibility to externalise harm to other states, this would result in a market failure. Transboundary pollution is an example of such a cross-border externality which justifies centralisation. The second justification of centralisation is the prevention of a so-called 'race to the bottom'.[30] This race to the bottom could emerge when states engage in a destructive competition whereby they, in order to attract industry, reduce environmental standards below efficient levels. Whether such a race to the bottom exists is of course an empirical issue. It has to be shown that the (as such positive) competition between jurisdictions turns into a negative spiral between jurisdictions to compete with inefficient regulations and that, moreover, industry reacts to this race to the bottom. If the latter is the case, then it would result in industry moving to so-called pollution havens.[31]

---

29 See *inter alia*, *Revesz, R.*, 'Federalism and Interstate Environmental Externalities', *University of Pennsylvania Law Review*, 1996, Vol. 144, 2341–2416.

30 *Revesz, R.*, 'Rehabilitating Interstate Competition: Rethinking the "Race-to-the-bottom" Rationale for Federal Environmental Regulation', *New York University Law Review*, 1992, Vol. 67, 1210–1254.

31 See on the pollution haven hypothesis, *Vogel, D.*, Trading up: Consumer and Environmental Regulation in a Global Economy, Cambridge, MA, Harvard University Press, 1995.

Currently, EU environmental law may not be sufficiently able to remedy transboundary externalities and the race to the bottom. Several important proposals to deal with transboundary externalities (*inter alia* resulting from air pollution) were withdrawn by the European Commission, as they could apparently not receive sufficient support in the council.[32] In addition, there may also be a serious danger of a race to the bottom for the following reasons: the European Member States still hold strongly to their sovereignty and (with a few exceptions) the European Commission (as guardian of the treaties) is in fact only allowed to verify whether the Member States formally transposed the obligations resulting from environmental directives correctly in Member State law. That is, to a significant extent, limited to a formal implementation. The EU authorities largely lack enforcement powers (comparable to the Environmental Protection Agency in the EU) that would allow them to control factual implementation in the Member States, let alone environmental quality.[33]

Of course, the European Commission will strongly react against an implementation and enforcement deficit, but that largely concerns the failure of Member States to formally incorporate the environmental *acquis*. In addition, both the EU Court of Justice and changes in the treaties have created more possibilities to force the Member States to go beyond a mere formal implementation. The Francovich case law created the possibility to hold Member States liable for damage resulting from the lack of implementation of directives.[34] Case law also imposed a duty on Member States to effectively enforce national legislation implementing (environmental) directives.[35] The Court also increasingly uses the possibility to impose a penalty payment upon those Member States that consistently failed in implementation.[36]

Moreover, since the beginning of this century, several initiatives were taken to force Member States to use the criminal law to enforce legislation transposing environmental directives.[37] That was precisely the reason why an environmental

---

32 See in that respect *De Sadeleer, N.*, 'UE: le mauvais côté de la "Better Regulation"', *La Libre Belgique*, 2015, 54–55, available at: http://tradeven.cluster015.ovh.net/wordpress/wp-content/uploads/2018/12/BetterRegulation2.pdf.

33 It is only on rare occasions (and only if Member States voluntarily agree to it) that Commission officials go on a mission to a Member State to verify whether particular environmental protection measures have indeed been implemented. See Jans & Vedder, *supra* n. 23, 167.

34 CJEU, Case C-60/90 Francovich and others v. Italian Republic [1990], ECLI:EU:C:1991:428.

35 See further Jans & Vedder, *supra* n. 23, 163–170.

36 See further on the enforcement of European environmental law, Jans & Vedder, *supra* n. 23, 163–179.

37 See *inter alia*, *Comte, F.*, 'Criminal Environmental Law and Community Competence', *European Energy and Environmental Law Review*, 2003, Vol. 12, 147–156; *Comte, F.*, 'Environmental Crime and the Police in Europe: A Panorama and Possible Paths for a Future Action', *European Environmental Law Review*, 2006, Vol. 15(7), 190–231 and *Hedemann-Robinson, M.*, 'The Emergence of European Union Environmental Criminal Law: A Quest for Solid Foundations', Environmental Liability, 2008, Vol. 16(3), 71–91.

crime directive[38] was promulgated. However, this directive merely forces Member States to impose criminal sanctions in their domestic legislation, transposing European environmental law. But the problem is that this will not necessarily make a significant difference in practice, as in theory a Member State could do very little or nothing concerning the effective enforcement of the domestic legislation, implementing the environmental *acquis*.

The basic problem is that what really happens as far as the enforcement of national legislation transposing the *acquis* is concerned is simply largely unknown. It is, for example, unknown how many agents in particular Member States have been appointed to monitor the compliance with the domestic legislation; it is equally unknown, at least not communicated to the European Commission, how many installations have to be monitored and how many violations occur. There is also no information on how many cases would be dismissed by public prosecutors, nor on the sanctions effectively imposed. There is a policy document which to an important extent deals with this problem: Recommendation 2001/331, providing for minimum criteria for environmental inspections.[39] This document prescribes in a detailed manner how inspections should be carried out, how inspection visits should take place and that specific plans aiming for environmental inspections have to be developed. Member States should also report in detail, *inter alia* on staffing, details of environmental inspections carried out and an evaluation of the success or failure of the plans, among others. The problem is, however, that this is a recommendation that is not applied in practice. In practice, Member States still resist even the communication of data on enforcement actions to the European Commission, let alone supervision by the European Commission of monitoring activities by the Member States authorities.

The result is that within this framework, there is a significant danger that European environmental law could remain largely ineffective. Member States could theoretically (and it has to be feared in practice as well) still compete simply by having perfect paper transposition of the law, but no effective enforcement. As long as this remains below the radar of the European Commission and the Court, they could get away with it.[40] The result is not only that the race to the bottom between Member States could continue notwithstanding formal harmonisation (competition consisting of differing enforcement levels), but that also the effective influence that EU environmental law should have on increasing

---

38 Directive 2008/99/EC of 19 November 2008 on the protection of the environment through criminal law (2008) OJ L328/28.

39 Recommendation 2001/331 of 4 April 2001 providing for minimum criteria for environmental inspections in the Member States, [2001] OJ L118/41.

40 It has, moreover, to be feared that this race to the bottom increased after the enlargement process. See *Faure, M. & Johnston, J.S.*, 'The Law and Economics of Environmental Federalism: Europe and the United States Compared', *Virginia Environmental Law Journal*, 2009, 205–274.

environmental quality in the Member States and creating a level playing field for industry will be frustrated.

10. THE NEED FOR RADICAL CHANGES

It thus becomes clear that in order to maintain the effectiveness of EU environmental law in its important task of remedying market failures, radical changes must be implemented. The suggestion to award enforcement competences to the EU authorities in the environmental domain is at this moment an absolute no-go, which is, as such, remarkable. Similar EU enforcement competences do exist – for example, in the domain of fisheries policy.[41] Autonomous enforcement powers of the European Commission equally exist in the domain of competition policy. And as far as food safety is concerned, the Food and Veterinary Office has, on the one hand, far-reaching control competences, but can equally monitor the functioning of enforcement agencies within the Member States.[42] It cannot be understood why these competences could be awarded to the EU level in those other domains and not to guaranteeing environmental quality. Vesting powers of investigation and auditing at the EU level could enhance the level of implementation of EU law.[43] If autonomous inspection powers are still considered a bridge too far, the commission should at least be awarded auditing powers to verify the quality of the work exercised by the environmental inspection authorities within the Member States. And the very least is that the Member States should disclose data on enforcement of national legislation implementing the environmental *acquis*, with auditing by the European Commission.

It is undoubtedly important, as many chapters in this book stress, to focus on a reshuffling of environmental law and to carefully address the question of the potential added value of a codification. If performed carefully, such a codification might contribute to the quality of EU environmental law and with that hopefully also to improved environmental quality in the EU. At the same time, it is important not only to focus on codification and harmonisation, but to equally focus on the fundamental problem of the lacking enforcement of EU environmental law (at least lacking information on that point) at the Member State level.

In addition to focusing on harmonisation and codification, it is important to focus on the possibility to provide EU authorities (some) autonomous

---

41 Regulation (EC) No 768/2005 establishing a community fisheries control agency and amending Regulation (EC) No 2847/93 (2005) OJ L347.

42 See *Hedemann-Robinson, M.*, 'Environmental Inspections and the EU: Securing an Effective Role for a Supranational Union Legal Framework', *Transnational Environmental Law*, 2017, Vol. 6(1), 49–50.

43 See Hedemann-Robinson, *supra* n. 42, 50.

enforcement powers, or at least auditing powers concerning inspections exercised by Member State authorities – or, at the very least, data on enforcement within the Member States. The real improvement of environmental quality in the EU will, after all, be crucially dependent upon the enforcement of environmental law in practice. In addition to the codification question, enforcement should therefore undoubtedly also be addressed.

POSSIBILITIES OF AND LIMITS TO CODIFICATION OF EU ENVIRONMENTAL LAW

Ludwig KRÄMER*

The present chapter will discuss some aspects of codifying EU environmental law. It will limit itself to the more formal side, because the question of how substantive environmental law should be organised is an eminent political one. Indeed, whether air or water pollution should mainly be based on emission limit values or quality objectives, whether economic instruments – taxes, pollution allowance trading systems or other instruments to internalise the externalities of economic activities – should be used is not a question of greater or less intense codification, but depends on political choices.[1] For this reason, only the more procedural provisions of EU environmental law will be discussed.

* Head of unit of the Environmental Department of the European Commission (retired).

[1] In water policy, the EU went from emission limit values, laid down in Directive 76/464, OJ 1976, L 129, p.23, to quality objectives, see Directive 2008/105, OJ 2008, L 348 p.84; the same change occurred in air pollution, where Directive 84/360, OJ 1984, L 188 p.20 established the principle of emission limit vales, which was abandoned by Directive 96/61, OJ 1996, L 257 p.26.

After clarifying the EU terminology concerning the approximation of different pieces of legislation and the constitutional framework of codification (1), a number of examples will be discussed, where a codification would be possible (2). A third section will describe the principal limits which oppose, at present, such a codification at EU level (3).

1. CODIFICATION IN EU LAW

The terminology of the TFEU with regard to common, EU-wide legislative provisions is not coherent. While the provisions on the internal market (Article114ss. TFEU) refer to the approximation of laws, Article 191(2) TFEU mentions 'harmonisation measures' in a provision which concerns national safeguard measures and which has remained, until now, irrelevant in practice. Both 'approximation' and 'harmonisation' refer to melting, in one way or the other, national provisions into common, EU-wide rules.

In contrast to this, 'codification' of EU legal provisions refers to the activity of bringing different EU-wide provisions into one legal frame. Such a codification takes therefore as a point of departure the existing environmental provisions of EU law and tries to establish common legislative provisions which concern the different sectors of environmental law, such as on water, air, soil, waste or permits.[2]

EU environmental law does not require or even favour unified EU-wide provisions on the protection of the environment. While Article 191(2) TFEU suggests that EU environmental policy – and hence also the specific measures adopted in the context of this policy – aim at a high level of environmental protection, this requirement is nuanced by the addition that the diversity of situations in the various regions of the Union shall be taken into account. And the EU legislature shall furthermore take into account 'the economic and social development of the Union as a whole and the balanced development of its regions' (Article 191(3) TFEU). The influence of the diversity of the environment within the EU was also underlined by two further provisions: on the one hand, EU-wide environmental provisions concerning town and country planning, the quantitative management of water resources and land use must be adopted by unanimous decision of the EU legislature. The objective is to give to each Member State a veto right in order to ensure that its specific

2 'Codified legislation' by the EU Commission still has a different meaning: it refers to the process by which all later amendments of a directive or a regulation are incorporated into one legal text. This process is conducted for information purposes only; the codified version has no legal value of its own. Also, the recitals of the legislative act and of its later amendments are not included in the process.

national environmental situation is duly taken into consideration, when EU provisions are adopted.[3] On the other hand, whenever EU legislation is adopted on the basis of Article 192 TFEU, Member States have the right to maintain or introduce more stringent protective measures (Article 193 TFEU). The TFEU thus very deliberately accepts that EU environmental provisions are not unified and common for all EU Member States and regions, but that they are different from one Member State to the other.

These provisions of Articles 191ss TFEU may be compared with the internal market provisions of Articles 114ss TFEU. The objectives of the provisions concerning the internal market aim at the 'establishment and functioning of the internal market' (Article 114(1) TFEU). The functioning of the internal market requires that the trade in goods and services is not exposed to 'disguised restrictions' or 'arbitrary discrimination' (Article 114(6) TFEU) and that there is no 'obstacle to the functioning' of the market (Article 114(6) TFEU). Such a provision would be completely misplaced in the environmental chapter, as there is no 'functioning of the environmental sector': actors on the internal market trade, but the environment has no actors in this sense.

Additionally, once a provision under Article 114 TFEU is adopted, it is valid for all Member States. Deviations from that common provision may be explicitly authorised by the Commission, but only under very restricted conditions (Article 114 (4) and(5) TFEU); and when a deviation is approved, the Commission is obliged to examine how the deviation from the common rules may be remedied as quickly as possible (Article 114(7) TFEU). All these provisions show that the internal market provision aim at a level playing field among the different economic actors on the market and therefore at rules that are, as far as any possible, uniform. The contrast to the environmental chapter of the TFEU is obvious and considerable.

Codification of EU environmental law has to overcome two other basic obstacles under the EU treaties. As the competence to adopt environmental legislation is shared between the EU and the EU Member States, the EU may, under the principle of subsidiarity, adopt measures only:

> if and in so far as the objectives of the proposed action cannot be sufficiently achieved by the Member States, either at central or at regional and local level, but can rather by reason of the scale or effects of the proposed action, be better achieved at Union level (Article 5(3) TEU).

And under the principle of proportionality, the action of the EU 'shall not exceed what is necessary to achieve the objectives of the Treaties' (Article 5(4) TEU).

---

3 The same concept underlies the provision of Article 172(2) TFEU which concerns trans-European networks and which requires 'the approval of the Member State concerned', when guidelines and projects of common interest relate to the territory of a Member State.

It follows from all this that codification of EU environmental law is not a question of approximation or harmonisation of national environmental legislation. Rather, it is the aligning of different provisions in EU environmental law, in order to improve environmental provisions – whether this increases transparency, effectiveness or substantive protection, or whether it pursues other objectives. Codification is only allowed when the codified provisions are 'better' – whatever that means – than the previous, more dispersed provisions and when such a codification is 'necessary'. As fixed criteria on the question, what is 'better' and 'necessary' lack an explanation of if, when and how to codify, which lends the EU legislature a certain level of discretion in terms of codification At the end of the day, it would have to be the Court of Justice which would, in the case of divergence of opinions, have to decide whether a specific codification measure is compatible with EU law. National and EU administrations, however, exercise a rather strict self-control, in order to avoid the adoption of codifying provisions, as there is a general consensus not to make environmental provisions too effective.

EU Member States sometimes codified their national environmental law, without necessarily using the term 'code'.[4] This national legislation aimed exclusively at improving the national environmental legislative situation and took thus into consideration the respective national specificities. The national codifying legislation is marked by the following facts:

- It does not deal with all aspects of environmental law, but leaves certain areas or problems out, which are then covered by specific pieces of legislation;
- As it is general, it is relatively frequently amended or completed by executive provisions, guidance instruments, administrative or technical instructions; and
- Its interpretation is often influenced by the jurisprudence of the EU Court of Justice, though that influence is not always reproduced in textual amendments.

In view of these specificities of national environmental legislation, it is of little value to analyse which areas were covered and why, which amendments were introduced and which areas of environmental law were omitted or regulated by specific national legislation. The following will rather try to describe if and

4 See for example Netherlands, Wet milieubeheer of 13 January 1979; Vlaanderen, Decreet houdende algemene bepalingen inzake milieubeleid of 5 April 1995; Sweden, Miljöbalk 1998; France, Ordonnance 2000–14 concernant le Code de l'environnement; Poland, Environmental Protection Act of 27 April 2001. Switzerland adopted a Bundesetz über den Umweltschutz of 7 October 1983. Germany generated a draft of an Umweltgesetzbuch (produced by academic professors) in 1998. At the international level, the IUCN Draft Covenant on Environment and Development (5th ed. 2015) deserves mention.

what codification efforts were undertaken – or omitted – at the EU level in environmental law matters.

2. POSSIBILITIES OF CODIFYING EU ENVIRONMENTAL PROVISIONS

2.1. ACCESS TO ENVIRONMENTAL INFORMATION

A right of citizens to have access to environmental information at the national level was introduced in 1990 and updated in 2003.[5] General provisions on access to documents held by EU institutions which went less far followed in piecemeal provisions in 1993/1994. After the introduction into the treaty of a general provision on access to information in 1998, a regulation on the general access to documents was adopted in 2001.[6] When the EU adhered to the Aarhus Convention,[7] new provisions on access to environmental information became necessary.[8] The EU was not willing to generalise the provisions of the Aarhus Convention to all information held by its institutions and bodies. It rather maintained the different approaches and also refused to align Regulation 1049/2001 to the requirements of the Aarhus Convention, although there are several obvious contradictions to the convention[9] and the convention prevails over EU secondary legislation.[10] The result is that access to environmental information held by EU authorities is more difficult than access to information held by national authorities. This situation persists at present.

---

5 Directive 90/313 on the freedom of access to information on the environment, OJ 1990, L 156 p.58; later replaced by Directive 2003/4, OJ 2003, L 41 p.26.

6 Regulation 1049/2001 regarding public access to European Parliament, Council and Commission documents, OJ 2001, L 145 p.43.

7 Decision 2005/370 to adhere the Aarhus Convention, OJ 2005, L 124 p.1; the Convention is reproduced in the annex to this Decision.

8 Regulation 1367/2006, OJ 2006, L 264 p.13.

9 Regulation 1049/2001 only applies to three EU institutions, not to all of them and not to EU bodies or agencies. The regulation requires refusal of access to documents, when disclosure undermines the protection of international relations, defence and military matters or the financial, monetary or economic policy of the EU or of a Member State; the Aarhus Convention allows, but does not require the refusal of disclosure when international relations or national defence are adversely affected; it does not allow refusal of disclosure on financial, monetary or economic policy matters. Regulation 1049/2001 requires refusal of disclosure of 'legal advice'; the Aarhus Convention does not allow a refusal based on such an argument. Regulation 1049/2001 requires refusal of disclosure when the protection of the purpose of inspections, investigations and audits would be undermined; the Aarhus Convention allows refusal of disclosure only when the ability to conduct an enquiry of a criminal or disciplinary nature is concerned. See for further details *A. Berthier and L. Krämer*, The Aarhus Convention. Implementation and compliance in EU law. Bruxelles 2015.

10 See Article 216(2) TFEU.

2.2. REPORTING REQUIREMENTS

Most pieces of EU environmental legislation provided that Member States should report at regular intervals on the implementation of the specific directive or regulation and that the Commission should regularly issue a comprehensive report on the implementation of the legislative act. As the details concerning these reporting obligations differed, Directive 91/692 was adopted.[11] The directive provided implementation reports for the different environmental sectors – *inter alia*, water, air and waste – every three years, based on a questionnaire which was drawn up by comitology procedure. The Commission then had to publish a synthesis report for each sector every three years.

Directive 91/692 became quickly obsolete, however, because environmental directives which were adopted after 1991 were not adapted to its system; additionally, the Commission did not insist on the drawing up of the national reports which delayed its own reporting. The national reports and subsequently the questionnaires less and less covered a whole sector, but remained incomplete. Also, translation problems had the effect that the synthesis Commission reports became very short and did not reflect the implementation of legislation in a given sector. Thus, in 2018, Directive 91/692 was repealed.[12] The Commission made a general assessment of all reporting obligations in the environmental legislation, covering 181 such obligations in 58 legislative texts.[13] However, its review proposal only covered eight legislative acts,[14] providing even for specific provisions for each of them.

A good illustration of this is the situation in the nature conservation area. Directive 2009/147 on the conservation of wild birds provided for Member States and the Commission to produce implementation reports every three years;[15] the Habitats Directive 92/43 requested the production of implementation reports every six years.[16] In contrast, the regulation on trade in endangered species only provided for general reporting obligation;[17] the regulation on invasive alien species provided for national reports every six years, but only one report – in 2021 – from the side of the Commission.[18] In 2018, the Commission proposed

---

11 Directive 91/692; OJ 1991, L 377 p.48.

12 Decision 2018/853, OJ 2018, L 150 p.155.

13 Commission, COM (2017) 312 and SWD (2017) 230.

14 Commission, COM (2018) 381. A more profound reconsideration would also be necessary, because, as the Commission itself recognises, the individual citizens have, under Directive 2003/4 (fn 5) and Regulation 1367/2006 (fn.8) a subjective *right* to have access to information on the environment and the omission to establish a report shortens this right.

15 Directive 2009/147, OJ 2010, L 20 p.7, Article 12.

16 Directive 92/43, OJ 1992, L 206 p.7, Article 17.

17 Regulation 338/97, OJ 1997, L 61 p.1, Article 15(4).

18 Regulation 1143/2014, OJ 2014, L 317 p.35, Article 24.

to have the reporting period for both directives established at six years and also to reduce the reporting frequency under the CITES Regulation 338/97.[19]

Sometimes, the reporting obligations are in direct opposition to the legal obligations of the EU: the Aarhus Convention requires the contracting parties to establish a report on the state of the environment every three to four years.[20] The EU Regulation on the European Environment Agency provides such a report only every five years, and this is what the Agency does in practice.[21]

2.3. PUBLIC PARTICIPATION IN DECISION-MAKING[22]

The provisions on public participation in decision-making are scattered. A 2003 directive provides for such a participation with regard to some directives, but only refers to two directives as regards projects – environmental impact assessment and permits of industrial installations – and six directives as regards plans and programmes.[23] However, as regards EU plans and programmes, there are numerous legislative acts in environmental law,[24] as well as in environmental-related sectors[25] such as climate change,[26] energy, agriculture,[27] fisheries,[28] industry,[29] food, transport and trans-European networks, where projects, plans or programmes are to be established, without there being detailed provisions on early participation of the public when all options of the project or plan are

19 Commission, COM (2018) 381.

20 Aarhus Convention (fn.7), Article 5(4).

21 Regulation 401/2009, OJ 2009, L 126 p.13, Article 2(h).

22 See also *L. Krämer*, The EU and public participation in environmental decision-making. in: *J. Jendroska* and *M. Bar* (eds): Procedural Environmental Rights: Principle X in Theory and Practice. Intersentia, Cambridge 2017, p.121.

23 Directive 2003/35, OJ 2003, L 156 p.17. The six directives concern waste, hazardous waste, batteries, packaging and packaging waste, nitrate pollution of waters and air quality.

24 See for example Directive 2009/71/Euratom, OJ 2009, L 172 p.18, on nuclear installations; Directive 2015/ 2193 on medium combustion plants, OJ 2015, L 313 p.1.

25 The requirement to provide for public participation in projects, plans or programmes related to the environment stems from the Aarhus Convention which is, as mentioned, binding on the EU and its Member States. The requirement is further elaborated in Regulation 1367/2006 (fn.8).

26 See for example the work programme concerning the eco-design of energy-related products, Directive 2009/125, OJ 2009, L 285 p.10; action plan for the energy performance of buildings, Directive 2010/31, OJ 2010, L 153 p.13.

27 See for example the Commission strategy for bioeconomy, COM(2012) 60 and SWD (2017) 374; the different plans under the Structural Funds, Regulation 1303/2013, OJ 2013, l 347 p.320; a forest strategy, Decision 1386/2013, OJ 2013, L 354 p.171, Annex no.28 (viii).

28 See for example action plans to combat structural fishing overcapacity under Regulation 1380/2013 on the Common Fisheries Policy, OJ 2013, L 354, p.22, Article 22.

29 See for example Regulation 1025/2012 on industrial standardization OJ 2012, L 316 p.12 and the annual action plans on industrial standardization, COM (2018) 686; the strategy on sustainable production and consumption, Decision 1386/2013, OJ 2013, L 354 p.171, annex, no.43(v).

open, on the relevant documents which must be made accessible and on a non-technical summary of the project or plan. Neither does EU law differentiate between consultation and participation, nor does it provide for effective, proportionate and dissuasive sanctions for cases of non-compliance.

EU law also frequently requires the drawing up of plans or programmes by Member States. The different legislative acts cannot all be enumerated here; some examples concerning environmental legislative acts must suffice. They concern:

- management plans for extractive waste;[30]
- flood risk management plans;[31]
- air quality plans;[32]
- programmes of measures on marine water resources;[33]
- action plans for the sustainable use of pesticides;[34]
- action plans on the management of noise issues;[35]
- renewable energy action plans;[36]
- programmes on consumer information on energy efficiency;[37]
- emergency plans for offshore oil and gas operations;[38]
- action plans for the pathways of invasive alien species;[39]
- long-term strategy for the renovation of buildings:[40]
- integrated plans on energy and climate;[41]
- corrective action plans to reduce greenhouse gas emissions.[42]

No attempt was made in these provisions to reach common standards for the participation of the public, nor is there a cross-reference to Directive 2003/35.

30 Directive 2006/21 on the management of waste from extractive industries, OJ 2006, L 102 p.15, Article 5.

31 Directive 2007/60 on the assessment and management of flood risks, OJ 2007, L 288 p.27, Article 7.

32 Directive 2008/50 on ambient air quality, OJ 2008, L 152 p.1, Articles 23 and 24.

33 Directive 2008/56 concerning the marine water strategy, OJ 2008, L 164 p.19, Articles 5, 11 and 13.

34 Directive 2009/128, OJ 2009, L 309 p.71, Article 5.

35 Directive 2002/49 on the management of environmental noise, OJ 2002, L 189 p.12, Article 8.

36 Directive 2009/28 on renewable energies, OJ 2009, L 140 p.16, Article 4.

37 Directive 2012/27 on energy efficiency, OJ 2012, L 315 p.1, Article 12.

38 Directive 2013/30 on the safety of offshore oil and gas operations, OJ 2013, L 178 p.66, Article 29.

39 Regulation 1143/2014 (fn.18), Article 13.

40 Directive 2018/844, OJ 2018, L 156 p.75, Article 1 (inserting an Article 2a into Directive 2010/31).

41 Regulation 2018/1999 on the governance of the energy union and climate action, OJ 2018, L 328 p.1, Article 3.

42 Regulation 2018/842 on binding annual greenhouse gas emission reductions, OJ 2018, L 156 p.26, Article 8.

2.4. ACCESS TO JUSTICE

Access in environmental matters to the EU courts is regulated by the general provision of Article 263(4) TFEU. The Court of Justice rejected all attempts to facilitate access in environmental matters, with the consequence that no action by an environmental organisation was, until today, ever declared admissible. Article 9(3) of the Aarhus Convention had no significant impact on this practice of the court.

A proposal for a directive on access to national courts in environmental matters was not adopted.[43] As regards the environmental impact assessment of projects and the permitting procedure of industrial installations, access to courts is granted.[44] The Court of Justice cautiously tries to enlarge access in other environmental areas in order to comply with the spirit of the binding provision of Article 9(3) of the Aarhus Convention.

Under the directive on environmental liability, persons may draw the attention of public authorities on situations of damage to the environment and suggest restorative measures. When the invitation is well reasoned, a refusal by the authorities to become active may be challenged in court.[45]

No further attempts to reach a common approach on access to justice in environmental matters exist.

2.5. PERMITS

The directive on (large) industrial installations[46] contains, in Articles 4 to 21, detailed provisions concerning the application for a permit, the right to obtain a permit when the directive's requirements are respected, details on permit conditions, general principles which have to be respected, monitoring requirements, the updating of permit conditions, the participation of the public in the permit procedure and provisions on the site closure. In contrast, the directive on nuclear installations[47] does not require any of these conditions, but only requests Member States to establish a legislative framework for such installations. Furthermore, the directive on medium combustion plants[48] also

43 Commission, COM (2003) 624.

44 Directive 2003/35 (fn.23), Article 2; Directive 2010/75 on emissions from industrial installations, OJ 2010, L 334 p.17, Article 25; Directive 2011/92, OJ 2012, L 26 p.1, Article 11.

45 Directive 2004/35, OJ 2004, L 143 p.56, Articles 12 and 13.

46 Directive 2010/75 (fn.44).

47 Directive 2009/71/Euratom (fn.24), Article 4. The directive refers to 'nuclear safety' only; however, nuclear installations are not either covered by Directive 2010/75, so that there are no permit requirements for them in EU law. Nuclear installations are covered by Directive 2011/92 on the environmental impact assessment.

48 Directive 2015/2193 (fn.24), Article 5.

omits almost all of the detailed permit requirements of Directive 2010/75, but deals with some requirements in a single article.

The directive on waste[49] and the directive on the landfill of waste[50] both required waste installations to obtain a permit, but concentrated on waste-related permit conditions, failing to refer to general details of the permit procedure. Installations which dispose of their own non-hazardous waste at the place of production, or which recover (incinerate) waste, may be exempted by Member States from the permit requirement, without any explanation for this exemption.[51] Additionally, waste water treatment installations are only subject to a permit requirement without any further specification.[52] Discharges of pollutants into surface or groundwater are not subject to a permit requirement by EU law, although Member States may, of course, provide for such permits.[53]

2.6. ENVIRONMENTAL IMPACT ASSESSMENT

Already in 1985, the EU adopted a directive on the environmental impact assessment of certain public and private projects which were listed in annexes to the directive.[54] These provisions were fine-tuned and updated in 2011 and 2014.[55] The directive contained detailed provisions on the impact assessment procedure and the participation of the public. It requested a description and assessment of the 'direct effects and any indirect, secondary, cumulative, short, medium and long-term, permanent and temporary, positive and negative effects of the project on the environment'.[56] However, for projects with an impact on the territory of another Member State – not even a third country – it provided for an intergovernmental consultation instead of a participation of the citizens of the neighbouring state,[57] in contradiction to the participation requirements of the Aarhus Convention, which prohibits any discrimination.

When the EU adopted legislation on the protection of natural habitats,[58] the Commission tried twice to ensure that projects which were to be realised within a protected area ('Natura2000' area) underwent an environmental impact assessment according to Directive 85/337. However, the Council refused and only

49 Directive 2008/98, OJ 2008, L 312 p.3, Article 23.
50 Directive 1999/31, OJ 1999, L 182 p.1, Articles 7 to 9.
51 Directive 2008/98 (fn.49), Article 23.
52 Directive 91/271, OJ 1991, L 182 p.40, Article 11.
53 Directive 2000/60 on surface water, OJ 2000, L327 p.1; Directive 2006/118 on groundwater, OJ 2006, L 372 p.19.
54 Directive 85/337, OJ 1985, L 140 p.75.
55 Directive 2011/92, OJ 2012, L 26 p.1; Directive 2014/52, OJ 2014, L 124 p.1.
56 Directive 2011/92 (fn.44) Annex IV, fn.1.
57 Ibid., Article 7.
58 Directive 92/43 (fn.16).

accepted that projects which were 'likely to have a significant effect' on the site should undergo an 'appropriate assessment of its implications for the site', noting that the opinion of the general public should be requested, 'if appropriate'.[59]

In 2001, the EU adopted a directive on the environmental impact assessment of plans and programmes which did not refer to the detailed provisions of Directive 85/337.[60] The directive referred to the consultation of the public, not to 'participation', and left practically all procedural details to the Member States.[61] For transnational plans or programmes, it repeated the intergovernmental consultation provision of Directive 85/337.

When the EU prepared its regulations of the trans-European networks in the transport and the energy sectors, no participation of the public was ensured, contrary to such a requirement for national plans or programmes.[62] The two regulations which were eventually adopted referred in general terms to Directive 2011/92 and provided for some derogations,[63] but an attempt of the Commission to have for transnational projects a transnational environmental impact assessment established was not adopted by the legislature.

2.7. SAFEGUARD (EMERGENCY) MEASURES

Article 191(2) TFEU provides that EU environmental measures shall contain a safeguard clause which allows Member States to take provisional measures for non-economic environmental reasons; such measures should be supervised – Article191(2) TFEU refers to 'inspection' – by the EU.

EU environmental law is very dispersed in this regard. Horizontal legislative acts give Member States the possibility not to apply the EU provisions in certain circumstances. Examples are the directive on access to environmental information which contains in Article 4 a long list of possibilities for Member States to refuse disclosure of environmental information.[64] A similar list is contained in Article 4 of the regulation on environmental information held by EU institutions,[65] although the two provisions are not aligned. Under the environmental impact assessment directive,[66] a Member State may exempt, 'under exceptional circumstances', a project from the requirements of an impact

59 Ibid., Article 6 (3).
60 Directive 2001/42, OJ 2001, L 197 p.30.
61 Ibid., Article 6.
62 Directive 2001/42 (fn.60), Article 4(1), expressly requires that an environmental impact assessment is made, before a plan or a programme is submitted to the legislative procedure.
63 Regulation 347/2013, OJ 2013, L115 p.39, Article 9; Regulation 1315/2013, OJ 2013, L 348 p.1, Article 36.
64 Directive 2003/4 (fn.5).
65 Regulation 1049/2001 (fn.6).
66 Directive 2011/92 (fn.44), Article 2(4).

assessment; it is not specified whether this provision is limited to non-economic circumstances. The Commission shall be informed of the exemption, but no further control is foreseen.

As regards nature conservation, the birds directive protected all wild birds in Europe. It allowed derogations from, *inter alia*, the killing, capturing, selling and hunting of birds in order to protect some general interests, but also 'to permit on a selective basis, the capture, keeping or judicious use of certain birds in small numbers.[67] The Habitats Directive provided that Member States were allowed to deviate from the protection requirements for fauna and flora species, in order:

> to allow under strictly supervised conditions on a selective basis and to a limited extent, the taking or keeping of certain specimens of the species listed in Annex IV in limited numbers specified by the competent national authorities.[68]

As can be seen, no alignment was made between the provisions of the two directives, as regards prior authorisations, the strictly supervised conditions and the 'judicious use'.

In the water sector, legislative arrangements made the use of safeguard measures almost superfluous. For example, the water framework directive[69] fixed as a legal objective that a good quality of surface water should be reached by 2015. It allowed, however, each Member State to unilaterally prolong this delay by up to twelve years 'in exceptional circumstances', without any control by the Commission.[70] Furthermore, it allowed temporary deterioration of the water quality[71] and the designation of water stretches which were too polluted to reach a good water quality.[72]

The directive on the pollution of waters by nitrates from agricultural activity determines that the amount of livestock manure applied to land each year shall not contain more than 170 kg/ha nitrogen.[73] However, Member States may fix other amounts, provided that these are based on objective criteria. The Commission has to approve such derogations, but has done so during some 25 years now in more than 30 derogation decisions. With such generous practice, a safeguard clause does not appear necessary.

The directive on ambient air quality of 2008, which in part introduced a prolongation of the compliance dates established by a directive of 1999, allowed

---

67 Directive 2009/147 (fn.15), Article9(1)(c). This directive had been preceded by Directive 79/409, OJ 1979, L 103 p.1 which contained the same provision.

68 Directive 92/43 (fn.16), Article 16(1).

69 Directive 2000/60 (fn.53).

70 Ibid. Article 4(4).

71 Ibid. Article 4(6).

72 Ibid. Article 4(5).

73 Directive 91/676, OJ 1991, L 375 p.1, Annex III no.2.

Member States to postpone compliance with the new air quality limit values until 2011 at the latest.[74] No further postponement or derogation was permitted, but in the follow-up of the diesel scandal it became apparent that Member States did not enforce the full application of the directive, in particular not for PM2.5, PM10 and NOx limit values. Although the directive required that Member States should take action to ensure that the non-compliance with the limit values was kept 'as short as possible', the non-compliance continued for years in several urban agglomerations. The Commission took court action against Member States for non-compliance with the directive only from 2015 onwards.[75]

The directive on industrial installations provided that, as a rule, Member States should set emission limit values for installations which respected the best available techniques; however, Member States were allowed to set, under certain conditions, less strict emission limit values.[76] Furthermore, for combustion plants, they were allowed to produce transitional national plans which provided for less stringent measures,[77] and malfunctions or breakdowns of installations were also allowed to temporarily disregard the respect the emission limit values.[78]

The framework directive on waste does not contain a safeguard or extensive derogation provision.[79]

2.8. INSPECTIONS

For industrial installations, Member States shall set up environmental inspection plans which cover all installations. Inspections shall take place at intervals between one and three years, and on complaints or incidents, non-routine inspections shall take place. On each inspection, a report has to be drawn up which is made available to the installation and made public.[80] Similar requirements are laid down for the inspection of installations to prevent major accidents, except that the inspection report need be made available to the public only on request.[81]

These requirements contrast the inspections for waste undertakings which shall only be subject to periodic inspections, without any further specifications

74 Directive 2008/152, OJ 2008, L 152 p.1, Article 22.

75 See Court of Justice, cases C-488/15 *Commission v. Bulgaria*, ECLI:EU:C:2017:267; C-336/16 *Commission v. Poland*, ECLI:EU:C:2018:94. Cases against Germany, France, Hungary, Romania, Italy and the United Kingdom were introduced are pending.

76 Directive 2010/75 (fn.44), Article 18(3) and (4).

77 Ibidem, Article 32.

78 Ibidem, Article 37. Even more generous are the provisions on breakdowns of waste incinerators, Article 46.

79 Directive 2008/98 (fn.51).

80 Directive 2010/75 (fn.44), Article 23.

81 Directive 2012/18, OJ 2012, L197 p.1, Article 20 and Annex V.

laid down in the waste Directive.[82] The directive on waste from the extractive industries requires site inspections prior to the commencement of the deposit of waste and at regular intervals thereafter.[83] No inspection requirements were laid down for the landfill of waste,[84] for waste-water treatment installations[85] or for establishments in ports which receive ship-generated waste.[86]

2.9. SANCTIONS

Most environmental legislative acts use the formula developed by the CJEU that Member States shall determine sanctions – the terms 'sanctions', 'fines' and 'penalties' are used without differentiation – for non-compliance and that such sanctions shall be effective, proportionate and dissuasive. The sanctions shall be transmitted to the Commission; however, the Commission does not compare the sanctions or examine whether they are really effective, proportionate and dissuasive. In practice, it therefore makes no difference whether the standard formula is inserted in an act.

The directive on trade with greenhouse gas emission allowances provides that an operator who does not surrender allowances for the emissions made shall pay a fine of 100 euro per tonne.[87] And following the 'diesel-gate' scandal in 2015, the Commission was given the possibility to charge car manufacturers with an administrative fine of up to €30,000 for each motor vehicle which does not correspond to the type approval for that type of vehicles.[88] It would be relatively easy to introduce, in EU law, such kind of sanctions for installations which emit too many pollutants or do not comply with permit requirements (for waste operators, in nature conservation legislation, etc.) if one wanted to make EU environmental law more effective.

The previous examples showed with great clarity that there is a very wide field for codification of environmental provisions at the EU level. This would not significantly change the repartition of competence between the Member States and the EU. It would not require a great intellectual or economic effort to realise such codification, and in the majority of cases, the substantive law would not change significantly.

---

82 Directive 2008/98 (fn.51), Article 23.

83 Directive 2006/21, OJ 2006, L 102, p.15, Article 17.

84 Directive 1999/31 (fn.31). However, landfills which receive more than 10 tons of waste per day or which have a capacity of more than 25.000 tons come under the provisions of Directive 2010/75 (fn.44).

85 Directive 91/271 (fn.52).

86 Directive 2000/59, OJ 2000; L 332 p.81; according to Article 11, ships may be inspected, whether they delivered the waste.

87 Directive 2003/87, OJ 2003, L 275 p.32, Article 16.

88 Regulation 2018/858, OJ 2018, L 151 p.1, Article 85(1).

3. LIMITS TO CODIFICATION

There are two main reasons why codification of environmental law at EU level does not take place: there is no need for such codification; and there are no persons, groups, associations or bodies who would press for codified provisions.

Producers, traders and importers are in favour of a common market (globalisation), which means more turnover and thus more profit. Uniform rules on this common market facilitate business, prevent unfair competition and provide for a level playing field. In contrast, environmental actors do not need this level playing field. Its main addressees are the local, regional and national administrations which are asked to enforce environmental law. However, these enforcement activities are themselves almost not controlled; this has as a consequence the fact that the enforcement of EU environmental law has become the most serious problem of environmental law. It has not yet generally been accepted that in the long term, different standards in environmental law also influence competition, market positions and profits.

Administrations in the different sectors can easily live with different environmental impact assessment provisions for nature protection projects, TEN projects or urban development planning, with sanctions which diverge or with participation rules that differ between one procedure or the other. Each official has his own little fief, where he is the master and does not have to look, for example, at permit conditions in sectors such as water or waste, when a permit for air emissions is requested. Furthermore, the local or regional provisions are embedded in a web of long-established, traditional national rules. Why should there be all of a sudden a sort of levelling of provisions at the EU level, although there does not appear to be any economic or administrative necessity?

In sum, national, regional and local administrations have no real interest in seeing EU environmental law codified. They arranged themselves with the system as it stands, which leaves them discretion for action and thereby reconfirms their factual power with regard to their area of activity. A generalised codification of environmental law might bring new uncertainties, require changes in existing practices or generate other inconvenience – for example, as regards delays, permit conditions or sanctions. Also, the aligning of formal conditions, for example on an environmental impact assessment, might all too easily lead to substantive changes: an EU environmental impact assessment for the Nordstream 2 gas pipeline through the Baltic Sea could substitute the present five national environmental impact assessments of Russia, Finland, Sweden, Denmark and Germany, but would not necessarily be in the interest of the five national administrations. A permit provision on the distance of wind turbines to private residences might disturb national noise policies and local habits and interfere with existing or emerging planning procedures.

These examples show at the same time that a differentiation between formal provisions for which a codification might be possible, and substantive environmental provisions, where greater prudence is required, is not always possible. Over the last 30 years, there has never been any initiative from any Member State to suggest that the different provisions of environmental law be aligned with each other.

Environmental academic lawyers in the EU are not interested in a codification. Their main area of activity is national environmental law and its evolution, and ultimately the impact of international and EU environmental law on the national law. At best, they compare the development of national environmental law or, in exceptional cases, suggest new pieces of legislation at EU level; but they are not committed to promoting an integrated European environmental law system, as this would, in their opinion, be too political an approach. There is no initiative from any group of environmental law academics to push for a codification of EU environmental law, and even new substantive or procedural environmental provisions at European level are very rare. The Avosetta Group, a loose grouping of environmental academics and one of the very few academic groups which keeps itself busy with environmental law in a transnational context, is a good example: its activities over recent decades practically never concerned measures to be taken at the EU level, but rather, the impact of EU measures on national environmental law.

A similar pattern can be observed with environmental organisations. National environmental organisations see as their vocation the promotion and defence of national environmental law and do not orient themselves towards EU initiatives. And EU environmental organisations – small, short in financial and human resources and with very few lawyers in their staff – are oriented to lobby for better provisions at the EU level, but are not dealing with the quality of the law, its coherence or its codification. Their approach towards EU environmental law is similar to the approach of vested interested groups which also lobby for better provisions to favour their specific interests, without keeping in mind the overall interest to establish an integrated, coherent and consistent system of environmental law. The result is, inevitably, piecemeal legislation.

The European Parliament, which normally reacts on legislative initiatives from the Commission, but does not actively push for new laws, is neither interested nor equipped to work on horizontal questions such as codification.

In theory, the Commission administration could work towards a gradual integration of environmental law. In the past, thanks to the Commission's initiatives, remarkable progress in this regard was achieved in some sectors. Examples are competition law,[89] the enforcement of food law[90] or fisheries law.[91]

89 Regulation 1/2003 on the implementation of the rules on competition law laid down in Articles 81 and 82 of the Treaty, OJ 2003, L 1 p.1.

90 Regulation 2017/625 on official controls and other official activities performed to ensure the application of food and feed law, on animal health and welfare, plant health and plant production, OJ 2017, L 95 p.1.

91 Regulation 1380/2013 (fn.28).

Yet, these legislative acts, horizontal though they are, first of all try to organise a specific sector of EU law by creating framework legislation. They do not intend to provide, for example, for a code of food law or for competition law, and the different specific pieces of legislation continue to use different terms, procedures and requirements.

In any case, in the environmental law sector, the attempt to provide for coherent, integrated provisions on the reporting of Member States, in the form of Directive 91/692, failed and was abandoned. Framework legislation on substantive issues was established in the areas of water, air, waste and industrial installations, but no attempt was made to use identical or at least similar terms and procedures. Rather, each sector – that is, the national and EU administrations which are in charge of elaborating and monitoring the provisions – had its own preferences for terms and conditions. The Commission services were mainly interested in getting a Commission legislative proposal adopted and cared little, if at all, for harmonised terminologies. And as there was no other group of persons to press for codified terms, the present result was achieved, not more and not less.

This situation raises the question of whether a codification of environmental law at the EU level is necessary and desirable, or superfluous. There is no doubt that some codification would be useful, such as the delays for the establishment of national implementation reports, the conditions of a permit, procedural requirements for the granting of an authorisation at EU level or inspections and sanctions. However, on such questions, opinions will continue to differ, and, as law-making also implies the battle for (keeping or gaining) power, there would be a need for pressurising for codified terms.

The sketchy presentation of the actual situation of the potential pressure bodies shows that for a foreseeable time, it cannot be expected that the EU will move into any serious codification activity. This conclusion is completely independent of the uncertain evolution which the EU might take in the coming years, in order to meet the challenges of the growing populism, the departure of the UK from the EU, the challenges by the United States and China and the increasing pressure from migrants. It instead means that the time is not ripe in Europe for a codification of EU environmental law – or that Europe is not ripe for such a codification.

HARMONISING ENVIRONMENTAL STANDARDS FROM THE GUADALQUIVIR TO THE DANUBE DELTA

How can the Circle be Squared?

Nicolas de Sadeleer*

* Professor of EU law, Saint Louis University Jean Monnet chair.

1. INTRODUCTION

At first an obscure field in the 1970s, and having long remained the preserve of engineers and biologists, the environmental policy and the law which it gave rise have ended up asserting themselves both on public and private actors. Although it was not mentioned in the 1957 Treaty of Rome, environmental concerns have, through the various treaty reforms, gradually been able to establish themselves as one of the greatest values enshrined in the EU founding treaties. Environmental protection is not only a core objective of the Union; it has also been placed on equal footing with economic growth and the internal market.

However, the harmonisation process of environmental rules has been fraught with controversies since the inception of this policy. When it comes to decide which ecosystems and species to protect, which hazardous products to control or to ban, which factories to authorise, the thresholds for reuse and recycling waste, EU institutions and the Member States cross swords.

It is the aim of this chapter to explore some of the key issues arising in the harmonisation process of environmental rules. The discussion is structured in the following manner. The focus is firstly placed upon the drivers of the EU environmental policy and how they shaped that policy. In a second section, we shall contemplate the conundrum of legal bases upon which environmental measures can be adopted and the influence they exert on the nature of harmonisation. The third section addresses the numerous challenges faced by the protagonists of the European environmental policy and the hurdles to overcome in determining the common denominator among Member States.

2. GENERALITIES

2.1. THE ENVIRONMENTAL CRISIS

The scales and rates of the changes induced by human activities on ecosystems have been so significant on a geological time scale that it comes as no surprise that we are entering a new geological epoch, the Anthropocene. Indeed, overwhelming scientific evidence highlights the extent to which Earth's atmosphere (destruction of the ozone layer, emission of greenhouse gas (GHGs), etc.), lithosphere (e.g., quarrying, landscaping, urban sprawl, soil erosion, etc.), hydrosphere (pollution of water, salinisation, anthropologically induced floods and droughts, sedimentation of lakes and rivers, rising of sea level, etc.) and biosphere (changes in the vegetational character of major ecosystems, Earth's sixth major extinction, etc.) as well as other earth system processes (nutrient cycles, etc.) are now altered by human activities.[1] The environmental crisis underpinning these changes has become a critical issue confronting all of humanity.

What's more, the less visible but potentially drastic threats are manifold (climate change, health impairment resulting from exposure to chemical substances, microplastic waste, nanotechnology, etc.).

What about Europe? Thanks to EU environmental law and proper enforcement, much has been achieved over these last thirty years in the EU: a ban on lead in petroleum products; phasing out ozone depleting substances; reduction of nitrogen oxide emissions from road transport; improvement of waste water treatment and water quality; streamlining waste; reduction of acidification; and improvement of some aspects of air quality.[2] This significant progress demonstrates that environmental policy and law function properly, provided the Member States are committed to enforcing international rules as well as EU harmonised measures.

However, despite these achievements, the results of both the EU and the domestic environmental policies have at the very least been muted.[3]

Firstly, environmental degradation is manifest everywhere given that our continent has been significantly transformed by industrial, urban, transport, mining, agricultural and forestry activities. In addition, increasingly fragmented by transport infrastructures, subject to intensive urbanisation, cultivation or cattle grazing, polluted and eutrophised, the aquatic and terrestrial ecosystems sink to the lowest common denominator, losing both their cultural and natural specificity.[4] For animal and plant species, this results in a fragmentation and isolation of their habitats, constituting one of the most serious threats to their long-term survival. On account of the degradation of their habitats (urban sprawl, intensification of agricultural practices, etc.), which is only exacerbated by additional threats (excessive hunting, poaching, disturbances inflicted by tourism, etc.), wild species are suffering an unprecedented rate of extinction. Global warming and the depletion of the ozone layer are likely to precipitate much more profound changes to the distribution, structure and functions of European ecosystems.

Secondly, to make matters worse, every step forward – such as reductions in industrial pollution – appears to be cancelled out by the appearance of new phenomena, such as mass consumption and more diffuse sources of pollution proving more difficult to control (light pollution, air pollution, etc.), or unforeseen risks (biotechnology, nanotechnology, endocrine disruptors, etc.).

---

1 *K.T. Pickering and L.O. Owen*, An Introduction to Global Environmental Issues, 2nd. ed., (London-N.Y., Routledge, 1997), xxv.

2 *EEA*, The European Environment. State and Outlook (Copenhagen, 2005), 19.

3 *OECD*, Environmental Outlook to 2050 (Paris, 2012).

4 *N. de Sadeleer*, "The State of Biodiversity in Europe", in *Michael I. Jeffery, Karen Bubna-Litic* (ed.), Biodiversity Conservation, Law and Livelihoods: Bridging the North-South Divide, IUCN Academy of Environmental Law Research Studies, 2007, 181–192.

It comes thus as no surprise that the Member States are facing a daunting agenda of unfinished business, as well as a swathe of new challenges. By way of illustration, air pollution still significantly reduces life expectancy,[5] major rivers are still heavily polluted, the 2010 biodiversity conservation targets have not been met,[6] and the amount of waste increases in spite of recycling policies. As regard new challenges, the most pressing is climate change, whose impacts are becoming ever more frequent. Indeed, the overarching target to limit climate change to temperature increases below 2° C globally during this century[7] is unlikely to be met, in part because of GHGs from other parts of the world.[8] A closer look at GHG emissions within the EU reveals mixed trends: whereas emissions from large point sources have been reduced, at the same time emissions from some mobile and diffuse sources, especially transport-related, have increased substantially.[9]

The environmental impacts are closely linked to other challenges, such as unsustainable consumption patterns, economic growth[10] and others. As environmental challenges become more complex in a more populated and wealthy Europe, the uncertainties and the risks associated with them have increased.[11] Against this background, the European Environment Agency (EEA) is of the view that Europe points towards a number of systemic environmental risks 'which can be triggered by sudden events or built up over time, with the impact often being large and possibly catastrophic'.[12] Whatever the causes, the environmental crisis is perceived as a serious problem in Europe, because ecosystems provide a wide array of services that are usually taken for granted until they have gone missing.

2.2. THE ATTEMPT TO DEFINE THE CONCEPT OF ENVIRONMENT AT EU LEVEL

As far as EU treaty law is concerned, the concept of environment appears in several provisions of the Treaty on the European Union (TEU) and the

5 *EEA*, Air Quality in Europe – 2019, Report 10/2019, p. 66.

6 *EEA*, State of the Nature in Europe, Report 10/2020.

7 Article 2(1) a of the Paris Agreement under the United Nations Framework Convention on Climate Change.

8 *EEA*, Trends and Projections in Europe 2020. Tracking progress towards Europe's climate and energy targets, Report 13/2020, p. 6.

9 *EEA*, The European Environment – State and Outlook 2010 (Copenhagen, 2010), p. 34.

10 The relationship between that sort of economic integration and environmental protection has always been fraught with controversies. On the one hand, trade liberalisation and free competition increase the wealth of trading nations so they could afford to carry out an environmental policy. On the other hand, economic growth at all costs may result in greater pressures on ecosystems.

11 *EEA*, The European Environment – State and Outlook 2010, above, p. 20.

12 Ibid. p. 20.

Treaty on the Functioning of the European Union (TFEU) (i.e. Articles 3(3) and 21(2)(d)–(f) TEU, Articles 11, 114(3), (4), and (5), 191–193, and 194(1) TFEU), without, however, being defined, no doubt out of fear of circumscribing its scope to overly specific areas. Likewise, EU secondary law pays little attention to defining what is meant by the term 'environment'. Attempts to define its boundaries often involve its enumeration through examples.

What is meant by the concept of environment is ripe for discussion. Although everyone is agreed on the core of what is meant by this open concept, disputes arise about the boundaries surrounding its core content.

In English, the notion of environment has been defined as 'The set of circumstances or conditions, esp. physical conditions, in which a person or community lives. Also, physical conditions viewed to the possibility of life',[13] let alone 'the natural world, as a whole or in a particular geographical area, esp. as affected by human activity'.[14] In French, the concept, which appeared in 1972, is defined as: 'Ensemble des conditions naturelles (physiques, chimiques, biologiques) et culturelles (sociologiques) dans lesquelles les organismes vivants (en particulier l'homme), se développent'.[15] The CNRS defines it as 'l'ensemble des éléments physiques qui environnent un organisme vivant, qui se trouvent autour de lui'.[16] In German, *umwelt* is defined as 'Umgebung eines Lebewesen die auf es einwirkt u. seine lebenbedingungen beeinflusst',[17] whereas the concept of *milieu* in Dutch is defined as 'het geheel van uitwendige omstandigheden die van invloed zijn op de leefomstandigheden, het welzijn van de planten, dieren en mensen in een gebied of in het algemeen, zoals de toestand van de atmosfeer, van het water, van de bodem, enz'.[18] Needless to say, these very broad dictionary definitions are testament to the heterogeneous nature of the concept. If there is a catch-all concept, then this is it.

Immune to all efforts at legal classification, this chameleon-like concept may be limited under a narrow reading to NIMBY (not in my back yard) factors, whilst read more broadly it may be coterminous with the biosphere. Furthermore, it continuously overlaps with other concepts, such as ecology, nature, biodiversity, public health, worker protection, land use, living surroundings and sustainable development, which nevertheless have not succeeded in taking its place. In the 21st century, environmental issues cover questions that were ignored until a short time ago, such as global warming, genetically modified organisms (GMOs), product life-cycle analysis and electromagnetic radiation. Last, but not least, given that natural habitats are shrinking, sea levels are rising, glaciers are

13 Shorter Oxford English Dictionary, 5th ed., (Oxford, OUP, 2004).
14 New Oxford American Dictionary, (Oxford, OUP).
15 Le Nouveau Petit Robert de la Langue française (Paris, 2009).
16 *CNRS*, Trésor de la langue française (Paris, 1979).
17 Duden (Mannheim, 1981).
18 Van Dale (Utrecht, Antwerpen, 1999).

melting, fish stocks are fished outside safe biological limits[19] and rare natural resources are depleted, new issues gather momentum.

Taking things to extremes, one might say that there is, on the one hand, an objective dimension based on scientific criteria (state of species conservation,[20] pollution thresholds, ecosystem approach,[21] sustainable yields, total allowable catches, etc.), which seeks to protect the biosphere per se. Thresholds have been established pursuant to scientific analysis classifying ecological risk. Clearly, nature protection law as well as most of water law aim to protect ecosystems as such.[22] This scientific approach stands in opposition to a subjective or an anthropocentric vision of relations between humankind and our surroundings (including economic, aesthetic, cultural and recreational aspects), which focuses more on the quality-of-life dimension than the conditions favourable for life. Consequently, a species may be protected not by virtue of the role it plays within an ecosystem, but on the account of its appeal to a broader public or its economic value. As a result, the protection of the biosphere is justified as a function of the interests of humankind. In this respect, it should be pointed out that measures aiming to reduce noise, odours and air pollutants, as well as radiation, aim chiefly at improving the quality of human life.

Leaving aside this latent tension between two opposing viewpoints, one could ask what is still natural about a heavily 'artificialised' world. How can we distinguish the environment from nature, from ecology or from biology? Given that nature is totally subsumed by humans, we are, as consumers, surrounded by the artefacts of a commoditised nature.[23] Anxious to consume natural products, the uninitiated will fall into the depths of confusion on reading some of the judgments handed down by the CJEU in that regard. For instance, the use in most Member States of the term 'bio' for goods produced from organic agriculture (in French *biologique*, in Italian *biologico*, in Dutch *biologisch*) did not prevent the Spanish authorities from using the term *ecológico* in the indications of food products referring to the organic production method. As a result, the term *bio*

---

19 *EC*, Communication 'Towards more sustainable fishing in the EU: state of play and orientations for 2021', COM(2020) 248 final, p. 6.

20 Article 2 (i) of Directive 92/43/EC on the conservation of natural habitats and of wild fauna and flora.

21 CDB COP V, Decision V/6 on the ecosystem approach; Article 1(3) Marine Strategy Framework Directive 2008/56/EC.

22 Article 11(3)(l) Directive 2000/60/EC establishing a framework for Community action in the field of water policy.

23 *B. McKibben*, The End of Nature (New York, Anchor, 1989); *C. and R. Larrere*, Du bon usage de la nature, Pour une philospophie de l'environnement (Alto Aubier, Paris, 1997) 159; *Ph. Roqueplo*, Climats sous surveillance. Limites et conditions de l'expertise scientifique (Paris, Economica, 1993) 266.

has been customarily and continuously used on the grounds that term bears no relation to the organic method of production of that food. The Court of Justice of the EU (CJEU) agreed with the Spanish authorities in ruling that the term 'bio' must not be accorded specific protection in all Member States and in all languages. Accordingly, the term 'ecológico' was not likely to mislead Spanish consumers, since goods produced from this type of agriculture are in general referred to using the term *ecológico*.[24] Similarly, notwithstanding the presence of traces of lead, cadmium and pesticides, the term 'naturally pure' used on jars of jam will not be misleading for Austrian consumers.[25] In addition, the accidental presence of material derived from certain GMOs not exceeding a particular level in baby food is not subject to specific labelling requirements.[26]

2.3. DOES ENVIRONMENTAL PROTECTION REALLY MATTER AT THE EU LEVEL?

No other issue has produced as much controversy as does the EU environmental policy. Indeed, every environmental issue gives rise to conflicting opinions. Must the water quality be the same for a Swedish and a Bulgarian person? Should a Flemish person have easier access to nature than a Carpathian person, or vice versa? Do we have to breathe the same air in Madrid, London and Brussels as in Luleå? Should the sea sponges of the Black Sea be afforded better protection than the ones from the Irish Sea? Are the Greeks forced to comply with the same waste packaging recycling targets than an industrialised nation such as the Netherlands? Should an inhabitant of Molenbeek have the same life expectancy as a reindeer raiser from Pohjois-Pohjanmaa? Do the Cyprus Wheatear (*Oenanthe cypriaca*) or the Canarian Pine Tree (*Pinus Canariensis*) deserve EU protection although these endemic species are encountered at the outskirts of the continent and are likely to interest but a few naturalists? In other words, does environmental protection really matter? And in particular, is the EU – whose institutions are located in one of the most polluted area on the continent – much better placed to deal with the 'ecological', 'environmental', 'recreational', 'cultural' and 'ethical' expectations than a myriad of national political bodies? Ultimately, the answers to these questions may depend on one's cultural, ethnic, religious and historic background.

---

24 Case C-135/03 *Commission v Spain* [2005] ECR I-6906, paras. 36–41.

25 Case C-465/98 *Adolf Darbo* [2000] ECR I-2321, para. 33.

26 Case C-132/03 *Cadocons* [2005] ECR I-4167.

3. LEGAL CONUNDRUM

3.1. HOW CAN ONE DRAW THE DIVIDING LINE BETWEEN THE INTERNAL MARKET AND A GENUINE ENVIRONMENTAL POLICY?

Each piece of EU legislation must be rooted in one or more legal bases set out either in the TEU or in the TFEU. The determination of the relevant legal base is required in light of the principle of the allocation of powers, the duty to preserve the prerogatives of the EU institutions, the obligation to state reasons and the requirement of legal certainty.[27] Needless to say, the choice of legal basis of pieces of legislation aiming at protecting the quality of the environment represents a critical juncture in relations between institutions, as well as the relations between the Member States and the EU. Firstly, in defining the scope of the EU's intervention, the legal basis enables the EU to exercise its regulatory competence in such a field.[28] Moreover, the basis chosen determines not only which institution has the responsibility to take the action but also the procedure to follow and the objective pursued. Furthermore, it also determines the types of acts that can be adopted. Just as the powers of the Commission, the Parliament and the Council are capable of varying considerably depending on the procedure applied, they can also end up expressing contradicting preferences as regards the choice to be made between the different legal bases provided for.

It is not the case that every single provision even remotely relating to environmental issues must have been adopted under the only chapter of the treaty dedicated to environmental policy (chapter 19).[29] Regarding the EU environmental secondary legislation, it is possible to trace out the dividing line between the treaty provisions governing the internal market and the environment, respectively.

3.2. THE PREVALENCE OF MARKET INTEGRATION UNDER ARTICLE 114 TFEU

The rise of environmental policy was undeniably born out of the concern to avoid distortions of competition between undertakings. To give the national authorities free rein to enact unilateral product standards would have entailed the risk of fragmenting the internal market and hindering the free movement

27 Case C-370/07 *Commission v Council* [2009] ECR I-8917, paras. 37, 39, 46, and 48.

28 In accordance with the principle of conferral (Article 5(1) TEU), the legal base occupies centre stage inasmuch as it identifies the competence under which EU institutions act.

29 *N. de Sadeleer*, 'Environmental Governance and the Legal Bases Conundrum' (2012) *Oxford Yearbook of European Law*, 31(1): 1–29.

of goods within that market.[30] Against this backdrop, a significant number of product-oriented directives and regulations which have a direct impact on the internal market, and in particular those which lay down product standards, were adopted on the base of Article 100A EC, Article 95 EC and since December 2009, Article 114 TFEU, provisions empowering the EU institutions to enact all measures affecting the establishment and the functioning of the internal market, including those relating to environmental protection. It must be noted that this provision expressly refers, in the first, third and fourth paragraphs, to the protection of the environment. Moreover, in virtue of Article 3 TEU, the UE aims 'to promote ... the well-being of its peoples' and, in particular, 'a high level of protection and improvement of the quality of the environment'. It must be noted that environmental objectives must also be taken into account in virtue of Article 11 TFEU[31] and Article 37 EUCHR[32] within the context the internal market.

Article 114 TFEU has thus been selected as the genuine legal base for the harmonisation of the rules relating to products impairing the environment. Although this provision does not give EU lawmakers any general competence to harmonise national rules on health or environmental matters,[33] it has been applied for harmonising environmental pollution and risk issues ranging from vehicle exhaust emissions (Directive 70/220/EEC), GMOs (Directive 2008/1),[34] biocides (Regulation (EU) 528/2012),[35] pesticides (Regulation (EC) 1107/2009)[36] and chemicals (1907/2006 REACH regulation[37] and 1272/2008 CLP regulation[38]). That being said, the determination of the relevant level of protection can be dogged by controversies. In the *DecaDBE* case, the CJEU held

30 *N. de Sadeleer*, 'Trade v Environment in EU Law' 13:5 (2016) *US-China Law Review* 365–381.

31 The General Court stressed that in requiring that a high level of protection of the environment be maintained, Regulation No 1107/2009 on pesticides is applying both Article 114(3) TFEU and Article 11 TFEU that provides the integration of environmental protection requirements into the definition and implementation of the European Union's policies and activities, in particular with a view to promoting sustainable development. Case T-584/13 *BASF Agro* v. *Commission* [2018] ECLI:EU:T:2018:279, paras. 55.

32 Case C-444/15 *Associazione Italia Nostra Onlus* [2016] ECLI:EU:C:2016:978, paras. 61–63.

33 C-300/89 *Commission v Council* [1991] ECR I-2867; C-155/91 *Commission v Council* [1993] ECR I-939.

34 *N. de Sadeleer*, 'Marketing and Cultivation of GMOs in the EU. An Uncertain Balance between Centrifugal and Centripetal Forces' (2015)(4) *EJRR* 532–558.

35 Regulation (EC) No 528/2012 of the European Parliament and of the Council of 22 May 2012 concerning the making available on the market and use of biocides.

36 Regulation (EC) No 1107/2009 of the European Parliament and of the Council of 21 October 2009 concerning the placing of plant protection products on the market.

37 Regulation (EC) No 1907/2006 of the European Parliament and of the Council of 18 December 2006 concerning the Registration, Evaluation, Authorisation and Restriction of Chemicals (REACH), establishing a European Chemicals Agency (REACH).

38 Regulation (EC) No 1272/2008 on the classification, labelling and packaging of substances and mixtures (CLP Regulation).

that the prohibition on the use of certain hazardous substances in electrical and electronic equipment implies, in accordance with the requirement for a high level of protection, that the European Commission may 'grant exemptions only in accordance with carefully defined conditions' and that the conditions for exemption be interpreted strictly.[39] In this case, the fact that the directive had been enacted on the basis of Article 95 EC (Article 114 TFEU) did not have the effect of exempting the European Commission from the requirement to respect the obligation for a high level of protection under Articles 152 and 174 EC (Articles 168 and 191(1) TFEU). On another note, the difficulties of achieving a consensus within the European Commission can lead to belated decisions. By way of illustration, the General Court declared that the European Commission, by failing to adopt delegated acts to specify scientific criteria for the determination of endocrine-disrupting properties, has failed to fulfil its obligations under Regulation (EU) No 528/2012 on biocidal products.[40]

From an economic perspective, differentiated policies could be a source for distortions to competition. Due to their implementation in a disorderly fashion, national initiatives also risk turning out to be largely ineffective, as pollution does not respect international borders. In sharp contrast to Article 193 TFEU, Article 114 restricts Member States' powers to enact derogating provisions. By authorising the maintenance or adoption of more binding measures with the endorsement of the European Commission, Article 114 TFEU avoids the spectre of the creation of a multi-speed Europe on environmental questions.[41]

It is fair to say that against this backdrop, the Member States are not too willing to enact more stringent standards than the ones adopted by the EU within the framework of the internal market policy.

3.3. A GENUINE ENVIRONMENTAL POLICY UNDER ARTICLE 192 TFEU

On the other side of the dividing line, the genuine environmental legal base, Article 192 TFEU, embraces all acts for which an analysis of the aim and the content of the measure shows that they seek to achieve a high level of environmental protection and that they at most affect the establishment of the internal market on an ancillary base. The harmonisation pursued under that policy has to achieve a high level of environmental protection.

Here, since environmental objectives are predominant, considerations regarding the internal market become secondary. Despite their indirect or

---

39 Cases C-14/06 and 295/06 *Parliament and Denmark v. Commission* [2008] ECR I-1649, paras. 74 and 75.

40 Case T-521/14 *Sweden* v. *Commission* [2007] ECLI:EU:T:2015:976.

41 *I. Maletic*, The Law and Policy of Harmonisation in Europe's Internal Market (Cheltenham, Edward Elgar, 2013).

potential impact on the functioning of the internal market,[42] the vast majority of the EU directives aimed at protecting wildlife, different ecosystems, soils, marine environments, underground as well as surface water, air and the climate, procedural rights, environmental auditing and liability for environmental damage have been adopted on the basis of Article 192 TFEU.[43] In addition, the acts regulating the pollution emitted by listed installations and waste management[44] have also been adopted on the basis of this provision.

3.4. MUST MARKET INTEGRATION PREVAIL OVER ENVIRONMENTAL CONCERNS?

In spite of this clear theoretical differentiation, it is hardly easy to sketch out the dividing line between Articles 114 and 192 TFEU. In spite of their impact on the functioning of the internal market, several acts, which regulate the placing on the market of products, end up falling within the fold of environmental policy.[45] In fact, the choice remains a delicate one. Is environmental protection best assured through the adoption of uniform legislation? Or is it necessary to guarantee this protection through minimum harmonisation rules relying on Article 192 TFEU? One might answer these questions by stating that since they are reached on the basis of a consensus among Member States, maximum harmonisation rules adopted pursuant to Article 114 TFEU do not authorise the states to seek an absolute level of protection, even though in the wake of the Treaty of Amsterdam, the Council and the Parliament must endeavour to attain a high level of protection. In contrast, through the mediation of minimum harmonisation rules, Article 192 TFEU leaves untouched the Member States' powers to adopt a higher level of protection than that set by the EU harmonisation rule,[46] even where this mechanism may result in the emergence of European

42 Case C-155/91 *Commission v Council*, above; and Case C-187/93 *European Parliament v Council* [1994] ECR I-2857, paras. 24–26.

43 For an overview of the different acts founded on Article 192 TFEU, see *L. Krämer*, EU Environmental Law, 8th ed. (London, Sweet & Maxwell, 2016) 54–56; *D. Langlet and S. Mahmoudi*, EU Environmental Law and Policy (Oxford, OUP, 2016) 97; *N. de Sadeleer*, Commentaire Mégret. Environnement et marché intérieur (Brussels, ULB, 2010) 247–329.

44 However, product-related waste standards – packaging, hazardous substances in technical equipment – are based on Article 114 TFEU.

45 Directive 1999/94/EC relating to the availability of consumer information on fuel economy and CO_2 emissions in respect of the marketing of new passenger cars [1999] OJ L12/16; European Parliament and Council Regulation (EC) 443/2009 setting emission performance standards for new passenger cars as part of the community's integrated approach to reduce CO_2 emissions from light-duty vehicles [2009] OJ L 140/1.

46 Case C-194/01 *Commission v Austria* [2004] ECR I-4579, Case C-322/00 *Commission v Netherlands* [2003] ECR I-11267, Case C-184/97 *Commission v Germany* [1999] ECR I-7837, Case C-6/03 *Deponiezweckverband Eiterköpfe* [2005] ECR I-2753; C-534/13 *Fipa Group* [2014] ECLI:EU:C:2014:2393; Cases C-378/08, C-379/08 and C-380/08, *ERG* [2015] ECLI:EU:C:2010:126.

environmental law *à la carte*. It follows that air, water and soil emission standards are likely to differ from one Member State to another or from one region to another. Moreover, Member States with a low environmental profile are likely to argue for the adoption of EU harmonisation standards lacking vigour, arguing that more ambitious Member States could always reckon upon more stringent standards in accordance with Article 193 TFEU.[47]

This all begs a number of questions. Are the fears that economic cohesion may be undermined by more stringent national standards overstated? Should we conceive the environmental policy exclusively in terms of market unity, or in terms of ecosystem services? Does the importance of ecological challenges not imply, by contrast, that the Member States may move forward by adopting, if necessary, more stringent standards than the one provided for under the EU harmonisation rule?

Ultimately, perhaps this is simply just a false dichotomy. The choice of Article 114 TFEU as a legal basis for environmental measure does not mean that the internal market shall prevail over environmental considerations. Indeed, the court has recognised, on the basis of Article 11 and Article 114(3) TFEU, that in the context of the application of Regulation No 1107/2009 on pesticides, 'the protection of the environment takes precedence over economic considerations, with the result that it may justify adverse economic consequences, even those which are substantial, for certain traders'.[48] In spite of this weighing of interests, whenever the internal market measure aims at implementing the precautionary principle,[49] the EU institutions are called on to carry out an economic assessment of the economic and social effects to which the measure may lead.[50] Furthermore, one might be inclined to agree with this, where one considers that the Member States are merely transposing directives adopted on the basis of Article 192 TFEU, without seeking, however, to apply reinforced protection measures.[51]

3.5. OTHER LEGAL BASES

In addition, owing to the cross-cutting character of environmental policy, an array of other EU policies do integrate, in accordance with Article 11 TFEU, the requirements stemming from the environmental policy. It follows that environmental issues encompass a broad range of measures ranging from green

47 *L. Krämer*, EC Environmental Law, 6th ed. (Thomson, Sweet & Maxwell, 2007), 87.

48 Case T-475/07 *Dow AgroSciences and Others* v *Commission* [2011] EU:T:2011:445, para. 143; case T-483/11 *Sepro Europe* v *Commission*, [2013] ECLI:EU:T:2013:407, para. 85; and of 12 December 2014, Case T-269/11 *Xeda International* v *Commission* [2014] ECLI:EU:T:2014:1069, para. 138; Case T-584/13 *BASF Agro* v *Commission* [2018] ECLI:EU:T:2018:279, para. 55.

49 *N. de Sadeleer*, Environmental Principles, 2nd ed. (Oxford, OUP, 2020), 135–361.

50 Case T-584/13 *BASF Agro* v *Commission* [2018] ECLI:EU:T:2018:279, paras. 162 to 170.

51 *J.H. Jans*, 'Gold plating of European Environmental Measures?' 6:4 (2009), *JEEPL* 417–435.

energy, regulation of fisheries, cross-compliance in agriculture, product-policy and waste management or wildlife conservancy.

By way of illustration, Directive 2000/59/EC on port reception facilities for ship-generated waste and cargo residues – whose aim is to reduce the discharges of ship-generated waste and cargo residues into the sea by improving the availability waste facilities for ship-generated waste in harbours – is based upon Article 100 TFEU regarding transport policy. Directive 2010/31/EU on the energy performance of buildings was adopted, pursuant to Article 194(2) TFEU, as part of the energy policy.

The CJEU ruled that one regulation, which limited the use of driftnets, and another regulation on agricultural production methods, which were adopted on the common agricultural policy (CAP) legal basis, were rightly covered by the CAP.[52]

Likewise, the choice of the relevant legal bases for acts regulating radioactive materials has been embroiled with controversies. In *Greek Chernobyl I*, a case concerning the conditions for importing agricultural products originating in third countries following the nuclear accident at Chernobyl, the CJEU confirmed the applicability of the common commercial policy legal base when adopting a regulation governing imports of agricultural products originating in third countries following the accident at the Chernobyl nuclear power station.[53] By the same token, though a measure relating to radioactive substances could be considered as enhancing human health within the meaning of Article 191(1) TFEU, the CJEU ruled that Directive 2013/51/Euratom regarding the protection of human health against the dangers of radioactive substances in waters intended for human consumption was legitimately adopted on the basis of Article 31 EAEC Treaty.[54]

To sum up, given their transversal nature, environmental issues are likely to be regulated at the EU level within the framework of different policies.

4. THE CHALLENGE OF HARMONISING ENVIRONMENTAL STANDARDS

4.1. SUBSIDIARITY AND HARMONISATION OF ENVIRONMENTAL STANDARDS

The EU has no exclusive competence for protecting the environment. Pursuant to Article 4(2)(e) TFEU, the environment has been classified among the 11

52 Case C-405/92 *Mondiet* [1993] ECR I-6133, paras. 25–27; and Case C-336/00 *Huber* [2002] ECR I-7699, paras. 25–27.

53 Case C-62/88 *Greece v Council* (Chernobyl I) [1990] ECR I-1527.

54 Case C-48/14 *European Parliament v Council* [2015] ECLI:EU:C:2015:9, para. 39.

shared competences alongside the internal market, consumers protection and transports, *inter alia*. Accordingly, in virtue of Article 2(2) TFEU, the EU has the power to legislate and to adopt legally binding acts in the environmental area. Since environmental policy is not vested exclusively in the EU, the principle of subsidiarity enshrined in Article 5(3) TEU applies.[55] Moreover, subsidiarity comes much more to the fore in the environmental field than in other policies such as the internal market. Indeed, in sharp contrast to the harmonisation of the internal market, where Member States are usually unable to achieve the economic goals pursued by harmonisation,[56] environment policy entails constantly cooperation between all institutional players.

One needs to address the following question: which environmental issues are likely to be harmonised?

Firstly, there is no doubt as to the Member States' inability to solve environmental issues having a trans-boundary nature, such as ozone depletion, climate change, biodiversity, air and water pollution, among others. As a result, regulating these issues should be a matter for the EU and not chiefly for the Member States. Account must also be made of the fact that a number of EU environmental measures have cross-frontier elements. For instance, contaminated land, a rather localised form of pollution, is excluded from EU waste legislation[57] whereas contaminated land remediation must be tackled exclusively in accordance with Directive 2010/75 on industrial emissions and with Regulation 1013/2016 regarding their trans-frontier movements (when the contaminated land is treated abroad).[58] That being said, the directives do cover a number of plants and installations that do not have any trans-frontier impacts, such as landfills.[59] By the same token, Directive 2007/60/EC on the assessment and management of flood risks is covering all types of floods irrespective of whether the river basin encompasses more than one Member State.[60]

Secondly, given the significant discrepancies among the Member States regarding the stringency of their environmental policies, EU harmonisation ensures that a common playing field will apply in all Member States in a way that ensures a high level of environmental protection. In the absence of such a common regulatory approach, the efforts made by the most zealous Member

---

55 Case C-114/01 *AvestaPolarit Chrome* [2003] ECR I-8725, para. 56.

56 Case C-58/08 *Vodafone* [2010] ECR I-4999, paras. 77 and 78.

57 Article 2(1) (b) and (c) Directive 2008/98. See also Case C-1/03 *van de Walle* [2004] ECR I-7613, annotated by *N. de Sadeleer* (2008)3 *CMLR* 16.

58 Article 22 of Directive 2010/75/EU of 24 November 2010 on industrial emissions; and Regulation 1013/2016 on shipment of waste.

59 Directive 1999/31/EC of 26 April 1999 on the *landfill* of waste.

60 *L. Krämer*, EU Environmental Law, 8th ed. (Thomson, Sweet & Maxwell, 2016) 3.

States would easily be frustrated by the passivity of the others. This common playing field makes sense on the account that environmental policy entails significant costs. Accordingly, as a matter of solidarity, each Member State should commit itself to investing in environmental infrastructures (water treatment plants,[61] waste treatment plants,[62] etc.). Our view is that the absence of common standards amounts to a serious economic flaw. Tougher harmonised regulations on products, renewables, nature conservation and energy efficiency are not only good for the environment, but also for the competitiveness of the Member States economies. By the same token, several authorities complain that the Natura 2000 network hinders economic development, a statement that has never been supported by any serious economic studies. However, these criticisms are leaving aside the economic benefits – ecotourism, rural development and ecosystemic services, among others – of such a nature conservation policy. In order to be viable, tomorrow's economy should definitively be green.

Thirdly, given that the European Commission enjoys specific powers to require Member States to apply secondary law, the implementation of common environmental standards is likely to offer better protection for ecosystems than a highly variegated international law.

A fourth observation must be made. It is likely that unilateral measures would exacerbate the distortion of competition and create new barriers to free trade.

That being said, some environmental issues may also fall within the scope of an exclusive competence that is not subject to the principle of subsidiarity. In that connection, the opinion of the CJEU regarding a new generation trade agreement – the Free Trade Agreement between the EU and the Republic of Singapore – is a case in point. According to the Council and the 25 Member States which have submitted observations to the court, the provisions concerning environmental protection, set out in the envisaged free trade agreement, fell within the environmental competences shared between the EU and the Member States. However, the court took the opposite view: given that the parties are prohibited from applying measures adopted or maintained to implement a multilateral environmental agreement in a manner that would constitute a means of arbitrary or unjustifiable discrimination between the parties or a disguised restriction on trade, the agreement at issue has 'direct and immediate effects on the trade' and consequently fell under the exclusive competence regarding the common commercial policy.[63]

61 Directive 91/271/EEC of 21 May 1991 concerning urban waste-water treatment.
62 Article 16(1) to (3), Directive 2008/98 on waste.
63 Opinion 2/15 [2017] C:2017:376, para. 157.

4.2. AN EU ENVIRONMENT POLICY LEADING TO HARMONISATION OF NATIONAL PROCEDURAL AND SUBSTANTIVE STANDARDS

Driven by the fear of a disintegration of the internal market, concerns over portraying a less mercantile image of the EU, as well as the intention to safeguard ecosystems and species under threat, a European environmental policy has gradually emerged.[64]

Starting from a range of action programmes, EU environmental law has progressively grown from a sparse set of directives to a vast body of regulatory measures aiming both to regulate the main forms of pollution as well as to protect the main ecosystems along with some of their composite elements. Today it is possible to count more than three hundred regulatory measures that are around 8 per cent of EU law. Several EU agencies, 27 Member States, three EFTA States, hundreds of regions and *länder* and thousands of municipalities now implement EU secondary environmental law through a complex web of regulations that affect virtually every aspect of our lives.

Neither Article 192 nor Article 114 TFEU specifies that a particular legal act should be used in order to harmonise environmental measures. Accordingly, environmental standards have been harmonised at EU level haphazardly by directives and regulations. As a matter of fact, in environmental matters there has always been a mismatch with traditional legal categories.

4.2.1. Harmonisation through Regulations

Regulations, which for a long time played a secondary role, have been privileged as a means of enhancing a level playing field for traders, in particular with regard to harmonisation of the placing of certain goods posing environmental and health risks on the market and control of the import, export or transfer of goods involving ecological risks (chemical products, GMOs, etc.). For instance, chemicals (REACH and CLP regulations), pesticides and GMOs have been harmonised thanks to the adoption of regulations. Given that these sectors are product-related, it comes as no surprise that the EU institutions have lately favoured regulations adopted pursuant to Article 114 TFEU. The preference for regulations based on Article 114 TFEU could be explained by the fact that the more flexible nature of a directive entails a genuine risk of market fragmentation.

Regulations have also been adopted under Article 192 TFEU with the aim of formalising voluntary forms of participation for businesses; see, for example, the regulations on eco-labels or on environmental audits and where it is necessary

---

64 *N. de Sadeleer*, EU Environmental Law and the Internal Market (Oxford, OUP, 2014), 175–233.

to implement obligations flowing from international agreements to which the EU is a party.[65] On occasion, a choice has been made, within the context of environmental policy, for regulations aiming to set out product standards or to ban the import of endangered species[66] or invasive species.[67] Moreover, in some cases directives are amended, or even completed, by regulations.[68] On the other hand, the EU lawmaker has never used regulations to ensure the protection of water or the air, or the regulation of noise.

In practice, these regulations encapsulate a number of provisions requesting Member States to take specific actions.[69] Where these regulations require Member States to establish enforcement agencies and to develop enforcement policy, they are not self-executing.

4.2.2. Harmonisation through Directives

Given the importance conferred on subsidiarity, directives – and more specifically, framework directives[70] – are deemed to be the spearhead of EU harmonisation. The provisions of these framework directives are generally worded in very general terms, whilst regulations may be extremely precise.[71] By prescribing broad objectives but leaving the choice of implementation to Member State authorities, framework directives are well tailored to take into account the diversity of administrative and legal culture in the EU. In framing in fleeting terms the states' obligations to protect the ecosystems, these directives bear more

65 Regulation (EC) No. 2037/2000 on substances that deplete the ozone layer, see earlier in this chapter; Regulation (EC) No. 1013/2006 on the shipment of waste, see earlier in this chapter; Regulation (EC) No. 338/97 on the protection of species of wild fauna and flora by regulating trade therein.

66 Regulation (EEC) No. 348/81 on common rules for imports of whales or other cetacean products; Regulation (EEC) No. 3254/91 prohibiting the use of leghold traps in the EU; Regulation (EC) No 338/97 of 9 December 1996 on the protection of species of wild fauna and flora by regulating trade therein.

67 Regulation (EU) No 1143/2014 of 22 October 2014 on the prevention and management of the introduction and spread of invasive alien species.

68 See Regulation (EC) No. 166/2006 concerning the establishment of a European Pollutant Release and Transfer Register and amending Council Directives 91/689/EEC and 96/61/EC [2006] OJ L33/1; Regulation (EC) No. 850/2004 on persistent organic pollutants and amending Directive 79/117/EEC [2004] OJ L158/1. See also Art 19(3) of Directive 2003/87/EC establishing a scheme for greenhouse gas emission allowance trading within the EU ([2003] OJ L275/32–46) empowering the European Commission to enact regulations.

69 *L. Krämer*, 'On the Effectiveness of Monitoring the Application of EU Environmental Law' in New Perspectives on Environmental Law in the 21st Century (Barcelona, M. Pons, 2018) 15.

70 Regarding the technique of environmental framework directives, see *M. Bogaart*, 'The Emergence of the Framework Directive in EU Environmental Policy', in *M. Peeters and R. Uylenburg*, EU Environmental Legislation (Cheltenham, Edward Elgar, 2015) 48–79.

71 See the degree of precision reached by Regulation (EC) No. 1013/2006 on the shipment of waste ([2006] OJ L190/1) and European Parliament and Council Regulation (EC) No. 2037/2000 on substances that deplete the ozone layer ([2000] OJ L244/1).

resemblance to declarations of intent. In so doing, the lawmaker increases the discretion of national authorities in the choice of form and appropriate means for implementing EU law. In tolerating – let alone encouraging – administrative diversity, many of these directives keep uniformity at bay.

Clearly, the extent of such discretion compounds the difficulties faced by the European Commission in verifying in accordance with Article 17 TEU the compliance of EU environmental law in Member States. To make matters more complex, the air, water, waste management and nature conservation policies are highly decentralised, since the control over implementation is left, by virtue of Article 192(4) TFEU, to the Member States. In particular, the enforcement of the EU harmonised measures is entirely left to the Member States.[72] It follows that a decision as to whether to grant a license for operating a plant, to conduct an environmental impact assessment, to regulate waste streams or to prosecute environmental crimes are matters for national, regional and even to local authorities, not for the European Commission.

Accordingly, it is appropriate that the Member States establish control and oversight regimes in order to apply the policing measures associated with the conservation of environmental protection[73] and in order to punish infringements.[74] Given that the mechanics of enforcement diverge significantly among Member States, the adequacy of enforcement still remains a major issue. As the Guardian of the Treaties, the European Commission only exercises a relatively marginal control over the proper implementation of EU secondary law.[75]

By the same token, the financing of environmental projects is, by virtue of Article 192(4) TFEU, also a matter for the Member States. Remarkably enough, although the social and economic pillars of sustainable development dispose of funds made available for these purposes,[76] the title dedicated to the environment does not make any provision for structural financing. Moreover, the significance of the socio-economic funds dwarfs the LIFE Programme that is deemed to be one of the spearheads of EU environmental funding.[77] Furthermore, other

---

72 Given the absence of genuine liability rules and legal remedies, private enforcement still is far less prominent.

73 Recommendation 2001/331/EC of 4 April 2001 providing for minimum criteria for environmental inspections in the Member States [2001] OJ L118/41.

74 See Directive 2008/99/EC on the protection of the environment through criminal law. The Framework Decision was nullified in 2005 in Case C-176/03 *Commission v Council* [2005] ECR I-7879.

75 Given that the Commission does not have investigative powers of its own in the environmental area, it is largely reliant on the information provided by complainants, by public or private bodies, by the press or by the Member State concerned. See Case C-494/01 *Commission v Ireland* [2005] ECR I-3331, para. 43, Case C-135/05 *Commission v Italy* [2007] ECR I-3475, para. 28; and Case C-297/08 *Commission v Italy* [2010] ECR I-1749, para. 101.

76 Regulation (EC) 2012/2002 establishing the European Union Solidarity Fund [2002] OJ L311/3.

77 Launched in 1992, Life has financed 3115 projects contributing in €2.2 billion to the protection of the environment. The latest Financial Instrument for the Environment (LIFE+)

programmes of importance to the protection of the natural environment depend on the willingness of the Member States to provide the matching funds. By way of illustration, although the contribution to the agro-environmental schemes provided under Regulation (EC) 1698/2005 on rural development may be as low as 15% – unlike the first pillar of the CAP, these schemes are subject to co-financing – this appears to be a sufficient deterrent for state financial intervention.[78]

4.2.3. *Technical Directives Akin to Regulations*

Some directives are so precise and restrictive that they end up looking like regulations. This may be the case of the Emissions Trading System (ETS) Directive. The ETS was established by Directive 2003/87/EC. Constituting the *piece de résistance* of the EU's climate change policy, its main objective is to reduce GHGs in line with the commitments made by the EU and its Member States under the Kyoto Protocol, and lately under the Paris Agreement. Following its entry into force on 1 January 2005, the ETS was significantly amended[79] in 2004, in 2008, in 2009 and in 2018 – in particular in order to meet the political commitments made by the European Council. It has been gradually extended to 12,000 industrial plants as well as to airliners in relation to certain flights. The inclusion of aviation in ETS is deemed to be compatible with customary international law,[80] on the grounds that the EU and its Member States enjoy 'unlimited jurisdiction' over aircraft that are present with the territory of one Member State.[81]

Thanks to the ETS, the largest carbon market in the world has been created. It has subsequently been emulated both in China and in the USA. Harmonisation was justified on the one hand by the desire to coordinate the implementation of these international obligations and on the other hand out of concerns to avoid distortions of competition. The environmental objective of curbing GHG emissions stands alongside several ancillary objectives: 'sub-objectives of an economic nature'[82] consisting of the maintenance of the 'cost-effective and economically efficient manner';[83] 'economic development and employment';[84]

---

was adopted through Regulation (EC) 614/2007 concerning the Financial Instrument for the Environment (LIFE+) [2007] OJ L149/1. See Communication from the Commission, Mid-term review of the LIFE+ Regulation, COM(2010) 516 final.

78 *B. Jack*, Agriculture and EU Environmental Law (Farnham, Ashgate, 2009).

79 *N. de Sadeleer*, Commentaire Mégret. Environnement et marché intérieur (Brussels, ULB, 2010) 291–313.

80 Case C-366/10 *ATAA* [2011] ECLI:EU:C:2011:864, para. 125.

81 Ibid. paras. 124 and 125.

82 Case T-178/05, *UK v Commission* [2005] ECR II-4807, para. 60.

83 Directive 2003/87/EC of 13 October 2003 establishing a scheme for greenhouse gas emission allowance trading within the Community, Article 1.

84 Ibid. Preamble, 5th recital

and the presentation of the 'integrity of the internal market'[85] and the maintenance of competitive conditions.[86] A particular effect of this economic logic is to ensure that reductions in GHG emissions occur at the lowest cost.[87]

At the outset, the use of a directive in order to harmonise the area reflected the highly decentralised nature of the ETS from the start. In effect, within the ambit of the shared competence over environmental law, this instrument leaves a considerable margin of appreciation to the Member States, which should be assessed with reference to the principle of subsidiarity.[88] Accordingly, the Member States were charged with various tasks in relation to the organisation and control of this market.

Following the entry into force of the rules applicable to the third period (2013–2020) provided for under the amending Directive 2009/29/EC, the powers of the Member States have been restricted further. As it was necessary to reduce distortions of competition to a minimum, numerous aspects of the system are now governed by European Commission regulations. As a result, the ETS now oscillates between decentralisation and centralisation.

4.2.4. *Room for Manoeuvre Left by the Directives to the Member States*

Account must be made of the fact that the issue of harmonisation is more complex than just a matter of choice between Article 192 and 194 TFEU or other legal bases.[89] It is mostly the substantive content of the directives that determines the leeway left to the Member States in implementing their environmental obligations. The following cases illustrate the room for manoeuvre left to the state authorities in carrying out their environmental obligations.

4.3. THE BROAD DISCRETION GRANTED TO THE MEMBER STATES BY THE ENVIRONMENTAL DIRECTIVES

On the one hand, the CJEU is taking duly into account the discretion left to the national authorities by the recourse to framework directives. The following cases are testament to this judicial approach.

- The Court has, for example, held that when national courts review the legality of measures to combat agricultural pollution, they must take account of the discretionary power of the Member States, which is presupposed by the

85 Preamble, 7th recital.
86 Preamble, 7th recital.
87 Case C-127/07 *Arcelor Atlantique et Lorraine* [2008] ECLI:EU:C:2008:728 para. 32.
88 Case T-374/07 *Germany v Commission* [2007] T:2007:147, paras. 78 and 79; Case T-263/07 *Estonia v Commission* [2009] para. 52.
89 *D. Langlet and S. Mahmoudi*, EU Environmental Law and Policy (Oxford, OUP, 2016) 118.

complex nature of the assessments concerning the impact of the spreading of nitrates.[90]

- Similarly, Member States are endowed with broad discretion when they are required to ensure that their land-use policies take into consideration the need to maintain appropriate distance between Seveso establishments and buildings for public use.[91]
- The Water Framework Directive (WFD) 2000/60 is also a case in point given that it does not seek to achieve complete harmonisation of the rules of the Member States concerning water.[92] Accordingly, the Member States must be allowed a certain margin of discretion for determining whether the construction of a hydropower plant may in fact be an overriding public interest such that it could outweigh the preventive requirements of Article 4(7) of Directive 2000/60.[93] By the same token, the methods enabling the objective of ensuring that water-pricing policies provide adequate incentives for users to use water resources efficiently are left to the discretion of the national authorities.[94] Accordingly, the setting of the price of water services according to the volume of water actually consumed constitutes one of these methods. However, nothing in the WFD precludes that the water-pricing policy based on a price for water consumed by the users includes the costs of water distribution independent of their consumption.
- Regarding brownfields, it may be impossible to identify the polluter of a contaminated plot of land. Although Directive 2004/35/CE on environmental liability (ELD Directive) requires that a causal link exists between the operator and the damage, it does not preclude that national law could order the landowners to adopt preventive or remedial measures even when they are not the operator who had caused the damage.[95]

4.4. THE NARROW DISCRETION STEMMING FROM A TELEOLOGICAL AND SYSTEMATIC INTERPRETATION OF THE ENVIRONMENTAL OBLIGATIONS

On the other hand, even though most of the obligations laid down in framework directives provide for relatively fuzzy obligations, the discretion stemming from these obligations is by no means unfettered. In a swathe of cases, the CJEU has

---

90 Case C-293/97 *Standley* [2004] ECR I-2603, para. 37.

91 Case C-53/10 *Franz Mücksch* [2011] ECLI:EU:C:2011:585, paras. 40–1.

92 Case C-32/05 *Commission* v *Luxembourg* [2006] ECLI:EU:C:2006:749, para. 41; Case C-525/12 *Commission* v *Germany*, [2014] ECLI:EU:C:2014:2202, para. 50; and Case C-461/13 *Bund für Umwelt und Naturschutz Deutschland*, [2015] ECLI:EU:C:2015:433, para. 34.

93 Case C-346/14 *Commission* v *Austria* [2016] ECLI:EU:C:2006:749, para. 70.

94 Case C-686/15 *Vodoopskrba i odvodnja* [2016] ECLI:EU:C:2016:927, para. 21.

95 Cases C-378/08, C-379/08 and C-380/08, *ERG* [2015] ECLI:EU:C:2010:126, para. 63.

gradually been able to uncover their full potential, thanks to a teleological and systematic interpretation of these texts, thereby causing the objectives of nature conservation or the preservation of the environment to prevail over more literal interpretations. Accordingly, the purpose of the various directives at issue is the determining factor as to how to interpret the scope of complex technical concepts.

It is settled case law that given the aim of different directives to providing for a high level of protection of the environment, their provisions must be interpreted broadly. In particular, in an attempt to guarantee the effectiveness of the conservation regimes for vulnerable ecosystems, the CJEU has accordingly circumscribed the margin of appreciation of the national authorities in relation to the operations subject either to environmental impact assessments or to Strategic Environmental Assessments (SEAs), the designation of vulnerable areas, the qualification of waste and environmental information, as well as the quality of water bodies.

- As regards the interpretation of the scope of technical projects laid down in the annex of the EIA Directive, codified by Directive 2011/92/EU,[96] the CJEU held that 'the purpose of the directive would be undermined if some projects could escape an environmental impact assessment, though they were likely to have significant effects on the environment'.[97]
- Given the objective of SEA Directive 2001/42, which is to provide for a high level of protection of the environment, the provisions delimiting its scope must be interpreted broadly. It is settled case law that the Member States cannot exempt any plan or programme likely to have significant effects on the environment from the directive procedural requirements.[98] A regional regulation laying down the environmental requirements for the installation of wind turbines is subject to an SEA.[99]

  However, the SEA Directive authorises the Member States to exclude the plans and programmes determining the use of small areas at a local level provided that they have no significant effects on the environment.[100] Highlighting the aim of that directive of providing a high level of environmental protection, the CJEU held that a purely quantitative threshold

96 Directive 2011/92/EU on the assessment of the effects of certain public and private projects on the environment [2012] OJ L 26/1.

97 Case C-72/95 *Kraaijeveld* [1996] ECR I-5403, para. 39; Opinion of AG Elmer in Case C-72/95 *Kraaijeveld* [1996] ECR I-5403.

98 Case C-295/10 *Valčiukienė* [2011] ECLI:EU:C:2011:608, para. 53; Case C-567/10 *Inter-Environnement Bruxelles* [2015] C:2012:159, para. 37, and Case C-473/14 *Dimos Kropias Attikis* [2015] C:2015:582, para. 50; C-290/15 *d'Oultremont* [2016] ECLI:EU:C:2016:816, paras. 39 and 40.

99 C-290/15 *d'Oultremont* [2016] ECLI:EU:C:2016:816, para. 54.

100 Article 6(3).

regarding the size of the plan would lead, in practice, to exempting an entire class of plans or programmes in advance from the requirement of environmental assessment. Small areas at the local level cannot thus be defined exclusively with reference to the size of the area concerned.[101]

Moreover, although that SEA Directive 2001/42 does not expressly apply to the repeal of a plan,[102] the CJEU held in *Inter-Environnement Bruxelles* that the total or partial repeal of a plan or programme does fall within the scope of that directive. In effect, 'it is possible that the partial or total repeal of a plan or programme is likely to have significant effects on the environment'.[103] Lastly, Article 2(a) of the SEA Directive expressly includes within its scope measures modifying plans and programmes. Accordingly, a plan or programme that is intended to give more specific expression to and implement a master plan established by a hierarchically superior measure that has not itself been the subject of such an environmental assessment may not be exempted from the obligation to carry out an environmental assessment under SEA Directive 2001/42.[104]

- With respect to natural habitats, the CJEU has interpreted rather strictly the obligations related to the designation of sites intended to guarantee the favourable conservation of habitats or endangered species, which must comply with scientific criteria.[105] A plan or project is subject to an impact assessment whenever the effects are deemed to be significant. The court held that it does not entail significant effect when 'it is considered not likely to adversely affect the integrity of the site concerned and consequently, not likely to give rise to deterioration or significant disturbances within the meaning of Article 6(2)'.[106]
- By the same token, a somewhat strict interpretation applies to the designation of areas as vulnerable to pollution from nitrates of agricultural origin,[107] as well as the designation of bathing waters.[108]
- Following the judgment in *Bund für Umwelt und Naturschutz Deutschland*, the Water Framework Directive (WFD) 2000/60 entails obligations that are more binding than any Member States really expected.[109] The Member

101 Case C-444/15 *Associazione Italia Nostra Onlus* [2016] ECLI:EU:C:2016:978.

102 The directive refers expressly not to repealing measures but only to measures modifying plans and programmes. See para. 36.

103 Case C-567/10 *Inter-Environnement Bruxelles* [2015] ECLI:EU:C:2012:159, para. 38.

104 Case C-473/14 *Dimos Kropias Attikis* [2015] ECLI:EU:C:2015:582, para. 59.

105 *N. de Sadeleer and C.H. Born*, Droit international et communautaire de la biodiversité (Paris, Dalloz, 2002) 496–499.

106 Case C-127/02 *Waddenzee* [2004] ECLI:EU:C:2004:482, para. 36.

107 Case C-258/00 *Commission v France* [2002] ECR I-5959.

108 Case C-56/90 *Commission v UK* [1993] ECR I-4109, case note (1993) 6:1 *JEL* 125.

109 Case C-461/13 *Bund für Umwelt und Naturschutz Deutschland eV* [2015] ECLI:EU:C:2015:43, paras. 50 and f. See *H. Van Rijswick and C. Backes*, 'Ground Breaking Landmark Case on Environmental Quality Standards', 3–4 (2015) *JEEPL* 363–377.

States are called on to divide the ecological quality ratios (EQRs) for each surface water category into five different classes (high, good, moderate, poor and bad). Article 4(1)(a)(i) of Directive 2000/60 states that deterioration of the status of all bodies of surface water should be prevented. The CJEU interpreted the concept of 'deterioration of the status' of a body of surface water as not entailing a classification of that body of water in a lower class.[110] Accordingly, the duty to prevent deterioration of the status of bodies of surface water applies whenever the body is deteriorated irrespective of any change of class. This obligation amounts thus to a standstill. Accordingly, the prohibition of deterioration of the quality of a water body is a binding requirement and not a political slogan.

- The CJEU has classified contaminated soils and polluted waters as waste where such matters appear by definition to be precluded from the scope of ambit of the waste framework directive.[111]
- The right to obtain access to environmental information has been interpreted somewhat broadly by the CJEU. A Dutch association for the protection of bees had made a request, on the basis of Directive 2003/4 on access to information in environmental matters, to disclose the authorisations of several plant protection products and one biocide. Bayer, the holder of a large number of those authorisations, objected to that disclosure, on the ground that it would infringe copyright and adversely affect the confidentiality of commercial or industrial information. Under that directive, authorities may in principle refuse access to environmental information held by them in order to protect the confidentiality of commercial or industrial information, but they must nevertheless release information on emissions into the environment. The Dutch authority considered that a number of documents (laboratory studies, field studies, experiments conducted on the effects of the substance on bees, etc.) did not relate to 'information on emissions into the environment' within the meaning of the second subparagraph of Article 4(2). It took the view that from the legislative history of the directive, it could be inferred that the emissions clause does not cover 'discharges or other releases of substances into the environment'.[112] However, endorsing a broad interpretation of the notion of 'emissions', the CJEU dismissed that interpretation. First, it held that no distinction must be made between 'emissions into the environment'

110 Case C-461/13 *Bund für Umwelt und Naturschutz Deutschland* [2015] ECLI:EU:C:2015:433, para. 55.

111 Case C-1/03 *Van De Walle* [2004] ECR I-7613, case note (2006) 43 *CMLR* 207–223; and Case C-252/05 *Thames Water Utilities* [2007] ECR I-3883, para. 27.

112 Opinion Kokott in C-442/14 *Bayer CropScience and Stichting De Bijenstichting* [2016] C:2016:213, para. 55.

within the meaning of Article 4(2) and 'discharges' and 'releases'.[113] Nor should the concept of 'emissions'be restricted to emissions emanating from certain industrial installations covered by Directive 2010/75.[114]
- Finally, the Court has made adjustments to theories on direct effect[115] and consistent interpretation.[116]

To sum up, one is driven to the conclusion that the CJEU has narrowly interpreted the Member States' room for manoeuvre. The stage is therefore set for the CJEU to play the role of a counterweight: the low level of binding force of the EU legal arrangements has been compensated for by the *effet utile* of the directive. It is significant that Member States adopt and implement salient regulatory measures with a view to achieving the environmental goals set forth by the various environmental directives.

5. CONCLUSION

Painting a portrait of EU environmental law is certainly a challenge. However, at this stage of our reflections we may nevertheless sketch out a few observations.

An initial observation points to the disparate nature of this area of law. This brief overview of the EU regulations and directives has given us the impression of a largely unfinished edifice, consisting of an array of disparate rules, scattered around within different sectoral regimes and with legislation varying widely between them.

This 'Balkanisation' of secondary law is a result both of the variety of legal bases as well as the diverse nature of harmonisation measures. Whereas the majority of environmental directives protecting ecosystems or regulating certain types of pollution relied on Article 192 TFEU, Article 114 is the legal basis of regulations governing the placing on the market of products or substances which are harmful to the environment. There is no doubt that as a result of the unadventurous nature of the EU policy, certain matters fall within the purview of subsidiarity (listed installations, quality objectives for different ecosystems ...), whilst other sectors have been almost completely harmonised (movement of waste, restrictions on the placing on the market or use of chemical substances).

A third point which needs to be made is that the harmonisation of the majority of the subject matters is still incomplete. In fact, unlike the Member

---

113 Case C-442/14 *Bayer CropScience and Stichting De Bijenstichting* [2016] ECLI:EU:C:2016:889, para 63.

114 Para. 71.

115 Case C-72/95 *Kraaijeveld* [1996] ECR I-5403; Case C-201/02 *Wells* [2004] ECR I-723, para. 67; and Case C-97/11 *Amia SpA*, above, paras. 34–35.

116 Case C-97/11 *Amia SpA* [2012] ECLI:EU:C:2012:306, paras. 29–30.

States, the EU is not capable of regulating everything, nor does it seek to be able to do so. The obligation to comply with the principle of subsidiarity prevents the European Union lawmakers from harmonising in areas of law where the Member States are better placed to enact legislation (mobile telephones, nuisances created by small industrial facilities, town planning, etc.). The very nature of harmonisation is thus flexible.

As far as the most advanced Member States are concerned, this policy is not particularly innovative, given that it generally limits itself to incorporating the *acquis* of the best. However, for a number of southern and central European countries, this policy has obliged them to overhaul their legal regimes in order to afford better protection to their environment.

As a result of the tangled web of contradictory rules, which is riddled with ambiguities, the EU courts are not only the guardians of the temple of law, but they have also turned into the architect. In effect, the increasingly frequent recourse by the EU lawmaker to catchall formulae can account for the growing importance of preliminary references pursuant to Article 267 TFEU.

Last but not least, in spite of the accumulation of directives and regulations, along with the resulting national rules, the pressure on ecosystems continues to grow, natural spaces have been seriously diminished, species are disappearing at a worrying rate, chemical substances are continuing to accumulate and the coasts are ever more smothered with concrete, *inter alia*. The gap between the rules and the problems, which the law is supposed to regulate, has never been so marked.

EUROPEAN MULTILINGUALISM AND HARMONISATION OF ENVIRONMENTAL LAW

Valentina JACOMETTI*

1. INTRODUCTION: MULTILINGUALISM AND TERMINOLOGY PROBLEMS WITHIN THE EUROPEAN UNION

As is well known, one of the main features of the European Union (EU) is the recognition of integral multilingualism: the languages of all Member States are recognised as official languages of the EU. This figure currently stands at 24. Without going into detail, in a very general way it can be said that the recognition of multilingualism on the legal level implies that the treaties and legal acts of general application are drafted and published in all official languages.

Consequently, the multilingual character of EU law inevitably involves a high degree of complexity, together with relevant translation problems that are likely to increase with the accession of new Member States.[1]

* Associate Professor of Comparative Private Law, University of Insubria, Italy.

[1] The literature on European multilingualism is quite extensive, see among others: *S. Šarčevič* (ed.), Language and Culture in EU Law, Routledge, 2015; *D. Cosmai*, The Language of Europe. Multilingualism and Translation in the EU Institutions: Practice, Problems and Perspective, Editions de l'Université de Bruxelles, 2014; *E. Wagner, S. Bech & J.M. Martínez*, Translating for the European Union Institutions, 2 ed., Routledge, 2014; *G. Ajani, G. Peruginelli, G. Sartor & D. Tiscoronia* (eds.), The Multilanguage Complexity of European

As we are speaking of legal rules, this complexity involves both language and legal problems, as each legal language mirrors a specific legal culture and consequently varies from one legal system to another. The problem is not only that of understanding EU legal rules, but rather, that of their uniform application in order to achieve an effective harmonisation of the laws of EU Member States, and not a merely nominal and apparent one. In fact, since the EU law-makers' task should be to harmonise the laws of EU Member States, they should ensure a high degree of consistency between adopted legal provisions so that the latter can be interpreted in the same way and produce the same effects in all Member States.

However, although this seems of undoubted importance for achieving the ultimate goals of the European Union, it does not always occur as a consequence of a number of issues deriving from the drafting and implementation of EU legislation, such as, in particular, those related to legal terminology, interpretation and translation specific to the EU context.

Indeed, one central problem of multilingual legislation is that of terminology and translation of legal concepts,[2] because of the conceptual differences between the various legal systems. Moreover, with regards to the EU, even though the legislature is necessarily multilingual, it cannot rely upon a common terminology at the European level. In addition, sometimes EU law-makers do not seem to be aware of the extensive differences that exist at a conceptual and terminological level within the European legal area. This clearly causes problems that are difficult to resolve, in particular in view of the intense move towards harmonisation within the European context. However, such a harmonisation does seem difficult to achieve, if the significant dissimilarities between the different legal systems and the barriers they engender in the creation of a common European legal language are not appropriately understood.

In fact, on the one hand, the problem of terminological correspondence should theoretically not arise within the EU, where the meaning of legal terms in all languages can be considered to derive from the same conceptual system, that of the EU legal system, which is an autonomous system with respect to those of the Member States.[3] However, the fact that EU legal rules then have to be applied in practice in the different EU countries must not be overlooked,

Law, Methodologies in Comparison, 2007; *R.L. Creech*, Law and Language in the European Union, Europa Law Publishing, 2005; *B. Pozzo* & *V. Jacometti* (eds.), Multilingualism and the Harmonisation of European law, Kluwer Law International, 2006.

2 See *T. Gallas*, *'Drafting multilingue: missione impossibile'*, in *E. Ioriatti Ferreri* (ed.), La Traduzione del diritto comunitario ed Europeo: riflessioni metodologiche, 2007, pp. 27 ff.; *A.L. KJær*, 'Legal translation at the European Union: A research field in need for a new approach', in *K. Kredens* & *S. Gozdz-Roszkowski* (eds.), Language and the Law: International Outlooks, 2007, p. 69.

3 On the relationship between language, translation and autonomy of EU law see *A.L. KJær*, Theoretical Aspects of Legal Translation in the EU: The Paradoxical Relationship between Language, Translation and the Autonomy of EU Law, in *S. Šarčevič* (ed.), *supra* note 1, pp. 90 ff.

or underestimated: this application necessarily means referring to the concepts and rules existing in the relevant national legal systems, as interpreted and applied by national courts and legal scholars. It should be kept in mind that in general, EU law does not create 'fundamental' concepts of its own – because it cannot, and does not want, to do so – since it is conceived as a subsidiary law aimed at creating rules to be inserted within the context of existing 'fundamental' concepts of the different national legal systems. Conversely, EU law does create new concepts of its own that are of a more specific and detailed nature. However, the EU lawmakers rarely define these concepts, and consequently, in order to give content to them it is necessary to refer to the underlying legal cultures of the Member States.

2. CRITICAL ISSUES IN THE ENVIRONMENTAL LAW FIELD

From a general point of view, one cannot avoid noting that much of the critical issues regarding terminology and its impact on harmonisation of EU law can be found in the environmental law field. In particular, legal terms in this field are often used in a contradictory way. Furthermore, in spite of the recurrent use of the legislative drafting technique of introducing specific definitions in legislative texts with the exact objective of achieving harmonisation, quite often these definitions are not very useful to this purpose. In fact, either the definitions do not relate to legal terms, or they define terms too broadly, without specifying all the conditions and consequences related to the relevant term. Naturally this leaves room for discretion, and therefore differences, in the national implementation and leads to the consequence that the actual application of EU law inevitably requires reference to the legal institutions existing in each individual Member State. In fact, notwithstanding the role played by the EU Court of Justice, the application and effects of EU law also depend on the interpretation given by national courts and legal scholars, which, obviously, may differ from one another as they, directly or implicitly, refer to the interpretative criteria, principles and concepts belonging to their own legal system.

Conversely, it should be noted that according to EU drafting guidelines, EU legal acts should be drafted respecting 'the multilingual nature of union legislation' and 'concepts or terminology specific to any one national legal system are to be used with care'.[4] This means that drafters should use neutral

---

4 The Joint Practical Guide of the European Parliament, the Council and the Commission for persons involved in the drafting of European Union legislation, 2015, point 5, available at http://eur-lex.europa.eu/homepage.html. However, it should be observed that at the moment of implementation into the legal systems of the Member States, there can sometimes be a new operation of 'intralingual' translation from the 'neutral' language of the European legislation to the specific national legal language (see the example of the German implementation of the Directive 2003/87/EC at para. 4).

terminology as much as possible. However, the clarity of terms, especially 'neutral' terms, can be impaired by the political dimension of the drafting process. In fact, notwithstanding the widespread idea that EU law is the product of the technocrats-bureaucrats of the EU institutions, if one looks at the concrete drafting process of EU law, it is evident that politics strongly influence both the substance of the rules and the choice of terminology. Thus, quite often the terms are intentionally ambiguous, probably because of the difficulties in attaining a political agreement among Member States as to the definition and use of shared concepts.

In particular, in some sectors – such as environmental law – the use of a terminology which is non-technical from a legal perspective can be the result of a choice of EU law-makers to assign the task of defining legal concepts to other sciences in the vain hope to avoid the difficulties connected with the use of legal terms that are deeply connected with national legal systems. Indeed, in the environmental law field, where legal and scientific issues are necessarily mingled, the indispensable dialogue that the lawyers establish with the 'technicians' – that is, biologists, engineers and so on – has created the illusion that it would be possible to transfer the task of defining legal concepts to other sciences. By contrast, instead, if it is true that the interchange with other sciences can help the understanding of some phenomena to be regulated, the responsibility to give content to legal rules is up to lawyers. Additionally, lawmakers should not be misled by the ease of translating terms belonging to natural sciences which refer to objects that exist in the real world and so always have the same referent in all languages. On the contrary, since these apparently neutral terms from other sciences do not provide any useful information from a legal point of view, lawyers end up facing very difficult issues of interpretation.

As a result, terminology problems at the EU level can lead to considerably different outcomes in actual implementation by Member States and consequently have a significant impact on the process of harmonisation. This impact is intensified by the fact that in the environmental field, the EU has operated mainly by way of directives: it is known that directives need to be transposed into national law before they can be applied. National implementation measures may differ considerably from one country to another, and in many cases they make implicit reference to the national interpretation of the legal terms contained in the relevant directive. The problem is that the national interpretation varies significantly from one Member State to the next.

In addition, these issues are worsened by the minimum harmonisation approach which was, until recently, followed by EU directives. This approach has been conceived for technical regulations concerning objects and phenomena existing in the real world, as was almost all the initial Community legislation. By contrast, when the European legislature started to deal with strictly legal issues, where terms refer to concepts that do not have an objective referent, the minimum harmonisation approach has often led to unsatisfactory results. Even when the EU law-makers seek to provide an almost complete regulation of a particular subject matter, national implementation measures can still introduce definitions and rules of a wider scope, provided that they comprise the minimum required by the EU directives, thus allowing for national laws that diverge from one another.

3. THE EXAMPLE OF EU EMISSION ALLOWANCES: THE LACK OF A LEGAL CLASSIFICATION AT EU LEVEL ...

Among the several examples occurring in the field of EU environmental law, I would like to consider the question of the lack of a legal definition of greenhouse gas emission 'allowances' in the EU legislation that introduced them in the EU system, as it appears to be particularly significant with regards to its impact on harmonisation. The legal framework for greenhouse gas emission allowances is provided by Directive 2003/87/EC (Emissions Trading Directive), which created the EU emissions trading system (EU ETS),[5] an EU-wide trading scheme for greenhouse gas emission allowances, that is, a market of tradable pollution rights.[6] The advisability of analysing the legal definition of emission allowances results from the specific characteristics of emission allowances and from the different positions that exist on their legal nature in the various European legal systems where the EU ETS was implemented.

In principle, it can be said that emission allowances enable an entity to emit a certain amount of pollutants. However, such an allowance also includes the right to be sold and transferred, and this makes it substantially different from a traditional emission permit. Consequently, emission allowances should be considered a *sui generis* instrument, whose legal nature and regulation require a new definition by the legal system. Without such a definition, an emissions trading system cannot be expected to work properly and efficiently. Indeed, emissions trading systems are artificial markets created with the aim of using market incentives to control pollution in a more efficient way, but at the same time they are necessarily integrated in a regulated framework. In order for such

5 Directive 2003/87/EC of the European Parliament and of the Council establishing a scheme for greenhouse gas emission allowance trading within the Community, OJ 2003 L 275/32. On the Directive and the European emissions trading system and their implementation in Member States, see among others: *M. Peeters, M. Stallworthy & J. de Cenra de Larragán*, Climate Law in EU Member States, 2012; *M. Faure & M. Peeters*, Climate Change and European Emissions Trading, 2008; *J. Delbeke* (ed.), Environmental Law: The EU Greenhouse Gas Emissions Trading Scheme, 2006.

6 On emissions trading in general, see among others: *S. Weishaar* (ed.), Research Handbook on Emissions Trading, 2016; *J. Quiggin, D. Adamson & D. Quiggin* (eds.), Carbon Pricing: Early Experiences and Future Prospects, 2014; *D. Freestone & C. Streck* (eds.), Legal Aspects of Carbon Trading: Kyoto, Copenhagen and Beyond, 2009.

a market to function efficiently it is necessary that the object of the market – emission allowances – is well defined, protected by law and tradable.[7] The legal qualification of emission allowances has an impact on several significant issues, such as: the governing law; the rights granted to allowance holders and the protection of these rights; the circulation of allowances and relevant rights; the type of applicable liability; whether and how security rights can be created over emission allowances; the accounting and tax treatment of allowances; the treatment of allowances in the event of insolvency proceedings; and the possibility of withdrawal of allowances, among others.[8]

Nevertheless, the EU legislature, having opted for the path of minimum harmonisation through a directive, confined itself to setting only the essential elements of emission allowances, without attempting to elucidate their legal characteristics or legal nature. The legal qualification, of course, may not be required at all if the institution or mechanism at stake is regulated in a complete manner. The situation is different instead where the regulation itself is full of gaps, as in the case of Directive 2003/87/EC.

In fact, here, as often happens in EU law, the law-maker seems to have adopted a compromise solution: a solution that does not provide a full regulation and applies ambiguous terms, thus leaving much discretion to individual Member States in the implementation of the new mechanism introduced by EU law. Therefore, one should refer to national laws implementing the directive in order to actually find out how allowances are regulated and protected.

From this perspective, it seems appropriate to begin with an analysis of the text of Directive 2003/87/EC. It may be noted that Article 3(a) actually contains a definition of 'allowance' as:

> an allowance to emit one tonne of carbon dioxide equivalent during a specified period, which shall be valid only for the purposes of meeting the requirements of this Directive and shall be transferable in accordance with the provisions of this Directive.

At first glance, one can already see that this definition refers firstly to the measurement unit of emissions, which constitutes technical-scientific data, while it says little about the object of the emissions trading scheme from a

---

7 See *B. Yandle*, Grasping for the Heavens: 3-D Property Rights and the Global Commons, Duke Environmental Law Policy Forum, 1999 (10), pp. 13 ff.

8 See *B. Holligan*, Commodity or Propriety? Unauthorised Transfer of Intangible Entitlements in the EU Emissions Trading System, MLR, 2020, pp. 979 ff.; *A. Hedges*, Carbon Units as Property: Guidance from Analogous Common Law Cases, CCLR 2016 (3), pp. 190 ff.; *K.F.K. Low & J. Lin*, Carbon Credits as EU Like It: Property, Immunity, TragiCO2medy?, Journal of Environmental Law, 2015 (27), pp. 377–404; *Commission Prada*, La régulation des marchés du CO2, Republique Française, 2010; *Bank of England, Financial Markets Law Committee*, Issue 116 – Emission Allowances: Creating legal Certainty, October 2009; *M. Wemaere, C. Streck, T. Chagas*, Legal Ownership and Nature of Kyoto Units and EU Allowances, in *D. Freestone & C. Streck* (eds.), Legal Aspects of Carbon Trading: Kyoto, Copenhagen and Beyond, 2009, pp. 35 ff.

legal point of view. Therefore, in order to understand the legal meaning of 'allowance', it is necessary to carry out a comparison of the various language versions of the directive, since according to the EU Court of Justice the meaning of EU legal terms cannot be inferred from a single language version, but should be derived from all legal versions of the relevant provision.[9] However, in the case of the Emission Trading Directive the comparative study does not help to clarify the issue of the legal qualification of allowances.

Table 1. Comparative table – Part 1

Directive 2003/87/CE			
English	**French**	**German**	**Italian**
Art. 3 (a)			
Definitions	*Définitions*	*Begriffsbestimmungen*	*Definizioni*
'allowance' means an allowance to emit one tonne of carbon dioxide equivalent during a specified period, which shall be valid only for the purposes of meeting the requirements of this Directive and shall be transferable in accordance with the provisions of this Directive	**"quota"**, le quota autorisant à émettre une tonne d'équivalent-dioxyde de carbone au cours d'une période spécifiée, valable uniquement pour respecter les exigences de la présente directive, et transférable conformément aux dispositions de la présente directive	**„Zertifikat"** das Zertifikat, das zur Emission von einer Tonne Kohlendioxidäquivalent in einem bestimmten Zeitraum berechtigt; es gilt nur für die Erfüllung der Anforderungen dieser Richtlinie und kann nach Maßgabe dieser Richtlinie übertragen werden	**«quota di emissioni»**, il diritto di emettere una tonnellata di biossido di carbonio equivalente per un periodo determinato, valido unicamente per rispettare le disposizioni della presente direttiva e cedibile conformemente alla medesima

Firstly, if one takes into consideration the English, French, German and Italian versions, it should be noted that on the one hand, by employing the term 'quota' in Italian and French, the EU law-maker adopted a kind of neologism, a somehow 'neutral' term, thus providing a possible solution to overcome the difficulties in defining the new mechanism. On the other hand, however, the EU lawmaker did not follow the same approach in other languages, such English and German, where it employed the words 'allowance' and 'Zertifikat'. In such a way, the lawmaker runs the risks of creating even more confusion: instead

9 Scholarship on this subject is quite extensive, see *inter alia I. Schübel-Pfister*, Sprache und Gemeinschaftsrecht – Die Auslegung der mehrsprachig verbindlichen Rechtstexte durch den Europäischen Gerichtshof, 2004; *A. Gambaro*, Interpretation of Multilingual Legislative Texts, in *K. Boele-Woelki & S. van Erp* (eds.), General reports of the 17th Congress of the International Academy of Comparative Law, 2007, pp. 51 ff.; *M. Darlén*, Multilingual Interpretation of European Union Law, 2009; *S. Pommer*, Interpreting Multilingual EU Law: What Role for Legal Translation?, European Review of Private Law 2012 (5&6), pp. 1421 ff.; *E. Paunio*, Legal Certainty in Multilingual EU Law, 2016.

of being a helpfully neutral term, 'quota' is simply a superimposed neologism, adding an extra layer of linguistic uncertainty.

Furthermore, whether the law-maker employed a neologism or an already existing term, the Directive does not specify all the conditions and all the consequences of the mechanism, and lawyers, in the actual application, will therefore end up referring to the legal institutions existing in each individual Member State.

On top of this, in the definition of Article 3(a), the expressions employed in the English, French and German versions – *allowance to emit, Zerifikat das zur Emission (...) berechtigt, quota autorisant à émettre* – seem to refer to the concept of 'authorisation in a wide sense', thus emphasising the public origin of allowances and almost seeking to purposely exclude the existence of a 'right'. By contrast, the expression employed in the Italian version – *diritto di emettere* – may lead to the conclusion that the EU lawmaker intended to grant a 'true' right to holders of allowances.

Table 2. Comparative table – Part 2

Directive 2003/87/CE			
English	**French**	**German**	**Italian**
Art. 12			
Transfer, surrender and cancellation of allowances	*Transfert, restitution et annulation de quotas*	*Übertragung, Abgabe und Löschung von Zertifikaten*	*Trasferimento, restituzione e cancellazione di quote di emissioni*
1. Member States shall ensure that allowances can be transferred [...] 4. Member States shall take the necessary steps to ensure that allowances will be cancelled at any time at the request of the person holding them. [...]	1. Les États membres s'assurent que les quotas puissent être transférés [...] 4. Les États membres prennent les mesures nécessaires pour que des quotas puissent être annulés à tout moment à la demande de la personne qui les détient. [...]	1. Die Mitgliedstaaten stellen sicher, dass Zertifikate übertragbar sind [...] 4. Die Mitgliedstaaten stellen durch die notwendigen Maßnahmen sicher, dass Zertifikate jederzeit gelöscht werden, wenn der Inhaber dies beantragt. [...]	1. Gli Stati membri provvedono affinché le quote di emissioni possano essere trasferite [...] 4. Gli Stati membri adottano i provvedimenti necessari per garantire che le quote di emissioni vengano cancellate in qualsiasi momento a richiesta della persona che le detiene. [...]
Art. 19			
Registries	*Registres*	*Register*	*Registri*
2. Any person may hold allowances. [...] 3. [...] to track the issue, holding, transfer and cancellation, as applicable, of allowances, [...]	2. Toute personne peut détenir des quotas. [...] 3. [...] suivre la délivrance, la détention, le transfert et l'annulation de quotas [...]	2. Jede Person kann Inhaber von Zertifikaten sein. [...] 3. [...] Vergabe, Besitz, Übertragung und gegebenenfalls Löschung von Zertifikaten zu verfolgen [...]	2. Qualsiasi persona può possedere quote di emissioni. [...] 3. [...] controllare, se del caso, il rilascio, il possesso, il trasferimento e la cancellazione delle quote di emissione [...]

Moreover, even looking at other articles of the Directive is not much more helpful. In particular, Article 12 – concerning the transfer, surrender and cancellation of allowances – and Article 19 – concerning registers of allowances – do not say much about the kind of entitlement on allowances or their transfer. Indeed, these articles merely provide that Member States shall ensure that allowances can be transferred between persons and cancelled at the request of the holder and that any person may hold allowances.[10] Furthermore, these articles are not much clearer from the point of view of terminology: while the English version talks of 'holding' allowances and the French speaks of 'détention' both in Article 12 and in Article 19, the terminology of the German and Italian versions is more confused. Thus, the German version speaks of 'Inhaber' in Article 12 and 'Inhaber' and 'Besitz' in Article 19, while the Italian version employs 'detiene' in Article 12 and 'possesso' in Article 19. The different language versions do not correspond to each other, and some versions seem to consider as equivalent concepts that have different meaning in the corresponding national legal systems, such as 'detenzione' and 'possesso' in Italy. What's more, the German version may also lead to further uncertainty, since the meaning of 'Besitzer' and 'Inhaber' is not the same in Germany and Austria.[11]

This is a clear example of a contradictory use of legal terms. Although it is unclear as to whether the highlighted inconsistencies are the result of a political compromise or of carelessness, they certainly can give rise to significant difficulties of transposition into national law and thus have a relevant impact on the harmonisation of EU law. The EU legislature seems to overlook the differences of meaning between the various terms used in the different language versions, while those terms recall concepts and institutions of the different legal systems of the individual Member States.

The only thing that seems clear is the desire of the EU law-maker not to take an explicit position with regards to the legal nature of emission allowances and to avoid any reference to the term 'property', not even to exclude the fact that the Directive is dealing with property.[12]

---

10 However, it should be noted that at least certain essential characteristics of allowances are to be found in Article 40 of the EU ETS Registry Regulation (Commission Regulation (EU) No 389/2013 establishing a Union Registry, OJ 2013 L 122/1) concerning the 'Nature of allowances and finality of transactions', which specifies that: 'An allowance or Kyoto unit shall be a fungible, dematerialised instrument that is tradable on the market'.

11 As to this issue, it should be borne in mind that according to German law, there is a distinction between 'mittelbarer' and 'unmittelbarer Besitzer', whereas in Austrian law, the distinction is between 'Besitzer' and 'Inhaber'. In Italian, see: *B. Pozzo*, Eigentum, in *A. Candian, A. Gambaro & B. Pozzo*, Property, Proprieté, Eigentum, 1992, pp. 261 ff.

12 As also evident in the aforementioned Article 40 of Registry Regulation, which provides that record of the Union Registry shall constitute prima facie and sufficient evidence of 'title' over an allowance, thus avoiding any reference to the term 'property' or the like. On the definition as property rights see *K.F.K Low & J. Lin*, Carbon Credits as EU Like It: Property, Immunity, TragiCO2medy?, Journal of Environmental Law, 2015, pp. 377 ff.

It would have been advisable to consider the legal nature of allowances early in the design process of the EU ETS, given its impact on relevant legal issues and the fact that in 2015 the European Court of Auditors also highlighted that the 'legal status of allowances should be further clarified in order to contribute to stability and confidence' and recommended the Commission to 'analyse the benefits of treating emission allowances as property rights across the EU'.[13] In spite of this, the EU law-maker is still reluctant to intervene on the issue. Indeed, on the one hand, the EU legislature established that not only derivatives of emission allowances, but also the allowances themselves are 'financial instruments' covered by the Markets in Financial Instruments Directive II (MiFID II),[14] thus likely enhancing the harmonisation of the qualification of emissions allowances at least in the field of financial markets.[15] On the other hand, at a more general level, in 2017 the EU Court of Justice refrained from defining the nature of emission allowances.[16]

4. ... AND THE DIFFERENT LEGAL DEFINITIONS OF ALLOWANCES AT THE NATIONAL LEVEL: THE LACK OF HARMONISATION

Failing clear guidance from EU law, the determination of the legal nature of allowances is then left to the Member States. Given the dissimilarities between their legal systems, national lawmakers have obviously come up with different attitudes and solutions.

In the United Kingdom,[17] for example, the emissions trading regulations were silent on the legal nature of allowances and simply recalled the definition of

---

[13] *European Court of Auditors*, Special Report No 6, 'The integrity and implementation of the EU ETS', 2015, para. 92, available at: http://www.eca.europa.eu/Lists/ECADocuments/SR15_06/SR15_06_EN.pdf.

[14] Annex I, section C, points (4) and (11) of Directive 2014/65/EU of the European Parliament and of the Council on markets in financial instruments, OJ 2014 L 173/349. By contrast, it should be noted that both emission allowances and derivatives of emission allowances are not included in the definition of 'commodity derivatives' under the MiFID (see Consultation Paper; ESMA's guidelines on information expected or required to be disclosed on commodity derivatives markets or related spot markets under MAR, 30 March 2016, ESMA/201/444, p. 13). See *K. Gorzelak*, The legal nature of emission allowances following the creation of a Union Registry and adoption of MiFID II – are they transferable securities now?, Capital Markets Law Journal, 2014 (9) 4, pp. 373–387.

[15] However, see below the remarks on the French implementing legislation.

[16] Judgment of the Court of Justice of 8 March 2017 in Case C-321/15 *ArcelorMittal Rodange and Schifflange SA v State of the Grand Duchy of Luxembourg*, EU:C:2017:179.

[17] As regards the United Kingdom, reference is made to the legislation in force before the definitive exit from the European Union in 2021.

Directive 2003/87/EC.[18] This is not overly surprising, since very rarely does the British legislature, unlike the continental ones, address qualification questions, usually leaving to the courts the task of dealing with these issues when they actually arise.

Indeed, the judgment of the England and Wales High Court in *Armstrong DLW GMBH and Winnington Networks Ltd* of 11 January 2012 contained an interesting attempt to define the theoretical characteristics of emission allowances on the grounds of the common law and Directive 2003/87/EC.[19] In order to establish the consequences of the theft of emission allowances, the court needed to determine, among other things, the legal status of emission allowances and classified them as *intangible property* under English common law.[20] In addition, it should also be reminded that the financial market regulations recalled the definition of financial instruments of the MiFID II, which also includes emission allowances.[21]

Similarly, the Italian law-maker merely reproduced the technical definition of allowances provided by Article 3 of the Emissions Trading Directive and avoided addressing the problem of the legal qualification of allowances,[22] and more recently implemented the MiFID II, thereby qualifying emission allowances as financial instruments for the purposes of financial markets regulation.[23]

From the standpoint of terminology, it should be noted that even the term used in the Italian version of the Directive and in the implementing legislation – 'quota di emissioni' – says little about the legal nature of the new instrument. Indeed, it seems almost to be disguising the intention of the legislator not to

---

18 Greenhouse Gas Emissions Trading Scheme Regulations 2012, regulation 3. See *M.J. Mace*, The Legal Nature of Emission Reductions and EU Allowances: Issues Addressed in an International Workshop, JEEP 2005, pp. 123 ff.

19 England and Wales High Court Case No: HC10C00532 between Armstrong DLW GMBH and Winnington Networks Ltd of 11 January 2012 (http://www.bailii.org/ew/cases/EWHC/Ch/2012/10.pdf).

20 The court reached this conclusion by applying a three-part test developed in the case *Re Celtic Extraction* (*Celtic Extraction Ltd and Bluestone Chemicals v Environment Agency*, [2001] Ch. 475): in order for emission allowances to be considered property, i) there must be a statutory framework conferring an entitlement on one who satisfies certain conditions; ii) the allowance must be transferable; and iii) the allowance must have value (see among others *A. Hedges*, *supra* note 8 at pp. 194 ff.; *K.F.K. Low & J. Lin*, *supra* note 9; *K. Anttonen, M. Mehling & K. Upston-Hooper*, Breathing Life into the Carbon Market: Legal Frameworks of Emissions Trading in Europe, EELR 2007, pp. 96 ff.; *A. Hobley & C. Rowe*, Transposition of the Emissions Trading Scheme Directive into UK Law and Associated Issues, JEEPL 2004, pp. 10 ff.

21 The Financial Services and Markets Act 2000 (Markets in Financial Instruments) Regulations 2017, regulation 2.

22 See Article 3(p) of Decreto legislativo 4.4.2006, n. 216, as well as Article 3(pp) of Decreto legislativo 13.3.2013, n. 30, and Article 3(ss) of Decreto legislativo 9.6.2020, n. 47, that replaced the previous decrees.

23 Decreto legislativo 3.8.2017, n. 129.

address the issue through the use of a language which is non-technical from the legal point of view. The expression 'quota di emissioni', in fact, does not appear attributable to concepts existing in Italian law, and it instead seems to recall the ordinary meaning of the word 'quota', understood as a fraction of a larger whole. This – as often happens with words taken from common vocabulary – provides no useful information from a legal perspective and confronts lawyers with difficult interpretation problems.

Unlike English courts, however, Italian courts have not yet had the occasion to address this issue, and the few legal scholars who addressed it are still quite divided. In brief, we observe that some scholars tend to focus their attention on the public origin of emission allowances and therefore classify them as administrative permits or licenses, while other scholars consider that allowances should be classified as movable goods.[24]

As for Germany, the implementing statute largely reproduced the provisions of the Directive and did not include a positive definition of allowances, even if the German law-maker departed from the Directive in naming allowances, abandoning of the term 'Zertifikat' and replacing it with 'Berechtigung'.[25] As the term 'Zertifikat' is generally used in the field of securities, in the past this change of terminology was considered a consequence of the fact that initially the German implementing statute explicitly said that allowances were not financial instruments.[26] By contrast, following the implementation of the MiFID II, emission allowances are now classified as financial instruments for the financial market regulation in Germany.[27]

From another point of view, it should be noted that according to §7 (3) TEGH, the transfer of allowances requires 'Einigung' and 'Eintragung' (agreement and registration) on the emissions allowances register, as required for immovable property.[28] However, given the lack of a positive definition, German legal scholars are also rather divided on the legal qualification of allowances. In particular, here too one can observe the opposition between those

---

24 For an analysis of the problem of the legal nature of allowances in the Italian legal system, see *V. Jacometti*, Lo scambio delle quote di emissione, 2010, pp. 422 ff. More recently, *F. Gaspari*, Tutela dell'ambiente, regolazione e controlli pubblici: recenti sviluppi in materia di EU Emissions Trading Scheme (ETS), Riv. it. dir. pubbl. com. 2011, pp. 1149 ff.; *C. Camardi*, Cose, beni e nuovi beni, tra diritto europeo e diritto interno – things, goods and news rights between European and national law, Europa e diritto privato 2018 (3), pp. 955–1019.

25 §3(3) Treibhausgas-Emissionshandelsgesetz – TEHG, 21.07.2011, which replaced the previous statute of 08.07.2004.

26 §15 TEGH, original version. See *T. Holzborn & A. Israel*, Rectliche Aspekte des Handels mit Emissionsrechte, ET 2005, pp. 740 ff.; *U. Ehricke & K. Köhn*, Die Regelungen über den Handel mit Berechtigungen zur Emissions von Treibhausgasen, WM 2004, pp. 1903 ff.

27 Zweites Finanzmarktnovellierungsgesetz – 2. FiMaNoG. 23.06.2017.

28 See *M. Appel & A. Burghardt*, Phishing of European Emission Allowances and Resulting Legal Implications, CCLR, 2012 (3), pp. 228–245 ff.

scholars who consider that allowances have a public nature and those who affirm that allowances represent a private law right.[29]

Finally, in France the implementing provisions introduced an explicit legislative classification of emission allowances in the *Code de l'environnement*.[30] In particular – apart from the 'technical' definition originally contained in Article L. 229-7 of *Code de l'environnement* and now replaced by the direct reference to the Directive in Article L. 229-5 – Article L. 229-11 (previously Article L. 229-15[31]) defines allowances from a legal point of view, providing that allowances are 'biens meubles' existing only in electronic form, which are negotiable and which grant their holders the same rights.

The choice of the French law-maker is therefore quite clear: emission allowances are movable goods and therefore the object of property rights.[32] This choice is even more definite when one considers that the French version of the Emissions Trading Directive seems to define allowances as authorisations to emit one tonne of CO2eq for a given period.[33]

Finally, for the sake of completeness, it is worth noting that with the implementation of the MiFID II, emission allowances have been assimilated to financial instruments, but have not been included in the definition of the latter, in contrast to what is provided by the MiFID II and by other national implementing provisions, mentioned above.[34]

---

[29] For an overview on the German implementation of the emissions trading system and the problem of qualification, see among others: *A. Pardon*, Die Rechtsinhaberschaft an Emissionsberechtigungen und ihre Übertragung, 2012; *W. Frenz*, Emissionshandelsrecht, 2012.

[30] Ordonnance n. 2004-330 portant création d'un système d'échange de quotas d'émission de gaz à effet de serre (15.04.2004).

[31] The relevant provisions of the *Code de l'environnement* were recently amended by the Ordonnance n°2019-1034 relative au système d'échange de quotas d'émissions de gaz à effet de serre (2021–2030) (9.10.2019).

[32] For an overview on the French system and the issue of legal qualification of emissions allowances, see *C. Cheneviere*, Le système d'échange de quotas d'émission de gaz à effet de serre, LGDJ, 2018; *Commission Prada, supra* note 8.

[33] See para. 3 above. See *R. Peylet*, Un marché de nouveaux biens meubles, les quotas d'émission de gaz à effet de serre, RJEP/CJEG 2005 (621) pp. 213 ff.; *M. Pâques & S. Charneux*, Du quota d'émission de gaz à effet de serre, REDE 2004, pp. 266 ff.

[34] See Article L531-1 introduced by the Ordonnance n. 2016-827 relative aux marchés d'instruments financiers (23.06.2016). With regards to the reference to emission allowances in the MiFID and MiFID II, it is worth noting that the terminology used in the MiFID directive was inconsistent as the French version seemed to include futures relating to 'autorisations d'émissions' of any kind within financial instruments, while according to a comparative reading of the different language versions of the MiFID one may assume that the provision dealt only with transactions relating to 'quotas d'émission', since other language versions speak of 'quote di emissioni' (in Italian), 'emission allowances' (in English), 'Emissionsberechtigungen' (in German). With regard to the German version, it is also worth noting that the MiFID employed the terminology used by the German lawmaker ('Berechtigung') and not that used by the EU law-maker in the Emissions Trading Directive

5. CONCLUSION

From this brief overview, it is evident that given the ambiguous terminology and the lack of a definition of the legal nature of emission allowances at the EU level, the exact legal nature of allowances and their regulation are necessarily dependent on the relevant national legal systems, with the consequent and unavoidable differences that exist between Member States.[35] Indeed, emission allowances belong to a new kind of tool, which has a specific legal nature that requires a new definition by the legal system. Perhaps, however, to ensure uniformity and consistency between Member States, it would have been desirable that this new definition had been adopted at the EU level rather than being left to national law-makers.

The example of emission allowances shows the impact of terminology issues on the process of harmonisation of EU law, since the lack of common terms and general legal concepts at the EU level can lead to significantly different results in the actual legal practices of Member States.

('Zertifikat'). Over time, the EU legislator seems to have become gradually more aware of the impact of terminology, and thus the MiFID II consistently employs the terminology of the Emissions Trading Directive.

35 *M.J. Mace*, *supra* note 16; *K. Anttonen, M. Mehling & K. Upston-Hooper*, *supra* note 18. See also the European Commission's Final Report, 'Legal Nature of EU ETS Allowances' (December 2018), available at https://op.europa.eu/en/publication-detail/-/publication/9d985256-a6a9-11e9-9d01-01aa75ed71a1 – also intended to address the European Court of Auditors' 2015 report (see *supra* note 12) – that, while recognising that the approach in the Member States differs, generating certain legal uncertainty, suggests that 'greater clarity on the definition of the legal nature of emission allowances might not provide legal certainty'.

INTERNAL HARMONISATION OF ENVIRONMENTAL LAW

Learning from the Member States?

Anna VANHELLEMONT*

1. INTRODUCTION

The concept of harmonisation covers various meanings. A very broad and general definition would be that harmonisation consists of the bringing together of legal ideas to allow a functioning in unison.[1] In the context of the European Union, harmonisation is mostly used in the sense of approximation of laws between different legal systems (i.e. external harmonisation). However, it can also be understood as harmonisation within one legal system or one branch of law. A definition for this so-called internal harmonisation could be:

> Internal harmonisation is the legal process in which incoherencies within one legal system are resolved in a coordinated and integrated manner.

* Doctoral researcher in Environmental Law at Hasselt University, Belgium.

1 *M. Andenas, C. Baasch Andersen & R. Ashcroft*, Towards a Theory of Harmonisation, in *M. Andenas & C. Baasch Andersen* (eds), Theory and Practice of Harmonisation, 2011 p. 576.

In this chapter, we will scrutinise the idea of internal harmonisation of environmental law in three Member States, namely, the Netherlands, Belgium (Flemish region)[2] and France. Of course, the inclusion of experiences in all Member States would be very useful in order to determine best practices of harmonising environmental legislation. However, this would not be feasible in the context of this chapter and shall be the topic of further research.

In the second section, we will scrutinise the development of environmental legislation in each Member State. We will take a look at the evolution and existing environmental legislation before any harmonising steps had been taken, the reasons and motives for harmonisation, the starting point and following process and the current state of environmental legislation. Following this, in section three, we will partially conduct the same exercise at the EU level. A clear overview of the national reasons, processes and instruments will be useful, as we can consider whether these motives are similar to the ones identified at the EU level, and how the legal process may be transposed to this supranational level. Finally, some concluding remarks will be made on the possibility of further harmonising EU environmental legislation.

The main research question throughout this contribution is: can the EU learn from legal processes of environmental internal harmonisation in the Member States?

2. HARMONISATION OF ENVIRONMENTAL LEGISLATION IN THE MEMBER STATES

At the national level, we can observe several initiatives to internally harmonise environmental legislation. Across the EU, environmental codes and general environmental acts have been adopted in the different Member States. Although this process has not yet taken place in all states, there is a clear on-going trend towards improving the quality and organisation of environmental legislation.

In this section, the situation in the Netherlands, Belgium (the Flemish region) and France will be scrutinised. This includes a short overview of the evolution and previous environmental legislation, a search for motives and reasons that ultimately led to the review and internal harmonisation of environmental law and the (legal) process that took place. To conclude each part, the current state of environmental law will be discussed, including possible future steps.

2 Since 2004, the Walloon Region also has its own environmental code, which can be consulted online at http://environnement.wallonie.be/legis/menucode.htm. It currently only consists of two books, the first containing common general provisions and the second containing legislation on water.

2.1. THE NETHERLANDS

The 1875 Nuisance Act (*Hinderwet*), which aimed to prevent and limit environmental danger, damage and nuisance caused by industries, can be considered the first piece of environmental legislation in the Netherlands. During the 20th century, many other acts were introduced to tackle specific environmental problems, thus adopting a sectoral approach to environmental law.[3] This sectoral legislation was considered unclear, complex and only provided partial solutions to environmental issues. As a result, difficulties with the implementation and enforcement of the legislation rose.

Hence, the need for a general, more uniform regulation for several topics was clear early on in the development of Dutch environmental law. The work group Duk (named after its chairman) had already advised in 1974 on the idea of a more effective and uniform regulation of participation and appeal in environmental cases, proposing a general law on the topic.[4] Furthermore, the coordination of environmental permitting was also considered a topic that exceeds the sectoral boundaries of environmental law, and one which needed a more integrated approach. In 1975, the Institute of Public Administration (*Instituut voor Bestuurswetenschappen*) was commissioned to analyse the current environmental legislation and proposals in order to determine potential similarities, differences, gaps and overlaps.[5]

The starting point of the 1976 proposal for an act containing general provisions on environmental health (*Wet algemene bepalingen milieuhygiëne*) was the idea that all general environmental topics would be included in the law, though at different points in time. The first version of the general environmental act only included two topics: the permitting procedure and appeal. This was also based on the findings that the former legislation on environmental participation and appeal was incoherent, did not provide sufficient information, lacked the option for appeal in certain circumstances and included differing deadlines.[6]

The first 1979 version of this act included harmonised provisions for the permitting procedure and appeal for nine different sectoral acts. In the following years, new chapters were added on topics such as advising, environmental reporting and financial provisions.[7] Although this act already provided harmonisation between different pieces of environmental legislation, the need for more coherence and integration also grew. Furthermore, in addition to procedural harmonisation, substantial harmonisation was deemed necessary.

3 *B.A. Beijen* (ed.), Hoofdlijnen milieubestuursrecht, 3rd ed., 2015, pp. 60–61.
4 Rapport van de Werkgroep Inspraak en Beroep Milieuhygiëne (Report of the Working Group on Participation and Access to Justice in Environmental Matters), 1974.
5 Memorie van toelichting (Explanatory memorandum), 14311, nr. 3, 1976–1977, p. 2.
6 Memorie van toelichting, 14311, nr. 3, 1976–1977, p. 2.
7 *M.N. Boeve & F.A.G. Groothuijse*, Omgevingsrecht, 4th ed., 2013, p. 9.

This trend resulted in the adoption of the 1993 Environmental Management Act (*Wet milieubeheer*), which replaced both the Nuisance Act, the Act on General Principles for Environmental Health and, later on in its development, several sectoral acts. The Environmental Management Act consists of 22 chapters, of which two are not yet completed (namely, chapter 3 on international issues and chapter 6 on environmental zoning).

Several motives and objectives can be examined in the development of the Dutch Environmental Management Act. Firstly, the need for more uniform and comprehensive legislation of environmental law was recognised very early on. This need was based on the previous state of environmental legislation, including incoherencies, lack of information and gaps in legislation. Furthermore, a more integrated approach to environmental legislation could ensure that environmental issues were not pushed from one sector to another. The term 'harmonisation' is also explicitly used in the report that accompanies the first proposal for the Environmental Management Act.[8]

Furthermore, in 2010 the act containing general principles of environmental policy (*Wet algemene bepalingen omgevingsrecht*) entered into force, introducing one integrated environmental permit for all activities potentially affecting the environment. This environmental permit replaces and integrates about 25 permits, exemptions and notifications that all existed separately and followed different procedures.[9]

However, the harmonisation and integration trend in the Netherlands has not yet come to an end. In the future, the environmental legislation in the Netherlands will be even further integrated in the Environmental Act (*Omgevingswet*) which was adopted and published in 2016 and will normally enter into force on 1 January 2022.[10] A first motive for the adoption of this new act can again be found in the fragmented nature of environmental legislation (i.e. it is spread over dozens of acts), which leads to coordination issues and reduced recognition and usefulness. Even though past legislative revisions were very necessary and resulted in a more harmonised system of environmental law, Dutch environmental legislation is still perceived as being too complex and fragmented, mainly due to its sectoral structure. This also entails problems with clarity, predictability and coherence.[11] Two other reasons include the need to adapt the legislation to current and future developments (e.g. the requirement of sustainable development) and the application issues that resulted from the co-existence of many different acts with different procedures, instruments and rules.[12] In order to resolve these issues, the Dutch government found the

8 Voorlopig verslag (Preliminary report), 14311, nr. 4, 1977, p. 5.

9 Memorie van toelichting, 30844, nr. 3, 2006–2007, p. 3.

10 The progress can be followed at https://aandeslagmetdeomgevingswet.nl/.

11 Memorie van toelichting, 33962, nr. 3, 2013–2014, p. 14.

12 Memorie van toelichting, 33962, nr. 3, 2013–2014, p. 6.

optimisation of sectoral legislation insufficient and chose instead a fundamental review of all environmental legislation.[13]

This most recent comprehensive review of Dutch environmental law serves four objectives. Firstly, environmental legislation should be clear, predictable and easy to use. Secondly, the environment should be central in coherent policy, decision-making and regulation. Thirdly, an active and flexible approach should leave enough room for the balancing of interests in order to attain environmental aims. Finally, decision-making for environmental projects should be quicker and better.[14]

The new environmental act contains 23 chapters, of which 19 are currently completed.[15] It concerns the physical environment and activities that (can) have an influence on this environment.[16] The term 'environment' is used in a broad sense, including constructions, infrastructure, water, soil, air, landscapes, nature and heritage.[17] This shows the shift from a sectoral and media-oriented to an integrated and area-oriented approach; the act lays down one environmental vision based on protecting the entire physical environment. An illustration of this integrated vision is the 'disappearance' of the separate sectoral planning instruments at the local level.[18]

The act provides an integrated environmental framework, building upon well functioning parts of environmental law that were already in existence and (partially) replacing 26 pieces of environmental legislation, including the Environmental Management Act. This revision entails substantive changes for some parts of environmental law, while others are transferred to the new act without any changes. As already mentioned, not all chapters are yet complete. The first proposal provided a structure for all environmental legislation, of which several parts were still to be added in separate proposals (for example, concerning soil, noise and nature).[19] Besides reducing the legislative body of environmental law, the Environmental Act will be executed in only four administrative measures (*Algemene Maatregelen van Bestuur*) instead of the previous 120 measures.[20]

The introduction of this new environmental act has not been without critique. For example, the Council of State criticised the use of framework legislation,

---

13 Memorie van toelichting, 33962, nr. 3, 2013–2014, p. 18.

14 Memorie van toelichting, 33962 nr. 3, 2013–2014, p. 7.

15 The most recent consolidated version of the act (of 30 December 2020) can be consulted online at https://aandeslagmetdeomgevingswet.nl/regelgeving/stelsel-omgevingswet/tekst-toelichting-omgevingswet-amvb/ (consulted on 4 March 2021).

16 Article. 1.1 Omgevingswet (Environmental Act).

17 Article 1.2 Omgevingswet.

18 *Gemeente Haarlem & G32*, Vergelijkend Rapport Omgevingswet, https://www.platform31.nl/uploads/media_item/media_item/79/24/Was-Wordt-lijst_Haarlem_en_G32-1487674019.pdf, 2016, p. 10.

19 Memorie van toelichting, 33962 nr. 3, 2013–2014, p. 8.

20 *B.A. Beijen* (ed.), Hoofdlijnen milieubestuursrecht, 3rd ed., 2015, p. 67.

both for the sake of legal certainty and the shift of powers from the legislative to the executive branch.[21] The council poses the question of whether the delegation and the extent of these powers is justified in the field of environmental law.[22] However, future practices will show whether the goals of the Environmental Act are met, and whether the obtained flexibility and potential lack of legal certainty prove to be an issue.

2.2. ENVIRONMENTAL LAW IN BELGIUM (FLEMISH REGION)

The development of environmental law in Belgium has mostly been parallel to the developments on the international and European level, which started in the 1970s. Until the mid-20th century, environmental protection was not yet a national issue in Belgium. However, environmental law experienced a great expansion during this period of time. This development did not occur in a systematic way, but tended to happen haphazardly. New environmental legislation was mainly introduced to counter a concrete incident or in response to international or European obligations.[23] A list including all previous and current European, Belgian and Flemish environmental legislation can be consulted online.[24] This shows an extensive number of laws, decrees and other measures that apply to the environment in the Flemish region.[25] Flemish environmental law was mainly developed on a sectoral basis, with an absence of uniformity in the decision-making and enforcement rules, making the existing legislation very complicated.[26]

Currently, this sectoral approach to environmental law is still very clear, even though most general and horizontal provisions are included in the Decree of 5 April 1995 concerning the general provisions relating to environmental policy.[27] This decree can be considered a partial codification of environmental law.

21 In its 2018 report, the Council of State mentions that 95 per cent of the legislation originated in the executive and not the legislative branch.

22 Nederlandse Raad van State, Jaarverslag 2018, https://jaarverslag.raadvanstate.nl/2018/wp-content/uploads/sites/6/2019/03/WEBVERSIE_Jaarverslag_2018.pdf, pp. 23–24.

23 *H. Bocken*, The Inter-University Commission for the Revision of Environmental Law in the Flemish Region: Objectives and Procedures, in *H. Bocken & D. Ryckbost* (eds) The Codification of Environmental Law: Proceedings of the International Conference, 1996, p. 4.

24 For the thematic index, see: https://navigator.emis.vito.be/thematische-index. For the legal index, see: https://navigator.emis.vito.be/juridische-index.

25 A similar list can be consulted for the Walloon region at: http://environnement.wallonie.be/legis/index.htm.

26 *H. Bocken*, The Inter-University Commission for the Revision of Environmental Law in the Flemish Region: Objectives and Procedures, in *H. Bocken & D. Ryckbost* (eds) The Codification of Environmental Law: Proceedings of the International Conference, 1996, p. 4.

27 However, several horizontal measures still exist separately, for example on the topic of access to environmental information.

It originated from the proposals of the Interuniversity Commission for the Revision of Environmental Law in the Flemish Region (*Interuniversitaire Commissie voor de Herziening van het Milieurecht in het Vlaamse Gewest*), chaired by Hubert Bocken. The Bocken Commission was founded in 1989 and published its final report in the beginning of 1995. During this five-year period, three decrees that were drafted according to the proposals of the Bocken Commission were already approved.[28] Criticism was voiced on this phased communication of the commission's proposals, proclaiming that the Flemish Council[29] should have waited until the final report to include all proposals in one global draft of decree. The Belgian Council of State formulated several points of critique on this phased introduction of legislation, stating that it could lead to interpretation problems and application issues of the separate parts, because they lack a broader context. Nevertheless, the timely revision of Flemish environmental law was prioritised.

The primary aim of the Bocken Commission was a to attain a comprehensive codification and revision of the Flemish legislation on environmental protection. This included the objective to achieve a systematic body of law that comprised all rules of environmental law, based on a clear notion of the objectives and instruments of environmental policy.[30] The first idea was to bring together all environmental legislation in one integrated framework decree, which would then be considered a Flemish Environmental Code. The proposed Flemish Draft Decree on Environmental Policy of the Bocken Commission not only included horizontal environmental measures (e.g. on access to information, enforcement and decision-making), but also provided for separate chapters on the different sectors of the environment (e.g. water, soil, waste and noise).[31]

Though intellectually and politically sound, this environmental code was considered too ambitious, as in reality environmental policy is in constant evolution. In practice, it was decided that besides the framework decree with general provisions, separate sectoral environmental legislation should stay in existence. This decision was also founded on the fact that certain sectoral acts were too specific to be included in a general code. Furthermore, this approach provided for the option to develop new sectoral legislation in order to counter new ecological challenges. Even though the choice was made for sectoral legislation to stay separate, the development of the general framework decree was still

---

28 Two of them were sectoral decrees, concerning waste, and one was a decree on environmental agreements.

29 Former title of the Flemish Parliament (from 1980–1995).

30 *H. Bocken*, The Inter-University Commission for the Revision of Environmental Law in the Flemish Region: Objectives and Procedures, in *H. Bocken & D. Ryckbost* (eds), The Codification of Environmental Law: Proceedings of the International Conference, 1996, p. 4.

31 *H. Bocken et al*, The Flemish Draft Decree on Environmental Policy: An Outline, in *H. Bocken & D. Ryckbost* (eds), The Codification of Environmental Law: Proceedings of the International Conference, 1996, pp. 11–40.

considered primordial.[32] The project for the revision of environmental law in the Flemish region was based on objectives such as improving the effectiveness of environmental protection law, the rationalisation and simplification of environmental legislation and the more efficient use of environmental policy instruments.[33] In short, the aim was to harmonise the legal basis of environmental legislation in Flanders, rendering it more effective and less complex.[34]

The proposed draft decree would be the first part of a more comprehensive framework decree on environmental policy, providing environmental law with more internal cohesion. The objective of this framework decree was twofold: it should allow the transposition of Flemish environmental legislation in a decree containing general provisions on environmental policy and a series of sectoral decrees.[35] As already mentioned, the existence of separate sectoral legislation was found necessary, because this legislation is mostly very specific, which makes it more difficult to integrate into one framework act. Furthermore, in order to face new ecological challenges, the adoption of new sectoral legislation in the future cannot be ruled out. On the other hand, for new issues that have an impact on the entirety of the environment and which should be regulated uniformly, the framework decree is the ideal instrument. This decree can be considered the basis of all other environmental legislation and is referred to in sectoral acts. As a part of the revision project, sectoral legislation would also be reviewed and, if necessary, introduced in a way that is coherent with the general provisions found in the framework decree.[36]

The 'annexation technique' for legislation (*aanbouwwetgeving*) used in Flanders is similar to the Dutch example, which served as an important reference in this revision project. The 1995 proposal shows the same characteristics of major reform as the Dutch Environmental Management Act (and even the upcoming Dutch Environmental Act). This 'annexation technique' was also recommended by the Belgian Council of State in an advise for a previous legal proposal.[37] The council considers the technique useful for major revisions, as the different legislative parts can be drafted separately, and one will not prevent the realisation of the other. Furthermore, supplementing the technique – and if deemed necessary – the legislation would be coordinated after finalisation.

32 Ontwerp van decreet (Draft decree), Stuk 718 (1994–1995), nr. 1, p. 3.

33 *H. Bocken*, The Inter-University Commission for the Revision of Environmental Law in the Flemish Region: Objectives and Procedures, in *H. Bocken & D. Ryckbost* (eds), The Codification of Environmental Law: Proceedings of the International Conference, 1996, p. 3.

34 *H. Bocken*, The Inter-University Commission for the Revision of Environmental Law in the Flemish Region: Objectives and Procedures, in *H. Bocken & D. Ryckbost* (eds), The Codification of Environmental Law: Proceedings of the International Conference, 1996, pp. 4–11.

35 Ontwerp van decreet, verslag, Stuk 718 (1994–1995), nr. 4, p. 2.

36 Ontwerp van decreet, memorie van toelichting, Stuk 718 (1994–1995), nr. 1, p. 3.

37 It concerns a proposal on a decree concerning the universities in the Flemish Community: Gedr. St., Vlaamse Raad, 1990–1991, 502- nr. 1, p. 185.

The first version of the decree only included a title on general provisions and a title on decision-making and participation. This first title consisted of definitions, objectives and principles, which steer environmental policy and serve as interpretation guidance for the other provisions in the decree. The second title provides for environmental reports, environmental policy plans and annual environmental programmes on the different levels of government. Furthermore, this title already contains a section on environmental quality standards, laying down the basic principles on which the Flemish government should establish the specific standards.

Since the decree was first introduced, it has undergone many changes and additions. A few months after the first two titles were adopted, the third title on corporate environmental management was added to the decree.[38] In 2002, the fourth title on environmental impact and safety reporting was introduced.[39] This title was followed shortly in 2004 by title five on general, sectoral and integrated environmental conditions (which never entered into force),[40] title 11 on strategic environmental consultation[41] and title 10 on environmental agencies.[42] In 2007, title 16 on monitoring, enforcement and safety measures[43] and title 15 on environmental damage and liability were added, the latter as a transposition of the EU Environmental Liability Directive.[44] Title six on environmental agreements was introduced in 2012.[45] In 2014, a new title five on the exploitation of classified facilities was adopted, replacing the former title. Furthermore, title eight on climate was added.

A further step of integration and harmonisation in Flemish environmental law entailed the introduction of the environmental permit with the 2014 Decree on the Environmental Permit (*Decreet betreffende de omgevingsvergunning*), which entered into force in 2017.[46] Similar to the Dutch example, this permit concerns both environmental and spatial aspects of a project and is the result of an integrated permitting procedure.

2.3. CODIFICATION OF ENVIRONMENTAL LAW IN FRANCE

The French jurisprudence had been asking for a codification of French environmental law for many years before the decision was made in 1990 to

38 Stukken (Legislative documents) 719 (1994).
39 Stukken 1312 (2001–2002).
40 Stukken 1846 (2003–2004).
41 Stukken 2196 (2003–2004).
42 Stukken 2122 (2003–2004).
43 Stukken 1249 (2006–2007).
44 Stukken 1252 (2006–2007).
45 Stukken 1710 (2011–2012).
46 Decreet betreffende de omgevingsvergunning (Decree on the Environmental Permit), 25 April 2014.

commission a report on the feasibility of such a French Environmental Code.[47] In 1991, the commission handed in a report to the Ministry of the Environment.[48] In this report, they concluded that an 'authentic' codification of environmental law was necessary. This need for an environmental code consisted of several aspects. First, it would help to better know the content of environmental law. Second, it would make environmental legislation more easily accessible for everyone, which would lead to better application of the law. Also, specifically for the branch of the environment, it was deemed important that environmental law was recognised as a legitimate and non-controversial social value.[49]

The main incentive for the introduction of an environmental code was the existing patchwork of environmental legislation that was formed by many legal texts adopted in the 19th and 20th centuries, which led to difficulties in accessibility and comprehensibility. Introducing a French Environmental Code could serve as the official starting point of French environmental law.[50] Other reasons for the revision of environmental law were the need to improve the quality and coherence of the law. The process of codification to ameliorate environmental legislation was selected because it could achieve all those aims by resolving contradictions, removing repetitions, cleaning up ambiguities and drafting better legal texts.[51]

On the topic of completeness of the French Environmental Code, the aim of exhaustiveness was considered against the aims of synthesis and simplification. The decision was made to include the fundamentals of environmental law in a first chapter of the code, while also allowing for miscellaneous rules to be included in the code, as long as they were governed by those fundamental principles.[52]

The French Environmental Code was finally introduced in 2000 by ordinance 2000-914,[53] and the code was finalised in 2007 with the adoption of fifth book concerning the prevention of pollution, risks and nuisances.[54] The legislative

47 On 23 January 1976, the politician Jean Lecanuet declared that it would be necessary to start drafting an environmental code, in order to facilitate the use of the law by practitioners.

48 'Reflexions Préliminaires sur l'éventualité d'une Codification du Droit de l'environnement, Rapport pour le Ministère de l'environnement', Paris, May 1991.

49 *M. Prieur*, Pourquoi une Codification, Revue Juridique de l'Environnement, numéro special,. Le code français de l'environnement, 2002 (9), p. 10.

50 *M. Prieur*, Pourquoi une Codification, Revue Juridique de l'Environnement, numéro special,. Le code français de l'environnement, 2002 (9), p. 10.

51 *G.J. Martin*, French Experiences of the Codification of Environmental Law, in *H. Bocken & D. Ryckbost* (eds) The Codification of Environmental Law: Proceedings of the International Conference, 1996, p. 118.

52 *G.J. Martin*, French Experiences of the Codification of Environmental Law, in *H. Bocken & D. Ryckbost* (eds) The Codification of Environmental Law: Proceedings of the International Conference, 1996, p. 119.

53 Ordonnance n° 2000-914 du 18 septembre 2000 relative à la partie Législative du code de l'environnement.

54 Commission Supérieure de Codification, Dix-Huitième Rapport Annuel, 2007, p. 6.

part of the French Environmental Code consists of seven books and contains most acts and decrees related to the environment, which were all developed and adopted at different stages. The first book contains common provisions (i.e. general principles, information and participation, institutions, protection agencies and financial and procedural provisions); the second book contains provisions on physical environments (i.e. legislation on water and air); the third book deals with natural spaces (i.e. provisions on natural heritage, the coastline, parks and reserves, sites, landscapes, access to nature and the prevention of natural risks); the fourth book includes legislation on flora and fauna (i.e. on the protection of flora and fauna, hunting and freshwater fishing); book five is on the prevention of pollution, risks and nuisances (i.e. classified facilities and structures, chemical products and biocides, GMOs, waste, the prevention of natural risks and acoustic and visual nuisances, the protection of the living environment and nuclear safety); book six contains specific provisions for certain regions; and book seven concerns the protection of the environment in the Antarctic.

The French Environmental Code can be considered comprehensive, although several more specific rules that could be considered part of a broader environmental policy can still be found in separate pieces of legislation (e.g. the Forest Code, Mining Code and Energy Code).

An interesting note is that the entire body of French law has been mostly codified since the entry into force of the Environmental Code. The Superior Commission on Codification has been reporting on this evolution annually since 1991.

3. LEARNING FROM THE MEMBER STATES

3.1. THE STATE OF EU ENVIRONMENTAL LEGISLATION

EU environmental law has evolved a great deal since the first action programme for the environment was adopted in 1973.[55] EU environmental policy developed into an important and extensive EU policy, covering many legal acts and topics and constituting several specific EU environmental institutions and bodies. A search on the EUR-Lex website containing all EU law for active regulations and directives on the subject matter of the environment already returns 434 results.[56] Even though topical summaries of EU environmental legislation are provided

55 Declaration of the Council of the European Communities and of the representatives of the governments of the Member States meeting in the Council of 22 November 1973 on the programme of action of the European Communities on the environment.

56 This includes 306 regulations and 128 directives (consulted on 4 March 2021).

online,[57] this is still a very large number of legal acts to consider, which may lead to accessibility and comprehensibility issues. Other problems have also been noted in the field of EU environmental law. Effective implementation and enforcement of EU environmental legislation are hampered by several factors. The existing environmental legislation is too specific and detailed and is not built around a systematic and harmonious concept; it has mostly been fragmentary and random. EU environmental law was never meant to cover the entire field of the environment and consists mainly of specific measures adopted to tackle specific problems.[58] It was developed ad hoc, without strategic thinking on how to organise a specific sector.[59] Furthermore, environmental legislative acts are considered inflexible, incomprehensible and too numerous. Contradictions between separate pieces of environmental legislation also occur.[60]

In general, the fragmentation of EU environmental law can already be noticed in its division in specific sectors which are regulated separately, even though all elements of the environment are interconnected, and actions affecting one part may also affect others. Regulating each sector individually may lead to counterproductive regulation, as issues may be pushed from one sector to another.[61] Furthermore, legislation on one topic is typically spread over different acts, which may lead to issues of accessibility and comprehensibility.[62] Specific examples of the incoherencies in EU environmental legislation can be found in the differing reporting obligations contained in the directives,[63] the different instruments used across the sectors[64] and the existence and absence of inspecting provisions in different environmental acts.[65]

---

57 See for example: https://eur-lex.europa.eu/summary/chapter/environment.html?root_default=SUM_1_CODED=20&locale=en.

58 *B. Iwanska*, The Need to Consolidate EU Environmental Law; A Polish Perspective, in *R. Macrory* (ed.), Reflections on 30 years of EU Environmental Law, Europa Law Publishing 2005, p. 494.

59 *L. Krämer*, EU Environmental Law, 8th ed., 2016, p. 482.

60 *C. Demmke*, Towards Effective Environmental Regulation: Innovative Approaches in Implementing and Enforcing European Environmental Law and Policy, 2001, p. 16; https://jeanmonnetprogram.org/archive/papers/01/010501.html.

61 *D. Owen*, Mapping, Modelling and the Fragmentation of Environmental law, Utah Law Review, 2013 (2019), p. 228.

62 See, for example, the legislation on waste. Even though there is framework legislation on this topic, there are also acts on waste management operations, specific waste streams, reporting on waste and even issues overlapping with other sectors, such as waste water.

63 An overview of the reporting obligations arising from EU environmental legislation can be found in Annex 3 to the Fitness Check on reporting and monitoring, SWD(2017) 230 final. See also: *A. Vanhellemont*, Environmental Reporting by the EU Member States and the Commission – Current Practices, Legislative Action and a Way Forward, JEEPL, 2020 (17)2, pp. 189–228.

64 For example, the different plans, permits and maps provided in separate pieces of environmental legislation.

65 Certain EU environmental acts contain provisions on inspections – for example, the Industrial Emissions Directive and the Waste Shipment Regulation – while others do not

These issues are similar to the ones experienced at the Member State level. The sectoral approach and haphazard development of EU environmental law has led to an extensive body of legislation, which is both fragmented and complex. The same need to internally harmonise environmental legislation as experienced in the Member States also seems to exist at the EU level.

3.2. HARMONISATION STEPS

Several harmonisation steps have already been taken at the EU level. In general, the commission's Better Regulation Agenda and Regulatory and Fitness (REFIT) programme offer options for further harmonisation of environmental legislation. As a result of this, codified versions of older directives have been adopted, different environmental directives have been re-casted into a single directive, and the use of framework directives and daughter directives has increased.[66] However, even though these initiatives are based on general policy principles that can be applied to separate pieces of environmental legislation, they do not offer a comprehensive (re-)view on environmental policy as a whole.

A clear example of more harmonised environmental legislation is the Industrial Emissions Directive, which regulates all pollutant emissions (i.e. including water, air, waste, noise, etc.), taking into account the entire environmental performance of an industrial installation.[67] More general action aimed at EU environmental policy as a whole includes the 2019 regulation on the alignment of reporting obligations in the field of legislation related to the environment.[68] However, this regulation does not cover all pieces of environmental legislation and can once again be considered a rather specific instrument.

Other initiatives include projects such as the Make it Work Project, an initiative introduced in 2014 by the Netherlands, the UK, Sweden and the Czech Republic, which aims to identify concrete opportunities to improve the quality of EU environmental law and to establish a more coherent and consistent framework for the EU environmental *acquis*.[69] Also, at Oslo University, researchers are working on a project on consistency in environmental law.[70]

---

and fall back on the non-binding provisions of the 2001 recommendation on environmental inspections (which is also limited in scope).

66 For a more extensive discussion, see: *B. Beijen*, Seeking coherence among environmental directives, in *M. Peeters & R. Uylenburg* (eds), EU Environmental Legislation, Edward Elgar, 2014, pp. 80–84.

67 Directive 2010/75/EU of the European Parliament and of the Council of 24 November 2010 on industrial emissions (integrated pollution prevention and control) (Recast), *OJ* L 334.

68 Regulation (EU) 2019/1010 of the European Parliament and of the Council of 5 June 2019 on the alignment of reporting obligations in the field of legislation related to the environment, *OJ* L 170.

69 http://minisites.ieep.eu/work-areas/environmental-governance/better-regulation/make-it-work.

70 https://www.jus.uio.no/english/research/areas/natural-resources/projects/consistency/.

3.3. OPTIONS FOR FURTHER HARMONISATION

The question remains as to which (concrete) options for more comprehensive internal harmonisation exist at the EU level, and whether inspiration can be drawn from the national level.

The introduction of an Environmental Framework Directive has been suggested by Beijen, containing at least generally applicable definitions of core concepts, terms and main environmental instruments that are used in all sectors of the environment. Such a framework directive could then be the basis for revising existing directives and introducing new environmental legislation. More specific provisions would still be contained in sectoral directives, which would then function as a type of daughter directive to the general framework. Additionally, these sectoral directives can be complemented by more detailed daughter directives. This idea would constitute a pyramid structure, though without any hierarchical relations between the directives.[71]

An even more comprehensive EU Environmental Code including all horizontal legislation and common provisions that are currently regulated separately in sectoral legislation is also an option. This could be based on a similar structure as the Dutch Environmental Management Act and the Flemish decree containing general provisions relating to environmental policy. Of course, in this case, the separate sectoral legislation would also remain in existence. However, any discrepancies in the procedural elements, such as reporting, inspections and used instruments, would be resolved.

A more ambitious project, consisting of one EU environmental code including all environmental legislation at the EU level, similar to the French Environmental Code and future Dutch Environmental Act, would probably not be feasible, at least not as a first step. Instead of providing simplification and accessibility, this may even prove to be more unclear. Furthermore, it would be difficult to assess which specific provisions could be included in the code. A goal of comprehensiveness entails the difficult question of where to draw the line. Finally, the codification of all environmental legislation would surely entail a very costly operation, whereas the benefits of this one EU environmental code are less obvious or certain.

The 'annexation technique' used for the harmonisation and codification of environmental legislation in the Member States offers a useful perspective for the procedure that could be followed at the EU level. Instead of initiating a complete overhaul including all environmental legislation, the more practical and feasible option would be a step-by-step improvement of EU environmental law. This procedure would entail scrutinising different topics and pieces of

[71] *B. Beijen*, Seeking coherence among environmental directives, in *M. Peeters & R. Uylenburg* (eds), EU Environmental Legislation, 2014, pp. 84–86.

legislation separately, looking for ways in which they could be harmonised. Every step should be accompanied by an assessment of the proposed changes: do the advantages of harmonisation outweigh the costs? Also, it could very well be that certain issues require specific solutions, while others may be resolved with a more general revision that is applied across the entire body of law. Most importantly, the main aim of protecting the environment through effective legislation should be remembered throughout any operation of reviewing and improving environmental law. Practically speaking, it would be possible to establish a code consisting of several books (e.g. the first containing all common and general provisions and several other books containing sectoral legislation), following the French example.

An important side note should be made on the difference between the different legislative levels and the transferability of arguments in favour of codification of domestic environmental law to the EU level. As several of these arguments relate to making environmental law more understandable for practitioners, ensuring ecological progress and getting better compliance, the question arises as to whether this is relevant for EU legislation. EU environmental law is not addressed directly at citizens and stakeholders who have to comply with the rules, but instead, at the national legislators. This entails that the stakeholders in the Member States are not directly confronted with EU environmental legislation (except for directly applicable regulations). They only have to apply the domestic rules implementing EU environmental law. In this sense, they may not even be aware that this legislation originates from the EU level.[72]

4. CONCLUSION

Looking at the cases of the Netherlands, Belgium and France, we can note that at the national level many harmonisation and codification steps have been taken in the field of environmental law. Issues of fragmentation and inconsistency in environmental legislation were already noted as early as the 1970s. This is especially interesting, as the starting point of a real EU environmental policy can be situated in this time period. Since then, EU environmental legislation has expanded and now shows similar problems as faced in the Member States.

Certainly, internal harmonisation – and possibly codification – of EU environmental legislation should be considered. Several options for a more harmonised body of EU environmental law were put forth in this chapter. Nevertheless, the starting point should not be the inclusion of the entire body of EU environmental law in one harmonised and codified act, but a

[72] *Michael Faure*, To codify or not to codify EU environmental law: That's not the question, in *B. Vanheusden, T. Iliopolous and A. Vanhellemont* (eds.), Harmonisation in EU Environmental and Energy Law, Intersentia, Cambridge 2022, pp. 9–25.

step-by-step analysis and improvement of the legislation, always assessing the impact of certain changes and considering the advantages and charges. This especially entails examining the relevance of arguments in favour of harmonisation and codification for EU legislation, as it has a different finality than national laws.

It is clear that further research on the internal harmonisation of EU environmental law is necessary, including an impact assessment of the different options for harmonisation and codification. The risk exists that the proposed options are merely costly operations, without any substantial benefits. 'Better' or more qualitative legislation will only have a positive impact if it also leads to better implementation and more effective legislation that aids in reaching the main goal of protecting the environment. Moreover, it is possible that specific action will already provide solutions for certain issues. Harmonising for the sake of harmonising should be avoided.

ACCESS TO ENVIRONMENTAL JUSTICE IN THE EU

Interpretation, Harmonisation and the Search for Consistency

Alison Hough*

1. INTRODUCTION

The principle of consistency is a common-sense tenet underpinning the rule of law, which requires that legal interpretations be consistent, vertically and horizontally.[1] The principle and the related doctrine of consistent interpretation

* Senior Lecturer, Faculty of Business and Hospitality, Midlands Campus, Technological University of the Shannon (TUS), Athlone, County Westmeath, Ireland.

1 *E. Herlin-Karnell & T. Konstadinides*, The Rise and Expressions of Consistency in EU Law: Legal and Strategic Implications for European Integration 2013, Cambridge Yearbook of European Legal Studies, pp. 139–167.

are important tools for the harmonisation of EU law.[2,3] This chapter conducts an examination of the case law of the Court of Justice of the European Union (CJEU) in the area of Article 9 of the Aarhus Convention UNECE 1998[4] as an exposition of the failure of the court to uphold the doctrine of consistency horizontally. The case law of the CJEU applying Article 9 of the Aarhus Convention to the issue of standing rights before national courts of Member States can be negatively contrasted with the case law of the CJEU when it applies the same article to standing rights for reviewing acts of the EU institutions before the CJEU under Regulation (EC) 1367/2006 (hereinafter 'the Aarhus Regulation'). This results in an undesirable lack of harmonisation in the application of the Aarhus Convention principles across the multi-level governance system of the EU.

The case law of the CJEU regarding access to justice in environmental matters (and the provisions of Article 9 of the Aarhus Convention) before the national courts is marked by its emphasis on the need for broad access to justice[5] and consistency of interpretation with the provisions of the Aarhus Convention (even where those provisions have not been implemented in directly relevant EU law measures/do not meet the conditions for direct effect). On the other hand, when NGOs attempt to review environmental decisions of the EU institutions before the General Court, the CJEU has repeatedly refused access in what appears to be a failure to apply the same principles and requirements of consistency and broad access to justice to the EU institutions and its own procedures.[6]

This restrictive approach to review is in direct opposition to the pronouncements of the Aarhus Convention Compliance Committee on the issue in their draft decision in C32 I & II.[7] It also stands in contrast to the approach

2 *M. Brenncke*, Hybrid Methodology for the EU Principle of Consistent Interpretation, 2017, Statute Law Review, 39(2) pp. 134–154.

3 *P. Craig & G. DeBurca*, EU Law: Texts, Cases and Materials, 2020, 7th Ed. Oxford University Press, pp. 217 & 310.

4 The Convention on Access to Information, Public Participation in Decision-making and Access to Justice in Environmental Matters, known as 'the Aarhus Convention', United Nations Economic Commission for Europe, (available at <www.unece.org/fileadmin/DAM/env/pp/documents/cep43e.pdf>). It was signed on 25 June 1998 and approved on behalf of the European Community by Council Decision 2005/370/EC of 17 February 2005 on the conclusion, on behalf of the European Community, of the Convention on access to information, public participation in decision-making and access to justice in environmental matters (OJ 2005 L 124, p. 1).

5 *A. Ryall*, Access to Justice in Environmental Matters: The Evolving EU Jurisprudence, 2016, IPELJ, 23(4) pp. 115–124. p. 5.

6 *C. Poncelet*, Access to Justice in Environmental Matters – Does the European Union Comply with its Obligations? 2012, JEL, 24(2) pp. 287–309. *G. Garcon*, The Rights of Access to Justice in Environmental Matters in the EU – The Third Pillar of the Aarhus Convention: Validity and Scope of the Review Procedures under Regulation (EC) 1367/2006, 2013, EFFL (8), p. 78.

7 Aarhus Convention Compliance Committee, Draft findings and recommendation of the Compliance Committee with regard to Communication ACCC/C/2008/32 (Part II) concerning compliance by the European Union, www.unece.org/env/pp/compliance/Compliancecommittee/32TableEC.html.

of the court in the area of economic interests such as competition and state aid cases, where affected individuals have *locus standi* without having to demonstrate a particular concern which marks them out from others similarly affected. The contrast with cases involving economic interests has already been the subject of an examination by Krämer,[8] who states: 'This is, without doubt, due to the fact that the ECJ allowed the admissibility of applications on economic grounds much more easily than in environmental matters'.

These conflicts in the case law on Article 9 of the Aarhus Convention can also be seen as a proxy for the many tensions in the broader EU legal order. This is apparent when carrying out an analysis of the case law through the lens of the principle of consistency. It seems apparent from an analysis of the case law that the doctrine of consistent interpretation is strictly adhered to when available as a vehicle for practical extension of the competence of EU law. However, it is not adhered to where it would act as a vehicle for the extension of international law competency into the legal order of the European Union. The contradictions in the case law also play out the struggle of the perceived of lack of transparency and democratic deficit that dog the institutions of Europe on the heels of the Brexit debate, and other polarities between environmental protection (often seen as opposed to economic growth) and economic interests, as well as institutional efficiency versus transparency and accountability.

2. THE DOCTRINE OF CONSISTENCY AND HARMONISATION

Consistency and consistent interpretation in the EU legal order are receiving increased attention in international law academic discourse. Herlin-Karnell and Konstadinides highlight the importance of the integrity of the legal order as represented through the appearance of consistency, pointing to MacCormick's contention that the law should make sense if considered as a whole, by being rational and orderly.[9] It is clear that it is central to the rule of law and contributes to legal certainty.[10]

One of the issues with application of the doctrine of consistent interpretation to the relationship between the Aarhus Convention and EU law is the hierarchy

8 *L. Kramer*, Access to Environmental Justice: The Double Standards of the ECJ. 2017, JEEPL (14) pp. 159–185, p. 167.

9 *E. Herlin-Karnell & T. Konstadinides*, The Rise and Expressions of Consistency in EU Law: Legal and Strategic Implications for European Integration, Cambridge Yearbook of European Legal Studies, 2013 pp. 139–167.

10 *G. Betlem*, The Doctrine of Consistent Interpretation – Managing Legal Uncertainty, 2002, Oxford Journal of Legal Studies, 22(3) pp. 397–418.

of norms required by the doctrine. In order to avoid an inconsistent approach to EU law, certain norms must be accorded priority over others.[11] This touches on an unanswered question relating to the supremacy of EU law in relation to international law.

Betlem[12] highlights the three levels on which the doctrine operates:

1) On the national law, giving effect to EU law in Member States;
2) Within EU law, giving effect to primary EU law over secondary EU law; and finally,
3) EU law in relation to international law.

The doctrine of consistent interpretation often manifests in EU law as 'indirect effect' where a provision does not have direct effect, but a measure of national law must nevertheless be interpreted in accordance with it (e.g. Van Colson).[13,14]

One issue with the doctrine is the potential for mission creep, with the doctrine providing justification for the CJEU to grant competence to the EU in areas where there are no directly applicable measures of law.

The doctrine is subject to the *contra legem* limit, and so cannot be used to require a court to arrive at a decision that would conflict with national law, but operates in the realm of judicial discretion to interpret the law.[15]

Herlin-Karnell and Konstadinides point to the TFEU for support for the value of consistency as a legal principle in the EU legal order including references in Article 7, Article 13 and also Article 256 which refers to the power of the CJEU to review decisions of the General Court to ensure consistency.[16] From these provisions it can be seen that the EU institutions have an obligation of consistency with the law in their actions.

The examination of the case law of the CJEU dealing with Article 9(3) reveals a strategic enforcement of the principle of consistency where it furthers the extension of EU competence and the project of integration, but a failure to uphold the same principle when it comes to application of Article 9(3) to the EU institutions in a way that would fetter the powers of those institutions to determine absolutely their own procedures.

---

11 *G. Betlem*, The Doctrine of Consistent Interpretation – Managing Legal Uncertainty, 2002, Oxford Journal of Legal Studies, 22(3) pp. 397–418, p.398.

12 *G. Betlem*, The Doctrine of Consistent Interpretation – Managing Legal Uncertainty, 2002, Oxford Journal of Legal Studies, 22(3) pp. 397–418.

13 Case C-14/83.

14 *M. Brenncke*, Hybrid Methodology for the EU Principle of Consistent Interpretation, 2017, Statute Law Review, 39(2) pp. 134–154, p.135.

15 *M. Brenncke*, Hybrid Methodology for the EU Principle of Consistent Interpretation, 2017, Statute Law Review, 39(2) pp. 134–154, p.144.

16 *E. Herlin-Karnell & T. Konstadinides*, The Rise and Expressions of Consistency in EU Law: Legal and Strategic Implications for European Integration, 2013, Cambridge Yearbook of European Legal Studies, pp. 139–167.

Harmonisation (or the process of approximation of EU standards) in EU law is critical to the operation of the single market, but more broadly to coherent European integration.[17] The elements by which harmonisation operate are positive harmonisation (making of common legal rules and standards) and negative harmonisation (the removal of barriers to harmonisation).[18] The doctrines of direct effect and indirect effect/consistency[19,20] are crucial to the functioning of harmonisation, in that they are tools used by the CJEU to ensure that harmonisation occurs as it should.

The failure of consistency at the EU level in relation to Art 9(3) of the Aarhus Convention arises in two instances. Firstly, the EU institutions (primarily the EU Commission and the CJEU) have failed to implement laws in a manner consistent with Art 9(3) of the Aarhus Convention (through the legal rules proposed and the case law expounded). Secondly, the failure of the CJEU to apply the same principles (the 'interpretative obligation' to EU level case law (in the interpretation of the Aarhus Regulation) as it does to national level case law involving access to justice represents a failure of consistent interpretation.

These failures undermine the principle of consistency in the EU legal order. The implied acceptance of a hierarchy of norms is disrupted when those norms are refused application in the same manner across the whole system. It also undermines the perceived integrity of the EU legal order, showing Member States that it is possible in certain circumstances for the institutions like the CJEU to act 'politically' and ignore international law rules. It also creates circumstances where regulatory acts which breach EU environmental law go unchallenged until they are implemented at the Member State level, at which stage they can then be challenged through Art 267 reference. This approach requires the implementation of a breach of EU environmental law before it can be challenged, allowing the EU institutions themselves to procure disruptions of harmonisation (and leaving a bad measure unchallenged where the implementing measure never occurs). It also deprives NGOs and citizens of their right to review decisions because, as is highlighted by many academics[21] and reports,[22] there are extensive problems with the idea that Art 267 provides a complete system of

17 *P. Craig & G. DeBurca*, EU Law: Texts, Cases and Materials, 2020, 7th Ed. Oxford University Press, p. 641.

18 *M. Costa & S. Peers*, Steiner & Woods EU Law, 2020, 14th ed. Oxford University Press, p. 340.

19 *P. Craig & G. DeBurca*, EU Law: Texts, Cases and Materials, 2020, 7th Ed. Oxford University Press, p. 217.

20 *M. Costa & S. Peers*, Steiner & Woods EU Law, 2020, 14th ed. Oxford University Press, p. 136.

21 *P. Craig & G. DeBurca*, EU Law: Texts, Cases and Materials, 2020, 7th Ed. Oxford University Press, pp. 566–567.

22 *Milieu*, Study on EU implementation of the Aarhus Convention in the area of access to justice in environmental matters (2019), pp. 90 & 120–124. https://ec.europa.eu/environment/aarhus/pdf/Final_study_EU_implemention_environmental_matters_2019.pdf.

access to justice, due to problems accessing Art 267 review at the Member State level, or the absence of the required implementing measure.

This damages the project of EU harmonisation and also plays into narratives which abound at the national level in many countries that judicial review is the enemy of public administration and to be feared. This is simply not borne out by the evidence,[23] and in fact one of the rationales for the access rights in the Aarhus Convention is improved public administration.[24]

Judicial review ensures that all institutions of government are subject to the law and held accountable before it[25,26] – an essential element of the broad, substantive conception of the rule of law espoused by the EU Commission.[27]

3. CASE LAW OF THE CJEU ON ART 9 AS APPLIED BY THE MEMBER STATES' COURTS

It is clear from the case law on Article 9 that the CJEU generally strives for what Ryall describes as the doctrine of consistent interpretation.[28] For example, in Fish Legal, Case 279/12, the CJEU stated (when discussing access to environmental information) that in becoming a party to the Aarhus Convention, the EU undertook to ensure the general principles would be given effect to. In adopting Directive 2003/4 the EU legislature intended to '... ensure consistency of European Union law with the Aarhus Convention'.[29]

This approach of ensuring consistency with the Aarhus Convention can also be seen in 'LZ No. 1' (also known as Slovak Brown Bears No. 1),[30] delivered in 8 March 2011. In this decision, the court held that while Article 9(3) was not directly effective in EU law, national courts had an obligation to interpret national law in accordance with the objectives of Article 9(3) in a manner that would allow NGOs to challenge a decision, if the decision breached any provisions of EU law affected by Article 9.

---

23 *M. Sunkin*, The Impact of Public Law Litigation, in Public Law in *M. Elliott & D. Feldman* (eds.), 2015, Cambridge University Press.

24 Recitals 9, 10 and 11 to the Aarhus Convention, https://unece.org/DAM/env/pp/documents/cep43e.pdf.

25 *D. Feldman*, Democracy, The Rule of Law and Judicial Review, 1990, the Federal Law Review, 19(1).

26 *R. Ruebner*, Democracy, Judicial Review and the Rule of Law in the Age of Terrorism: The Experience of Israel – A Comparative Perspective, 2003, Georgia Journal of International and Comparative Law, 31(3).

27 COM(2019) 163 final 'Further strengthening the Rule of Law within the Union' https://eur-lex.europa.eu/legal-content/EN/TXT/?uri=CELEX%3A52019DC0163.

28 *A. Ryall*, Access to Justice in Environmental Matters: The Evolving EU Jurisprudence, 2016, IPELJ 23(4) pp. 115–124.

29 Case C-279/12 *Fish Legal and Emily Shirley v Information Commissioner and Others* [2013] ECLI:EU:C:2013:853, para. 36.

30 Case C-240/09.

The court found that while the Aarhus Convention does not have direct effect in EU law, it is an integral part of the EU legal order,[31] and it stated at paragraph 30 that it is important for the national court:

> to interpret, to the fullest extent possible, the procedural rules relating to the conditions to be met in order to bring administrative or judicial proceedings in accordance with the objectives of Article 9(3) of that convention and the objective of effective judicial protection of the rights conferred by EU law, in order to enable an environmental protection organisation, such as the zoskupenie, to challenge before a court a decision taken following administrative proceedings liable to be contrary to EU environmental law.

Further, when specifically discussing the fact that the EU had legislated for implementation of Article 9(3) through the 'Aarhus Regulation',[32] the CJEU stated:

> Where a provision can apply both to situations falling within the scope of national law and to situations falling within the scope of EU law, it is clearly in the interest of the latter that, in order to forestall future differences of interpretation, that provision should be interpreted uniformly.

Throughout the judgment there is a strong sense of the importance of the doctrine of consistency.

Finally, it is worth highlighting the strong statement in paragraph 49 of the judgment that 'it is inconceivable that Article 9(3) of the Aarhus Convention be interpreted in such a way as to make it in practice impossible or excessively difficult to exercise rights conferred by EU law.'

As will be seen in later case law on challenging acts of EU institutions, the CJEU has arrived at precisely the situation they describe as inconceivable in LZ No. 1.

The decision in LZ No.1 marked an important exposition of the CJEU's conceptualisation of its role as mediator of the Aarhus obligations to Member States.[33]

---

31 The Convention on Access to Information, Public Participation in Decision-making and Access to Justice in Environmental Matters, known as 'the Aarhus Convention', was signed on 25 June 1998 and approved on behalf of the European Community by Council Decision 2005/370/EC of 17 February 2005 on the conclusion, on behalf of the European Community, of the Convention on access to information, public participation in decision-making and access to justice in environmental matters (OJ 2005 L 124, p. 1).

32 Regulation (EC) 1367/2006.

33 *P. Oliver*, Access to Information and to Justice in EU Environmental Law: The Aarhus Convention, 2013, Fordham Int'l L.J. (36), pp. 1423, 1433.

Again in 'Djurgården',[34] a decision of the CJEU of the 15 October 2009, Sweden was acknowledged to have discretion in terms of laying down standing requirements for NGOs who could challenge under Article 10(a) of the environmental impact assessment (EIA) directive,[35] but that discretion had to be exercised in a way that was consistent with EU law measures providing for 'wide access to justice' and the Aarhus Convention.[36]

In Commission v Ireland[37] of 16 July 2009, the CJEU ruled that Ireland's costs regime was not aligned with the 'not prohibitively expensive' requirement (i.e. the NPE rule), and as the court's discretion not to award costs against an unsuccessful litigant was discretionary, it failed to provide sufficient legal certainty. This was in breach of Article 10(a) of the EIA Directive[38] as amended, which implements Article 9 of the Convention.

In the 'Trianel' Case[39] delivered 12 May 2011, the CJEU again required the national court to interpret and apply provisions of national law in a manner consistent with EU law provisions (Article 10(a) of the EIA Directive[40] that NGOs meeting the criteria in Article 1(2) be deemed to have standing) and the Aarhus Convention. Here, an NGO challenged a provision of German law that provided NGOs only had standing in cases where they could show infringement of a rule granting personal rights, and not in cases where they sought to protect the public interest rather than individuals' rights. Of particular interest is that the court identified that environmental law is an area of law for the most part 'address[ing] the public interest and not merely the protection of the interests of individuals as such' and therefore that NGOs should have *locus standi* in any case where EU environmental law rules were being infringed. Anything less, according to the court, 'would be contrary to the objective of giving the public concerned wide access to justice and at odds with the principle of effectiveness if such organisations were not also allowed to rely on the impairment of rules of EU environmental law'.

The same approach is reinforced in many more recent cases. For example, dealing with Article 9(2) of the Aarhus Convention, the CJEU in 'LZ No. 2',[41] delivered 8 November 2016, found (at paragraph 58) that Article 9(2) limited:

> the discretion available to the Member States when determining the detailed rules for the legal actions which it envisages inasmuch as that provision has the objective of

---

34 Case C-263/08.

35 85/337/EC.

36 *A. Ryall*, Access to Justice in Environmental Matters: The Evolving EU Jurisprudence, 2016, IPELJ, 23(4) pp. 115–124, 110.

37 Case C-427/07.

38 Case C-85/337.

39 Case C-115/09 *Trianel* [2009] ECLI:EU:C:2011:289.

40 85/337/EC.

41 Case C-243/15.

> granting 'wide access to justice' to the public concerned, which includes environmental organisations meeting the conditions laid down in Article 2(5) of the convention.

In the case of 'Protect Natur'[42] 20 December 2017, Austrian law required that in order to earn the standing to bring a court challenge to a permit on grounds of infringement of the Water Framework Directive (WFD),[43] the NGO was obliged to raise that specific ground of the WFD during the administrative procedure. The NGO had made a submission during the administrative procedure based on the Habitats Directive[44] instead. The court ruled they had therefore not fulfilled the requirements under national law to have standing to raise a challenge under the WFD, and that Article 9 of the Aarhus Convention was not directly effective. The CJEU found that this was an overly restrictive approach to standing and was contrary to the broad access to justice required by the Aarhus Convention.

The court reiterated its approach of requiring national courts to interpret procedural rules governing bringing of actions to the fullest extent possible, in accordance with:

> both the objectives of Article 9(3) of the Aarhus Convention and the objective of effective judicial protection of the rights conferred by EU law, in order to enable an environmental organisation, such as Protect, to challenge before a court a decision taken following an administrative procedure that may be contrary to EU law.[45]

In the 'Klohn' Case,[46] delivered on the 17 October 2018, the court held that even where a measure[47] contained in a directive had not yet been transposed into national law, that law must still be interpreted to the fullest extent possible '... in such a way that persons should not be prevented from seeking, or pursuing a claim for, a review by the courts, which falls within the scope of that article, by reason of the financial burden that might arise as a result'.[48]

Hence, the 'Member State's courts are under an obligation to interpret national law in conformity with that directive' where transposition had not taken place by the required date, even where the provisions were not directly effective. In this way the doctrine of consistency, while it reinforces direct effect,

42 Case C-664/15 Protect Natur [2017] ECLI:EU:C:2017:987.
43 2000/60/EC.
44 92/43/EEC.
45 Para. 54.
46 Case C-167/17 Klohn [2018] ECLI:EU:C:2018:833.
47 The Article 10(a) requirement that judicial review in EIA matters under the EIA Directive 85/337/EC as amended not be prohibitively expensive implementing Art. 9(4) of the Aarhus Convention.
48 Para. 36.

can also be seen to run in parallel to it as highlighted by Herlin-Karnell and Konstadinides.[49]

In 'NEPP',[50] a judgment of 15 March 2018, the applicants challenged a planning permission granted for Eirgrid's North-South Interconnector (138km high-voltage power line to connect the Irish and Northern Ireland (UK) markets). They were unsuccessful due to prematurity after a five-day leave application. Questions of costs and the NPE rule were referred to the CJEU for determination. The element of uncertainty in the costs provisions before the national court was criticised, as was the requirement that the existence of costs protection hinged on the potential for environmental damage. Following the trend of the other judgments in this area the CJEU emphasised, in relation to Article 9(3) and Article 9(4) of the Aarhus Convention, that '… it is for the national court to give an interpretation of national procedural law which, to the fullest extent possible, is consistent with them.'

The court also held that costs protection must be available even to cases considered premature, especially where the rules were uncertain regarding the correct time for bringing the action. Member States must provide the cost protection even for claims determined to be frivolous or vexatious. The court initially distinguished, for application of the NPE rule, between the elements of the claim that fall under EU environmental law and those that did not (which therefore did not benefit from costs protections of Art 9(4)), but went on to take a holistic approach to the costs issue that considered the overall effectiveness of the right to access justice.

Overall, the CJEU has taken a strong purposive approach to implementing the provisions of Article 9 of the Aarhus Convention even in areas where no legislative measure has been passed by the EU. As pointed out by Van Wolferen,[51] this represents an extension of competence. Environment is an area of shared competence.[52] The CJEU has utilised the doctrine of consistency as a vehicle to carve out a larger area of competence than that which would have been available to it otherwise,[53] and in the opinion of some commentators went beyond what was legally permissible in all the circumstances.[54] It is, however,

---

49 *E. Herlin-Karnell & T. Konstadinides*, The Rise and Expressions of Consistency in EU Law: Legal and Strategic Implications for European Integration, Cambridge Yearbook of European Legal Studies, 2013 pp. 139–167.

50 Case C-470/16 NEPP [2018] ECLI:EU:C:2018:185.

51 *M. Van Wolferen*, Case C-243/15 Lesoochranárske zoskupenie vlk v Obvodný úrad Trenčín, 2017 JEEPL 14(1) p. 136, https://doi.org/10.1163/18760104-01401008.

52 Article 4(2) TFEU.

53 *J. Jans*, Who is the referee? Access to Justice in a Globalised Legal Order, 2011, REA, 4, NR. 1, pp. 87–99, p. 91. *M. Van Wolferen*, Case C-243/15 Lesoochranárske zoskupenie vlk v Obvodný úrad Trenčín, 2017 JEEPL 14(1) p. 136, https://doi.org/10.1163/18760104-01401008.

54 *J. Jans*, Who is the referee? Access to Justice in a Globalised Legal Order, 2011, REA, 4, NR. 1, pp. 87–99, p. 98.

consistent with the environmentalist approach of the Aarhus Convention to take the interpretation that results in a high degree of environmental protection.[55]

4. THE CASE LAW OF THE CJEU ON CHALLENGES TO ACTS OF EU INSTITUTIONS UNDER THE 'AARHUS REGULATION'.

As can be seen from the above case law, the CJEU has taken a strong position on both broad access to justice and consistency of Member States' laws with the provisions of the Aarhus Convention. This can be contrasted with the courts' approach to standing before the court for NGOs with the purpose of challenging an act of an EU institution.

The EU signed the Aarhus Convention in 1998 and ratified it in 2005, making it part of the community legal order by way of Council Decision 2005/370/EC of 17 February 2005.[56]

Several measures were created to give effect to the provisions of the Aarhus Convention (whose regime is as yet incomplete), creating directives for public participation[57] and access to environmental information.[58] All attempts to create an access to justice directive have failed,[59] and questions remain over the effectiveness of the right across the EU.

The EU also applied the provisions of the Aarhus Convention to its own bodies and institutions via the 'Aarhus Regulation',[60] which has been in effect from 28 June 2007. This regulation made provision for access to environmental information from European Community institutions, public participation in their decisions and access to justice to challenge acts of such institutions.

The 'Aarhus Regulation' provides that NGOs could request an 'internal review' of administrative acts of Community bodies and institutions.[61] It also provides that where they wished to challenge the outcome of such internal review, they could 'institute proceedings before the Court of Justice in accordance with the relevant provisions of the Treaty'.[62] However, this ability to challenge administrative decisions is limited by Article 2(1)(g) of the regulation,

55 *B. Peters*, Unpacking the Diversity of Procedural Environmental Rights: The Convention on Human Rights and the Aarhus Convention. JEL 2018 (30) pp. 1–27. doi:10.1093/jel/eqx023.
56 OJ 2005 L 124, p. 1.
57 2003/35/EC.
58 2003/4/EC.
59 COM/2003/0624 final – https://eur-lex.europa.eu/procedure/EN/2003_246.
60 Regulation (EC) 1367/2006.
61 Article 10.
62 Article 12(1).

which restricts the definition of administrative acts to a 'measure of individual scope under environmental law, taken by a Community institution or body, and having legally binding and external effects'. It is also restricted by the standing rules of the CJEU which are the 'relevant provisions of the Treaty' referred to in Article 12, above.

The standing rules find their basis in Article 263(4) Treaty on the Functioning of the European Union (TFEU), which allows an individual to challenge a decision addressed to another where they are 'directly and individually concerned' by the measure:

> Any natural or legal person may, under the conditions laid down in the first and second paragraphs, institute proceedings against an act addressed to that person or which is of direct and individual concern to them, and against a regulatory act which is of direct concern to them and does not entail implementing measures.

The 'direct and individual concern' requirement has been the subject of a very restrictive interpretation in the 'Plaumann' decision,[63] made on the 15 July 1963. Here, the court declared that a producer/importer of clementines adversely affected by the decision of the commission to place a higher tariff on clementines than had been applicable under national law was not 'individually concerned' on the basis that such a commercial activity may be practised by any person and was not such as to distinguish the applicant.[64]

'Direct and individual concern' therefore meant being able to show that you were distinguished from all others affected by the measure by some special effect the measure had on you and only you.

4.1. JOINED CASES C-401/12 – C-403/12 AND JOINED CASES C-404/12 & C-405/12

In the Joined Cases C-404/12 P and C-405/12 (sometimes referred to as 'Stichting Natuur'), handed down on the 13 January 2015, the 'Plaumann' interpretation of the standing rules can be seen restricting the ability of NGOs to challenge administrative acts of the EU institutions.

The decision concerned challenges by two NGOs (Stichting Natuur en Milieu and Pesticide Action Network Europe) to the adoption by the European Commission of regulations setting out maximum residue levels of certain

63 Case C-25/62 Plaumann & Co. v Commission [1963] ECLI:EU:C:1963:17.

64 *S. Marsden*, Direct Public Access to EU Courts: Upholding Public International Law via the Aarhus Convention Compliance Committee. Nordic Journal of International Law 2012 (81) pp. 175–204, p. 177.

pesticides in crops and food products. The NGOs sought access to internal review of the commission's decision under Article 10 of the Aarhus Regulation and were refused on the grounds that it was not an administrative act, but rather a legislative act, and not a measure of individual concern, and they did not meet the standing requirements for such a review under Article 2(1)(g) of the Aarhus Regulation.

The NGOs concerned successfully challenged this refusal in the General Court of the CJEU (in Case T-338/08 decided 14 June 2012) on the grounds that the standing requirements under Art 263 were inconsistent with the Aarhus Convention in the requirement for 'direct and individual concern' to establish standing. They also challenged the definition of administrative acts as a measure with individual scope as inconsistent with the Aarhus Convention, being overly restrictive and conflicting with the obligations of broad access to justice.

The decision of the General Court was overturned on appeal by the Grand Chamber of the CJEU (judgment dated the 13 January 2015) in the judgment in the Joined Cases C-404/12 P and C-405/12 P, reinstating the 'Plaumann' interpretation of the standing rule in Article 263 of the upholding the validity of the Aarhus Regulation and its definition of administrative acts as ones of individual scope.

The Grand Chamber acknowledged at paragraph 44 that international agreements bind EU institutions and prevail over the acts laid down by those institutions. However, it went on to make the claim at paragraph 45 that:

> the EU institutions which have power to negotiate and conclude such an agreement are free to agree with the non-member States concerned what effects the provisions of the agreement are to have in the internal legal order of the contracting parties. If that question has not been expressly dealt with in the agreement, it is for the courts having jurisdiction in the matter and in particular the Court of Justice, within the framework of its jurisdiction under the FEU Treaty, to decide it, in the same manner as any other question of interpretation relating to the application of the agreement in question in the European Union on the basis in particular of the agreement's spirit, general scheme or terms.

The court acknowledged that provisions of an international agreement could be relied on for a finding that an act of secondary EU legislation is illegal, provided the following conditions were satisfied:

1. The nature and broad logic of that agreement do not preclude it; and
2. Those provisions appear, as regards their content, to be unconditional and sufficiently precise.

The court held at paragraph 46 that Article 9(3) of the Aarhus Convention was not sufficiently unconditional and precise, and therefore could not have direct effect as it did not meet these conditions. The court's interpretation of the conditionality of Article 9(3) rested on the perceived requirement for conditions to be laid down for standing – only members of the public who meet the conditions – 'if any' – laid down in national law are entitled to exercise the rights under Article 9(3). As Krämer[65] has pointed out, the court has misconstrued a provision allowing parties to lay down conditions regulating standing as a provision requiring parties to lay down conditions, which it is not. This would seem to be a significant flaw in the court's reasoning.

The court then moves into a diffuse analysis of two economic decisions[66] raised in argument, the 'Fediol'[67] decision, where a measure implementing the GATT could be reviewed for legality in light of the provisions of that international agreement, and the Nakajima v Council[68] decision, where anti-dumping measures could be reviewed against the provisions of the WTO law to which they gave effect, on grounds that the Aarhus Regulation, unlike the measures at issue in those cases, did not create specific obligations based on specified provisions of the Aarhus Convention and that the Aarhus Regulation did not confer rights on individuals.

Both these contentions seem to be inaccurate representations of the Aarhus Regulation, and are also the opposite of what the CJEU itself stated about the Aarhus Regulation in 'LZ No. 1',[69] as can be seen in paragraph 41,[70] where the CJEU declared the Aarhus Regulation an implementation of Article 9(3). Additionally, Article 9(3) is specifically referenced in paragraph 18 of the preamble to the Aarhus Regulation.

Finally, it seems overly prescriptive to require that a measure of EU law giving effect to an international agreement can only be interpreted by the CJEU in light of that agreement where the terms of the international agreement are capable of direct effect.

This is in direct contrast to the cases examined above, where the CJEU consistently held that even if a particular provision of Article 9 of the Aarhus Convention did not have direct effect, where the EU had legislated to give effect

---

65 *L. Kramer*, Access to Environmental Justice: The Double Standards of the ECJ, JEEPL 2017(14) pp. 159–185, p. 180.

66 For a detailed consideration of the applicability of the comparison of these cases, see: *L. Kramer*, Access to Environmental Justice: The Double Standards of the ECJ, JEEPL 2017(14) pp. 159–185.

67 Case C-69/89 Nakajima v Council EU:C:1989:254.

68 Case C-70/87 Fediol v Commission EU:C:1991:186.

69 Case C-240/09.

70 LZ No.1, Case C-240/09, para. 41: 'In that connection, it is irrelevant that Regulation No 1367/2006, which is intended to implement the provisions of Article 9(3) of the Aarhus Convention, only concerns the institutions of the European Union and cannot be regarded as the adoption by the European Union of provisions implementing the obligations which derive from Article 9(3) of the Aarhus Convention with respect to national administrative or judicial proceedings'.

to the particular provisions then the national court was obliged to interpret all measures of domestic and EU law in light of the obligations of that agreement.[71]

The decision also appears to try to reserve unto the CJEU the status as ultimate arbiter of the effect of the Aarhus Convention within the legal order of the EU. This would seem to be a failure of the doctrine of consistent interpretation, as was highlighted by Marsden when discussing the same issue regarding C32 Part 1.[72]

Such statements were repeated in Joined Cases C-401/12 and C-403/12 ('Milieudefensie'), a judgment delivered on the same day as C-404/12 and C- 405/12, above, on identical grounds. Paras. 52–61 are identical to the crucial passages of C-404/12 and C-405/12 at paras. 44–53.

4.2. 'C32 EU, PARTS I & II'[73]

This case concerned a communication in 2008 by the NGO ClientEarth[74] to the Aarhus Convention Compliance Committee (ACCC) regarding the obstacles to access to administrative and judicial review at the EU level, such as that the Aarhus Regulation unduly restricted the categories of reviewable decisions, that it did not provide for an effective remedy as it did not expressly provide for substantive as well as procedural review, that individuals lacked standing and that the proceedings were prohibitively expensive for NGOs. ClientEarth also raised the issue that the 'Plaumann' standing rules excluded NGOs from accessing direct judicial challenge before the CJEU to EU institutions' administrative decisions under Art 263(4) rules for annulment actions, separate to the route of review under the Aarhus Regulation.

The infringement proceedings were long-running with a preliminary finding in 2011 in C32 Part I[75] that the ACCC would make no finding of infringement. Instead, they would await the outcome of several cases pending before the CJEU, which would provide the CJEU with an opportunity to address the problematic standing rules.

---

71 E.g. see above references to LZ No. 1 Case C-240/09 paragraph 30, LZ No. 2 Case C-243/15 para. 58, Protect Natur Case C-664/15 para. 54, Klohn Case C-167/17 para. 36.

72 *S. Marsden*, Direct Public Access to EU Courts: Upholding Public International Law via the Aarhus Convention Compliance Committee. Nordic Journal of International Law 2012 (81) pp. 175–204, p. 201.

73 ACCC/C/2008/32 (European Union).

74 Communication in ACCC/C/2008/32, 1st December 2008 https://unece.org/DAM/env/pp/compliance/C2008-32/communication/Communication.pdf.

75 Findings and Recommendations in ACCC/C/2008/32 (part I) (European Union) adopted 14th April 2011 https://unece.org/fileadmin/DAM/env/pp/compliance/CC-32/ece.mp.pp.c.1.2011.4.Add.1.e.pdf.

These pending cases included the Joined Cases C-401 (C-405/15) are discussed above. As is apparent from the discussion of these cases, the CJEU declined the opportunity to change course, resulting in C32 Part II, where the ACCC concluded its long running examination of the issue in 17 March 2017 with a finding of infringement.[76]

The ACCC's draft findings against the EU deconstructed the Aarhus Regulation, in particular Article 2(1)(f): '"administrative act" means any measure of individual scope under environmental law, taken by a Community institution or body, and having legally binding and external effects'.

The substance of ACCC's findings were that:

1. The Aarhus Regulation is flawed because it excludes all parties other than NGOs from access to review mechanisms for acts of EU bodies and institutions. Article 9(3) provides for access to justice by NGOs but cannot be used to exclude access by all others. In particular, Article 9(3) it requires that individuals have access to justice, and this is not allowed by the Aarhus Regulation (paragraph 94 of the draft finding).
2. The restriction of review to administrative acts of individual scope by Article 2(1)(g) is in breach of Article 9(3) of the Aarhus Convention (paragraph 53).
3. The restriction to administrative acts adopted under environmental law by Article 2(1)(g) and (f) was a breach of Article 9(3), as this article provides for access to review where there is a contravention of environmental law, which is broader than acts adopted under environmental law (paragraph 101).
4. The requirement in Article 2(1)(g) of the Aarhus Regulation that the administrative measure has 'legally binding and external effect' is another impermissible barrier to the right to challenge decisions and does not have a basis in Article 9, paragraph 3, of the Convention (paragraph 104).
5. The committee stated that the exclusion in Article 2(2) of the Aarhus Regulation of all bodies acting in and administrative review capacity also fell foul of Article 9(3). However, in the absence of concrete examples, the ACCC declined to make a finding of non-compliance on this point (paras. 111, 112).

Based on these findings, the ACCC called on the EU to amend or replace the Aarhus Regulation, and called on the CJEU to interpret EU law in a way which, 'to the fullest extent possible, is consistent with the objectives of article 9,

[76] Draft Finding ACCC/C/2008/32 (part II) (European Union) 17 March 2017, available at: https://www.unece.org/fileadmin/DAM/env/pp/compliance/C2008-32/Findings/C32_EU_Findings_as_adopted_advance_unedited_version.pdf.

paragraphs 3 and 4', presumably intentionally echoing the language of the CJEU itself in multiple decisions on the same articles of the convention when dealing with Member States Courts (e.g. 'LZ No. 1'[77] para 30, 'Protect Natur'[78] paragraph 54, 'Klohn'[79] paragraph 36).

The ACCC findings in 2011 and 2017 were clear that the EU needed to act immediately to change their laws. This is a position widely agreed by Europe's leading environmental lawyers, including Krämer[80] and others[81] and many leading environmental NGOs, such as ClientEarth[82] and the EEB.[83]

It is also important to note that aside from the ACCC's findings in relation to the Aarhus Regulation, they also made findings regarding general annulment action of regulatory acts under Article 263(4)[84] which provides for direct recourse to the CJEU to challenge regulatory acts or omissions, and took issue with the 'Plaumann' interpretation[85] of the treaty requirement of 'direct and individual concern'. The ACCC found that the CJEU had interpreted this phrase too restrictively in a manner not required by the treaty language, and this unduly restricted standing in relation to environmental matters by requiring a complainant to be peculiarly or uniquely affected by the measure complained of.

The EU responded with a proposal for a Council Decision rejecting the findings on the 17 June 2017.[86] This argued that that the ACCC was overstepping its jurisdiction by attempting to direct the jurisprudence of the CJEU, and that it was prevented by the principles of EU law from accepting the infringement. It claimed that alteration of the standing requirements would require alteration of the EU treaties. It referred to the special legal order of the EU and argued that it had created a reservation to this extent on accession. However, an examination

---

77 Case C-240/09.

78 Case C-664/15.

79 Case C-167/17.

80 *L. Kramer*, Access to Environmental Justice: The Double Standards of the ECJ, (2017) JEEPL 14(2).

81 *H. Schoukens*, Access to Justice in Environmental Cases after the Rulings of the Court of Justice of 13 January 2015: Kafka Revisited? (2015) Utrecht Journal of International and European Law, 31(81), pp. 46–67. DOI: http://doi.org/10.5334/ujiel.di accessible at https://utrechtjournal.org/articles/10.5334/ujiel.di/.

82 ClientEarth, EEB & J&E Joint Position Paper on Amendment of the Aarhus Regulation (2021) https://www.clientearth.org/latest/documents/position-paper-amending-the-aarhus-regulation-an-internal-review-mechanism-that-delivers-the-eu-green-deal/.

83 *EEB*, Commission Proposal to strengthen access to justice tackles main obstacle but fails overall (2020) https://eeb.org/commission-proposal-to-strengthen-access-to-justice-tackles-main-obstacle-but-falls-short-overall/.

84 Art 263 TFEU https://eur-lex.europa.eu/LexUriServ/LexUriServ.do?uri=CELEX:12008E263:EN:HTML.

85 Case C-25/62 Plaumann & Co. v Commission [1963], https://eur-lex.europa.eu/legal-content/EN/TXT/?uri=CELEX%3A61962CJ0025.

86 COM(2017) 366 final, dated 17 June 2017, available at: http://www.consilium.europa.eu/en/press/press-releases/2017/07/17/aarhus-convention/.

of the accession documents reveals no such reservation, just a recognition that the necessary legislative provision had not yet been made at the EU level, and until such time as the EU exercised competence in this area, the matter would remain within the competence of Member States[87] (as is standard for an area of shared competence, like the environment).

The ACCC responded on the 30 June 2017 with a clarification[88] refuting most of these arguments, on grounds substantially already dealt with in the draft finding from March 2017.

The EU eventually rejected the council proposal COM(2017) 366 to outright reject the decision of the ACCC, instead agreeing a decision (Council Decision 2017/1346 of the 17 July 2017) that required the ACCC's findings to be amended, to remove all references to the jurisprudence of the CJEU and to change the reference to the EU 'endorsing' the finding to the milder 'takes note of' the findings (essentially requiring them to take no further action).

Therefore, the EU did not accept the findings of the Compliance Committee at the Meeting of the Parties (MoP) and instead sought to have the amendment to the findings in Council Decision 2017/1346 approved.

The position by the EU as regards the ACCC finding was unprecedented and resulted in negotiations over the week of the 2017 Meeting of the Parties to try to reach a consensus, rather than have a step taken that might set an unfortunate precedent for the Meeting of the Parties,[89] potentially undermining its integrity and that of the ACCC.

This position causes a problem for the application of the doctrine of consistency as a tool for harmonisation of EU procedural environmental law. As stated at the outset, the doctrine of consistency is based upon a convention of accepting a hierarchy of norms. In the usual course of international law, a signatory to an international treaty accepts that it will interpret its laws in conformity with the norms contained with the treaty.[90] However, the EU appears to have adopted a position which disrupts the usual hierarchy upon which the doctrine of consistency rests.

---

87 The Declaration of Approval of the European Union of the Aarhus Convention, dated 17 September 2005, available at: https://treaties.un.org/Pages/ViewDetails.aspx?src=IND&mtdsg_no=XXVII-13&chapter=27&clang=_en#EndDec.

88 ACCC Clarification, Contained in the Annex to the Open Letter: Addressing the EU's non-compliance with the Aarhus Convention dated 4 July 2017, available at: https://cidce.org/wp-content/uploads/2016/08/to-Env-Mins-re-COM-rejection-of-Aarhus-C32-findings-4July.pdf.

89 Full Summary of the Budva Meeting of the Parties, Sixth Session of the Meeting of the Parties to the Aarhus Convention, available at: https://www.unece.org/environmental-policy/conventions/public-participation/aarhus-convention/tfwg/envppmop/envppmop6mopp3highlights/full-summary-of-budva-meetings.html.

90 E.g. see Art 27 of the Vienna Convention.

5. CASE LAW OF THE CJEU AFTER THE MEETING OF THE PARTIES

In 'Mellifera Ev',[91] a judgment of the General Court of the 27 September 2018,[92] an association intent on the protection of bees sought annulment of the decision to grant renewal of authorisation for glyphosate (considered by them to be harmful to bees). This was refused under the Aarhus Regulation restriction that it was not an administrative act of legal scope. According to Berthier,[93] the General Court refused to take account of the findings of the ACCC in C32 Part II, dismissing them as a 'simple project',[94] and that it had been released on the 17 March 2017, after the challenged measure had been adopted. If by 'simple project', that court is implying the decision is of no effect because it is only a draft, this would seem like a disingenuous argument. The decision is only a draft due to the refusal of the EU to accept the finding of the ACCC (as explained above). This decision was upheld on appeal.[95]

Case C352/19/P 'Brussels Capital Region',[96] delivered on 3 December 2020, shows how the refusal to interpret Union law in light of the Aarhus Convention serves to exclude a diversity of actors from accessing justice – in this case the Brussels Regional Capital. This case concerned the EU Commission decision to renew the authorisation of glyphosate for use in the EU and was heard on appeal from the General Court. The CJEU stated that it would not interpret Art 263, specifically the 'direct concern' requirement, in light of Art 9 of the

---

91 Case T-12/17 Mellifera Ev & Ors v EU Commission, available at: https://curia.europa.eu/juris/document/document.jsf?text=&docid=206172&pageIndex=0&doclang=en&mode=lst&dir=&occ=first&part=1&cid=7086325.

92 *L. Squintaini*, Case Law of the Court of Justice of the European Union and the General Court, JEEPL 2019 (16) pp. 91–104.

93 *A. Berthier*, Article 9(3) of the Aarhus Convention remains a dead letter in the European Union legal order, published 5 November 2018, available at https://www.clientearth.org/article-93-of-the-aarhus-convention-remains-a-dead-letter-in-the-european-union-legal-order/.

94 I am indebted to L. Squintaini (above) and A. Berthier (ibid.) for their comments on the other language versions of the judgment, as well as the analysis in *M. Pagano*, The 'Mellifera' Case and Access to Environmental Justice Under the Aarhus Regulation: New Findings, Old Story, EU Law Analysis, posted 19 October 2018, available at: http://eulawanalysis.blogspot.com/2018/10/the-mellifera-case-and-access-to.html.

95 Unfortunately even though the judgment was handed down on 20 September 2020, it has not yet been translated to English so I have had to rely ClientEarth and others commentary on the appeal decision, Case C-784/18 Mellifera Ev v The Commission, 20 September 2020, available at: https://curia.europa.eu/juris/document/document.jsf?text=&docid=230612&pageIndex=0&doclang=FR&mode=lst&dir=&occ=first&part=1&cid=9485987. Analysis available at *S. Betchel*, Digging a moat to protect the castle walls: CJEU solidifies barriers to NGO standing | ClientEarth.

96 Brussels Capital Region v EU Commission, Case C-352/19/P, available at: https://curia.europa.eu/juris/document/document.jsf?text=&docid=234927&pageIndex=0&doclang=en&mode=lst&dir=&occ=first&part=1&cid=7086625.

Aarhus Convention, and that the 'interpretative obligation' could not arise in relation to the EU Treaties, only secondary law.

The 'Carvalho'[97] judgment was given in an action before the General Court seeking annulment of a number of EU Climate Action measures on grounds that the targets in them are not ambitious enough. This action was deemed inadmissible by the General Court, and one of the unsuccessful grounds argued was that the Plaumann standing rule was inappropriate for application in environmental cases. The Aarhus Regulation did not feature in this case. This case was appealed to the Grand Chamber, with judgment[98] handed down to much public attention on the 25 March 2021, and again was unsuccessful on Plaumann grounds.

A recent judgment (27 January 2021), ClientEarth v EIB,[99] heard on appeal before the General Court of the CJEU under the Aarhus Regulation, was a rare successful application for annulment of a decision. The decision concerned was the rejection of a request for internal review of a financing decision on environmental grounds. The project concerned a biomass incinerator designed to generate energy from burning wood, was deemed to meet the EU's environmental objectives, and this was challenged by ClientEarth based on the lack of evidence that the woody biomass would be sourced in an environmentally sustainable manner.

The request for review was refused by the EIB on grounds that it was not a decision made 'under' environmental law.

In a surprising decision, the General Court found that it was and therefore annulled the refusal (which means the EIB will have to remake the decision). In doing so it tenuously indicated that the CJEU had an interpretative obligation arising from the need for consistency between EU and international law (at para. 107), and with the CJEU's own decision making in relation to the Aarhus Convention, citing the example of Edwards, C260/11.

This represents a dramatic departure for the court, but one which will likely be overturned on appeal. This was the trajectory in a previous progressive General Court decision in Joined Cases 404–405/12. The appeal has already been lodged, so it remains to be seen whether this will represent another anomaly or a new point of departure for the CJEU which resolves this basic inconsistency. In any event, it is an encouraging acknowledgement of recognition within the court of the need for consistency with international law.

---

97 Case T-330/18 8 May 2019.

98 Case C-565/19 P Carvalho & Ors. v The EU Parliament, The Council and the EU Commission [2021] ECLI:EU:C:2021:252, available at: https://curia.europa.eu/juris/document/document.jsf?text=&docid=239294&pageIndex=0&doclang=en&mode=lst&dir=&occ=first&part=1&cid=5821389.

99 Case T-9/19 ClientEarth v EIB, 27th January 2021, available at: https://eur-lex.europa.eu/legal-content/EN/TXT/?uri=CELEX%3A62019TJ0009.

In reviewing this matter, it should be borne in mind that since the Plaumann standing criteria was first applied to environmental cases in 1995[100] (in Case T-585/93 Stichting Greenpeace), there has been no change in the jurisprudence of the CJEU on this issue. Signing and ratifying the Aarhus Convention in 2005 and passing the Aarhus Regulation in 2006 produced no change in the standing requirements.[101] In fact, if anything, the right to review was subject to even more restrictions after the ratification of the Aarhus Convention due to the requirements of the Aarhus Regulation,[102] with the criteria of 'individual scope' (Article 2(1)(g)) and the restriction to administrative acts made 'under' environmental laws (Article 2(1)(g) and (f)), and the restriction of the right of review to NGOs only under Articles 10 and 12. Widely hailed changes brought in by the Lisbon Treaty[103] to standing requirements (dispensing with the 'individual concern' requirement in certain circumstances) also did not produce the improvements expected in the situation.[104] Reviewing the history of the restrictive approach to standing in light of these developments would seem to suggest that there should be no expectations of radical change in this area as a result of the new public consultations and studies being undertaken by the commission, and the recent legislative proposal to amend the Aarhus Regulation seems to confirm this.

It is quite clear that a different interpretation of 'direct and individual concern' is possible, and rests in the hands of the CJEU,[105] and that also that the Aarhus Regulation is not fit for purpose.[106]

The conflict between the EU legal measures and the Aarhus Convention also raises the prospect that a Member State could be subject to a finding of breach of rights by an international law body like the ACCC, while being unable to remedy the breach because it arises as a result of an EU law measure. As is usual, such a Member State would not be able to shift blame to the EU where such a problem

100 *S. Marsden*, Direct Public Access to EU Courts: Upholding Public International Law via the Aarhus Convention Compliance Committee. Nordic Journal of International Law 2012 (81) pp. 175–204, p. 179.

101 e.g. Case C-355/08 P WWF-UK v Council [2009] ECR I-73. Case T-37/04 Região Autónoma dos Açores v Council [2008] ECR II-103.

102 *S. Marsden*, Direct Public Access to EU Courts: Upholding Public International Law via the Aarhus Convention Compliance Committee. Nordic Journal of International Law 2012 (81) pp. 175–204, p.179.

103 Article 263(4) TFEU.

104 e.g. Case T-16/04 'Arcelor'.

105 *M. Eliantonio*, Towards an Ever Dirtier Europe? The Restrictive Standing of Environmental NGOs before the European Courts and the Aarhus Convention, 2011, Croatian Yearbook of European Law & Policy, Vol. 7 No. 7, available at: https://hrcak.srce.hr/94667.

106 'C32 Part II' Draft Finding ACCC/C/2008/32 (part II) (European Union) 17 March 2017, available at: https://www.unece.org/fileadmin/DAM/env/pp/compliance/C2008-32/Findings/C32_EU_Findings_as_adopted_advance_unedited_version.pdf.

arises. In this way, the inconsistency present in the EU legal order undermines the implementation of the international law norms of the Aarhus Convention.

The lengths to which civil society will have to go to establish full and proper access to justice for NGOs remains to be seen, as does whether individuals will ever be allowed access rights (i.e. whether full implementation of Article 9 of the Aarhus Convention will ever be achieved).

6. THE AARHUS REGULATION REVIEW

Council Decision (EU) 2018/881 instructed the commission to carry out a study into how they should respond to the ACCC's findings, and to submit a proposal for a new Aarhus Regulation.[107]

A public consultation was launched in December 2018.[108] The public consultation informed a consultant's report carried out by Milieu,[109] which examined access to justice issues in the EU at large, in a detailed report running to hundreds of pages informed by public consultation with academics, officials and NGOs in all of the EU Member States.

The European Commission produced draft legislation[110] on 14 October 2020 intended to address the findings of the Compliance Committee by proposed amendment of the Aarhus Regulation, and implementing the proposals suggested in the Milieu report.

The EU Commission sought an opinion on compliance from the ACCC in relation to the legislation. The ACCC indicated in their advice issued on 12 February 2021[111] that the EU Commission's proposals fell short of what is required to meet the obligations of the Aarhus Convention. Even though the proposal removed the 'individual scope' and 'under environmental law' provisos, it did not fully resolve the access to justice issues identified by the ACCC – namely, that the draft legislation did not address the problem of an

---

107 Council Decision (EU) 2018/881 of 18 June 2018, requesting the commission submit a study on the Union's options for addressing the findings of the Aarhus Convention Compliance Committee in case ACCC/C/2008/32 and, if appropriate in view of the outcomes of the study, a proposal for a Regulation of the European Parliament and of the Council amending Regulation (EC) No 1367/2006.

108 'EU implementation of the Aarhus Convention in the area of access of justice in environmental matters', available at: https://ec.europa.eu/environment/aarhus/consultations.htm.

109 *Milieu*, Study on EU implementation of the Aarhus Convention in the area of access to justice in environmental matters (2019), available at: https://ec.europa.eu/environment/aarhus/pdf/Final_study_EU_implemention_environmental_matters_2019.pdf.

110 COM(2020) 642 final, Proposal for a Regulation to amend the Aarhus Regulation, available at: https://ec.europa.eu/environment/aarhus/pdf/legislative_proposal_amending_aarhus_regulation.pdf.

111 ACCC/M/2017/3 Advices, available at: https://unece.org/sites/default/files/2021-02/M3_EU_advice_12.02.2021.pdf.

overly restrictive approach to standing rights and still restricted categories of reviewable decisions. It also did not address the fact that under the Plaumann case law on Art 263(4)) and individuals/NGOs, the CJEU continues to interpret Art 263(4) in a manner incompatible with broad access to justice (although it would be difficult to see how the proposal could have addressed this due to separation of powers issues).

The proposals did not remove seek to remove the impugned restriction that the measure must have 'legally binding and external effects'. The ACCC found that there was no basis in the convention for including the phrase 'legally binding' effects. They felt that this potentially limited the categories of decisions which are reviewable (as also highlighted in the 2017[112] decision). The ACCC felt that it would exclude acts that properly fell within the terms of Art 9(3) of the Aarhus Convention. ClientEarth gave the ACCC several examples of decisions that had been refused review on ground that they did not entail 'legally binding and external effects'.[113]

The commission's legislative proposals for revising the Aarhus Regulation also introduced further restrictions, limiting the categories of reviewable acts to 'non-legislative act adopted by a Union institution or body'[114] and excepting 'those provisions of this act for which Union law explicitly required implementing measures at Union or National level'.[115]

The ACCC also highlighted that excluding provisions for acts or omissions for which 'implementing measures' required at the Union or national level was unnecessarily restrictive. The Milieu Study[116] on implementation of access to justice found that 'most types of acts will result in implementing measures'. The justification offered by the EU Commission for this exclusion was that the measure could be later challenged by individuals/NGOs when the implementing measure was challenged (when eventually adopted), and in particular, implementing measures at the Member State level could be challenged effectively through the Art 267 reference procedure whereby a national court refers a question of law to the CJEU. It was argued that this mechanism provided adequate access to

112 ACCC/C/2008/32 Part II (2017) https://unece.org/fileadmin/DAM/env/pp/compliance/CC-57/ece.mp.pp.c.1.2017.7.e.pdf.

113 Paras. 62–68 of the Communication from the Communicant 23 Feb 2015, available at https://unece.org/DAM/env/pp/compliance/C2008-32/communication/frCommC32_23.02.2015/frCommC32_comments_on_CJEUs_ruling_of_15.01.15.pdf.

114 COM(2020) 642 final, Proposal for a Regulation to amend the Aarhus Regulation, available at: https://ec.europa.eu/environment/aarhus/pdf/legislative_proposal_amending_aarhus_regulation.pdf.

115 COM(2020) 642 final, Proposal for a Regulation to amend the Aarhus Regulation, available at: https://ec.europa.eu/environment/aarhus/pdf/legislative_proposal_amending_aarhus_regulation.pdf.

116 *Milieu*, Study on EU implementation of the Aarhus Convention in the area of access to justice in environmental matters (2019), pg. 113, available at: https://ec.europa.eu/environment/aarhus/pdf/Final_study_EU_implemention_environmental_matters_2019.pdf.

justice (Para 39, Part II, 2017). This requirement introduces the potential for unacceptable delays waiting for an 'implementing measure' to be adopted and also means that the right to challenge a measure might vary from country to country due to uneven implementation of access to justice rights across the EU, as highlighted in the Milieu Study[117] on the implementation of access to justice principles in the EU. If an NGO or individual cannot get standing before their national court, they would not be able to challenge the measure. If access to justice is prohibitively expensive, they will be similarly excluded. The ACCC was very clear in the 2017 decision that the Art 267 reference procedure for a preliminary ruling did not provide sufficient access to justice (para. 90, Part II, 2017). There also seems to be a fundamental illogicality in requiring that a measure that contravenes environmental law must be implemented before it can be challenged.

The EU has also argued that the special legal character of the EU legal order[118,119,120] requires that acts requiring implementing measures only be reviewable through the implementing measures, referring to the need for the court closest to the citizen to make the decision (an inaccurate usage of subsidiarity), and that Art 267 represents a complete system of access to justice. This argument posits that the ACCC has ignored or failed to understand the special character of the EU legal order. However, the ACCC addressed this in the 2021 advice, stating that the EU had not presented any evidence that allowing review at the EU level would affect the special legal order of the EU. They also discuss at length the reasons why the arguments based on subsidiarity are flawed (paras. 32–35), because the ACCC are requiring that decisions of EU bodies are reviewed at the EU level, which does not conflict with any existing rules on subsidiarity or competence. They also point out that Art 267 procedure does not provide a complete system of access to justice. In fact, it could be argued that subsidiarity requires review of EU decisions directly at EU level. Art 5 TEU makes it clear that EU action is required by the principle of subsidiarity where the objective cannot be effectively achieved by action at national level. Clearly, review of EU bodies' decisions cannot effectively be done at national level, or at

---

117 *Milieu*, Study on EU implementation of the Aarhus Convention in the area of access to justice in environmental matters (2019), available at: https://ec.europa.eu/environment/aarhus/pdf/Final_study_EU_implemention_environmental_matters_2019.pdf.

118 See Comments on the draft findings in ACCC/C/2008/32 Part II from the Party Concerned 18 October 2016. Comments on the draft findings in ACCC/M/2017/M from the Party concerned dated 1 February 2021, available at: https://unece.org/sites/default/files/2021-02/frPartyM3_01.02.2021_comments.pdf.

119 Commission Note on Access to Justice (2020) COM(2020) 643 final, available at: https://ec.europa.eu/environment/aarhus/pdf/communication_improving_access_to_justice_environmental_matters.pdf.

120 Commission Proposal to Amend the Aarhus Regulation (2020) COM(2020) 642 final, available at: https://ec.europa.eu/environment/aarhus/pdf/legislative_proposal_amending_aarhus_regulation.pdf.

all, as the national courts have no jurisdiction to review an EU administrative decision, they can only refer the matter to the CJEU.

The 2020 Commission proposal to amend the Aarhus Regulation is not encouraging, as it does not acknowledge some of the core features of the ACCC's findings in C32 and suggests that the Commission still does not accept those findings or the necessity for the Aarhus Convention to be applied at the EU level. This creates an on-going inconsistency in the EU legal framework and creates an accountability gap for EU level administrative decision-making.

7. POST-SCRIPT: POLITICAL AGREEMENT ON A REVISED AARHUS REGULATION

The Commission Proposal to amend the Aarhus Regulation was amended in Parliament[121] and then passed through the trilogue process. As a result of the European Parliaments intervention, heavily influenced by a number of eNGOs such as ClientEarth, the EEB, Justice and Environment, CAN-E and the EJNI, the proposal was amended significantly in a manner that brought it more into line with the requirements of the Convention and the ACCC findings in C32. As a result, the following changes were introduced, finalised in the political agreement reached on the 12 July 2021:[122]

a. Restrictions such as those excluding implementing measures were removed from the definition of administrative acts/omissions which could be the subject of requests for internal review and judicial review.
b. Rights of review and access to justice for individuals were introduced. There were two categories, both of which must be represented by a lawyer or eNGO who must confirm compliance with the requirements.
    i. Individuals experiencing impairment of a right, where they can show that they are particularly affected in comparison to the public at large. Extensive recitals clarified that this is not to be interpreted restrictively in the manner of "direct and individual" concern in the Plaumann decision.

121 The European Parliament's amendments to the Commission Proposal dated 20 May 2021 can be found here: https://www.europarl.europa.eu/doceo/document/TA-9-2021-0254_EN.html.

122 This analysis is based on the informal consolidated text submitted by the EU Commission to the ACCC on 23 July 2021, available at: https://unece.org/sites/default/files/2021-07/frPartyM3_23.07.2021_annex1.pdf 1. The final version of the Regulation is not yet available. The draft legislation is expected to be published in late September 2021, and to come into force 20 days after publication in the Official Journal in the usual manner, in advance of the Aarhus Convention Meeting of the Parties on 18 October 2021, except for the provisions on individual access to justice in Art 11(1)(a) which will take effect 18 months after the entry into force of the revised regulation.

ii. Public Interest Ground: Where a complaint is of public interest, and is supported by 4000 individuals from five Member States with a minimum of 250 from each Member State, evidenced by physical or digital signatures.

c. Recitals implementing the "not-prohibitively-expensive" requirement of Art 9(4) as regards costs, and guaranteeing both substantive and procedural review were introduced.

This move towards compliance by the EU institutions with the Aarhus Convention, while incomplete (proposals on review of State Aid decisions and access to information were rejected), represents a significant threshold moment in the EU's relationship with the Aarhus Convention and the ACCC (and has had a cautiously positive preliminary reception from the ACCC[123]). It is to be hoped that this change in attitude will influence the CJEU in its interpretation of case law, particularly that brought under the revised Regulation when it is finally introduced.

8. CONCLUSION

As can be seen from cases dealing with Article 9 of the Aarhus Convention and relevant EU law provisions,[124] the CJEU has championed broad access to justice and insisted on adherence to the doctrine of consistency in a manner that has increased the practical competence of the EU. On this level the doctrine of consistency has largely been effective in harmonising standing rules for environmental matters across Member States.

This can be contrasted with the approach towards Article 9(3) obligations when it comes to allowing NGOs to challenge acts of EU institutions, as is apparent in decisions of the CJEU in Joined Cases C-401-403/12 ('Milieudefensie'), Joined Cases 404–405/12 ('Stichting Natur') and 'Melifera Ev'. The access to review and challenge provisions of the Aarhus Regulation and associated standing requirements have been interpreted in a narrow fashion, with a spurious reliance on temporal arguments, ignoring the doctrine of consistency and the obligation to interpret EU law in a manner which gives effect to the provisions of the Aarhus Convention. This, in turn, has resulted in an internal inconsistency in EU law, apparent both within the case law on Article 9 with regard to national courts

123 Report by the Compliance Committee on Compliance of the European Union, dated 26 July 2021, available at: https://unece.org/sites/default/files/2021-08/M3_EU_report_to_MOP7_advance_unedited.pdf.

124 e.g. LZ No. 1 (Case C-240/09), Trianel (Case C-115/09), Commission v Ireland (Case C-427/07), 'Protect Natur' (Case C-664/15), Klohn (Case C-167/17) and Djurgården (Case C-263/08).

and EU courts standing rules, and within the CJEU standing jurisprudence in a broader level when one compares the cases on standing in the economic area to that in the environmental area, as well as an external inconsistency between the rules and laws of the EU and the international law obligations of the Aarhus Convention.

This case law threatens to undermine the integrity of EU law on an internal level, but also threatens the integrity of the Aarhus Convention and the effectiveness of the Compliance Mechanism. It is to be hoped that the steps taken by the Commission to review the Aarhus Regulation will lead to changes in the area, but until this manifests in actual access to justice for both individuals and NGOs before the CJEU, it is important to continue to monitor these developments closely. The position adopted by the EU regarding the ACCC's advice[125] and the recent decisions of the Grand Chamber of the CJEU do not instil confidence that this will soon be resolved. However, recent developments in the negotiation of the revised Aarhus Regulation offer hope for meaningful engagement with the Convention as it applies at the EU level.

On a broader level, such approaches to public participation and access to justice can be criticised as contributing to the perception of a culture problem within European institutions, which is often characterised as pitting environmental interests against economic interests and growth, and also adding fuel to the fires of the crisis of faith in EU institutions, as exemplified by Brexit.

One can conclude that in circumstances where the hierarchy of norms is unclear, or simply not accepted, the doctrine of consistency ceases to function as a meaningful mechanism for the harmonisation of EU environmental law. It appears that the limits of the usefulness of the doctrine of consistency are exceeded when consensus cannot be reached on its application. For now, at least, harmonious application of standing rights for challenging the acts of EU institutions and bodies remains out of reach.

---

125 Comments on the draft findings in ACCC/M/2017/M from the party concerned dated 1 February 2021, available at: https://unece.org/sites/default/files/2021-02/frPartyM3_01.02.2021_comments.pdf.

ENVIRONMENTAL PROTECTION AND SYMBOLIC VALUE OF HARMONISING ENVIRONMENTAL LAWS

Is Further Harmonisation the Solution?

Costanza Di Francesco Maesa*

1. INTRODUCTION

For a long time, but especially and more rapidly so during the recent years, the environment and the natural resources of our planet have been exploited and polluted by both private individuals and corporate entities. The consequence of such behaviour is that serious challenges, such as climate change, various forms of pollution, as well as unsustainable consumption and production, threaten people's health, as well as the very survival of the flora and fauna worldwide.

In such a context, international and European environmental policies and laws aimed at protecting the environment are becoming more and more important. A high level of protection of the environment has become a primary objective of the EU.[1] To that extent, several European acts have been adopted.

---

* Costanza Di Francesco Maesa is a Professor of Law and Biotechnology at the University of Siena, a teaching assistant, under the direction of Professor Massimiliano Montini, in Advanced European Law and Sustainable Development Law at the University of Siena and a post-doctoral researcher at the University of Florence.

1 See Articles 3(3) TEU, 191-193 TFEU. More recently, see also the European Green Deal strategy, and particularly the Communication from the Commission to the European Parliament, the

In particular, to resolve the original fragmentation occasioned by the inclusion of environmental provisions into different pieces of sectoral legislation protecting different interests, such as water, soil or air, harmonisation has played an important role in dealing with environmental protection in a more integrated manner.[2]

Furthermore, the number of actors competent to monitor the implementation of environmental laws, as well as the amount of environmental compliance networks composed of European environmental inspectors, police officers, prosecutors, judges, auditors and heads of environmental protection agencies,[3] has considerably increased in recent years. Even mechanisms designed to enhance compliance with environmental legislation and oversee the correct application of European environmental legislation at the national level have been adopted.[4]

However, air, water and soil pollution has not significantly diminished, the effects of climate change are in the public eye and the problem of waste disposal has not yet been solved in many countries.

From the foregoing, it may be deduced that the problem does not stem from the lack of harmonised environmental rules or from the absence of actors responsible for implementing and enforcing environmental legislation, nor does it stem from the lack of networks allowing those actors to communicate between the most adequate ways of enforcing environmental obligations.

The reasons for the inadequate protection of the environment must thus be sought elsewhere. It is the system of environmental governance, particularly with regard to mechanisms ensuring access to justice, which has to be rethought. Ensuring accountability mechanisms and an effective system of judicial and

---

European Council, the Council, the European Economic and Social Committee and the Committee of the Regions, 'The European Green Deal', COM/2019/640 final; the proposal for a Regulation of the European Parliament and of the Council 'establishing the framework for achieving climate neutrality and amending Regulation (EU) 2018/1999 (European Climate Law)', COM/2020/80 final, and the Communication from the Commission to the European Parliament, the Council, the European Economic and Social Committee and the Committee of the Regions, 'EU Biodiversity Strategy for 2030 Bringing nature back into our lives', COM/2020/380 final.

2 For a list of around 40 of the principal European acts, see Commission Staff Working Document, Environmental Compliance Assurance, Scope, concept and need for EU actions, SWD(2018)10 final, Annex 2.

3 In particular, the main European networks are the following: European Union Network for Implementation and Enforcement of Environmental Law (IMPEL); EnviCrimeNet; European Network of Prosecutors for the Environment (ENPE); EU Forum of Judges for the Environment (EUFJE); European Organisation of Supreme Audit Institutions (EUROSAI); European Network of the Heads of Environment Protection Agencies (NEPA), particularly its Better Regulation Interest Group (BRIG).

4 About the Commission's role, see section 3.1. About EIR, see Communication from the Commission, Environmental Implementation Review 2019: A Europe that protects its citizens and enhances their quality of life, COM(2019)149 final. About the EEA, see Regulation (EC) No 401/2009 of the European Parliament and of the Council of 23 April 2009 on the European Environment Agency and the European Environment Information and Observation Network, OJ L 126, 21.5.2009, pp. 13–22. See also Communication from the Commission, EU actions to improve environmental compliance and governance, COM(2018)10 final.

administrative review of the decisions taken with respect to environment-related matters is unavoidably necessary to ensure an adequate protection of the environment on the European territory. Whether harmonisation should be considered a useful tool in this respect is scrutinised in this chapter.

In order to do so, the first section (1) gives a working definition of the concepts of harmonisation, also focusing on the symbolic nature that this notion may assume, while the second section (2) analyses the main problems emerging in respect of the enforcement of environmental obligations and of access to justice in the environmental field. In the conclusion, eventually the question of whether more harmonisation is needed is answered.

2. NOTION OF HARMONISATION

The definition of the term 'harmonisation' is particularly important considering the multifaceted nature of this concept at the EU level in general, and in the field of EU environmental law in particular.[5] However, since the crux of the analysis is not related to the general concept of 'harmonisation', but rather to that concept as regards EU environmental measures, this chapter provides a formulation of the concept of harmonisation for this purpose only.

First of all, it should be noted that an unequivocal definition of the term 'harmonisation' does not exist in any European primary or secondary legislative act. Furthermore, in the English version of the treaty, other terms such as 'approximation' are used without a clear distinction from the term 'harmonisation'.[6] Admittedly, from the wording of the provisions of the treaties and the jurisprudence of the ECJ, it may be inferred that the main aim of harmonisation is to create similar rules in a given field, and in the European legal context it particularly refers to the approximation of laws between different legal systems.[7] As regards the form of harmonisation measures, there are different methods of harmonisation at the disposal of the European legislature, which may choose whether to have recourse to minimum or maximum harmonisation instruments.[8]

---

5 For a definition of the notion of harmonisation, see *E.J. Lohse*, The Meaning of Harmonisation in the Context of European Community Law – a Process in Need of Definition, in *M.T. Andenæs, & C.B. Andersen* (eds), Theory and Practice of Harmonisation, Edward Elgar 2012, p. 282 et seq. See also *M.G. Faure*, The Harmonization, Codification and Integration of Environmental Law: A Search for Definitions, EELR 2000, p. 174 et seq.

6 See *Lohse, supra* note 5; *N. Lochner*, (1962) Was bedeuten die Begriffe Harmonisierung, Koordinierung und gemeinsame Politik in den Europäischen Verträgen? Zeitschrift für die gesamte Staatswissenschaft 1962 (118), p. 35.

7 See *Faure, supra* note 5, p. 174; *M. Boodman*, The Myth of Harmonization of Laws, American Journal of Comparative Law 1991 (39) p. 699, 700–701. See also *A. Jeammaud*, Unification, uniformisation, harmonisation: de quoi s'agit-il? in *F. Osman* (ed.), Vers un code européen de la consommation/Towards a European consumer code, 1998 p. 35, 43.

8 See *P. Craig & G. De Búrca*, EU Law: Text, cases and materials, sixth edition, 2015, p. 626 et seq.; *A. Mc Gee & S. Weatherill*, The Evolution of the Single Market-Harmonisation or

That general meaning of the term 'harmonisation' also applies to EU environmental measures, even if the peculiarities of environmental law give it a peculiar function. The dual objective inherent in European environmental acts, namely, the objective of achieving the effective protection of the environment and that of achieving the integration, establishment and proper functioning of the internal market,[9] gives harmonisation in the environmental field a peculiar function. Harmonisation in the environmental field is not a 'substantive goal in itself', but is rather 'an instrument concerning the form of environmental legislation', which serves the goal of 'integration of environmental policies'.[10] Since it is the integration of environmental policies and not the approximation of laws of different legal systems which is the objective to be achieved, the adoption of more and more similar rules is not always the objective pursued by European harmonising environmental laws. Consequently, in some cases Member States (MS) are free to adopt more or less stringent national environmental standards than those established at the EU level, provided that these are compatible with the treaty. The reason for this is that, for instance, differences in emission and quality standards do not hinder the free movement of goods.[11]

The definition of the notion of harmonisation given above concerns mainly the adoption of substantive environmental laws. However, to give a coherent and useful definition of the term with regard to environmental policies, a broader definition is needed. From a wider and more accurate perspective, which takes into account the progress made by the European integration process so far,[12] harmonisation is an 'active, steered process originating from an independent entity', which begins with the 'conscious creation of a concept at the European level by various actors and included in various normative instruments, which has the intent and the potential to develop towards a common European law'.[13] In this regard, actors are not only European institutions responsible for enacting secondary legislation, but also European and national actors charged with the task of implementing and enforcing European environmental rules. Instruments are not only secondary legislation, but also primary legislation and specific mechanisms, such as infringement proceedings and procedures aimed at ensuring that private parties have access to justice in environmental matters,

---

Liberalisation, MLR 1990 (53), pp. 578, 582; *M. Dougan*, Minimum Harmonization and the Internal Market, CMLRev 2000 (37), p. 853.

9 See ECJ, Case C-64/09, Commission v France [2010] ECR I-3283. See also *J.H. Jans & H.H.B. Vedder*, European Environmental Law After Lisbon, 2012, p. 97 et seq.

10 The expressions in the text are those of *Faure, supra* note 5, p. 174.

11 See Article 193 TFEU. About it, see Case C-6/03, Deponiezweckverband Eiterköpfe [2005] ECR I-2753, para. 58; Joined cases C-379/08 and C-380/08, ERG et al. (ERG II) [2010] ECR I-2007; Case C-2/10, Azienda Agro-Zootecnica Franchini [2011] ECR I-6561.

12 See *U. Everling*, Rechtsvereinheitlichung durch Richterrecht in der Europäischen Gemeinschaft, RabelsZ 1986 (50), p. 193.

13 *Lohse, supra* note 5.

so that the obligations enshrined in secondary legislative measures are correctly implemented and enforced. According to this broader and more accurate definition, harmonisation, therefore, does not only entail decision-making, but also administrative and judicial implementation and enforcement.

However, to delimit even further the notion of harmonisation, another clarification is needed. From a functional perspective, formal approximation and similarity in norms, both substantive and procedural, is not enough to achieve the objective of protecting the environment. Rather, it is only through a substantive, and not a merely formal, or symbolic, application of European environmental measures, that harmonisation may serve its function of effectively pursuing the objective of protecting the environment.[14] The current analysis therefore scrutinises whether European environmental measures have, in some cases, only a symbolic, and not substantive, value.

Finally, a coherent definition of the notion of harmonisation must also take into account the strict interrelationship between this concept and that of environmental governance, which can be defined as 'an inclusive system of actors, institutions and norms that establishes responsibility and accountability, and builds trust and capacity to cooperate in policy-making, decision-making, implementation and enforcement, in the field of environment'.[15] Accountability and responsibility are the other two concepts which play an essential role in ensuring that European environmental objectives are achieved in practice and which, consequently, help to give the notion of harmonisation a substantive value in addition to a merely formal one.

In the absence of an integrated and harmonious system of enforcement of environmental rules where adequate mechanisms of accountability and responsibility of the actors involved are in place, harmonisation of European environmental laws risks being no more than a vague concept with a merely symbolic value.

3. ENVIRONMENTAL ENFORCEMENT MECHANISMS

As we have seen above, it is in the last stage of the harmonisation process, that is, in the enforcement phase, that the major problems lie. After the implementation phase,[16] the enforcement phase is aimed at ensuring that the European acts or

---

14 About the difference between formal and substantive harmonisation, see *Faure*, *supra* note 5, p. 175.

15 Development of an assessment framework on environmental governance in the EEP EGA Study, EU Member States, Policy Summary, Background Final report – May 2019, p. 3.

16 The term 'implementation' is intended in the text in a narrow sense. In broader sense, the implementation process is composed of four different phases. See *J.H. Jans & H.H.B. Vedder*, *supra* note 9, p. 139.

the national laws implementing them, in case of directives, are enforced. Their correct enforcement must be monitored and, if necessary, adequate sanctions must be applied in respect of the perpetrators of the offences. Specific actors responsible for monitoring the compliance with environmental rules and adequate mechanisms to ensure the effective enforcement of those rules need to be established. Furthermore, appropriate accountability and responsibility mechanisms aimed at ensuring that the actors charged with monitoring the correct implementation of European environmental laws may be held accountable and liable in case of bad performance of their tasks are particularly important.

However, no adequate accountability mechanisms or effective judicial and administrative remedies are provided for in the European legal framework. As a result, a private party or a public authority cannot oblige the competent actor to take a position in respect of a particular alleged violation of environmental law. Owing to space constraints, the system of implementation of European environmental law is not analysed in detail in the present chapter.[17] Only the features which risk depriving of substance the notion of harmonisation are analysed in the ensuing sections.

3.1. COMMISSION'S INFRINGEMENT PROCEEDINGS

A brief overview of the role of the different actors in the implementation process is nevertheless necessary to identify the shortcomings of such a system. Implementation of European acts is generally undertaken by the MS.[18] In turn, the commission is charged with ensuring that European laws are effectively applied.[19] In that regard, the most important instrument available to the commission is the infringement proceedings.[20] By this procedure, as a power of last resort, the commission may bring a matter before the Court of Justice if it considers that an MS failed to fulfil its environmental obligations.

17 For an in-depth analysis of the implementation and enforcement system of European environmental law, see *M. Hedemann-Robinson*, Enforcement of European Union environmental law – Legal Issues and challenges, 2007; *M.E. Hall*, Environmental Law in the European Union: New Approach for Enforcement, Tulane Environmental Law Journal, 2007 (20), p. 277; *P. Koller & L. Cashman*, Implementing EC environmental law. Compliance promotion and enforcement by the European Commission, JEEPL 2009 (6); *L. Etherington*, Digging beneath the surface: Transposition, implementation and evaluation of European environmental law, Journal of Environmental Policy & Planning, 2006 (8), p. 107 et seq.

18 See Articles 4(3) TEU, 291 TFEU and 192(4) TFEU. About enforcement duties, see Case 365/97, Commission v Italy [1999] ECR I-7773, para. 85.

19 See Article 17 TEU. This system of implementation has been called 'executive federalism' by *L. Lenaerts & P. van Nuffel*, European Union Law, 2013, p. 688 et seq.

20 Articles 258–260 TFEU.

The commission may particularly initiate infringement proceedings in view of breaches of European environmental obligations on three occasions: in non-communication cases, in non-conformity cases or in bad application cases.[21] The latter cases usually originate in complaints of NGOs or private parties about an activity at a specific location breaching European environmental legislation if no action is taken to remedy the situation at the national level. In such an event, the commission may initiate infringement proceedings against an MS.[22] The onus of proof to demonstrate that an infringement of EU environmental law occurred is placed on the commission, which, in general, may not make use of any presumption of culpability, but must provide evidence of 'sufficient probative value' in order to prove its allegation.[23] However, the commission has neither investigatory and inspection powers nor adequate resources to verify complaints or to launch own-initiative inquiries.[24] It is consequently dependent on national administrative or judicial authorities in its search for information and evidence. Relying on the duty of sincere cooperation[25] between the Union and the MS is nevertheless not a sound course of action for obliging MS to carry out systematic inspections of installations and sites on their own territory[26] at the risk of being sanctioned by the ECJ.[27]

In that regard, infringement proceedings suffer from several problems and limitations which considerably restrict the commission's power and ensure the commission's unaccountability for the decisions it takes. Similarly, there are no effective judicial and administrative procedures to review the commission's decisions taken within infringement proceedings. Those problems are occasioned both by technical inadequacies of the legal mechanism itself and by the commission's unwillingness to be controlled by private parties or public authorities in the performance of its tasks. A structural reform of the commission's powers and of the resources allocated to it to deal with environmental cases would be necessary to solve those structural shortcomings. A more general reform of infringement proceedings as regards environmental

---

21 See, for detailed data, the annual reports on monitoring the application of EU law and *Hedemann-Robinson*, *supra* note 17, p. 40 et seq.

22 Article 258 TFEU.

23 Case C-96/81, Commission v Netherlands [1982] ECR I-1791; Case C-300/95, Commission v UK [1997] ECR I-2649; Case C-365/97, Commission v Italian Republic [1999] ECR I-7773; Case C-376/09 Commission v Malta [2011] ECR I-4017, para. 32; Case C-392/96, Commission v Ireland [1999] ECR I-5901.

24 See *Hedemann-Robinson*, *supra* note 17, p. 161 et seq.

25 Article 4(3) TEU.

26 See *Hedemann-Robinson*, *supra* note 17, p. 162; *R. Wägenbaur*, The European Community's policy on implementation of environmental directives, Fordham Int. LJ 1990-91, p. 462.

27 See, about the conflict of interest that may arise in those situations, *G. Winter*, On the effectiveness of the EC administration: the case of environmental protection, CML Rev 1996 (33), p. 711; *L. Krämer*, European Environmental Law Casebook, 1993, p. 395.

matters is nevertheless even more urgently needed to make sure that adequate accountability mechanisms are adopted.

The notion of 'accountability'[28] as the 'relationship between an actor and a forum, in which the actor has the obligation to explain and justify his or her conduct, the forum can pose questions and pass judgment, and the actor might face consequences' is being relied upon here.[29] According to this definition, commissioners theoretically have the obligation to explain and justify their conduct and the forum (i.e. third parties with an interest in the pursuance of infringement proceedings) can pose questions and pass judgment; as a result, commissioners may face consequences. However, in practice, that is not the case.

The lack of accountability mechanisms of commissioners is partly due to the double nature of the commission, which is not only responsible for enforcing policy, but also holds the monopoly on the proposal of legislative acts. Setting up forms of accountability for its members when performing its enforcement tasks is, therefore, a sensitive topic. However, that is not the sole problem created by the absence of a clear distinction between its enforcement and policy-making tasks.[30] The commission's decisions as to whether to launch or terminate infringement proceedings may be strongly influenced by political reasons, rather than the merits of the case, and when that happens, third parties cannot ask the commission for the reasons underpinning its decision or hold somebody accountable for the decision.

That is even more so since it is difficult to identify who should be held accountable for such a decision, if that were possible in the first place. Theoretically, decisions over the initiation of infringement proceeding and over subsequent legal steps in the proceedings are taken by the College of Commissioners. In practice, however, it is the Legal Unit within the DG Environment, together with the Commission's Legal Service, which decides whether a proposal to launch an infringement proceeding should go before the college[31] and usually the details of the cases are not discussed at the college meetings. In that regard, allegations that an individual commissioner or a number of commissioners blocked, on political grounds, the initiation of infringement proceedings are nothing new.[32]

---

28 See *M. Busuioc, D. Curtin & M. Groenleer*, Agency growth between autonomy and accountability: the European Police Office as a 'living institution', Journal of European Public Policy, 2011 (18), p. 852.

29 *M. Bovens*, Analysing and assessing accountability: a conceptual framework, Eur. Law J. 2007 (13), p. 452.

30 See *Hedemann-Robinson*, *supra* note 17, p. 179; *E. Hattan*, The implementation of EU environmental law, JEL 2003 (15), p. 275.

31 See *Hedemann-Robinson*, *supra* note 17, p. 181.

32 See *R. Macrory & P. Purdy*, The enforcement of EC environmental law against Member States, in *J. Holder* (ed.), The impact of EC Environmental Law in the United Kingdom, 1997, p. 35; *R. Williams*, The European Commission and the enforcement of environmental law: an invidious position, YEL 1994 (14), p. 354.

Enforcement and policy-making tasks are strictly intertwined, and political interference may seriously influence the decision-making of the legal unit.[33] The legal unit within the DG Environment lacks independence; in its directorate there are also units responsible for environmental policy and conflicts of interests on infringement cases may arise between the units within the directorate.[34] In the *Prestige* case, which could serve as an example of political interference with the decision to initiate infringement proceedings, the politically influenced advice of the executive level of the legal unit was followed, and the case was never transmitted to the college.[35]

The lack of independence from political influence of the actors charged with taking decisions about environmental enforcement actions, coupled with the absence of adequate mechanisms to ensure their accountability, risks seriously undermining the commission's credibility and the public trust in the commission's role as the enforcer of environmental obligations.

The commission has in fact an unfettered discretion in deciding whether or not to pursue infringement proceedings, and there are no remedies for private parties against the commission's decisions. Neither public authorities nor private persons can compel the commission to initiate infringement proceedings. They have likewise no legal recourse against the commission's decisions not to start proceedings, or to discontinue or stay proceedings that have been instituted.[36] The commission's decision whether to initiate infringement proceedings or to terminate proceedings which have already been started cannot be reviewed by the court, either in an annulment action,[37] or by means of an action for failure to act under Article 265 TFEU.[38] A decision of the commission not to start an infringement procedure will likewise not give rise to non-contractual liability on the part of the Union.[39] As a result, the right to an effective remedy before a tribunal[40] risks being seriously compromised as well.

Another factor which seriously hinders the credibility of the commission is the lack of transparency. The current legal framework allows the commission not to grant private parties access to information and documents relating to environmental infringement proceedings on the ground that those documents

33 See the European Ombudsman's Decision 1288/99/OV.

34 See *Hedemann-Robinson*, *supra* note 17, p. 182.

35 See, for in-depth analysis, *Hedemann-Robinson*, *supra* note 17, pp. 183–184.

36 Case C-48/65, Lütticke v Commission [1966] ECR I-0019.

37 Article 263 TFEU. See Case C-247/87 Star Fruit v Commission [1989] ECR I-0291, Case T-479 and 559/93 Bernardi v Commission [1994] ECR II-1115; Case T-201/96 Smanor v Commission [1997] ECR II-1081.

38 See Case C-48/65, *supra* note 36; Case C-247/87, *supra* note 37; Case C-371/89, Emrich v Commission [1990] ECR I-1555.

39 Joined Cases C-205/10 P, C-217/10 P and C-222/10 P, Eriksen et al. v. Commission [2011].

40 This right is enshrined in Article 47 of the Charter of Fundamental Rights of the European Union (CFR).

are deemed to be confidential. Despite being an important source of information for the commission, especially as regards bad application cases, complainants are still considered not to be parties to the procedure and are consequently denied access to these documents. Thus, it is not even possible for them to verify if those decisions have been influenced by political considerations. Without transparency, there can be no public scrutiny over the commission's activities.

The unaccountability of the commissioners dealing with environmental cases is aggravated by another factor, that is, the diffuse character of the EU political authority in the European environmental enforcement mechanism. As a result of the latter, national political actors may 'use the nature of intergovernmental bargaining to transfer political costs to the EU. But, increasingly, the EU institutions might use the fact that its policy choices will have to be enforced by national governments to evade accountability too.'[41] In such a situation, environmental enforcement risks are caught in a vicious circle: national authorities do not effectively enforce environmental obligations and do not carry out on-site inspections so as not to be sanctioned by the commission and then claim that the commission is not efficient in ensuring effective enforcement of environmental laws, while the commission claims that it cannot discharge its burden of proof in bad application cases and stresses that the enforcement of harmonised environmental laws is a task of the Member States.

3.2. JUDICIAL REVIEW

In the absence of adequate accountability mechanisms, another way for interested private persons and NGOs to ensure compliance of the decisions of the commission, on which increasingly more powers regarding environmental matters have been conferred both by the treaties and by secondary legislation,[42] is to challenge those decisions via a judicial review procedure.

The main instrument to review the legality of acts adopted by EU institutions allegedly breaching European environmental law is the annulment proceedings.[43] The conditions under which third parties may challenge an act adopted by a European institution are nevertheless very strict. As a result, challenges to the commission's decisions adopted within the framework of

41 See, for an analysis of the current crisis in the Euro system, *L.M. Poiares Maduro*, A new Governance for the European Union and the Euro: Democracy and Justice, RSCAS Policy Papers, RSCAS PP 2012(11), p. 7.

42 See the Commission's powers under Articles 107–108 TFEU (*Jans & Vedder*, *supra* note 9, chapter 7, sections 7.3–7.4) or under Directive 2001/18 of the European Parliament and of the Council of 12 March 2001 on the deliberate release into the environment of genetically modified organisms and repealing Council Directive 90/220/EEC, OJ 2001 L 106/1.

43 Article 263 TFEU.

infringement proceedings have been repeatedly declared inadmissible by the ECJ on the ground that those decisions are acts which are not of direct and individual concern to private persons.[44] According to the ECJ's *Plaumann* test,[45] the practical possibilities of third parties to seek the annulment of European environmental measures are severely restricted.

European environmental measures are usually acts of a general nature, such as legislative measures concerning environmental protection standards, administrative decisions relating to the management of a specific environmental site or the commission's decisions under Articles 258-260 TFEU. Private parties have, therefore, many difficulties in demonstrating that they are affected by the act in question in a manner different from other persons. Consequently, numerous annulment actions brought by private persons to challenge acts by European institutions have been declared inadmissible on grounds of legal standing in a large number of cases.[46] Examples include challenges to European acts concerning conservation measures required in the fishing industry,[47] control of transnational shipment of waste,[48] allocation of funding under European financial instruments for the environment to a Member State in order to establish an interregional nature park,[49] as well as the decision of the European Investment Bank to co-finance a road project.[50] European environmental measures, including the decisions taken by the commission under Article 258 TFEU, are, thus, in practice, not subject to any substantive review.[51]

In that regard, the court has held that the application of the *Plaumann* test does not imply that the private parties' rights to an effective remedy and to a fair trial are violated and that no form of judicial protection is provided at all.[52]

---

44 See Cases C-247/87, *supra* note 37; T-479 and 559/93, *supra* note 37; T-201/96, *supra* note 37.

45 Case C-25/62, Plaumann & Co v Commission [1963] Reports of cases 199, paras. 95, 107; Case C-50/00P, Unión de Pequeños Agricultores v Council [2002] ECR I-6677; Case C-263/02P, Commission v Jégo-Quéré [2004] ECR I-3425. See *M. Lee*, EU Environmental Law: Challenges, Change and Decision-Making, 2005, p. 139 et seq.

46 Case C-503/07P, Saint-Gobain Glass Deutschland v Commission [2008] ECR I-2217; Case C-362/06P, Sahlstedt et al. v Commission [2009] ECR I-2903; Case T-330/18, Armando Carvalho et al. v European Parliament and Council of the European Union, Order of the General Court [2019], and its appeal before the Court of Justice in Case C-565/19 P, Armando Carvalho et al. v European Parliament and Council of the European Union [2021] ECLI:EU:C:2021:252.

47 Case C-131/92, Arnaud et al. v Council [1993] ECR I-2573, C-263/02P, *supra* note 45.

48 Case C-209/94P, Buralux SA, Satrod SA and Ourry SA v Council [1996] ECR I-0615.

49 Case T-117/94 Associazione Agricoltori della Provincia di Rovigo et al. v Commission [1995] II-455.

50 Case T-460/92, Tate et al. v European Investment Bank [1993] ECR II-1257.

51 See Case C-87/89, Sonito v Commission [1990] ECR I-1981. See, critically, *L. Krämer*, Public interest litigation in environmental matters before European courts, JEL 1996 (8), p. 13.

52 Case C-321/95P, Stichting Greenpeace Council et al. v Commission [1998] ECR I-1651, para. 32.

In the court's view, NGOs and private parties could bring legal proceedings at the national level, in the course of which, if necessary, a question of interpretation of EU law could be referred by the national judge to the ECJ under the preliminary rulings procedure.[53] However, this argument is weak, and the option does not ensure an adequate judicial protection.[54] As noted by the Aarhus Compliance Committee (ACCC):

> [w]hile the system of judicial review in the national courts of the EU MSs, including the possibility to request a preliminary ruling, is a significant element for ensuring consistent application and proper implementation of EU law in its MSs, it cannot be a basis for generally denying members of the public access to the EU Courts to challenge decisions, acts and omissions by EU institutions and bodies; nor does the system of preliminary review amount to an appellate system with regard to decisions, acts and omissions by the EU institutions and bodies. Thus, with respect to decisions, acts and omissions of EU institutions and bodies, the system of preliminary ruling neither in itself meets the requirements of access to justice in Article 9 of the Convention, nor compensates for the strict jurisprudence of the EU Courts.[55]

In the same vein, the committee also affirmed that the 'direct concern' requirement referred to in Article 263(4) TFEU, as interpreted by the court, and the third limb of that provision, introduced in Article 263(4) TFEU with the Lisbon Treaty, are not in compliance with Article 9(3) of the Aarhus Convention (AC).[56] In accordance with the ECJ's interpretation given to that provision, NGOs acting purely to promote a public, that is, environmental protection, as opposed to a private or a specific interest, would always be excluded from challenging a European decision through the annulment procedure.[57]

---

53 Case C-321/95P, *supra* note 52, para. 33. See, critically, *A. Ward*, Judicial Review of Environmental Misconduct in the European Community: Problems, Prospects and Strategies, YEEL 2000 (1), pp. 154–156.

54 *Hedemann-Robinson*, *supra* note 17, pp. 362–365.

55 Aarhus Convention Compliance Committee (ACCC), Findings and recommendations with regard to communication ACCC/C/2008/32 (part II) concerning compliance by the European Union [2017] paras. 56-57; Findings and recommendations with regard to communication ACCC/C/2008/32 (Part I) concerning compliance by the European Union [2011] para. 90.

56 ACCC (part II), *supra* note 55, paras. 65–78.

57 However, the European Commission recently published, on 6 March 2020, a Roadmap (<https://ec.europa.eu/info/law/better-regulation/have-your-say/initiatives/12165-Access-to-Justice-in-Environmental-matters>) proposing an amendment of the Aarhus Regulation. The roadmap makes clear that internal review shall become available for more acts of the institutions. See, on this point, *S. Bechtel*, 'Commission takes first step towards better NGO access to the European Court of Justice', available online <https://www.clientearth.org/commission-takes-first-step-towards-better-ngo-access-to-the-european-court-of-justice/>.

3.3. *LOCUS STANDI* OF NGOs

In recent years, a trend towards interpreting NGOs' *locus standi* more consistently with Article 9(3) AC has been upheld by the court,[58] but only with regard to legal protection against decisions taken by national authorities. The most prominent decision in that sense is the *Protect* judgment,[59] where the court stated that 'by denying environmental organisations any right to bring an action against such a decision to grant a permit, the relevant national procedural law is contrary to the requirements flowing from a combined reading of Article 9(3) of the AC and Article 47 of the Charter'.[60] The referring court shall thus interpret 'the procedural rules relating to the conditions to be met in order to bring proceedings [...] in order to enable an environmental organisation [...] to challenge before a court a decision taken following an administrative procedure that may be contrary to EU environmental law'.[61] Should such an interpretation be impossible, the referring court must disapply in the proceedings before it any conflicting national procedural rule which denies environmental organisation the standing to bring an action against a decision allegedly breaching EU environmental law.[62]

At the same time, the *Plaumann* test continues to apply with respect to decisions taken by European institutions. The court is thus applying a double standard of protection.[63] This creates an apparent discrepancy between the rights of NGOs and private parties to challenge national decisions related to the environment and the rights of the same persons with regard to European decisions related to the environment. According to the case law of the court, while national courts are bound by the principles enshrined in the *Slovakian Brown Bears* and *Protect* judgments, the court does not consider itself bound by them. The serious consequences of this situation have been clearly identified by the ACCC, which affirmed that 'if the examined jurisprudence of the EU Courts on access to justice were to continue, unless fully compensated for by adequate administrative review procedures, the Party concerned would fail to comply with Article 9, paragraph 3, of the Convention'.[64]

---

58 Case C-237/07, Janecek [2008] ECR I-6221; Case C-263/08, Djurgården-Lilla Värtans Miljöskyddsförening [2009] ECR I-9967; Case C-115/09, Bund für Umwelt und Naturschutz Deutschland [2011] ECR I-3673; Case C-240/09, Lesoochranárske zoskupenie VLK (Slovakian Brown Bears) [2011] ECR I-1255.

59 Case C-664/15, Protect Natur-Arten-und Landschaftsschutz Umweltorganisation (Protect case) [2017] ECLI:EU:C:2017:987.

60 Case C-664/15, *supra* note 58, para. 52.

61 Case C-664/15, *supra* note 58, para. 54.

62 Case C-664/15, *supra* note 58, paras. 52–56.

63 See *L. Krämer*, Access to Environmental Justice: the Double Standards of the ECJ, JEEPL 2017 (14), pp. 159–185.

64 ACCC (part I), *supra* note 55, paras. 80–82.

3.4. ADMINISTRATIVE REVIEW

Given the failures of EU law, as interpreted by the ECJ, in complying with the AC, the ACCC scrutinised whether the Aarhus Regulation[65] nevertheless compensates those failures by introducing adequate administrative review procedures.[66] In that regard, Article 10 AR provides NGOs with the possibility to ask for the internal review of European acts under certain conditions. According to Article 10 AR, public authorities or private parties other than NGOs do not have access to internal review. The wording of that provision is significantly narrower than that of the corresponding AC's provision, which provides for 'members of the public' which meet the criteria, if any, established in the law, to be given access to administrative or judicial procedures.[67] In that regard, the ACCC stated that 'by barring all members of the public except NGOs meeting the criteria of its Article 11', the AR 'fails to correctly implement Article 9, paragraph 3'.[68]

Furthermore, the combined reading of Articles 10, 11 and 2(1)(f-g)-(2) AR provides that only measures which meet some cumulative criteria can be challenged. The measures must be 'of individual scope', 'legally binding', having 'external effects' and be adopted 'under environmental law'. However, these requirements have been claimed to fail to correctly implement Article 9(3) AC.[69] In the ACCC's opinion, Article 9(3) AC encompasses a broader range of acts. In particular, Article 9(3) AC provides a right of challenge where 'any act or omission whatsoever by a Community institution or body, including any act implementing any policy or any act under any law – contravenes law relating to the environment';[70] not only 'administrative act[s] under environmental law', as defined in the AR.[71] In that regard, for instance, it is not clear if treaty rules on structural funds, fisheries, development aid, agriculture or industrial policy may be challenged under Articles 2 and 10 AR. In accordance with a strict interpretation of those provisions, it seems that they are not included therein and that they fall outside the scope of application of the internal review procedure.

Another obstacle to the right to bring administrative review of European institutions' decisions is the requirement whereby measures which can be

---

65 Regulation (EC) No 1367/2006 of the European Parliament and of the Council of 6 September 2006 on the application of the provisions of the Aarhus Convention on Access to Information, Public Participation in Decision-making and Access to Justice in Environmental Matters to Community Institutions and Bodies (Aarhus Regulation), OJ 2006 L 264/13.

66 ACCC (part II), *supra* note 55, para. 83.

67 Article 9(3) AC.

68 See ACCC, Findings on communication ACCC/C/2006/18 (Denmark) (ECE/MP.PP/2008/5/Add.4), paras. 30–31; ACCC (part II), *supra* note 55, para. 93.

69 See ACCC (part II), *supra* note 55, Communicant's comments of 23 February 2015, paras. 42–49.

70 ACCC (part II), *supra* note 55, para. 99.

71 The expression 'environmental law' is defined in Article 2(1)(f) AR.

challenged must be 'legally binding' and have 'external effects',[72] considering that some measures which do not have legally binding and external effects are covered by the wording of Article 9(3) AC. Furthermore, several administrative acts and omissions[73] are exempted from administrative review.

Moreover, the AR is not even clear on the applicable standards of review, with the result that it is not clear whether only a 'marginal' review or, on the contrary, a full review of the merits of the case should be undertaken. The European institution to which the request for internal review is addressed therefore has a wide leeway in deciding on the request. Moreover, the possibility for the European institution not to consider the request if it is 'clearly unsubstantiated',[74] in the absence of clear criteria on the standards of review, gives it a broad power to disregard any request it does not want to deal with. Such a theoretical risk has materialised in practice, given that so far only two procedures have led to a final decision,[75] and only one of them led to an actual review.

As a general conclusion on the compliance with the AC of the administrative review procedure provided for in the AR, the ACCC affirmed that 'the Regulation does not correct or compensate for the failings in the European Union jurisprudence, and leaves the Party concerned in non-compliance with Article 9, paragraphs 3 and 4, of the Convention.'[76]

4. CONCLUSION

The foregoing analysis reveals that an adequate protection of the environment is not impaired by the absence of harmonised European environmental rules. Adequate accountability mechanisms of the actors responsible for enforcing and monitoring the enforcement of European environmental laws are, on the contrary, lacking. The analysis showed that there are no effective judicial or administrative mechanisms to challenge EU institutions' acts and omissions which may be contrary to EU environmental law, either. In that regard, further harmonisation of national enforcement procedures is not an effective solution. It risks creating even more European legislation possessing merely symbolic value.

---

72 See Article 2(1)(g) AR.

73 See Article 2(2) AR.

74 Article 10(2) AR.

75 See *J.H. Jans & H.H.B. Vedder*, *supra* note 9, p. 248; *G.J. Harryvan & J.H. Jans*, Internal Review of EU Environmental Measures. It's True: Baron van Munchausen Doesn't Exist! Some Remarks on the Application of the So-Called Aarhus Regulation, REALaw 2010 (2), pp. 51–63; *M. Pallemaerts*, Access to Environmental Justice at EU Level. Has the 'Aarhus Regulation' Improved the Situation?, in *M. Pallemaerts* (ed.), The Aarhus Convention at Ten. Interactions and Tensions between Conventional International Law and EU Environmental Law, 2011.

76 ACCC (part II), *supra* note 55, para. 120.

The adoption of further European harmonising acts will not resolve the shortcomings deriving from the dual standard of protection applied by the ECJ with respect to the interpretation of the *locus standi* requirements of NGOs and members of the public at the national and the European level. Nor will it solve the serious problems of conflict of interest, lack of resources and lack of powers of the actors responsible for enforcing and monitoring the enforcement of European environmental obligations. No amount of harmonisation would ameliorate any of that, since, when in the form of general EU measures, they will not be subject to scrutiny by the public, and no one could ensure that those harmonised rules are followed.

Hence, if not accompanied by the establishment of an integrated and harmonious system of enforcement where adequate mechanisms of accountability of the actors involved and where effective judicial and administrative review procedures are in place, harmonisation in the environmental field risks having only a symbolic value.

Only the setting up of adequate judicial and administrative review procedures and accountability mechanisms of the European institutions charged with monitoring the compliance of European environmental obligations would solve the problem of having merely symbolic European environmental harmonising measures. Without the adoption of adequate accountability and review mechanisms, there will be no enforcement of European environmental laws. Furthermore, allowing civil society to hold EU institutions to account for the legality of their decisions will increase the legitimacy of the EU institutions itself, which is essential for a Union that claims to be based on the rule of law.

While being conscious that the proposed solution is not the one upheld by the EU legislator, it seemed necessary to highlight that it is desirable that in a more or less distant future such a solution will be taken into consideration.

PART II

HARMONISATION IN ENVIRONMENTAL LAW

BRIDGING THE GAP BETWEEN SOIL AND CLIMATE CHANGE IN THE EU

The Issue of Soil Organic Carbon

Matteo FERMEGLIA*

1. INTRODUCTION

Nobody could deny that soil plays a crucial role in the provision of all vital ecosystem services. However, besides acting as the benchmark for food production, water storage and supply, biodiversity – let alone added cultural and social services[1] – soils are also garbled by the upsurge of climate change.[2] The impacts of soil exploitation on a massive scale for energy and food production reveal a core, yet overlooked, ecological function of soil: carbon pooling. This ecological function serves as a yardstick for several ecologic functions carried

* Ph.D., Assistant Professor of International and European Environmental Law, University of Hasselt. Email: matteo.fermeglia@uhasselt.be.

[1] See *Adhikari, Kabindra, and Alfred E. Hatermink*. 2016. Linking Soils to Ecosystem services – A global review, (2016) 262 Geoderma, 101–111.

[2] For a general overview of the issue, see *R. Lal*, Soil Carbon Sequestration to Mitigate Climate Change (2004) 123(1–2) Geoderma, 1–22.

out by soil in order to halt greenhouse gas emissions or, in turn, even worsen it: soil organic matter (SOM). SOM stores a significant amount of greenhouse gas (GHG) – mainly CO_2 – in the form of soil organic carbon (SOC) stocks. Similarly, other GHGs, namely, nitrous oxide (N_2O) and methane (CH_4), are also produced and stored (or trapped) in soils under anaerobic conditions, like peat and permafrost.[3] Soils are thus the second-largest active store of GHG after the oceans, with around 1.500 billion tonnes of carbon found in SOM worldwide.[4] In Europe, the total SOC stock amounts to 73–79 billion tons.[5] Hence, the 2011 European Commission (EC) Communication on the Resource Efficiency Roadmap called upon Member States to adopt measures aimed to reduce erosion and enhance SOM, with a view to an overall non-regression of SOM levels – especially in soils with less than 3.5 per cent SOM.[6] Notwithstanding the key role played by soils in the global carbon cycle and the dire ecological interrelations between climate change and its functions, however, the issue of SOM protection has been traditionally marginalised even in the lingering debate about a European comprehensive regime on soil protection.

This chapter will thus first outline the interplay between SOM ecological functions and the threats thereto posed by climate change. Next, it will analyse the legal instruments arguably aimed at tackling the issue of soil integrity in relation to GHG emissions at the EU level. Lastly, it will envision a set of potential solutions as to a comprehensive and effective regulatory approach to SOM protection in the EU.

2. WHY SOIL ORGANIC MATTER(S)?

SOM is generated through the carbon cycle as a result of the release into soil of the CO_2 absorbed by plants through the photosynthesis from ambient air in the form of organic compounds by plant roots, or through the decay of plant material or soil organisms when they die. Microbial breakdown of organic matter ultimately releases the nutrients, which plants use to grow. Importantly, during this process of decomposition, part of the carbon sequestered is released

3 In fact, such stocks amount to approx. 50 per cent of the estimated global belowground organic carbon pool: see *Charles Tarnocai et al.*, Soil organic carbon pools in the northern circumpolar permafrost region, (2009) 23(2) Global Biogeochemical Cycles, 1–11.

4 *IPCC*, Climate Change 2014: Synthesis Report. Contribution of Working Groups I, II and III to the Fifth Assessment Report of the Intergovernmental Panel on Climate Change. Intergovernmental Panel on Climate Change (IPCC), 2015.

5 See *EEA*, Climate change, impact and vulnerability in Europe 2016: An indicator based report, Report no. 1/2017, 161. However, this evaluation is still controversial, and might well be underestimated.

6 See Commission Communication COM (2011) 571 final, Roadmap to a Resource Efficient Europe, 15, and Commission Staff Working Document Accompanying the Communication SEC (2011)1067 final, 42, respectively.

as CO_2 through soil respiration, while other carbon is converted into stable organic compounds that are locked into the ground (i.e. SOC), and some carbon is partly exported from soils to rivers and oceans as dissolved organic carbon or part of erosion material.[7]

Solid scientific evidence shows that climate change will impinge on the integrity of SOM stocks both in rural and urban areas.[8] Yet the extent and magnitude to which this will happen is still a matter of considerable debate.[9] Temperature and precipitation patterns certainly constitute the most relevant factors controlling SOC dynamics. Higher temperatures may yield plant production, thereby increasing carbon inputs to soils; however, it will also increase microbial decomposition of SOM, thus spurring GHG emissions from SOC.[10] Likewise, an increase in the frequency of extreme weather events may exacerbate soils' susceptibility to erosion, salinisation, slaking, compaction and other degradation processes, leading to further GHG losses.[11] Furthermore, such impacts may differ depending on the kind of soils, with specific reference to permafrost and peat. SOC contained in the northern permafrost region is estimated to account for approximately 50 per cent of the estimated global underground organic carbon pool.[12] Peat soils account for 20 per cent of the carbon in European soils (CO_2, CH_4 and N_2O) and are mostly located in Sweden, Finland and the British Isles.[13] Hence, overall, effective and coordinated mitigation are increasingly being promoted to encourage sustainable land management, in order to ensure protection of soil carbon stocks as a crucial ecosystem function to achieve the pivotal 1.5° C target set out in the Paris Agreement.[14] In fact, land use change represents the largest source of CO_2 emissions from soils in Europe, especially drainage of organic soils, which amount to 20–40 tCO2e/ha/year.[15] Without action targeted at soils' carbon pooling function, SOM decomposition is likely to exceed levels gained from increased plant growth, thus resulting in a positive climate feedback from SOC released into the atmosphere.[16]

---

7 See *European Commission*, Soil: The Hidden Part of the Carbon Cycle, 2011.

8 See *R. Schils et al.*, Review Of Existing Information On The Interrelations Between Soil And Climate Change, CLIMSOIL project Final Report, 2008; see also *B.G. Rawlins et al.*, A review of climate change impacts on urban soil functions with examples and policy insights from England, UK, (2015) 31 Soil Use and Management, 46–61.

9 See *P. Smith*, Soils and Climate Change, (2012) 4 Current Opinion in Environmental Sustainability, 539–544.

10 See, *inter alia*, *M. Fernandes-Martinez et al.*, Global trends in carbon sinks and their relationship with CO2 and temperature, (2019) 9 Nature Climate Change, 73–79.

11 See *EEA*, supra n 5, 158.

12 See *Tarnocai et al.*, supra n 3, 1–11.

13 See *EEA*, Soil Organic Carbon, 2012.

14 IPCC, 1.5° Report – Summary for Policymakers, 2018, 23–24. See also *Calum Brown et al.*, Achievement of Paris climate goals unlikely due to time lags in the land system, (2019) 9 Nature Climate Change, 203–208.

15 See *R. Schils et al.*, supra n 8, 13.

16 See *A. V. Gallego-Sala et al.*, Latitudinal limits to the predicted increase of the peatland carbon sink with warming, (2018) 8 Nature Climate Change, 907–913.

3. SOM PROTECTION IN THE EU: A PATCHY FRAMEWORK

The multi-faceted, cross-cutting aspects of soil protection are reflected in a notable degree of fragmentation among different legal instruments addressing soil protection and management, either as a single ecological aspect of ecosystems in a given area (e.g. waters, biodiversity, forestry, etc.), or as a subject of protection against actual or potential threats in relation to its human uses (e.g. agricultural practices).[17] Significantly, this also holds true at the EU level. The importance of ensuring a high level of soil protection has been widely recognised in EU 7th Environmental Action Programme. Moreover, the proposal for a Soil Framework Directive (SFD) issued by the EC comprised carbon pooling as a primary function of soil.[18] Consequently, the decline of SOM was encompassed as a major threat to soil integrity, which should have been taken into account by Member States when drafting programmatic instruments aimed to mitigate risk and enhance reparation and protection measures.[19] After the withdrawal of the SFD in 2013 due to fierce opposition by some Member States, barely any express reference to SOM can be found in the EU *acquis*.[20] Nevertheless, a set of scattered legal tools currently governing SOM can be pinpointed among three building blocks: (1) EU Environmental Law; (2) EU Climate Law; and (3) EU Common Agricultural Policy (CAP).

3.1. EU ENVIRONMENTAL LAW

Within EU environmental legislation, the legal tools addressing soil issues are to be found in the area of water, waste, air, chemicals and biodiversity policies.

The Water Framework Directive, by establishing good water body status conditions, and therefore controlling pollution from point sources to water, may contribute to enhancing soil biodiversity protection, albeit indirectly.[21] Soil quality and water issues are strictly interlinked: while fully healthy soils can prevent the risk of floods and protect underground waters, SOM can hold 3–5 times its weight in water, if correctly preserved.[22]

---

17 See, *inter alia, I. Hannam*, International And National Aspects Of A Legislative Framework To Manage Soil Carbon Sequestration, (2004) 65(3) Climatic Change, 1–23.

18 Commission Proposal for a Soil Framework Directive, COM (2006) 232 final, art. 1, lett. f.

19 Ibid. art. 4 and the Commission Communication, Towards a Thematic Strategy for Soil Protection, COM (2002) 179.

20 See *N. Glaesner et al.*, Do Current European Policies Prevent Soil Threats and Support Soil Functions?, (2014) 6 Sustainability, 9538–9563.

21 European Parliament and Council Directive No. 2000/60/EC, art. 4.

22 See Commission Staff Working Paper SEC(2011) 1067 final, 41.

The Waste Framework Directive (WFD), while setting out an overarching waste management hierarchy, importantly includes composting as a method of recycling organic material as an alternative to disposal.[23] Compost, as a soil conditioning and fertilising material, indeed entails the potential to replace SOC lost from soil. Provisions are also made in the directive to ensure the protection of soils, as well as water air and wildlife.[24] In particular, Article 22 WFD calls on the Commission to 'carry out an assessment on the management of bio-waste with a view to submitting a proposal if appropriate'. The assessment shall examine the opportunity of setting minimum requirements for bio-waste management and quality criteria for compost and from bio-waste, in order to guarantee 'a high level of protection for human health and the environment'.[25] It is therefore to be expected that in future the Commission will consider possible further actions to support composting and digestion of bio-waste across the EU.

However, the potential impacts of this policy for soil organic carbon across the EU are likely to be limited, because no obligation exists to produce high-quality compost across the EU. Moreover, the support for bio-waste must be coordinated with the policies promoting renewable energy sources (RES), to the extent that the latter could result in waste incineration being promoted over waste recycling, thus hindering the amount of bio-waste composted and its use as a soil improver for maintaining or enhancing SOC levels.

The Nitrates Directive (ND) may have significant potential to contribute to the protection of soil through the implementation of measures to obtain good ecological status in all water bodies, as well as the implementation of the codes of good agricultural practices in vulnerable zones.[26] The ND requires Member States to identify and designate Nitrate Vulnerable Zones (NVZs).[27] Farmers located in NVZs are required to comply with action programme measures to reduce nitrate leaching, more specifically by reducing fertiliser-N inputs in soils. However, the actual impact of N fertilisers on SOM potential for carbon sequestration is unclear, and ultimately not significant.[28] Likewise, the Sewage Sludge Directive (SSD) is the most important directive for the protection of soil, as soil protection from sewage sludge used on agricultural land is one of the main goals of this directive.[29] Since sludge represents a source of some carbon in agricultural soils, the SSD can contribute to this.

With regard to air policies, the Industrial Emission Directive (2010/75/EU) and the National Emission Ceiling Directive, although they consider soil

[23] European Parliament and Council Directive No. 2008/98/EC, art. 22.
[24] Ibid. art. 13.
[25] Ibid. art. 22.
[26] Council Directive No. 91/676/EEC, art. 3 and 4.
[27] Ibid. art. 3, para. 2.
[28] *S. Khan et al.*, The Myth of Nitrogen Fertilization for Soil Carbon Sequestration, (2007) 36 Journal of Environmental Quality, 1821–1832.
[29] Council Directive No. 86/278/EEC, art. 1.

primarily as a medium with regard to pollution of industrial emissions, could play a relevant role inasmuch as they aim to control emissions, which may negatively affect SOM, such as NO_x, SO_2 and heavy metals.[30]

Lastly, effective tools to enhance soil quality can be drawn from biodiversity law. Inasmuch as higher soil quality contributes to enhanced biodiversity levels, instruments such as the Natura 2000 framework under the Habitats and Birds Directive are capable of ensuring increases in SOC levels in croplands and grasslands.[31]

3.2. EU CLIMATE LAW

SOM arguably holds a pivotal role when it comes to EU Energy and Climate policies. Soils provide for biomass, which are increasingly relied on to reduce the share of fossil fuels throughout the energy supply chain.[32] At the same time, soils can offset GHG emissions by capturing and storing carbon – also through artificial carbon capture and storage – and are key to adapting to climate change (e.g. by flood regulation owing to the structuring effect of SOM or food production).[33] The EU Adaptation Strategy as a general framework to enhance climate adaptation aims to prompt a series of actions at the Member State level, addressing key soil threats, including SOM degradation.[34] However, such actions are voluntary and often rely on action under other instruments (e.g. the LIFE programme, the CAP or the Floods Directive) to deliver meaningful policy goals.[35]

The Renewable Energy Directive (RED) hence becomes central to SOM protection.[36] The 2018 RED aims to foster the uptake of RES, thus furthering implications for soil protection in terms of land use change and land management, specifically regarding expansion in bioenergy and biofuel use.[37] In this perspective, the RED sets out sustainability criteria targeted at protecting certain

[30] See Parliament and Council Directive No. 2010/75/EU, art. 1, and Parliament and Council Directive No. 2016/2284/EU, art. 1, respectively.

[31] See *A. Hagyó and G. Tóth*, The impact of environmental policy on soil quality: Organic carbon and phosphorous levels in croplands and grasslands of the European Natura 2000 network, (2018) 223 Journal of Environmental Management, 9–15.

[32] See *A. Frelih-Larsen et al.*, Updated Inventory and Assessment of Soil Protection Policy Instruments in EU Member States, Final Report to DG Environment, 2017, 172.

[33] *J.R. Porter et al.*, 'Food Security and Food Production Systems', in *C.B. Field et al.* (eds), Climate Change 2014: Impacts, Adaptation, and Vulnerability. Part A: Global and Sectoral Aspects. Contribution of Working Group II to the Fifth Assessment Report of the Intergovernmental Panel on Climate Change (Cambridge University Press, 2015).

[34] See the Commission Communication COM(2013) 216 final, An EU Strategy on Adaptation to Climate Change, 8.

[35] See *Frelih-Larsen et al., supra* n 32, 170 ff.

[36] Parliament and Council Directive No. 2018/2001/EU.

[37] Ibid. whereas 82.

valued land areas based on high carbon or high biodiversity value that would potentially link to SOM protection.[38] Moreover, it contains specific provisions to support the use of degraded land for biofuel feedstock cultivation.[39]

The Climate Action Regulation (CAR) lays down the 2021–2030 targets for GHG emission reductions for each Member State from sectors outside the EU Emissions Trading Scheme (ETS).[40] As such, it offers the legal basis to address GHG emissions associated with soil management and agriculture.[41] However, the CAR does not state explicitly how this will be achieved. Therefore, it is left up to Member States to determine how to deliver the target and what actions are to be undertaken in which sector. Without a policy framing the importance of action on soils and steering the GHG benefits of action consistently, it is difficult to ascertain Member States' degree of ambition with regard to GHG mitigation in the agricultural sector. Yet, importantly, CAR Article 7 allows Member States to account for net removals from land use, land use change and forestry (LULUCF), including from managed croplands and grasslands, which can be used to compensate for exceeding their annual GHG emission targets – albeit within pre-determined limits.[42] Furthermore, the LULUCF Regulation enacted to implement Article 7 CAR comprises SOC as a carbon pool, for the purposes of balancing GHG emissions and removals in the LULUCF sector.[43] Overall, however, neither holistic soil management nor specific actions to address SOM are required as part of EU climate policy.

3.3. COMMON AGRICULTURAL POLICY

Unsurprisingly, the field where SOC and soil as a carbon pool actually plays a more central role in the EU is the Common Agricultural Policy (CAP). In Europe, land used for agriculture with organic soils emitted on average 16 to 17 tonnes of CO2 per hectare in 2016,[44] while GHG emissions from the agricultural sectors amount to approximately 10 per cent of total EU GHG emissions, and 22.3 per cent of overall non-CO2 GHG emissions.[45]

---

38 Ibid. art. 26.

39 Ibid. art. 29.

40 Parliament and Council Regulation No. 2018/842/EU amending the Regulation no. 525/2013/EU.

41 Ibid. art. 2.

42 Ibid. art. 7. The total amount, which can be used to offset emissions from other CAR sectors is total of 280 million GtCO2 EU-28 wide.

43 Parliament and Council Regulation No. 2018/841/EU, Art. 4 (1) and Annex I (B).

44 See *UNFCCC*, European Union 2018 inventory report.

45 See *EUROSTAT*, Agri-Environmental indicator – greenhouse gases emissions, 2019; *European Commission*, In-depth Analysis in support of the Commission Communication COM(2018) 773, 159.

The CAP supports carbon sequestration in soil and maintenance of high SOM levels primarily through good agricultural and environmental conditions (GAEC) standards no. 4 (on soil cover) and 6 (specifically directed at SOM).[46] Thus, Member States must define national or regional minimum requirements for GAEC taking into consideration the specific characteristics of the area concerned, including soil and climatic conditions. However, such a framework might be hampered by implementation failures at the Member State level.[47] The lack of clarity about the minimum appropriate practices for soil cover under GAEC4, GAEC5 (land management to limit erosion), and the limited scope of practices under GAEC 6 (ban on burning arable stubble), considerably constrain CAP's potential to prompt agro-environment climate measures in a synergic and coherent way to address their specific soil protection needs, such as SOM protection.[48]

In addition, a range of measures is provided under the Rural Development Programme for restoration, creation or management of permanent grassland habitats, wetlands, peatland, forests and other wooded land. Notwithstanding this, the CAP still has several weaknesses in terms of effective, climate-smart agricultural practices, which would indeed enable carbon sequestration, and operates rather in isolation from other EU's climate policies.[49] Moreover, the CAP as currently shaped – similarly to the RED – is intended to prevent the reduction of the soil carbon pool, but it is not directly aimed to improve this ecological function.

Significantly, in the post-2020 CAP reform, soil-related issues have been addressed in a twofold, more coherent way. Firstly, the greening and cross-compliance scheme will be replaced by a conditionality system.[50] Conditionality will link farmers' income support from CAP to the fulfilment of specific obligations, including GAEC standards, which will include preservation of rich soils such as peatlands and wetlands (GAEC2), as well as maintenance of SOM (GAEC3).[51] The conditionality mechanism operates also with regard to Statutory Management Requirements (SMRs), which in turn relates to obligations arising out of other pieces of legislation, including the ND and WFD.

---

46 Council Regulation No. 73/2009/EU, Annex III.

47 See *C.B. Henriksen et al.,* Exploiting soil-management strategies for climate mitigation in the European Union: Maximizing "win-win" solutions across policy regimes (2011) 16(4) Ecology & Society, 22; *A. Matthews*, Research for Agri Commitee – The Future of Direct Payments, 2016 Brussels: European Commission.

48 See *J. Verschuuren*, Towards an EU Regulatory Framework for Climate-Smart Agriculture: The Example of Soil Carbon Sequestration, (2018) 7(2) Transnational Environmental Law, 301–322 and *Frelih-Larsen et al.*, *supra* n 32, 81 (yet noting that 17 MS defined additional requirements under GAEC6, such as crop rotation and application of soil organic manure).

49 See *Verschuuren*, *supra* n 48.

50 See *European Commission*, The Post-2020 Common Agricultural Policy: Environmental Benefits and Simplifications, 2019, 5.

51 See Ibid.

Furthermore, Member States will be mandated to commit their national direct payment and Rural Development budget (at least 30%) to the development of eco-schemes and Agri-Environment-Climate Measures (AECMs), respectively.[52] Payments will be granted to farmers and beneficiaries that utilise technologies able to maximise actions for climate change, including through the enhancement of soil health (including SOM conditions) on a voluntary basis.[53]

4. HARMONISATION OF EU LAW ON SOM

Given the overall inadequacy of the current patchy EU legal regime on soil protection to govern land management and broadly ensure SOM protection, the urgency for integrative concepts and underpinning methodologies to track progress towards the sustainable use of land and soil resources is clear. As shown in Section 2, soil quality is strictly connected to its functions. Thus, failing to properly address soil threats thwarts the multi-functionality of soils in terms of providing ecosystem services, including carbon sequestration and carbon pooling.[54] Previous research has demonstrated how all soil functions are somehow addressed in the current EU legislation, although very few provisions are expressively aimed to enhance soil functions.[55] At the Member State level, 54 per cent of the legal instruments currently in place to tackle soil ecosystem functions address soil carbon pooling (either directly or indirectly), whereas 59 per cent cover SOM degradation as a threat thereto.[56]

The following sub-sections will thus set out the conceptual framework for the implementation of a coherent and comprehensive regime for protection of SOM, further discussing the implications of such approach as a benchmark for the current EU legal framework governing soils as a carbon pool.

4.1. CONCEPTUAL FRAMEWORK FOR HARMONISATION

The multi-dimensional nature of the elements hampering soil's ecological integrity are truly hard to understand from an empirical standpoint, and therefore to address from a legal standpoint. The ability of legislation to achieve effective soil carbon management will depend on the legal and institutional elements that protect physical processes associated with soil carbon sequestration and the

---

52 See Ibid. 6.

53 See Ibid.

54 See *L. Greiner et al.*, Soil function assessment: review of methods for quantifying the contributions of soils to ecosystem services, (2017) 69 Land Use Policy, 224–237, at 225.

55 See *N. Glaesner et al.*, supra n 20, 9558.

56 See *Frelih-Larsen et al.*, supra n 32, 24–25.

establishment and maintenance of carbon sinks and reservoirs. Such elements should be incorporated within procedures that regulate and manage the land use activities generating losses of soil carbon, leading to land degradation and contributing to the greenhouse effect. Legislation and policy reform should be approached from a sound conceptual basis, preferably with an overall societal goal of sink management and enhancement.[57]

Thus, a clear understanding of the principal processes and consequences of land degradation is essential, in order to provide direction as to how environmental legislation can be framed to support successful management and control of soil carbon sequestration.[58] In this regard, the 2006 EC Soil Thematic Strategy first enshrined the concept of soil functions and pitched it in the EU environmental agenda.[59] Carbon pool was enlisted as one of soils' primary functions. However, such an approach has been utterly abandoned in the wake of the withdrawal of the SFD.

The next sub-sections will hence illustrate two assessment methodologies currently available for policy-making at the EU level, both of which importantly rely on soils' ecosystem functions as the core element of analysis.

4.1.1. *The Soil Function Assessment (SFA) Method*

The uptake of a genuine ecosystem approach in the development of a comprehensive environmental policy aiming to address land and soil ecosystems shall draw from the Ecosystem Services (ES) approach.[60] In sum, ES aims to quantify the goods and services provided by ecosystems to society.[61] The capacity of soils to deliver ES is largely determined by its functions, and each individual soil function can be seen as providing a soil-related contribution to ES.[62] Carbon pooling has been identified as the most prominent soil function assessed in most ES studies thus far, both because of its prominence among soils' numerous and multi-faceted ecosystem functions, and because it is easier to calculate when compared to other soil properties.[63]

Based on the ES studies, a Soil Function Assessment (SFA) methodology can be carried out. SFA has already been adopted in some EU Member States (e.g. Germany and Austria) and consists of a static assessment of basic soil properties,

57 See *I. Hannam and B. Boer*, Drafting Legislation for Sustainable Soils: A Guide, 2004.

58 See *I. Hannam*, supra n 17.

59 See COM (2006) 231 final, supra n 20, 8–9.

60 See *C. Calzolari et al.*, A methodological framework to assess the multiple contributions of soils to ecosystem services delivery at regional scale, (2016) 261 Geoderma, 190–203.

61 See *J. Bouma*, Soil science contributions towards sustainable development goals and their implementation: linking soil functions with ecosystem services, (2014) 177(2) Journal of Plant Nutrition and Soil Science, 111–120.

62 See *L. Greiner et al.*, Soil function assessment: review of methods for quantifying the contributions of soils to the ecosystem, (2017) 69 Land Use Policy, 224–237.

63 Ibid. 228.

such as SOC content, texture (clay and silt contents), pH, stone content, bulk density (or pore volume) and soil hydromorphic properties (e.g. indications on stagnant soil horizons, drainage and water logging data).[64] The steps required to link key soil properties and soil processes to soil functions, and to link soil functions to ES and related benefits, are displayed in the figure below.

Figure 1. SFA's workflow

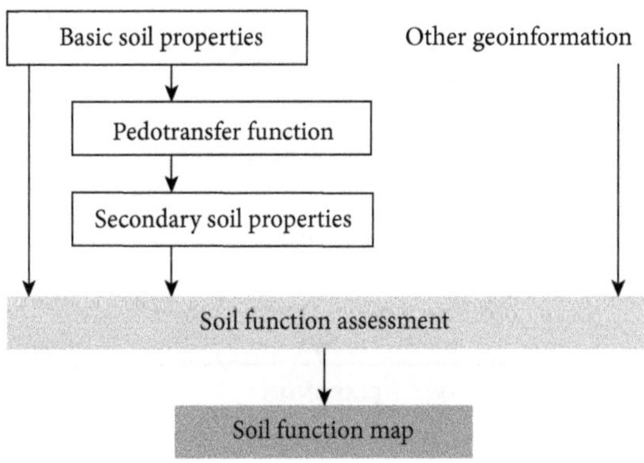

Source: Lucie Greiner et al. (2017).

Building on the data on soil properties as the benchmark dataset, which could well be integrated with other secondary properties (e.g. the carbonate content or the nutrient status), relevant soil functions can be assessed. SFA's viability, however, heavily depends on soil mapping and data availability, and might prove particularly useful for ES studies in land-use planning.

4.1.2. The DPSIR Method

The DPSIR method is based on the interplay between driving forces, pressures, states, impacts and responses. The DPSIR method assumes a chain of causal links starting with driving forces (i.e. economic sectors, human activities), through pressures (e.g. emissions, substance runoff, waste disposal) to states (i.e. physical, chemical and biological) and impacts on ecosystems, human health and functions, eventually leading to political responses (i.e. prioritisation, target-setting, indicators). The DPSIR method has been extensively adopted by the European Economic Area (EEA) since the early 2000s as an integrated approach for reporting (e.g. in the EEA's State of the Environment Reports) and only recently has been extended to soil quality assessment.[65] Similarly to the

64 Ibid. 233.
65 See *EEA*, Land systems at the European level – analytical assessment framework, 2018.

FSA, the DPSIR method casts its primary focus towards soil functionalities. Yet, unlike FSA, DPSIR devises the analysis according to different land processes (e.g., agriculture and forest land use), with the aim of linking the assessment with targeted and effective policy responses, as displayed in the figure below.

Figure 2. Basic components of the land system and their relation to the DPSIR framework

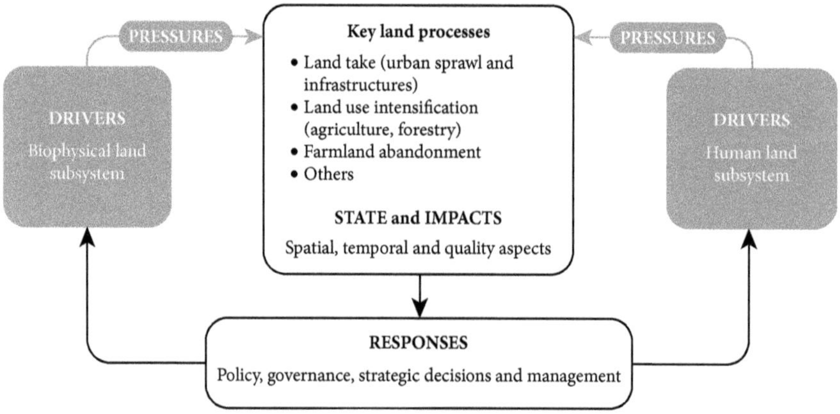

Source: EEA (2018).

To acquire relevance in the law- and policy-making process, the DPSIR method should be used to inform policy-relevant questions. For example, the relevant policy question might concern predicted impacts on land system in terms of SOC concentration as a result of the intensification of certain agricultural practices across different territories. Firstly, the analytical process would map out all relevant drivers and pressures. Drivers and pressures are mostly related to the land processes, which in turn are defined as physical, biological or chemical processes that directly influence changes in ecosystem functions and services.[66] Significantly, the DPSIR assessment carefully takes into account different lands' geographical peculiarities. Next, the functional assessment is carried out, which measures the impacts – also in terms of eventual benefits – of each land process on the delivery of soils' environmental functions (i.e. carbon pooling). For example, intensification of certain agricultural practices and land uses would increase soil erosion and therefore lead to a decline in SOM. The ideal outcome of the assessment would thus be an analytical response to the underlying policy question, which shall in turn inform adequate measures to address specific pressures within a specific land ecosystem.[67] Hence, coming back to the policy question formulated above, the DPSIR analysis might suggest that the selected

66 Ibid.
67 Ibid.

agricultural practices increase food or energy production from biomass in a given territory with little impact on SOC in one area, while proving heavily detrimental to SOC stocks in others.

4.2. TOWARDS A COMPREHENSIVE EU REGIME ON SOM

EU policies governing land management and secure protection of nature and ecosystems need integrative concepts and underpinning methodologies to track progress towards the sustainable use of land and soil resources. At the 2017 Global Symposium on Soil Organic Carbon, the UN Food and Agriculture Organisation (FAO) firmly urged a rethinking of SOC governance.[68] Moreover, the importance of well-designed policy development was emphasised, which would encompass land uses and land management practices capable of increasing SOC with a thorough context-specific focus.[69]

Alternative approaches to align the current patchy and inconsistent EU framework with these recommendations have already been advocated, ranging from a revival of EU comprehensive soil regulation,[70] to the inclusion of agriculture in the ETS[71] and to mandatory Member State national action plans on SOM, following the approach already adopted on climate adaptation.[72] However, the experience gained thus far with the SFD and the long-standing struggle to regulate methane emissions from agriculture teaches us that all the above avenues for reform would have to navigate severe hurdles, inasmuch as they would impinge on the enjoyment of private vested property rights on land,[73] as well as stark Member State economic interests.[74] A crucial effort towards a comprehensive response is thus likely to be found in an international regime on SOM protection, similar to the regime adopted for fluorinated gases.[75] As noted elsewhere, such an international regime may spur more

68 See *FAO*, Unlocking the Potential of Soil Organic Carbon, Outcome Document of the Global Symposium on Soil Organic Carbon, 2017, 18.

69 Ibid. IX. The following widely applicable recommendations for maintaining or increasing SOC were also identified: control soil erosion; maintain ground cover; apply integrated nutrient management; encourage diversified farming systems; incentivise and empower farmers to manage SOC; and encourage collaboration between scientists, farmers and policy-makers to devise strategies for increasing SOC.

70 See *Glaesner et al.*, supra n 20, 9558.

71 See *Verschuuren*, supra n 48, 320.

72 See *Frelih-Larsen et al.*, supra n 32, 178–179.

73 See *Hannam and Boer*, supra n 57, and *Verschuuren*, supra n 48.

74 See *M. Petersen*, European Soil Protection Law after the Setback of December 2007 – Existing Law and Outlook (2008) 3 EEELR, 146–165.

75 See *B. Boer and I. Hannam*, Developing a Global Soil Regime, 2015 (1) International Journal of Rural Law and Policy, 1–13.

ambitious and coordinated solutions at the regional and domestic level.[76] In fact, several Member States enshrine international policies – such as the United Nations Convention to Combat Desertification, the Alpine Convention and the UNFCCC as important drivers of domestic decision making on soil issues.[77]

Without any of the above undertakings taking off in the short term, a viable option for harmonisation of EU law on SOM importantly builds on conceptually embedding soils' ecological functions as the fundamental underpinning throughout all relevant policies and regulations that already deal with soil protection. The ES approach has already been adopted in some EU Environmental policies, such as the 2011 Biodiversity Strategy, the 2013 Forest Strategy and – albeit to a minor extent – the CAP.[78] The SFA and DPSIR methodologies explained above are indeed apt to of deliver key empirical findings to steer regulation- and policy-making with a remarkable degree of accuracy. Both conceptual frameworks are consistent with the FAO recommendations on SOC, inasmuch as they prioritise soils with the highest carbon stocks in national and regional policies on soil conservation, while identifying the short- and long-term benefits of sustainable and carbon-neutral management practices for SOC sequestration and facilitating their implementation at the local level.[79] The missing link can thus be identified in a legal document outlining a Common European SOM Conservation Policy under the umbrella of EU Climate Action (art. 191 TFEU) directed at setting priorities and targets, and defining monitoring parameters, while not impinging on the subsidiarity principle by setting out specific obligations on land use and management. As such, this conservation policy would act as a political driver to channel integration and coherence towards strategic aims and objectives among the array of policy instruments dealing with land uses and SOC. In other words, SOM degradation as an actual threat to soils' carbon pooling ecosystem function should be clearly embraced as a priority throughout the EU's current environmental, energy, agricultural and climate policies. Such an approach would be consistent with the objectives brought forward by the EC in its 2050 climate neutral strategy and the pivotal European Green Deal, which acknowledges GHG emissions from soils as a matter of utmost importance and accommodates the development of specific agricultural techniques involving, for example, zero-tillage and the use of cover crops.[80]

---

76 See *M. Fermeglia*, Soil Functions and Soil Protection in the Era of Climate Change: A Multi-Level Perspective, in *L. Westra, K. Bosselmann, V. Zambrano* (eds.), Ecological Integrity and Land Uses: Sovereignty, Governance, Displacements and Land Grabs, 2019.

77 See *Frelih-Larsen et al.*, supra n 32, 174–175.

78 See *J. Bouma et al.*, Adoption of the Ecosystem Services concept in EU policies, (2018) 29 Ecosystem Services, 213–222.

79 See FAO, supra n 68.

80 See the Commission Communication COM(2018) 773 final A clean planet for all, 14 and the Commission Communication COM(2019) 640 final The European Green Deal, 12.

5. CONCLUSION

Scientific studies are increasingly delving into the core of soil's multi-faceted nature, its tangled interrelations within the whole ecosystem and its interplay with the staggering detrimental dynamics triggered by climate change. Yet, when it comes to developing a comprehensive legal response to the actual threats to soil climate functions, we are barely scratching the surface. This chapter has analysed the set of instruments currently available to ensure a comprehensive response to the compelling threats posed to SOM in the EU, with a view to highlighting their shortcomings and edges. Importantly, the manifold and complex challenges posed by SOM protection can provide an opportunity to deeply embed ecosystem considerations in EU environmental and climate law. To this end, this chapter has emphasised that governance programmes for sustainable use of soils at the EU level should expressly prioritise SOM protection throughout a vast range of sectors. Importantly, the staggering amount of data on soil conditions, coupled with scientifically sound methodological approaches, such as FSA and DPSIR, can prove instrumental to gauging the sensitivity level of trade-offs between environmental supply and socio-economic demands, thus gaining ground as a meaningful tool to inform harmonisation at the EU level.

TOWARDS MORE HARMONISATION IN THE TREATMENT OF WILD ANIMALS IN THE EU?

Elien VERNIERS*

* Doctoral Candidate in Environmental Law, specialising in Animal Law, Ghent University, Belgium.

1. INTRODUCTION

'The Fox and the Crow', one of the famous fables of Aesop, tells the story of a vain crow and a toady fox. The devious fox steals the crow's cheese. Yet, under European species protection law, it is the other way around: the fox is robbed of almost any protection and, compared to the treatment of the fox, the crow enjoys a much more favourable legal status.

This chapter will explore to what extent wild animals in the EU are differently treated, by analysing the legal regimes and case law (Section 3). Subsequently, the underlying motivations for the different treatment will be discussed, with a historical as well as a political explanation being presented (Section 4). The impact of different treatment cannot be ignored; therefore, this will be addressed, not only from a legal, but also from a policy-making point of view (Section 5). This chapter concludes with a section devoted to the 'issue of harmonisation', proceeding from a two-fold approach (i.e. animal welfare and species protection) (Section 6). Before delving into these topics, this chapter will set out the problem-setting and scope of this article (Section 2).

This research extends previous insights, by devoting attention to the differences between the birds directive and the habitats directive. This paper is also unique in that it links the harmonisation of species protection to the harmonisation of animal welfare. Consequently, the different treatment of wild animals in the EU will be tackled, both from an animal welfare perspective and from a species protection perspective.

2. PROBLEM-SETTING AND THE SCOPE OF THIS CHAPTER

2.1. THE DIFFERENT TREATMENT OF WILD ANIMALS IN THE EU

Two areas interfere with the treatment of wild animals at the European level: species protection and animal welfare.

2.1.1. Species Protection

Species protection, as part of nature conservation, is governed by several EU legal instruments, including the birds directive,[1] the habitats directive,[2] the Regulation on Invasive Alien Species[3] and the CITES Regulation.[4] Certain species protection instruments are inspired by animal welfare considerations, such as the directive concerning the importation into Member States of skins of certain seal pups and products derived from them[5] and the regulation on trade in seal products.[6,7] This can result in a web of legislation regarding the treatment of wild animals in the EU. For instance, the birds directive applies to almost

1 Council Directive 79/409/EEC on the conservation of wild birds, OJ 1979 L 103/1. *Consolidated version*: European Parliament and Council Directive 2009/147/EC on the conservation of wild birds, OJ 2010 L 20/7.

2 Council Directive 92/43/EEC on the conservation of natural habitats and of wild fauna and flora, OJ 1992 L 206/7.

3 European Parliament and Council Regulation (EU) No 1143/2014 on the prevention and management of the introduction and spread of invasive alien species, OJ 2014 L 317/35.

4 Council Regulation (EC) No 338/97 on the protection of species of wild fauna and flora by regulating trade therein, OJ 1997 L 61/1.

5 Council Directive 83/129/EEC on the importation into Member States of skins of certain seal pups and products derived therefrom, OJ 1983 L 91/30; Council Directive 85/444/EEC amending Council Directive 83/129/EEC on the importation into Member States of skins of certain seal pups and products derived therefrom, OJ 1985 L 259/70; Council Directive 89/370/EEC amending Directive 83/129/EEC on the importation into Member States of skins of certain seal pups and products derived therefrom, OJ 1989 L 163/37.

6 Recitals 1 and 9 European Parliament and Council Regulation (EC) No 1007/2009 on trade in seal products, OJ 2009 L 286/36.

7 *G. Van Hoorick*, Internationaal en Europees Natuurbehoudsrecht, 1997, pp. 257–258.

all wild bird species, while the habitats directive applies to a select number of wild animals (non-bird species) and the animal welfare regulations apply, in an extremely fragmented manner,[8] to wild animals.

The cornerstones of the EU's nature conservation legislation are the Birds Directive and the habitats directive. Therefore, the jumping-off point of this chapter will, in particular, be an examination of the extent to which both directives can converge even more closely.

The current legal basis for species protection in the Treaty on the Functioning of the European Union (TFEU)[9] is Title XX 'Environment' (Article 191 TFEU).

The Birds Directive will celebrate its 40th anniversary this year. While the original treaty from four decades ago establishing the European Economic Community (EEC Treaty) contained no provision to act in the area of environmental policy, the Birds Directive was adopted on the basis of Article 235 of the EEC Treaty.[10] This chapter allows for unanimous intervention by the Council 'if action by the Community should prove necessary to attain, in the course of the operation of the common market, one of the objectives of the Community and this Treaty has not provided the necessary powers'.[11]

However, when adopting the habitats directive, the EEC Treaty did contain a specific legal basis for environmental legislation (Articles 130 R-T) due to an amendment by the Single European Act.[12] The Habitats Directive was adopted on the basis of Article 130 S.[13]

2.1.2. Animal Welfare

In the field of animal welfare, certain legislative instruments exist which intervene in animal welfare aspects at the EU level – for example, the regulation on the protection of animals during transport and related operations,[14] the regulation on the protection of animals at the time of killing,[15] and the directive on animals used for scientific purposes.[16] European animal welfare law mainly

---

8 *A. Nurse & D. Ryland*, Mainstreaming after Lisbon: Advancing Animal Welfare in the EU Internal Market, European Energy and Environmental Law Review 2013 (June), pp. 101, 104.

9 Consolidated version of the Treaty on the Functioning of the European Union, OJ 2012 C 326/47.

10 First recital of the preamble of the Birds Directive (non-consolidated version).

11 *W. Wils*, The Birds Directive 15 Years Later: A Survey of the Case Law and a Comparison with the Habitats Directive, Journal of Environmental Law 1994 (6)2, pp. 219, 223.

12 Single European Act, OJ 1987 L 169/1.

13 *Wils*, *supra* note 11 at p. 224; *Van Hoorick*, *supra* note 7 at p. 26.

14 Council Regulation (EC) No 1/2005 on the protection of animals during transport and related operations and amending Directives 64/432/EEC and 93/119/EC and Regulation (EC) No 1255/97, OJ 2005 L 3/1.

15 Council Regulation (EC) No 1099/2009 on the protection of animals at the time of killing, OJ 2009 L 303/1.

16 European Parliament and Council Directive 2010/63/EU on the protection of animals used for scientific purposes, OJ 2010 L 276/33 (recitals 1, 2, 6 and 12).

targets domesticated animals; but, to a limited extent, wild animals[17] are also covered.[18]

Unlike species protection, animal welfare still lacks a specific legal basis. Since the Lisbon Treaty,[19] animal welfare has been mentioned in the context of Article 13 of the TFEU. Nonetheless, this article is a mere integration clause, where animal welfare must be taken into account when 'formulating and implementing the Union's agriculture, fisheries, transport, internal market, research and technological development and space policies'.[20] European animal welfare legislation is based on secondary EU legislation, which, in addition to an animal welfare objective, primarily has another objective (e.g. Article 4 TFEU, Article 192 TFEU).[21]

2.2. TOWARDS MORE HARMONISATION

The term 'harmonisation' covers a wide range of connotations. In terms of a general interpretation, it means to encourage unification of legislation. However, at the EU level, harmonisation in legal jargon is also used as a specific term to indicate the degree of policy freedom that Member States retain when transposing European directives.[22,23] For example, regarding the birds directive, the European Court of Justice (ECJ) clarifies that 'With regard to Article 36 of the Treaty [...] a directive providing for full harmonization of national legislation deprives a Member State of recourse to that Article'[24] and 'As regards the degree of harmonization brought about by Directive 79/409 [...]. The Directive has therefore regulated exhaustively the Member States' powers with regard to the conservation of wild birds'.[25]

---

17 Council Regulation (EEC) No 348/81 on common rules for imports of whales or other cetacean products, OJ 1981 L 39/1; Council Directive 83/129/EEC on the importation into Member States of skins of certain seal pups and products derived therefrom, OJ 1983 L 91/30; Council Regulation (EEC) No 3254/91 prohibiting the use of leghold traps in the Community and the introduction into the Community of pelts and manufactured goods of certain wild animal species originating in countries which catch them by means of leghold traps or trapping methods which do not meet international humane trapping standards, OJ 1991 L 308/1.

18 *N. De Sadeleer*, EU Environmental law and the internal market, 2014, p. 294; *Van Hoorick, supra* note 7 at pp. 257–259.

19 Treaty of Lisbon amending the Treaty on European Union and the Treaty establishing the European Community, OJ 2007 C 306/1.

20 *E. Verniers*, Geen Europees biologisch logo voor ritueel geslacht vlees: Dierenwelzijn in de Europese Unie, NJW 2019, to publish (No. 407 – September 2019).

21 *De Sadeleer, supra* note 18 at p. 136; *Nurse & Ryland, supra* note 8 at pp. 103–104.

22 Article 288 TFEU: A directive shall be binding, as to the result to be achieved, upon each Member State to which it is addressed, but shall leave to the national authorities the choice of form and methods.

23 *De Sadeleer, supra* note 18 at pp. 231–232; *L. Lavrysen*, Handboek milieurecht, 2016, p. 109.

24 Case C-169/89, Gourmetterie Van den Burg [1990] ECR I-2143, para. 8.

25 Ibid. at para. 9.

Any reference in this paper to the objective of more harmonisation is intended to unify European legislation. This harmonisation can take two forms: on the one hand, more harmonisation between animal welfare and species protection; and on the other hand, more harmonisation within species protection. The core of this chapter mainly concerns the elimination of the differences between the Birds Directive and the habitats directive.

3. IDENTIFICATION OF THE DIFFERENT TREATMENT

To demonstrate the different treatment of wild animals in the EU, the applicable legislation as well as some case law will be examined.

3.1. LEGAL REGIMES: THE SCOPE OF APPLICATION

Depending on the type of animal, the Birds Directive applies to wild bird species, while the habitats directive applies to wild animal species.

3.1.1. Birds Directive

Article 1 (1) of the Birds Directive relates to 'the conservation of all species of naturally occurring birds in the wild state in the European territory of the Member States to which the Treaty applies'. Thus, in principle, the Birds Directive seeks to apply to all bird species,[26] including 'rare mutants'.[27] Nevertheless, the 'general system of protection' (Article 5 Birds Directive) is being mitigated by Articles 6 (marketing), 7 (hunting) and 9 (derogations) of the Birds Directive. In addition, ECJ case law has also had an impact on the scope of the application of the Birds Directive. In the van der Feesten case, the ECJ clarified that 'the Directive applies to bird subspecies which occur naturally in the wild only outside the European territory of the Member States if the species to which they belong or other subspecies of that species occur naturally in the wild within the territory in question'.[28] The Vergy case, on the one hand confirmed the van der Feesten case law,[29] while leading to a narrowing of the scope of the Birds Directive. The ECJ ruled that 'the Directive is not applicable to specimens of birds born and reared in captivity'.[30] When birds born and reared in captivity

26 Case C-247/85, Commission v. Belgium [1987] ECR 3029, paras. 18–22.
27 Ibid. at paras. 51–52.
28 Case C-202/94, van der Feesten [1996] ECR I-355, para. 18.
29 Case C-149/94, Vergy [1996] ECR I-299, paras. 16–18.
30 Ibid. at paras. 14–15.

are reintroduced into the wild, they once again fall with the scope of the Birds Directive.[31]

The broad scope of the Birds Directive results in protection for 'opportunistic'[32] bird species (e.g. Eurasian jay, Eurasian magpie, carrion crow), similar to the protection of other (more significant) bird species (e.g. little bustard, garganey).[33] Articles 2, 3, 5, 6, 10 and 13 of the Birds Directive apply to all birds, regardless of whether they are listed in Annex I.[34]

The criticism concerning the extensive protection of opportunistic (bird) species is that it is at the expense of the protection of more critical species.[35] The problem is, after all, that energy is wasted by using resources and personnel to secure opportunistic species, whereas this would be better spent on species that really need protection. Similarly, national courts[36] and the ECJ[37] have already had to deal with numerous cases concerning opportunistic species.

3.1.2. Habitats Directive

As an overall objective, Article 2 (1) habitats directive refers to 'ensuring biodiversity through the conservation of natural habitats and of wild fauna and flora in the European territory of the Member States to which the Treaty applies'. Nevertheless, this objective must be tempered because the tangible measures are limited to the 'species of wild fauna[38] of Community interest', as referred to in Article 2 (2) of the Habitats Directive.[39]

---

31 *N. De Sadeleer*, Bilan d'une décennie d'efforts législatifs en droit communautaire de la protection de la nature, in: *P. Van Pelt* (ed.) Recente ontwikkelingen in het Europees Milieurecht, 1995, pp. 199, 216.

32 *Opportunistic species* are species that do not depend on a particular habitat, adapt well to the changed living conditions caused by human intervention in the environment and are therefore able to expand considerably.

33 *J. Bouckaert*, Artikel 9 van de Vogelrichtlijn, 1989, pp. 26–27.

34 *Van Hoorick, supra* note 7 at p. 193.

35 *Bouckaert, supra* note 33.

36 For example: Court of Appeal (Antwerp, Belgium) [17 December 1982], note *A. Vandeplas*, De verdelging van houtduiven, *RW 1983–84*, pp. 1407–1409; Council of State (Belgium), Case n° 29.327 [12 February 1988], *Amén. 1988/2*, pp. 61–62; Council of State (the Netherlands), Case n° A-31 3865 (1981)/S1151 [7 August 1981], *Milieu en Recht 1982*, pp. 129–130; Council of State (the Netherlands), Case n° A-1.0511 (1982) [6 March 1986], *Milieu en Recht 1987*, pp. 16–19; Supreme Court (the Netherlands), Case n° 14122 [15 February 1991], ECLI:NL:HR:1991:ZC0150.

37 Case C-247/85, Commission v. Belgium [1987] ECR 3029, paras. 10–11, 30–31; Case C-262/85, Commission v. Italy [1987] ECR 3073, para. 11; Case C-236/85, Commission v. the Netherlands [1987] ECR 3989, para. 7; Case C-339/87, Commission v. the Netherlands [1990] ECR I-851, paras. 9–10.

38 NB: the text of the Habitats Directive refers to 'fauna and *flora*', but since this contribution is exclusively about animals, the reference is always confined to the 'animal species of Community interest'.

39 Article 2 (2) Habitats Directive: 'Measures taken pursuant to this Directive shall be designed to maintain or restore, at favourable conservation status, natural habitats and species of wild fauna and flora of Community interest.'.

An initial discrepancy arises: while the birds directive aims to preserve 'all species of naturally occurring wild birds in the European territory', is the scope of the Habitats Directive *in concreto* limited to the conservation of 'wild fauna species of Community interest'? These species of community interest are defined by Article 1 (g) of the Habitats Directive, which refers to species that are endangered, vulnerable, rare or endemic. These species are (or may be) listed in Annexes II[40] and/or IV[41] or V.[42,43]

A second difference between the two directives relates to the specific species protection measures, in particular, the difference between Article 5 of the birds directive and Article 12 of the Habitats Directive. Contrary to Article 5 of the birds directive, Article 12 of the Habitats Directive does not provide a general system of protection, but *a priori* limited the protection of wild animal species to those set out in Annex IV (a). The strict protection regime of Article 12 of the Habitats Directive (the 'second pillar')[44] therefore only applies to a small number of animal species.

Finally, the difference in scope means that the problem concerning opportunistic species does not occur here, precisely because of the limited scope of the Habitats Directive. After all, no opportunistic animal species has been included in Annex II (a), IV (a) or V (a) of the Habitats Directive. This results in a difference in treatment between, for example, the crow and the fox. While the Birds Directive does apply to crows, the Habitats Directive does not apply to foxes; yet, both animals are considered 'opportunistic' species.

3.1.3. *The Different Treatment in Legislation*

An initial difference that emerges from the legal framework above is the scope of application. While the Birds Directive establishes a general system of protection for all bird species on European territory (as referred to in Article 1), the Habitats Directive is limited to animal species of Community interest, listed in Annexes II (a), IV (a) and V (a). This means that all animals not listed in those annexes are the responsibility of the Member State itself and subject to national legislation. For example, keeping a certain mammal is only prohibited if prohibited by the national legislation of a Member State (with the exception of the animals listed on Annex IV (a) Habitats Directive).

---

40 Annex II (a): Animal species of community interest whose conservation requires the designation of special areas of conservation.

41 Annex IV (a): Animal species of community interest in need of strict protection.

42 Annex V (a): Animal species of community interest whose taking in the wild and exploitation may be subject to management measures.

43 Article 1 (g), last subparagraph.

44 *H. Schoukens & K. Bastmeijer*, Species Protection in the European Union: How Strict Is Strict?, in: *A. Cliquet, C-H. Born, D. Misonne, G. Van Hoorick & H. Schoukens* (eds.) The Habitats Directive in its EU Environmental Law Context: European Nature's Best Hope?, 2014, pp. 1, 3, 11.

3.2. CASE LAW

The different treatment for animals can also be demonstrated by case law. I will discuss three cases, all of which relate to the import ban on certain animal species.

3.2.1. Gourmetterie Van den Burg Case[45]

Gourmetterie Van den Burg was the defendant in a Dutch criminal case involving the red grouse. He was prosecuted and convicted for infringing Article 7 of the Dutch Law on Birds (the Vogelwet), which precluded the bird in question from being bought or sold on the domestic (Dutch) market. Van den Burg argued that he could not be convicted for violating this law, since the confiscated red grouse had been lawfully killed in the UK, in accordance with the Birds Directive.[46,47]

The Dutch Supreme Court ('Hoge Raad') accordingly referred to the ECJ for a preliminary ruling on the compatibility of the import ban of the red grouse, with regard to Articles 30 and 36 of the EEC Treaty.[48]

The ECJ observed that the red grouse is a species which does not occur within the Netherlands.[49] Additionally, the ECJ noted that it was indisputable that the national measure in question was in the nature of a measure having an effect equivalent to a quantitative restriction within the meaning of Article 30 of the EEC Treaty, which may be justified on the basis of protecting the health and life of animals (Article 36 EEC Treaty).

However, the ECJ recollected that set case law held that a directive providing for full harmonisation of national legislation deprives a Member State of recourse to Article 36 of the EEC Treaty. Consequently, regarding the degree of harmonisation brought about by the Birds Directive, it should be noted that the directive exhaustively regulated Member States' powers concerning the conservation of wild birds. As a result, Member States can solely invoke Article 14 of the Birds Directive to justify stricter protective measures.[50]

The ECJ limits the scope of Article 14 to migratory species, endangered species listed in Annex I of the Birds Directive, and endangered species within the meaning of the CITES convention. In terms of the other bird species covered by the Birds Directive, Member States are not authorised to adopt stricter

45 Case C-169/89, Gourmetterie Van den Burg [1990] ECR I-2143.

46 The red grouse (*Lagopus lagopus scoticus*) is listed on Annex III/1 to the Birds Directive and therefore constitutes an exception to the fundamental prohibition of trade in Article 6 (1) Birds Directive, in accordance with Article 6 (2) Birds Directive.

47 Case C-169/89, Gourmetterie Van den Burg [1990] ECR I-2143, paras. 1–2.

48 Ibid. at paras. 3–4.

49 Ibid. at para. 7.

50 Ibid. at paras. 8–9.

protective measures than those provided for under the directive, except in the case of species occurring within their territory.[51]

From the foregoing, it follows that the Netherlands was not empowered to afford the red grouse more protection than that provided for by the Birds Directive, because the red grouse is neither a migratory species nor a seriously endangered species set out in Annex I of the Birds Directive or the CITES.[52]

3.2.2. *German Crayfish Case*[53]

The German crayfish case concerned a German import restriction on imports of live European freshwater crayfish from Member States or from non-member countries in free circulation in other Member States. The German Federal Regulation on the Protection of Species ('Bundersartenschutzverordnung') made the importation of such crayfish subject to the grant of a licence. The underlying idea was to stop the crayfish plague caused by the importation of infected crayfish from North America, resulting in the virtual disappearance of wild native crayfish from European waters.[54]

The Commission appealed and found that the German rules in question were incompatible with Articles 30 and 36 of the EEC Treaty, on the grounds that the rules went beyond what was needed for the effective protection of native species of crayfish against disease and the risks of faunal distortion.[55]

The German government contends that the quantitative restriction is justified under Article 36 of the EEC Treaty on the basis of the protection of the health and life of animals (preventing epizootic disease).[56]

The ECJ assessed that it was not disputed that the purpose of the national measure in question is to protect the health and life of native crayfish, meaning that the measure is accordingly covered by the exception provided for in Article 36 of the Treaty. However, rules restricting intra-community trade are compatible with the Treaty, only insofar as they are indispensable for the purposes of providing effective protection for the health and life of animals.[57]

In this case, the German restrictions did not satisfy the principle of proportionality, because the objective could have been achieved by measures having less restrictive effects on intra-community trade. For example, instead of simply prohibiting imports of all species of live freshwater crayfish, Germany could have confined itself to health checks and only carrying out checks by sample.[58]

---

[51] Ibid. at paras. 10–14.
[52] Ibid. at paras. 15–16.
[53] Case C-131/93, Commission v. Germany [1994] ECR I-3303.
[54] Ibid. at paras. 1–3.
[55] Ibid. at para. 5.
[56] Ibid. at para. 6.
[57] Ibid. at paras. 17–18.
[58] Ibid. at paras. 19–25.

3.2.3. *Bluhme Case*[59]

In the Bluhme case, a preliminary ruling was referred to the ECJ in the context of criminal proceedings against Bluhme. Bluhme was tried for infringement of Danish legislation ('lov om biavl') prohibiting the keeping of bees on the island of Læsø, other than those of the Læsø brown bee subspecies (*Apis mellifera mellifera*).[60]

By analogy with the previous cases, the central question was whether the Danish national legislation did or did not infringe Article 30 of the EEC Treaty.[61]

The prohibition was motivated by the desire to protect the Læsø brown bee from extinction. It was also noted that the geographical scope of the prohibition was limited to Læsø and some neighbouring islands.[62]

Contrary to the previous cases, the ECJ accepted the import ban. When verifying the proportionality test, the ECJ held that the limitation of the geographical scope of the prohibition did not alter the fact that the Danish restriction constitutes a measure having an effect equivalent to a quantitative restriction.[63] Nevertheless, the limited geographical scope was compared to the recognised method of establishing areas in which a population can enjoy special protection (i.e. the SPA and SAC of the Birds and Habitats Directive).[64] With regard to the disappearance of the Læsø brown bee, the ECJ considered this risk to be undeniably genuine, in the event of mating with golden bees, due to the recessive nature of the genes of the brown bee.[65]

Subsequently, the ECJ arrived at the conclusion that the Danish legislative measure must be regarded as justified, under Article 36 of the Treaty, on the basis of the protection of the health and life of animals.[66]

3.2.4. *The Different Treatment in Case Law*

The discussed cases illustrate that, depending on whether the case concerns a bird or another animal, a different judgement is obtained. The explanation for these disparities is due to the difference in the scope for policymaking entrusted to Member States in the case of bird species on the one hand and other animal species on the other.[67]

59 Case C-67/97, Bluhme [1998] ECR I-8033.
60 Ibid. at para. 2.
61 Ibid. at para. 8.
62 Ibid. at paras. 6–7.
63 Ibid. at paras. 17–20.
64 Ibid. at para. 36.
65 Ibid. at para. 37.
66 Ibid. at para. 38.
67 *Supra* para. 10.

Articles 30 and 36 of the EEC Treaty have been invoked in all three court cases. The defence in each case was the 'protection of the health and life of animals'.

In the Gourmetterie Van den Burg case, invoking Article 36 was not allowed due to full harmonisation (i.e., Member States are deprived of any margin of policymaking) of the Birds Directive.[68]

By contrast, the invocation of Article 36 of the EEC Treaty was accepted in the German crayfish and Bluhme cases because the argument of 'full' harmonisation does not play a part in the Habitats Directive, which necessitated recourse to the classic provisions regarding the free movement of goods. For example, the strict protection regime of Article 12 of the Habitats Directive only applies to animals listed in Annex IV (a), while other animal species fall under the policy freedom of Member States. Since neither crayfish nor brown bees were covered by Annex IV (a) of the Habitats Directive, this resulted in these animals being dependent on a possible protection status provided by a Member State. It was this German and Danish protection status for the crayfish, *casu quo* the Læsø brown bee, that was challenged on the basis of Articles 30 and 36 of the E(E)C Treaty.

Both the German crayfish and the Bluhme cases were about fauna falsification, yet only in the Bluhme case was the import ban accepted. While the Danish ban was necessary and proportionate in relation to its aim of protection and therefore in conformity with Article 36 of the EC Treaty, the German ban did not meet the test of proportionality because it could be replaced by less restrictive measures.

The previous judgements reveal that, with regard to non-bird species, a case-by-case approach is used, because the Habitats Directive does not cover all animals, while the Birds Directive does cover all birds.

4. EXPLAINING THE DIFFERENCE IN TREATMENT

As indicated above, there exists a difference in treatment for wild animals in the EU. This section will examine the reasons for this difference and whether the *prima facies* major differences between the Birds Directive and Habitats Directive do have a logical explanation.

4.1. A HISTORICAL EXPLANATION

An initial explanation can be found in the historical course of international law. While the focus on wild animals (non-bird species) only began to emerge at the

68 Case C-169/89, Gourmetterie Van den Burg [1990] ECR I-2143, paras. 8–9.

end of the 20th century,[69] this was already the case for bird species at the very beginning of that century.[70] Historically, therefore, the attention given to birds has always been stronger than for other animal species.

The general principle of protection, as found in Article 1 of the Birds Directive, was first introduced by the Paris Convention of 1950.[71] Previously, the scope of application was limited to a specific category of bird species,[72] whereas Article 1 of the 1950 Paris Convention aimed at the protection of *all* wild bird species.[73]

The Habitats Directive, on the other hand, is based on the Bern Convention[74,75]

Article 2 of the Habitats Directive is modelled on Article 1 of the Bern Convention.[76] Both instruments provide for the conservation of wildlife as a general objective, but limit concrete measures to specific species.[77] However, the Habitats Directive does not completely follow the example of the Bern Convention, as the species lists of the latter are much more extensive and have only been adopted to a limited extent by the Habitats Directive. Appendix 2 of the Bern Convention has a much greater species coverage (approximately 120 animals more) than Annex IV (a) of the Habitats Directive.

The different predecessors of the directives explain the different protection status between birds and other animals. Whereas the Paris Convention of 1950 provided for a general protection status, the Bern Convention operated with a specific protection status that depended on the enumeration of a certain animal in the appendices.

---

69 Convention on International Trade in Endangered Species of Wild Fauna and Flora, Washington, 3 March 1973, in force 1 July 1975, 993 UNTS 243; Convention on the Conservation of Migratory Species of Wild Animals, Bonn, 23 June 1979, in force 1 November 1983, 19 ILM (1980), Cmnd 7888; Convention on the Conservation of European Wildlife and Natural Habitats, Bern, 19 September 1979, in force 1 June 1982, UKTS No 56 (1982), Cmnd 8738.

70 Convention for the Protection of Birds Useful to Agriculture, Paris, 19 March 1902, in force 6 December 1905, 191 CTS 91; International Convention for the Protection of Birds, Paris, 18 October 1950, in force 17 January 1963, 9134 UNTS 187; Benelux Convention on the Hunting and Protection of Birds, Brussels, 10 June 1970, in force 1 July 1972, 1214 UNTS 325.

71 International Convention for the Protection of Birds, Paris, 18 October 1950, in force 17 January 1963, 9134 UNTS 187.

72 For instance, the 1902 Paris Convention on the protection of *birds useful to agriculture*.

73 See also the Preamble: 'Considering that, in the interests of science, the protection of nature and the economy of each nation, *all* birds should as a matter of principle be protected;'.

74 Convention on the Conservation of European Wildlife and Natural Habitats, Bern, 19 September 1979, in force 1 June 1982, UKTS No 56 (1982), Cmnd 8738.

75 *Schoukens & Bastmeijer*, *supra* note 44 at pp. 12–13; *Van Hoorick*, *supra* note 7 at pp. 142, 224.

76 Article 1 (1) Convention on the Conservation of European Wildlife and Natural Habitats: 'The aims of this Convention are to conserve wild flora and fauna and their natural habitats, especially those species and habitats whose conservation requires the co-operation of several States, and to promote such co-operation'.

77 Article 1 (2). Convention on the Conservation of European Wildlife and Natural Habitats: 'Particular emphasis is given to endangered and vulnerable species, including endangered and vulnerable migratory species'.

4.2. A POLITICAL EXPLANATION

A second explanation for the differences between the Birds Directive and the Habitats Directive relates to the point in time when each directive was drawn up.

While the Habitats Directive has been in place since 1992, the Birds Directive dates back to 1979. The starting point of the Birds Directive was to offer the broadest protection possible to all birds (covered in Article 1, Birds Directive). This optimism was reflected in a strict policy with the result that opportunistic species, such as the European herring gull and the carrion crow, were also protected.

The legal cases (national and European) in the context of opportunistic species caused Member States to show reluctance in pursuing a 'gold-plating' approach *avant la lettre* to the adoption of the Habitats Directive.[78] Thus, when drafting the Habitats Directive, Member States (and political decision-makers) were much more cautious and did not wish to duplicate the far-reaching implications of the Birds Directive. The legal doctrine also criticised the extensive protection of opportunistic species.[79]

This was therefore anticipated by limiting the scope to the species of community interest. Instead of either following the example of the Birds Directive, on the one hand, or copying the extensive appendixes of the Bern Convention, on the other, policy-makers decided to create new (and more limited) species lists and classifications (i.e. Annex IV (a)).

5. THE SIGNIFICANCE OF THE DIFFERENT TREATMENT

So far, the existence of differences in treatment for wildlife in the EU has been demonstrated, and explanations for these differences have been explained. The following section examines whether these differences cause specific problems, addressing both policy and legal obstacles.

The key question concerns the EU's ambiguous attitude, whereby Europe does not trust Member States with regard to wild bird species and, for example, strictly regulates the protection of opportunistic bird species, while, with regard to the Habitats Directive, the EU places full confidence in Member States and allows them to regulate the protection of non-bird species with quasi-freedom.

5.1. POLICY BOTTLENECKS

Why Europe sets the bar so high for birds and so low for mammals, reptiles and fish is incomprehensible from a policy point of view. From the point of view of

[78] *Supra* para. 15.

[79] *Bouckaert*, *supra* note 33.

nature conservation, it is just as important to protect wild non-bird species as it is to protect wild bird species.

The safe conduct for Member States in respect of non-bird species does not benefit wild fauna in Europe. Various scientific studies have highlighted the decline in animal species occurring in the EU, but which fall outside the protection of the Habitats Directive. For example, a report by the European Environment Agency reveals an almost 50 per cent decline in 17 European grassland butterfly populations.[80] Butterflies examined in the report include the common blue,[81] which has declined significantly,[82] but the small heath,[83] the wall brown,[84] the small copper,[85] the meadow brown[86] and the dingy skipper[87] are also regressing.[88] None of them is listed in the annexes of the Habitats Directive. Another study regarding bee species in the EU finds that 9.1 per cent of EU bee species are threatened with extinction and a further 5.4 per cent of bees are considered to be 'near threatened'.[89] Furthermore, cross-border cooperation between Belgium and France reveals that, in addition to an absence of European legal protection, there is also a lack of national legal protection for bees.[90] A non-exhaustive list of examples of mammals that fall outside the scope of the Habitats Directive includes the Bavarian pile vole[91] (critically endangered), the broom hare[92] (vulnerable), the Corsican hare[93] (vulnerable) and the Cretan white-toothed shrew[94] (vulnerable).[95] Not only rare species, but also more common animal species are susceptible. For instance, while the garden dormouse[96] is not yet threatened,[97] this species declined more than almost any other rodent in Europe and may have disappeared from 50 per cent of its former ranges during the last 30 years.[98]

---

80 *C. van Swaay et al.*, The European Grassland Butterfly Indicator: 1990–2011, 2013, p. 19.

81 Polyommatus icarus.

82 *C. van Swaay et al.*, *supra* note 80 at p. 17.

83 Coenonympha pamphilus.

84 Lasiommata megera.

85 Lycaena phlaeas.

86 Maniola jurtina.

87 Erynnis tages.

88 *C. van Swaay et al.*, *supra* note 80 at p. 15.

89 *A. Nieto et al.*, European Red List of Bees, 2014, pp. viii, ix, 10 et seq.

90 *M. Folschweiller et al.*, Grensoverschrijdend actieplan voor wilde bestuivers. Interreg V SAPOLL project – Sauvons nos pollinisateurs-Samenwerken voor pollinators, 2019, p. 26.

91 Microtus bavaricus.

92 Lepus castroviejoi.

93 Lepus corsicanus.

94 Crocidura zimmermanni.

95 *A. Terry & H. J. Temple*, The Status and Distribution of European Mammals, 2007, pp. ix, 10, 12.

96 Eliomys quercinus.

97 IUCN Red List of Threatened Species classification = near threatened; *S. Bertolino et al.*, Eliomys quercinus. The IUCN Red List of Threatened Species, 2008, https://www.iucnredlist.org/species/7618/12835766.

98 *Terry & Temple*, *supra* note 95 at p. 18.

From a nature conservation point of view, there is no genuine justification for treating wild bird species differently from wild mammals and other species.

5.2. LEGAL BOTTLENECKS

The difference in treatment resulting from the directives constitutes a policy rather than a legal problem. Few cases reach the level of the ECJ. The Bluhme and German crayfish cases have already been discussed above.

The distinction in the scope and level of harmonisation (in a strict legal sense) between the two directives implies uncertainty about an analogous application of the Vergy and Gourmetterie Van den Burg cases to the Habitats Directive.

The protection of mammals and other non-bird species is regulated by national legislation, because the EU did not provide a similar level of harmonisation (scope for policymaking) for the Habitats Directive as is the case for the Birds Directive. As mentioned above, this needs to be nuanced with regard to the animal species listed in Annex IV (a), which are subject to the strict protection regime of Article 12 of the Habitats Directive.[99] Consequently, only these animals (the majority of which are reptiles) are subject to harmonisation.

In practice, the different protection status of the directives does not cause any problems, because Member States in fact provide protection status for animal species that do not fall within the scope of the Habitats Directive.

For example, Germany protects all mammals with the exception of certain mice, rats, the mink (Mustela vison), the coypu, the raccoon dog, the muskrat and the raccoon.[100] In the Flemish Region, the species decree provides for the protection of 15 mammals.[101] The Netherlands, similar to Belgium, have a list of specific animals that are protected. The Dutch list consists of 33 mammals, including the fox, the wild boar and the badger.[102] Opportunists often, but not always, fall outside the scope of protection.[103]

---

99 *Supra* para. 32.

100 Annex 1 (concerning §1) to the Decree on the Protection of Wild Species of Animals and Plants (Germany), [Verordnung zum Schutz wild lebender Tier- ind Pflanzenarten, BArtSchV], https://www.gesetze-im-internet.de/bartschv_2005/anlage_1.html.

101 Article N1 Decree of the Flemish Government on species protection and species management (Belgium), [Besluit van de Vlaamse Regering met betrekking tot soortenbescherming en soortenbeheer, het Soortenbesluit], http://www.ejustice.just.fgov.be/eli/besluit/2009/05/15/2009035724/justel.

102 Annex to Article 3.10 Act on the protection of nature (the Netherlands), [Wet houdende regels ter bescherming van de natuur, Wet natuurbescherming], https://wetten.overheid.nl/BWBR0037552/2019-01-01.

103 For example, the common vole is not protected in Germany and the Flemish Region, but it is protected in the Netherlands. On the other hand, the mole, for example, is protected in Germany, but not in the Netherlands or the Flemish Region.

Additional scientific research is required to clarify the differences in national species protection between Member States and whether these differences give rise to legal problems, but this falls outside the scope of this research. The general trend, however, is that the room for manoeuvre given to Member States is indeed being used, but to different extents.

In an oversimplified sense, both guidelines intend to achieve the same goal, but with a disparate approach. The aim of both directives is to protect as many bird and non-bird species as possible, which are in need of a protection regime.

The Birds Directive explicitly declared Article 1 of the Birds Directive applicable to all bird species in the European territory, while, at the same time, catching the opportunistic species by having them listed in Annex II ('huntable bird species').[104]

The Habitats Directive establishes a different method by including only a limited number of animal species in the strict protection regime and leaves the protection of the other animals to the discretion of Member States. With this method, opportunistic species once again fall outside the scope of any protection, but this time implicitly in the sense that, contrary to the Birds Directive, they were never *a priori* protected.

Admittedly, the working method of the Habitats Directive can be blamed for a lack of uniformity, because an exact protection status differs from one Member State to another, and from one animal to another. In Poland, for example, in a move to tackle an epidemic of African swine fever, the wild boar is hunted on a massive scale (outside the hunting season), whereas, in the Netherlands and Germany, the wild boar is protected outside the hunting season.[105] Even within the same Member State, there are inequalities, for example, the Brussels-Capital Region provides a general protection for the fox, while, in the Flemish Region, one third of the fox population is shot each year.[106] Applying Articles 7 and 9 of the Birds Directive by analogy could temper this.

Nevertheless, this lack of uniformity can be balanced by the principle of subsidiarity, which is respected. The principle of subsidiarity is reflected in the fact that the Habitats Directive, on the one hand, designates species of community interest and, on the other hand, allows Member States to provide for their own species protection which meets their respective needs and characteristics.

---

104 See Article 7, Birds Directive.

105 S. *Walker*, Planned wild boar cull in Poland angers conservationists, The Guardian, 11 January 2019, https://www.theguardian.com/environment/2019/jan/11/planned-wild-boar-cull-in-poland-angers-conservationists.

106 Question n°222 Q&A Flemish Parliament (Belgium) [*Vr. en antw.* Vl. Parl., vr. nr. 222, 14 December 2015 (P. DE BRUYN, antw. J. SCHAUVLIEGE)], https://www.vlaamsparlement.be/parlementaire-documenten/schriftelijke-vragen/1022172.

5.3. ANIMAL WELFARE BOTTLENECKS

The impact of the difference in treatment was discussed above from a nature conservation point of view. The conclusion was that, although species protection status for (bird) species is provided for in law, the differentiation in protection is difficult to justify, especially from a nature conservation point of view.

It has already been mentioned[107] that European animal welfare legislation applies to wild animals in a very restrictive and fragmentary manner. This is because animal welfare does not have an independent European legal basis and is therefore predominantly a competence for Member States, with varying standards of animal welfare as a result.[108]

National animal welfare legislation pervades European species protection.[109] In case C-100/08, the Belgian State justified the limit on trade in wild birds to birds having a metallic ring on imperative requirements concerning both biodiversity and animal welfare.[110]

Another striking example where animal welfare interferes with species protection concerns 'positive lists'. These are national lists, drawn up based on animal welfare considerations that enumerate which animals may be kept. If an animal is not on the list, it may not be kept due to animal welfare considerations, even though it may be kept on the basis of species protection law. An example is the Belgian positive list for mammals,[111] which allows only 42 mammals to be kept in Belgium. Recently, the Flemish government has also ratified a positive list for reptiles. This list was entered into force on 1 October 2019 and contains 422 reptiles.[112] The Netherlands also has a positive list for mammals based on animal welfare.[113]

In the past, such a positive list has already led to a preliminary ruling before the ECJ.[114] Animal breeders and animal keepers often disagree with the national

---

107 *Supra* para. 6.

108 *Nurse & Ryland*, *supra* note 8 at p. 104 et seq.

109 *De Sadeleer*, *supra* note 20.

110 Case C-100/08, Commission v. Belgium [2009] ECR I-140, paras. 91–93.

111 Royal Decree establishing a list of mammals not kept for production purposes that may be kept (Belgium), [Koninklijk besluit tot vaststelling van de lijst van niet voor productiedoeleinden gehouden zoogdieren die gehouden mogen worden], http://www.ejustice.just.fgov.be/eli/besluit/2009/07/16/2009024254/justel.

112 Decree of the Flemish Government establishing the list of reptiles that may be kept (Belgium), [Besluit van de Vlaamse Regering tot vaststelling van de lijst van reptielen die gehouden mogen worden], http://www.ejustice.just.fgov.be/eli/besluit/2019/03/22/2019030349/staatsblad.

113 Article 2.2 Act on an integral framework for keeping animals and related subjects (the Netherlands), [Wet houdende een integraal kader voor regels over gehouden dieren en daaraan gerelateerde onderwerpen, Wet dieren], https://wetten.overheid.nl/BWBR0030250/2019-01-01#Hoofdstuk2 and Article 1.4 Decree establishing regulations with regard to animal keepers (the Netherlands), [Besluit houdende regels met betrekking tot houders van dieren, Besluit houders van dieren], https://wetten.overheid.nl/BWBR0035217/2018-07-01#Hoofdstuk1.

114 Case C-219/07, Andibel and others [2008] ECR I-4475.

lists and do everything in their power to undermine them.[115] This was the scenario in the Andibel case, where it was argued that the Belgian positive list for mammals would disproportionately hinder intra-community trade.[116] The ECJ first accepted the existence of a positive list based on animal welfare,[117] insofar as it complies with various conditions listed in the judgement.[118] *In casu*, the Andibel case resulted in the Belgian positive list being amended to comply with the criteria listed by the court.

It remains to be seen whether these national lists will continue to give rise to new court cases requiring European intervention.

Finally, it should be noted that European species protection law has an impact on animal welfare. The limited scope of the Habitats Directive leaves the protection of foxes, for instance, to Member States. While the Brussels capital region actually protects the fox, this is not the case in Flanders, where the fox is hunted to such an extreme degree that the typical lifespan of the fox is reduced to only one year.[119] Note that the young and inexperienced fox population subsequently causes more damage than older onc.[120] The welfare of the fox as a wild species is therefore not achieved in the Flemish Region, because a fox should normally be able to live much longer in the wild (approximately up to four years old).[121]

6. IS (MORE) HARMONISATION THE PREFERRED SOLUTION AND HOW SHOULD THIS LOOK?

Successively, the different treatment of wild animals in the EU is identified; some explanations for, as well as the impact of, the difference in treatment were discussed. In this last part, (more) harmonisation is considered as a possible solution.

As stipulated,[122] harmonisation in this case should be understood as bringing legislation closer together in order to bridge differences. With regard to the treatment of wild animals in Europe, this issue can relate to harmonisation between two domains (i.e. harmonisation between animal welfare and species

115 For instance, a petition (e.g. 'Tegen Positieflijst' Platform Verantwoord Huisdierenbezit, the Netherlands) or legal cases (e.g. Andibel Case, Belgium) against positive lists.

116 Case C-219/07, Andibel and others [2008] ECR I-4475, para. 10.

117 Ibid. at para. 24.

118 Ibid. at paras. 33–36.

119 *K. Van den Berghe*, De vos vulpes vulpes in Vlaanderen: inventarisatie en synthese van de belangrijkste knelpunten, 1995, pp. 1–30.

120 Ibid. at pp. 11–12.

121 *S. Harris*, Age determination in the Red fox (Vulpes vulpes) – an evaluation of technique efficiency as applied to a sample of suburban foxes, Journal of Zoology 2009 (184), pp. 91, 92 et seq.

122 *Supra* para. 10–11.

protection), on the one hand, and harmonisation within the same domain (i.e., harmonisation between the Birds Directive and the Habitats Directive), on the other.

Although the emphasis of this chapter is on harmonisation within the area of species protection, the need for harmonisation between animal welfare and species protection is also briefly outlined below.

6.1. HARMONISATION BETWEEN ANIMAL WELFARE AND SPECIES PROTECTION

The interaction between the two domains has been demonstrated above. Questions can be raised about the feasibility of regulating wild animals from two different angles. For instance, from the species protection point of view, many animal species are protected, yet derogations are granted with regard to a number of animals that may be kept. In addition, animal welfare provides for an additional level by indicating, via positive lists, which animals can be kept from an animal welfare point of view, and does so without any deviation.

A mode of reasoning to avoid overlap and contradiction would be the integration and harmonisation of both domains, as both function as communicating vessels. Currently, the EU lacks a legal basis to harmonise on the basis of animal welfare. Nevertheless, this line of thought is an interesting area for further research.

6.2. HARMONISATION BETWEEN THE BIRDS DIRECTIVE AND HABITATS DIRECTIVE

6.2.1. *Current Status of Harmonisation of the Birds and the Habitats Directives*

As a preliminary remark, it should be noted that the ECJ consistently holds that EU rules do not seek to effect complete harmonisation in the area of the environment.[123]

6.2.1.1. Birds Directive

Article 14 of the Birds Directive allows, at first sight, stricter measures, but the ECJ has clarified, in the Gourmetterie Van den Burg case, that the Birds

[123] Case C-318/98, Fornasar and others [2000] ECR I-4785, para. 46; Case C-6/03, Deponiezweckverband Eiterköpfe [2005] ECR I-2753, para. 27; Case C-2/10 Azienda Agro-Zootecnica Franchini sarl and Eolica di Altamura Srl [2011] ECR I-6561, para. 48.

Directive is almost completely harmonised, and therefore the possibility to apply stricter measures is limited to migratory bird species, as well as endangered bird species listed in Annex I of the Birds Directive or within the meaning of the CITES convention. With regard to other bird species, only the Member State where the bird naturally occurs can apply those stricter measures provided for in Article 14 of the Birds Directive.

6.2.1.2. Habitats Directive

There is no provision in the Habitats Directive that is equivalent to Article 14 of the Birds Directive. Nevertheless, since that directive was adopted based on Article 130 S,[124] it should be noted that Article 130 T[125] allows for Member States to adopt more stringent protective measures. Under that provision, all that is required is for such measures to be compatible with the TFEU and notified to the commission.

In practice, this means that stricter measures are possible for 'harmonised species' (Annex IV (a) Habitats Directive). This prompts the question about to what extent the Gourmetterie Van den Burg and the Vergy cases can be applied by analogy to the Habitats Directive. This would mean that the stricter measures would have to be limited to the Member State's own territory, *casu quo* that the Habitats Directive would not be applicable to animal species born and reared in captivity.

6.2.2. The Aim of More Harmonisation

More harmonisation could help to eliminate the difference in the treatment of wild animals in the EU. This part examines the arguments in favour and those against more harmonisation.

6.2.2.1. Arguments in Favour of More Harmonisation

6.2.2.1.1. Solve Discrepancies between the Birds and the Habitats Directives

The problem concerning opportunistic species is a striking example of when a uniform approach would be more appropriate. As mentioned above, the Birds Directive, in theory, protects all birds. In order to resolve the aforementioned problem, political lobbying ensured that more and more of these 'harmful' birds were placed on Annex II. This allowed them to be hunted and tackled.

124 Currently Article 192 TFEU.
125 Currently Article 193 TFEU.

The Habitats Directive has *a priori* responded to such a problem by limiting itself to the protection of only a few species worthy of protection. The general principle of protection, as formulated in Article 1 of the Birds Directive, has therefore not been adopted by the Habitats Directive.

6.2.2.1.2. Solve Discrepancies under the Habitats Directive

Another issue that harmonisation could resolve is the ECJ's casuistic approach to cases that fall within the scope of Habitats Directive. For example, in the German crayfish case, an import ban was not accepted, whereas, in the Bluhme case, an import ban was permitted; the decision in each case was based on the doctrine of quantitative restrictions (i.e., Article 36 TFEU).

Harmonisation in the strictly legal sense is therefore an argument in supporting harmonisation as a general objective (which was previously referred to).[126]

6.2.2.1.3. Transpose *de facto* Harmonisation into *de jure* Harmonisation

Since the protection of the Habitats Directive is limited to Annex IV (a) on wild species, this creates a web of national legislation regarding other animal species. As a result, each Member State enacts national legislation protecting certain animal species. It may be advisable to regulate this at the EU level and thus transpose *de facto* harmonisation into *de jure* harmonisation. In Belgium, Annex I of the Species Decree contains a list of protected species. The species belonging to Category I are the only species protected from a Flemish point of view. Such a national list also exists in the Netherlands and many other countries. It is striking, for example, that the Dutch list contains 33 mammals, while the Flemish list contains 15 mammals. This results, once again, in different treatment.

6.2.2.2. Arguments against More Harmonisation. Main Argument: Principle of Subsidiarity

The objective of harmonisation must always be weighed against the principle of subsidiarity, so that it becomes clear when harmonisation should take precedence over subsidiarity.

The internal market and the environment are shared competences.[127] A shared competence implies that both the EU and Member States can legislate and

[126] *Supra* para. 10–11.
[127] Article 4 (2) (a) & (e) TFEU.

adopt legally binding acts in this area. The principle of subsidiarity determines the level (European or national) at which action must be taken.[128] The primacy of EU law prevents Member States from taking measures that deviate from those adopted by the EU. However, as long as no EU measures exist, Member States are free to pursue their own policies.

As mentioned above, the protection mechanism used by the Habitats Directive can be considered as a good example that expresses the principle of subsidiarity. It provides for uniform action for species of community interest in need of strict protection, as per Annex IV (a), while, at the same time, allowing for Member States themselves to take measures against other animal species.

An additional counterargument is that animal welfare is already delegated to Member States. Harmonisation of species protection for both bird and non-bird species does not prevent national differences, precisely because animal welfare legislation interferes with species protection. Therefore, in order to be fully unified, species protection cannot be harmonised at the European level without also tackling animal welfare. However, the EU has no legal basis for harmonising animal welfare.

6.2.3. *What, in Practical Terms, can Harmonisation Consist of?*

They are primarily two possibilities: choosing the improvement or the deterioration of the current situation.

6.2.3.1. The Path to Enhanced Protection: The Habitats Directive Following the Example of the Birds Directive

This approach is supported from a nature conservation point of view. As discussed above, there is no reason for nature conservation to treat bird species differently from other animal species. Raising species protection under the Habitats Directive to the same level as the Birds Directive will only benefit nature conservation.

In practice, this would mean that the scope of the Habitats Directive should be broadened by analogy with Article 1 of the Birds Directive. The Habitats Directive should institute a general protection status for all wild animal species on the territory of the EU. Article 12 of the Habitats Directive must also be amended to match Article 5 of the Birds Directive. Similar to the practice regarding the Birds Directive, certain animal species can be removed from the scope of the directive (cf. Annex II Birds Directive).

---

128 Article 5 TEU.

6.2.3.2. The Path to Reduced Protection: The Birds Directive Following the Example of the Habitats Directive

Taking the wrong path, the Birds Directive could be amended in line with the Habitats Directive. In reality, this would be a retrograde step for bird protection and might conflict with the standstill principle in Article 13 of the Birds Directive.

Some politicians will certainly welcome this option, because they no longer have to endure a cumbersome procedure if they want to tackle a certain opportunistic bird species. However, from a scientific point of view, this is not the recommended way forward. Above, reference has already been made to the decline in various animal species. Weakening the current protection status of birds would create a negative spiral with unprecedented repercussions for (European) nature conservation.

7. CONCLUSION

This paper examined the treatment of wild animals at the EU level. In particular, the differences between the Birds Directive and the Habitats Directive were investigated. Although, at first glance, the differences appear to be arbitrary, it was shown that they take a logical historical course. Moreover, they appear to have only limited legal implications. In the end, the issue of harmonisation, for which there are both pro and contra arguments, was tackled. The overall conclusion is that, although not necessary from a strict legal point of view, harmonisation can be encouraged from a nature conservation point of view.

HARMONISATION TRENDS OF ENVIRONMENTAL LIABILITY LAW THROUGH THE TOOLS OF CIVIL LAW

The Examples of Duty of Care and the Right to Personality

Georgios KALOGERAKIS*

1. INTRODUCTION

Since the time of Emperor Justinian (482–565 A.D.), the lack of harmonisation in civil law has been resolved by a single process: codification.[1] All the major codifications of the 19th and 20th centuries worked towards tidying up

* Doctoral Candidate in Civil Law, National and Kapodistrian University of Athens, Greece. Special thanks are due to Professor of Civil Law in the University of Athens, Mr. Antonios Karampatzos, supervisor of my doctoral research at the University of Athens, for his continued and kind support throughout my studies.

[1] *J. H. Merryman & R. Pérez-Perdomo*, The Civil Law Tradition: An Introduction to the Legal Systems of Western Europe and Latin America, 3rd ed., 2007, p. 6 et seq.

inhomogeneous civil law by systematising its primary material within a code. It is not within the scopes of this chapter to elaborate on how these codes were drafted. However, it should be emphasised that the majority of them are based on general clauses.[2] In these clauses, general rules and principles of civil law are codified in abstract and general terms, in such a way that they do not lend directly to their application, but require creative interpretation and subsumption by the judge in each specific case according to its circumstances (see for example the principle of good faith, abuse of rights, public morals, etc.).[3] The research question that this chapter tries to answer is: are the tools of civil law sufficient and, in particular, are the general clauses of each national civil code effective enough in harmonising environmental law regarding civil liability for damage to environmental goods?

All countries' civil codes have been deliberately designed to display a great deal of breadth and generality in their clauses. This serves to cover as many cases as possible, and allows for their constant adaptability to new legal phenomena, which in turn provides the necessary durability of the law.[4] Therefore, the civil code has been formulated in such a dynamic way that it can be applied in every possible case, even in fields of law that had not emerged when these codes were drafted (environmental and energy law, personal data, electronic transactions, etc.). It should be noted that when most of the civil codes entered into force, in the 19th and early 20th centuries, there was no specific environmental legislation. Despite that, their rules are naturally capable of responding to instances of environmental damage, even if the legislators did not have that in mind. Indeed, before environmental law was elevated to an autonomous field, many states applied civil law provisions to environmental disputes, while others still apply them in parallel with specific legislation. For example, German case law and theory also implements tort law (*Deliktsrecht*, §§823 et seq. BGB) or law governing the relations between neighbours (*Nachbarrecht*, §§903 et seq. BGB) on these cases;[5] the UK and US legal orders resort to fault-based negligence, along with the special category of strict liability torts ('*public nuisance*') that have been shaped in cases of pure environmental damage;[6]

---

2 For the importance of the general clauses and the model that these Codes followed, see *S. Rodotá*, The Civil Code within the European 'Constitutional Process', in: *M. Hesselink* (ed.), The Politics of a European Civil Code, 2006, p. 115, 122.

3 For the meaning and the characteristics of the general clauses, see *S. Grundmann*, General Standards and Principles, *Clauses Générales* and *Generalklauseln* in European Contract Law – A Survey, in: *S. Grundmann & D. Mazeaud* (eds.), General Clauses and Standards in European Contract Law: Comparative Law, EC Law and Contract Law Codification, 2006, pp. 1, 2–4.

4 Ibid. at p. 7.

5 *M. Kloepfer*, Umweltrecht (in German), 4th ed., 2016, p. 554et seq.; *T. Lytras*, Zivilrechtliche Haftung für Umweltschäden (in German), 1995, p. 50 et seq.

6 *N. Askounes Ashford & C.C. Caldart*, Environmental Law, Policy, and Economics: Reclaiming the Environmental Agenda, 2008, p. 211 et seq.; *E. Fisher, B. Lange & E. Scotford*, Environmental Law: Text, Cases and Materials, 2013, pp. 77–78.

the Dutch legal order is based principally on tort law in such disputes (Article 6:162 et seq. Dutch CC);[7] while in Belgium environmental civil liability is based on fault-based tort law (Article 1382 et seq. Belgian CC), and strict liability is introduced for particular instances by specific Acts.[8] It must also be noted that the 'Draft Common Frame of Reference' (DCFR): Principles, Definitions and Model Rules of European Private Law' has proposed a special strict liability rule (Article VI.-3:206) in cases of damages caused by dangerous substances or emissions – the main causes of environmental pollution– pointing out that there is some type of consensus among EU Members States regarding the utilising of civil law as the appropriate tool for the arising disputes.[9]

The diachronic importance of civil law in cases of environmental harm finds its legal base in Article 3 (3) of Directive 2004/35/CE:[10] this provision, interpreted in the light of Recital no 14 of the directive, refers to private law of each Member State regarding personal injury, damage to private property or any other economic loss arising from an environmental harm.[11] The directive does not regulate other aspects of civil liability, except some public law aspects of environmental harm and its restoration (for example, the preventive and remedial action of the operators or the competent authorities, the cost of the relevant measures and the recovery of it, etc.),[12] in order to unify the rules regarding those issues and to affirm the Member States' obligation to ensure environmental protection at the national level. In sum, the directive imposes an obligation to Member States to internalise the external environmental costs to the polluter through a strict liability system ('polluter pays'),[13] without prescribing the means and extent of such internalisation ('how much the polluter pays'). As a result, the rest of the conditions and elements of such liability, as well as the means and the extent of the remedy are left to be determined by the Member States. The aforementioned choice of the European legislator is dictated by the sovereignty of the Member States: environmental harm has a wide impact and deeply affects the local societies. As such, the conditions, the extent and the nature of the remedy (especially its possible punitive character, for example

---

7 *E. Brans*, Liability for Damage to Public Natural Resources: Standing, Damage and Damage Assessment, 2001, p. 243 et seq.

8 Ibid. at p. 296 et seq.

9 *C. von Bar & E. Clive* (eds.), Principles, Definitions and Model Rules of European Private Law – Draft Common Frame of Reference (DCFR), Full Edition, Vol. 4, 2009, pp. 3538–3539.

10 Council Directive 2004/35/CE on environmental liability with regard to the prevention and remedying of environmental damage (OJ 2004, L 143/56).

11 *P. Marburger*, EG-Umwelthaftungsrichtlinie und zivilrechtliche Umwelthaftung (in German), in: Festschrift für Eckard Rehbinder, 2007, p. 237, 238; *G. Wagner*, in: Münchener Kommentar zum Bürgerlichen Gesetzbuch (in German), Vol. 6, 7th ed., 2017, p. 2007.

12 *E. Brans*, Fundamentals of liability for environmental harm under ELD, in: *L. Bergkamp & B.J. Goldsmith* (eds.), The EU Environmental Liability Directive: A Commentary, 2013, p. 31, 38.

13 *C. Rodgers*, The Law of Nature Conservation, 2013, p. 146.

through the system of punitive damages) should be assessed on the basis of national law of each Member State.

This chapter is divided in two parts. The first part (section 2) examines the general duty of care in tort law and its implementation especially in case of environmental harms. Particularly, it will point out the function of this duty in these cases and how it could contribute to the achievement of a wider and more harmonised environmental approach of civil liability. The second part's analysis (section 3) is focused on the protection of environmental goods through the right to personality in order to find out whether the above right is a proper tool in instances of environmental offences, not only towards the remedy of personal damages, but also for the restoration of pure environmental damage. The aforementioned case studies will show the dynamic of civil law in accomplishing a harmonised treatment of liability rules in environmental law. It must be noted that tort law, alongside the right to personality and the law regulating the relations of the neighbours, constitutes the main concept of private law of the environment.[14]

2. THE GENERAL DUTY OF CARE IN ENVIRONMENTAL TORT LAW

Is it possible to utilise the general duty of care in order to 'codify' general principles of environmental law, such as, the prevention principle or the precautionary principle? And what advantages and disadvantages could offer the implementation of the general duty of care regarding the specific rules of environmental law? To answer the above questions, it is necessary to explore the content, the scope and the function of the general duty of care. Consequently, this general duty will be compared with equivalent duties set down by specific legislation (see Article 5 Directive 2004/35/CE) in order to find out its potential importance in harmonising environmental law.

2.1. THE FUNCTION OF GENERAL DUTY OF CARE AND THE PROTECTED LEGAL RIGHTS

The general duty of care ('Verkehrssicherungspflicht') constitutes an unwritten general rule of most of the Member States' civil law. As such, it finds its legal foundation not necessarily in specific provisions of the civil code, but mainly in the spirit and the system of tort law ('neminem laedere') in combination with the principle of good faith.[15] Tort law does not only operate in a repressive way,

14 *Kloepfer, supra* note 5 at p. 545 et seq.; *Lytras, supra* note 5 at p. 51.

15 *K. Roussos*, Schaden und Folgeschaden (in German), 1992, p. 7.

but also in a preventive one, imposing duties of care and protection of the other party's rights, even if that is not prescribed specifically in the law.[16] Breaching these duties leads to liability of the offender. As a result, the general clauses and the provisions of civil law should be interpreted on the aforementioned – preventive – way. Good faith, on the other hand, as it was being developed in most of the civil codes of Europe, has been established to fulfil a social role and to facilitate social coexistence, especially in cases where there is no explicitly recorded provision in the law.[17] In other words, it performs a social balancing role, imposing duties of appropriate and proportionate behaviour on both sides.[18] In the same way, not taking preventive measures when somebody foresees the danger which may occur from a risk source that he controls may constitute an abusive behaviour.[19]

The general duty of care aims to protect other parties' interests.[20] This entails not only property or financial interests, but interests of every nature, such as personal rights (life, health, private and family life, etc.). As an unwritten rule, it is distinguished by its pliable character. The extent and the intensity of this duty in each particular case depend on the needs and the circumstances (intensity and magnitude of danger, importance of the injured legal rights, cost of the measures, etc.).[21] In this context, this duty can be formed *ad hoc* by the judge. As a result, general duty of care contributes to the constant adaptability of the law to new circumstances and instances of offences which may not have been regulated by the legislator yet. However, the provisions of the civil codes are not designated to elevate environmental protection *eo ipso* to a protected legal right ('Rechtsgut').[22] All civil codes govern relations exclusively between individuals.

---

16 Ibid. at pp. 9–10. That the prevention belongs to the aims of European tort law is pointed out by Article VI.-1:102 of DCFR, which is entitled 'Prevention'. See *von Bar & Clive, supra* note 9 at pp. 3105–3106.

17 See *M. Hesselink*, CFR & Social Justice, 2008, pp. 49–50.

18 *D. Looschelders*, Schuldrecht – Allgemeiner Teil (in German), 16th ed., 2018, p. 28.

19 It is argued that good faith (through the prohibition of abuse of rights) can also fulfill its balancing and social function intergenerationally, allowing the possibility of the common use and enjoyment of environmental goods not only for the present, but for the future generations as well (see *I. Karakostas/E. Dacoronia*, Environment and Private Law in Greece, Annuaire international des droits de l' homme 2006 (1), p. 479, 487). In that way, the principle of sustainable development is being codified in civil law.

20 *P. Schlechtriem*, The Functions of General Clauses, Exemplified by Regarding Germanic Law and Dutch Law, in: *S. Grundmann & D. Mazeaud* (eds.), General Clauses and Standards in European Contract Law: Comparative Law, EC Law and Contract Law Codification, 2006, pp. 41, 45.

21 *D. Looschelders*, Schuldrecht – Besonderer Teil (in German), 14th ed., 2019, pp. 480–481; *D. Medicus & S. Lorenz*, Schuldrecht II -Besonderer Teil (in German), 18th ed., 2018, p. 465–466. For example, ultra-hazardous activities or the possesion of ultra-hazardous materials requires stricter preventive measures (see *L. Godden, J. Peel & J. McDonald*, Environmental Law, 2nd ed., 2019, p. 199).

22 *D. Medicus*, Zivilrecht und Umweltschutz (in German), JZ 1986 (17), pp. 778, 778–779; *Wagner, supra* note 11 at p. 2005; *R. Wilhelmi*, Risikoschutz durch Privatrecht: Eine Untersuchung zur negatorischen und deliktischen Haftung unter besonderer Berücksichtigung von Umweltschäden (in German), 2009, p. 43.

They were not formulated to enshrine the protection of the environment as a general principle. Consequently, the duties of care regarding environmental goods are established only insofar as: (a) they relate to the legal rights of one or more persons and tend to protect them from any damage that may occur to them through environmental harm;[23] and (b) the other party holds a risk source or carries out an activity that is likely to harm the environment and through it the person's legal rights.[24] The duty of care is not a duty of protection of the environment *per se*, it is a duty addressed to protect individual legal rights in cases where some person's conduct may put them in danger.[25] This also points directly to the limits of environmental protection through civil law.[26]

The duty of care imposes the obligation to take measures that tend to maintain the existing environmental situation, regardless of the specific provisions of environmental law. Otherwise, the breach of this duty is an illegal act and constitutes a tort (§823 BGB; Article 6:162 Dutch CC; Article 1382 Belgian CC; Article 914 Greek CC etc.).[27] Therefore, the holder of a risk source or an operator of an activity which may harm the environment is obliged to take preventive measures in order to prevent the danger that may occur or limit its magnitude.[28] This duty exists only insofar as individual rights are in a specific danger. Especially in Greek law,[29] some argue that the danger of an environmental harm imposes *per se* on the operator the obligation to take precautionary measures that may prevent or limit it.[30] This is justified because the environment is a common good and the wide impact of environmental harm can affect negatively, either now or in the future, individuals' rights (i.e. health, etc.). This opinion broadens the traditional concept of the duty of care, covering not only the immediate harm to individual rights, but also any future and possible harm which may occur to them through environmental harm. According to this opinion, it is sufficient for a holder of a risk source or operator to foresee the negative impact that his activity may have on the environment (not necessarily on specific individual rights) in order to take preventive measures.

---

23 See *Lytras, supra* note 5 at pp. 135–136; *Medicus, supra* note 22 at p. 780.

24 *Looschelders, supra* note 21 at p. 480; *Medicus & Lorenz, supra* note 21 at p. 465.

25 *Wilhelmi, supra* note 22 at p. 22; *M. Paschke*, in: *H.J. Koch, E. Hofmann & M. Reese*, Handbuch Umweltrecht (in German), 5th ed., 2018, p. 1165. *Medicus* (*supra* note 22 at p. 782) explains that the need for environmental protection does not establish duties of care *per se*, but it can be used itself as a criterion for the extent and the content of these duties.

26 *Medicus, supra* note 22 at p. 778. Cf. Articles 2 and 6 of Directive 2004/35/CE which introduce the concept of pure environmental harm (for example, biodiversity loss) independently from the damage to individual rights. See *C. von Bar*, Non-contractual Liability Arising out of Damage Caused to Another (PEL Liab. Dam.), 2009, pp. 529–530.

27 *Wilhelmi, supra* note 22 at p. 141.

28 *U. Diederichsen*, Die Haftung für Umweltschäden (in German), BB 1973 (11), p. 485,488.

29 See *I. Karakostas*, Environment & Law (in Greek), 3rd ed., 2011, pp. 362–366, 374.

30 Protection of the environment as a legal right ('Rechtsgut') has been proposed also in other legal orders, such as, for example in Germany (see *Diederichsen, supra* note 28, at p. 487). This approach remains, however, very controversial (see the critic of *Medicus, supra* note 22 at pp. 779–780).

2.2. THE PREVENTIVE MEASURES ESPECIALLY COMPARED TO DIRECTIVE 2004/35/CE

The general clauses and the provisions of civil law are interpreted in such a way that the prevention of environmental harm as well as the maintenance of the existing environmental situation can be achieved. Since these clauses serve, *inter alia*, a socially balancing role between a person's right to benefit from a dangerous activity and the need of society to be protected from the inherent dangers of it, some of the traditional principles of environmental law (such as the prevention principle, the precautionary principle or even the sustainability principle) could be founded in them. Furthermore, the implementation of good faith and the general duty of care in environmental cases reveals that there is a great deal in common between these two civil law principles and those of environmental law. Both have a social character, in the sense that they tend to protect the other party's interests and his enjoyment of a good; and both of them aim not at the improvement of the existing – environmental – situation, but act defensively to the maintenance of the *status quo*.[31] Due to their common aims and characteristics, it could be argued that even if these environmental principles were not specifically prescribed in the law, they could both spring from the good faith clause and the general duty of care. That is of great importance because through the civil law clauses, the aforementioned principles can also be codified as general principles of the private law of the environment and, as such, govern the relations between individuals.

Furthermore, it is argued that since Directive 2004/35/CE protects in parallel, but indirectly, personal legal rights, the obligations that it prescribes in detail could be used as important tools for the concretisation of the content of the general duty of care in environmental cases.[32] However, it should not be understood that the concept of the general duty of care is fully identified with the concept of other environmental principles. The first has a definitively wider scope and can be implemented even in fields that are not protected by the existing environmental legislation. That can be precisely shown through the comparison of the concept of the preventive measures imposed by the general duty of care and of these pursuant to Article 5 Directive 2004/35/CE.[33] The most important differences between these two are the following:

1) The scope of the preventive measures under Directive 2004/35/CE is defined in Article 2 (1) and 3. The directive covers only three categories of environmental damage, in contrast to the general duty of care, which can cover every possible case.

31 *Kloepfer, supra* note 5 at p. 189.
32 *Marburger, supra* note 11 at pp. 241–242; *Wagner, supra* note 11 at p. 2006.
33 Cf. also the comparison between these two made by *Marburger, supra* note 11 at pp. 241–242.

2) An abstract and non-specific danger is insufficient according to both legal statuses in order for the operator to be obliged to take preventive measures. However, Article 5 (1) Directive 2004/35/CE requires an *imminent threat* in such cases. On the contrary, it suffices that a particular activity can lead to a seriously foreseeable specific danger,[34] even if the danger is more remote and less imminent, in order for the general duty of care to emerge.
3) The *ratio* of the preventive measures is different. In the Directive the *ratio* can be detected in the imminent threat for the environment. On the other hand, the justification of emerging the general duty of care is that the operator holds a risk source that may threaten the interests and the legal rights of other persons.
4) The duration of the preventive measures also differs. In case of the preventive measures under the Directive, the operator is obliged to take these measures as soon as the threat becomes imminent. On the other hand, particularising and foreseeing of the danger leads to the obligation of the holder to take protective measures without delay.[35]
5) The cost of the preventive measures under the Directive is distributed according to Article 8. The costs of the preventive measures in other cases burden the holder of the risk source (operator) exclusively.

The above list shows that the duty of care according to civil law has a wider concept and offers a broader protection to the individuals' rights (and indirectly the environment).[36] Moreover, within each particular case, duties of care can at any time acquire the content that is imposed by the circumstances.[37] That is of great importance not only when there is no specific legislation (in which case the need for good faith's intervention is greater), but also when such legislation exists. The latter is crucial in this case: through the general duty of care and the *extra legem* handling of the law, the judge may not consider the measures laid down in the specific legislation sufficient, but he may impose stricter measures, aside from those delineated in the law.[38] This is so because

34 See *Godden, Peel &McDonald, supra* note 21 at p. 199; *Lytras, supra* note 5, at p. 138.

35 Cf. *Brans, supra* note 12 at p. 38.

36 *Wilhelmi, supra* note 22 at p. 285.

37 *Marburger, supra* note 11 at p. 242.

38 This is also the approach of Greek law (see *E. Poulou*, Environmental Protection through the Tools of Civil Law (in Greek), Essays in honor of G. Kallimopoulos, 2010, p. 561, 572). From the Greek case law, the Decision of Court of Appeal Athens No 10668/1986, EllDni 1985 (26), p. 509 is very characteristic: the plaintiff was a beekeeper who had placed hives in an area where an aluminum processing plant was operating. The plant had all the legal licences and complied with the environmental legislation. However, fluoride fumes were emitted from the plant; these emissions infected the flowers of the area, resulting in increased bee mortality. The Appeals Court awarded compensation to the plaintiff because the defendant plant failed to take the necessary preventive measures, such as the installation of fluoride filters. A failure to take additional measures compared with those delineated in the specific legislation constitutes a tort.

specific legislation, particularly of EU origin, mandates only a minimum of environmental protection and the needs of each particular case may require additional precautionary measures. Consequently, the implementation of tort law rules (as for example the general duty of care) for environmental protection can fill the gaps of the environmental legislation and in parallel harmonise the environmental civil liability, with the result that the elements of the liability (*causa*, fault, damage) can be defined in a homogenous way.

3. THE PROTECTION OF THE ENVIRONMENT THROUGH THE RIGHT TO PERSONALITY – THE TWO APPROACHES

The following section of this chapter points out the utilisation of the right to personality for environmental protection. This case will be examined through the comparison of the two approaches that have been developed accordingly: the approach of the ECHR[39] which protects the environment indirectly through other personal rights (under 3.1); and the unique approach of the Greek law which establishes a right to the enjoyment of environmental goods as an element of personality. Despite their differences, their contact point is that they tend to protect the undisturbed enjoyment by each person of the environmental goods.

3.1. THE PROTECTION OF ENVIRONMENT THROUGH THE RIGHT TO PRIVATE LIFE IN ECtHR'S CASE LAW

The case law of the European Court of Human Rights (ECtHR) can offer a very good example of indirectly protecting the environment against State's nuisance through other individual legal rights. Under the ECHR there is no explicit right to a healthy environment or to nature preservation in general.[40] However, the ECtHR has considered the quality of the surrounding environment in cases where a person was impacted negatively by unsafe or disruptive environmental conditions.[41] In these cases, the court has relied on

---

39 Convention for the Protection of Human Rights and Fundamental Freedoms, of the Council of Europe (1950).

40 Judgment of 22 May 2003, no 41666/98, *Kyrtatos v. Greece*, para. 52; Judgment of 9 July 2005, no. 55723/00, *Fadeyeva v. Russia*, para. 68.

41 The ECtHR has utilised Article 8, for example, in instances of noise pollution (see Judgment of 21 January 1990, no 9310/81, *Powell and Rayner v. UK*; Judgment of 8 July 2003, no 36022/97, *Hatton et al v. UK*), smell (Judgment of 9th December 1994, no 16798/90, *López Ostra v. Spain*), industrial pollution (Judgment *Fadeyeva v. Russia*; Judgment of 24 January 2019, no 54414/13, 54264/15, *Cordella v. Italy*), mining pollution (Judgment of 10 November 2004, no 46117/99, *Taşkın and Others v. Turkey*; Judgment of 27th January 2009, no 67021/01,

other individual rights protected by the ECHR (Article 2: right to life; Article 8: right to private and family life and home; Article 1 of Protocol 1: right to property, etc.). For the purposes of this chapter, we will focus mainly on Article 8 of ECHR and the indirect protection of environment through the individual's right to private and family life and home. This is justified because Article 8 has a naturally wider scope in comparison to other articles: it could include new elements of personality and cover plenty of the aspects of the individual's right to free and all-round development of his personality. As such it is often implemented by the ECtHR's case law as *ultimum refugium* in cases of environmental nuisance, when no other right can be implemented.

Article 8 is not violated every time an environmental deterioration occurs, because otherwise that would have as a result the establishment through case law of a general right to nature preservation.[42] In any case, certain conditions must be met in order to speak of a violation of this article. These can be summarised as follows: (a) actual interference by the state; (b) direct nature of this interference; (c) violation of the applicant's private sphere; and (d) severity and intensity of the interference. However, even if the above are fulfilled, such interference can be justifiable for one of the reasons mentioned in paragraph 2 of this article.

Article 8 applies in environmental cases both when the pollution is directly caused by the state (*positive interference*) and when state responsibility arises from the failure to regulate private-sector activities properly (*negative interference*).[43] Specifically, the ECtHR examines if a situation was a result of a sudden and unexpected turn of events or, on the contrary, was long-standing and well known to the state authorities. Then the court focuses on whether the state was or should have been aware that the hazard (or its interference) was affecting the applicant's private life and to what extent the applicant contributed to creating this situation for himself, being, for example, in a position to remedy it without a prohibitive outlay.[44]

The direct nature of the interference serves also as an admissibility criterion in ECtHR's case law. This is justified because the control mechanism of ECHR cannot accept an *actio popularis*.[45] The damage to the environmental good must have such an outcome, which at the same time leads to a current negative impact on a person's private sphere due to his close link with this good.[46] This link is both

Tătar v. Romania; Judgment of 10 February 2011, no 30499/03, *Dubetska et al v. Ukraine*), waste collection (Judgment of 10 January 2012, no 30765/08, *Di Sarno et al. v. Italy*) etc. For the above see also *W. Schabas*, The European Convention on Human Rights – A Commentary, 2015, pp. 387–388.

42 *C. Grabenwarter*, European Convention on Human Rights-Commentary, 2014, pp. 192–193.

43 Judgment *Hatton et al v. UK*, paras. 98, 119.

44 Judgment *Dubetska et al v. Ukraine*, para. 108. See also *Grabenwarter*, *supra* note 42 at p. 222.

45 Regarding the arising issues concerning admissibility in such cases and the prohibition of *actio popularis*, see notably Judgment *Cordella v. Italy*, paras. 100–109.

46 The potential danger is not sufficient, according to Court (see Judgement *Cordella v. Italy*, para. 104).

local (the person must be located close enough to the place of the deterioration so he endures its impact) and qualitative (the environmental good must be a part of his sphere of free development of personal/family life or home).[47] The individual's private sphere is not directly affected by each environmental deterioration. For example, the simple deprivation of the aesthetic enjoyment of the landscape or a biodiversity loss cannot constitute an infringement of that right.[48]

The environmental nuisance must also directly affect the applicant's private sphere, namely the individual's health or well-being or his home. All these concepts are interpreted broadly by the ECtHR. The court concludes that while there is no doubt that environmental pollution may negatively affect public health in general and worsen the quality of an individual's life, it is often impossible to quantify its effects in each specific case. With regard to health impairment, for instance, it is hard to distinguish the effect of environmental hazards from the influence of other relevant factors, such as age, profession or personal lifestyle.[49] It must be noted that the concept of health also includes mental health.[50] The causal link between the interference of the state and the harm of health is also evidenced by scientific reports and data, in which the recent ECtHR case law attaches significant evidential value.[51] 'Home' can be identified the physically defined area where private and family life develops.[52] The individual has the right to respect for his home, meaning not only the right to the actual physical area, but also to the peaceful enjoyment of the benefits of that area. Nonphysical breaches of that right are also included in the scope of Article 8, such us noise, emissions or smells. A serious breach results in the violation of a person's right to respect for his home if it prevents him from enjoying the amenities of his home.[53] Moreover, the court has elaborated that even if the person's health or his home are not harmed seriously by the deterioration, it is sufficient to be harmed in his well-being in order to establish a violation of Article 8.[54] 'Quality of life' on the other hand is a subjective characteristic which hardly lends itself to a precise definition.[55]

Furthermore, in all of the cases regarding environmental matters the court points out that the adverse effects of environmental nuisance must attain a certain minimum level of severity resulting in significant impairment of the

---

47 Judgment *Taşkın and Others v. Turkey*, para. 113.

48 Judgment *Kyrtatos v. Greece*, para. 53.

49 Judgment *Dubetska et al v. Ukraine*, para. 106.

50 See for example, Judgment of 6th February 2001, no 44599/98, *Bensaid v. UK*, para. 47.

51 See Judgment *Cordella v. Italy*, para 161 et seq. Cf. *Fadeyeva v. Russia*, paras. 80 et seq.

52 For the meaning of 'home', see the extensive analysis of ECtHR in Judgment of 26th March 2007, no 59909/00, *Giacomelli v. Italy*, para. 76.

53 See Judgment *Powell and Rayner v. UK*, para. 40: 'the quality of the applicant's private life and the scope for enjoying the amenities of his home have been adversely affected by the noise generated by aircraft using Heathrow Airport'.

54 Judgment *López Ostra v. Spain*, para. 51; *Kyrtatos v. Greece*, para. 52; *Taşkın and Others v. Turkey*, para. 113.

55 Judgment *Dubetska et al v. Ukraine*, para. 106.

applicant's ability to enjoy his home, private or family life.[56] The assessment of that minimum is relative and depends on the circumstances of the case, such as the intensity and duration of the nuisance, and its physical or mental effects. The general context of the environment should also be considered. If the detriment is negligible considering the environmental hazards inherent to life in modern cities, the claim cannot be regarded as admissible under Article 8.[57]

The state enjoys a certain margin of appreciation in determining the steps to be taken to ensure compliance with the convention, whether the case is analysed in terms of a positive duty for the state to take reasonable and appropriate measures to secure the applicants' rights under paragraph 1 of Article 8 or in terms of an interference by a public authority to be justified in accordance with paragraph 2. In both contexts, the state must strike a fair balance between the competing interests of the individual to respect his personal and family life or his home and those of the community as a whole (such as economic or development interests).[58]

3.2. THE IMPLEMENTATION OF THE RIGHT TO PERSONALITY FOR THE PROTECTION OF ENVIRONMENT IN GREECE

According to Article 8 ECHR, the simple deprivation of the enjoyment of an environmental good does not constitute in principle a violation of the right to private and family life or home, unless the injured party can prove a close link with that good. However, the opposite approach has been developed under the Greek CC, in the context of Article 57 (general right to personality). As it is stated in this article:

> Anyone whose personality is unlawfully insulted has the right to request that the offence be lifted and not be repeated in the future [...] Claim for damages under the provisions of tort law is not excluded.

Due to its general concept, Greek theory and case law apply it in a wide range of cases, from media insults to personal data breaches: the right to personality protects all of the personality's manifestations.[59]

---

56 Judgment *Kyrtatos v. Greece*, para. 54; *Fadeyeva v. Russia*, para. 69; *Dubetska et al v. Ukraine*, para. 105; *Fadeyeva v. Russia*, para. 69.

57 Judgment *Dubetska et al v. Ukraine*, para. 105; *Fadeyeva v. Russia*, para. 69.

58 For all of the above, see Judgement *López Ostra v. Spain*, para. 51; *Hatton et al v. UK*, para. 98; *Dubetska et al v. Ukraine*, paras. 140–141; *Giacomelli v. Italy*, para. 78. About the justification according to para. 2, see *Fadeyeva v. Russia*, paras. 94 et seq.

59 *Ap. Georgiadis*, General Principles of Civil Code (in Greek), 5th ed., 2019, p. 145; *A. Fountedaki*, Natural person and personality in Civil Code (in Greek), 2012, p. 133 et seq.

This unique right is often utilised in environmental cases not only in a defensive way (that is to prevent interferences to individual's private sphere, such as emissions and noise) but also to ensure the free and undisturbed enjoyment of environmental goods by each person.[60] To be more specific, Article 57 encompasses the concept of the person's vital space. This term includes every element necessary for the free and all-round development of personality. Among these, the enjoyment by each individual of the things that are common to all (*res communes omnium*) as well as communal things (a distinction from Roman law retained in Greek law) holds a special place.[61] The first category contains the air and the open sea, the second includes the waters with free and endless flow, streets, squares, harbours and bays, banks of floating rivers and large lakes and their banks (Article 967 Greek CC). Thus, the majority of environmental goods is included in this second category. It is argued in the light of Article 24 of the Greek Constitution, which enshrines the general protection of environment, that the right to personality not only protects the enjoyment of the things described in Article 967, but also the enjoyment of any environmental good (landscape's aesthetic, protection of traditional settlements, preservation of biodiversity, wild life etc.).[62]

To apply Article 57, it is sufficient for the offence to be illegal. Culpability is demanded only for a claim for damages. The offence consists of a disturbance or deprivation of the enjoyment of an environmental good (or intervention to individual's private sphere), of such a magnitude that disallows its communal use. No other prerequisite is needed. Since the right to personality is an absolute right, every disturbance of the individual's vital space is illegal *per se*, without the need to establish the opposition of the offence to a specific prohibitive legal provision.[63] The application of a specific rule of law which permits the conduct

60 From the remarkably rich Greek case law, see most notably the decisions of Court of Cassation (Areios Pagos) no 388/2016, Nomos (obstruction to the free use of a coast by an adjacent beach bar), no 43/2016, Nomos (smoke and smell from a neighbouring barbeque place), no 1574/2014, Nomos (emissions and depositions to the coast from a cement plant); decisions of Court of Appeal of Patra no 390/2011, Nomos (smells and environmental degradation due to the operation of a pigsty), Court of Appeal of West Macedonia 112/2012, Nomos (radiation of a mobile phone antenna), Court of Appeal of Larisa no 189/2015, Nomos (environmental degradation and destruction of flora from free grazing of wild pigs), no 373/2011, Nomos (environmental degradation due to the operation of a slaughterhouse); decision of Court of First Instance of Athens no 464/2014, Nomos (environmental degradation due to installation of transmission pylon).

61 *Fountedaki, supra* note 59 at pp. 228–299; *Karakostas/Dacoronia, supra* note 19 at pp. 483; *Poulou, supra* note 38 at p. 562; from the Greek case law, see especially decisions of Court of Cassation no 43/2016, Nomos; no 1574/2014, Nomos.

62 *Karakostas, supra* note 29, at pp. 294–293; *Poulou, supra* note 38 at p. 562. See decision of Court of First Instance of Piraeus no 464/2014, EEmpD 2014, 964.

63 *Fountedaki, supra* note 59 at p. 289; *Karakostas/Dacoronia, supra* note 19, at p. 484. See also decisions of Court of Cassation (Areios Pagos) no 1731/2006, NoB 2007, 353; Court of Appeal of Thessaloniki no 2025/2012, Arm 2013, 711; Court of Appeal of Larisa no 189/2015, Nomos and no 373/2011, Nomos.

in question (for example the non-exceedance of the legal limits or the issuance of an administrative licence) should be put forward by the other party.[64] Therefore, the most important aspect of the above approach (except that there is no need for the injured party to prove the fault of the defendant) is the reversal of the burden of proof. On one hand, it will suffice for the plaintiff to show that the defendant's conduct infringes his vital space; and on the other, the defendant must prove that the offence is not illegal but is permitted by a specific provision – a quite technical issue that the plaintiff is not always able to know *a priori*.

In cases of offences to the right to personality the injured party has a claim against the defendant to lift the offence and to not repeat it in the future. The object of these claims is the restitution *in natura* (restoration) of the thing's common or communal use and the reattribution of it to the community. Both claims do not require defendant's culpability. On the other hand, culpability remains a prerequisite only for the claim for damages, including the claim for moral damages.[65] In this context, Greek case law often awards moral damages on offences to environmental goods, which are included in individual's vital space.[66] However, Greek case law generally avoids awarding claims for property damage due to environmental offences. Despite the fact that Greek law has enshrined the 'polluter pays' principle in Article 29 of Act no 1650/1986,[67] the Courts have almost never applied this provision autonomously for the award of damages.[68] It is considered that, on one hand, the Greek judge is not familiar with the 'polluter pays' principle, and on the other hand, the plaintiffs prefer to invoke the right to personality because their main concern is to lift the environmental offence and to avoid a possible future repetition of it.[69] Furthermore, in some cases it is difficult to prove and calculate the existence and the magnitude of the damage.

The Greek approach of protecting the environment through the right to personality remains a unique approach in Europe.[70] Evidently, it differs

64 *Fountedaki, supra* note 59 at pp. 316–317; *Poulou, supra* note 39 at pp. 566–569.

65 *Fountedaki, supra* note 59 at pp. 368–369; see also decision of Court of Cassation (Areios Pagos) no 1574/2014, Nomos. Contra *Karakostas, supra* note 29, at pp. 302–303.

66 Thus, moral damages have been recognised, for example, to neighbours of high-voltage power transmission pylons (Court of Appeal of Athens 5560/2013, Isokratis), as well as to residents of seaside areas due to the arbitrary use and structures on the seashore (Court of Cassation 388/2016, Nomos).

67 Act 1650/1986 'Regarding the protection of Environment' (Official Gazette A' 160/16.10.1986).

68 There is only one case of utilising Article 29 in Greek case law in the decision of Court of First Instance no 464/2014, EempD 2014, 964.

69 *Karakostas, supra* note 29, at p. 403.

70 Article 57 of Greek Civil Code has been inspired by Article 28 of Swiss Civil Code (before the amendment of that Article in 1983). However, in Swiss Law there is no such approach of protecting the free and undisturbed enjoyment of the environment in this way. The aforementioned controversial approach has been proposed in Germany (see *H. Forkel*, Immissionsschutz und Persönlichkeitsrech (in German), 1968, pp. 24 et seq, 47 et seq; *G. Roth*, Materiellrechtliche und prozessuale Aspekte eines privatrechtlichen Umweltschutzes

significantly from that of the ECtHR, since it establishes a justiciable positive right for any person to live in a healthy and ecologically balanced environment.[71] It is not within the scope of this paper to criticise the above approach. Yet the all-encompassing nature of this right offers easy admissibility to the plaintiff, resulting in Article 57 having substituted specific provisions of environmental civil liability in practice (see for example Act no 1650/1986 'polluter pays principle'). Furthermore, the existence of a special environmental legislation neither changed the current situation nor was it especially beneficial from the aspect of civil law. On the other hand, Article 57 of Greek CC may offer the most proper example of a harmonised way of dealing with issues of environmental offences through the application of a general clause of civil law.

4. CONCLUSION

These two examples demonstrate that civil law does not lose its importance in environmental law: on one hand, even today the legal framework remains to some extent incomplete and fragmentary; and on the other, it refers explicitly to civil law regarding the private claims. Thus, civil law remains independent in relation to specific legislation and performs a separate function, complementing the specific environmental provisions and gaps.

However, the question remains: can civil law effectively contribute to the harmonisation of environmental law? Which is actually that crucial advantage that the utilisation of the general clauses of civil law could offer particularly in environmental protection? First of all, the creation of a legal system that protects the environment *per se*, exclusively restoring pure environmental damage is not always a step in the right direction. It does not in any way imply greater awareness or more qualitative environmental protection. On the contrary, making environmental protection an object of public interest without taking into account the safeguarding of individual's rights could lead to its legal neglect, turning the judicial protection of the environment a matter of environmental organisations exclusively. The individuals would have no real or effective motivation to claim the protection of the environment itself and take the initiative by embarking on a laborious judicial struggle. The privatisation of disputes about the environment provides a necessary incentive to protect the environment and offers a solution to the 'tragedy of the commons' from the reverse: I am not interested only in delineating my own use of common goods, but in having any interest (even financial, through the restitution of my damage, of property or of a moral nature) in order to stop the deterioration of

---

(in German), NJW 1972 (25), p. 921, 922 et seq) without success (cf. the critic of *Medicus, supra* note 22 at p. 780).

71 *Karakostas/ Dacoronia, supra* note 19 at p. 479.

common goods by another person. The admissibility to the court for anyone with a legitimate interest and the ability to request the lifting of an offence of a personal legal right (and maybe also some type of compensation) remains of key importance for maintaining the environmental quality. In parallel, the ease of admissibility is also enhanced by the following: the plaintiff in such cases only invokes claims based on civil law, while the defendant bears the burden of invocation of specific provisions that allow the conduct in question.[72] Thus, the *causa* of the liability and the calculation of damage and any other necessary element is based on civil law in a uniform way, without the need for invoking the sectoral environmental legislation.

As shown above, the implementation of the tort law in environmental offences has a wider scope in comparison with the environmental provisions, being able to regulate cases where there is no specific legislation and potentially providing better protection even where there are relevant legal provisions. The same can be argued for the right to personality, the main function of which is to facilitate the admissibility of the plaintiff's claim. All of the above, combined with the court's case-by-case judgment, can lead to a new dynamic in environmental protection.[73] However, it does not mean that there are no disadvantages to such a solution (specifically, legal uncertainty and possible inequality arising from case-by-case judgment). Furthermore, liability in civil law is fault-based. This means that the plaintiff bears the burden of proof for establishing the fault of the defendant in order to be awarded compensation. In particular, in the case of the general duty of care, the defendant's fault and its proof are partly objectified through the positive obligation to take protective measures. However, this fault-based system generally breaches the strict liability system applied in environmental law and can ultimately lead to opposite results. Moreover, the national-based nature of civil law and the different treatment of issues at national level do not favour the development of a uniform legal system within the EU.[74] Therefore, the practical benefits of civil law should not be overestimated when applying it to new areas of law such as environmental law.

Given the supplementary character of civil law in the national legal order and the structure of EU legal texts that refer to Member States' civil law, there necessarily arises the need of a harmonising approach between these two fields of law. Such an approach should take into account the basic principles of environmental law today as well as the need for an effective environmental protection and the individuals' legal interest to live in a healthy and ecologically balanced environment. Indeed, the majority of environmental law principles can be founded and codified in the general clauses of civil law, governing in such

---

72 *Godden, Peel &McDonald, supra* note 21 at p. 199.

73 *Wilhelmi supra* note 22 at p. 285.

74 *E. Orlando*, Liability, in: *L. Krämer & E. Orlando* (eds.), Principles of Environmental Law (Elgar Encyclopedia of Environmental Law series, Vol. VI), 2018, p. 272, 276.

a way the legal relations between individuals. As a result, civil law should be utilised by the legislator (and the judge), instead of taking *a priori* legislative actions that can lead to an unnecessary polynomy. The question of the lack of harmonisation cannot be solved by taking only new legislative initiatives, but also through the utilisation of some of the known and well tested tools of civil law, which are by nature intended to respond to new situations and legal phenomena. Consequently, the dynamic of civil law should not be underestimated in the legal protection of the environment; in some cases, it can even offer a more effective protection than the special provisions of environmental law.

PART III

HARMONISATION IN ENERGY LAW

HARMONISING OVERSIGHT OF THE EU LOW-CARBON POWER TRANSITION

With an Eye to Sustainability, Energy Justice and Security

Susann HANDKE*

1. HARMONISATION AND THE EU LOW-CARBON POWER TRANSITION

In early 2015, the European Commission (the Commission) announced the establishment of the Energy Union.[1] The realisation of this project will go far

* Independent Researcher, specialised in energy and climate law and governance, the Netherlands.

[1] Communication from the Commission, Energy Union Package: A Framework Strategy for a Resilient Energy Union with a Forward-looking Climate Change Policy, COM (2015) 80 final.

beyond the creation of competitive common markets for electricity and natural gas, which, from the late 1990s onwards, has been the aim of EU regulatory efforts in the energy sector. The description of the Energy Union hints at the great variety of policy fields that are involved. The Commission wants to pursue an 'ambitious' climate policy, while the EU energy sector must be able to supply 'households and businesses' with 'secure, sustainable, competitive and affordable energy'.[2]

The legislation that implements the Energy Union reflects this much more comprehensive approach, articulated in the five dimensions of EU energy and climate governance – energy security, internal energy market, energy efficiency, decarbonisation, as well as the compound of research, innovation and competitiveness.[3] Thus, the Energy Union seeks to integrate aspects of energy, market, environmental and social policies, foreshadowing a gradual harmonisation of related legislation, including oversight mechanisms.[4]

Since the inclusion of environmental and social concerns in the Energy Union exceeds the scope of past EU legislation on electricity, the Member States' harmonisation task becomes extensive and multi-focused. The extent to which legislation in this regard will be harmonised will have a major impact on the character of the Energy Union. The outcome of the Member States' harmonisation efforts will largely determine how EU citizens perceive this continent-wide project. Societal consensus and support will be vital, mainly because this unprecedented socio-economic transformation will eventually re-define the basis of the Union's economy. EU climate goals and actions are still evolving. The Union aims to achieve climate neutrality by 2050.[5] The legislation to implement the Energy Union prescribes how the Member States should embark on this transformation. A timely decarbonisation of electricity generation is crucial for the further progress of this process.

However, the establishment of the Energy Union is also influenced by external developments and actors, such as international law and global business practices. The international legal realm[6] and the global energy landscape impact the construction of the Union's energy future, both literally and imaginatively.

---

2 Ibid. at p. 2.

3 See Article 1 (2) (a) to (e) of the European Parliament and Council Regulation (EU) No 2018/1999 on the governance of the Energy Union and Climate Action, OJ 2018 L 328/1.

4 Section 4 discusses in detail the legislation of the 'Clean Energy for all Europeans' package that is relevant to this contribution. See, for an overview, European Commission, 'Clean Energy for all Europeans,' https://ec.europa.eu/energy/en/topics/energy-strategy-and-energy-union/clean-energy-all-europeans.

5 See Communication from the Commission, A Clean Planet for All: A European Strategic Long-term Vision for a Prosperous, Modern, Competitive and Climate Neutral Economy, COM (2018) 773 final; Council of the European Union, Long-term Low Greenhouse Gas Emission Development Strategy for the European Union and Its Member States, Document 6612/20; Communication from the Commission, The European Green Deal, COM (2019) 640 final.

6 See, for an assessment of how international, national, and subnational developments interact, *S. Handke*, The UN Climate Regime: Multilateralism, Polycentricity, and Divergent

The mitigation of climate change is a global effort; and international climate cooperation is primarily coordinated under the umbrella of the United Nations climate regime.[7] The EU played an important role in reaching the 2015 Paris Agreement, the regime's most recent treaty. The legislative package to create the Energy Union in part transposes the objectives of the Paris Agreement into EU law. Thus, the international legal realm largely corresponds with the Union's own approach.

International geo-economic developments pose a greater challenge to EU energy and climate governance. As this chapter shows, an increasingly interdependent global energy sector enables companies from outside the EU to enter the EU electricity sector. China State Grid, a large transmission company, is a case in point. This chapter presents the involvement of State Grid as a singular, unexpected phenomenon to which both the Commission and EU Member States need to find a response within the emerging regulatory framework in order to ensure the integrity of the EU internal debate and governance approach.

To help appraise the conversation about the EU energy future, this chapter ponders the question of what 'harmonisation' means in this context. The chapter focuses on the regulatory framework that facilitates the decarbonisation of the electricity sector as the energy system's 'first mover'.[8] It specifically explores components that shape the evolving oversight mechanisms to direct the EU low-carbon power transition. This chapter argues that EU oversight mechanisms will ideally lead to a harmonisation of Member States' governance approaches.

Harmonisation efforts to decarbonise power generation resemble the task of establishing the internal market[9] and the implementation of EU environmental law.[10] However, efforts to promote the energy transition go beyond sector-specific regulation. At times, Member States will enjoy more leeway to design

---

Energy Futures, in *M.O. Hosli, T. Garrett, S. Niedecken & N. Verbeek* (eds.) The Future of Multilateralism: Global Cooperation and International Organizations, 2021, pp. 257 et seq.

7 The UN climate regime consists of the 1992 United Nations Framework Convention on Climate Change, 1997 Kyoto Protocol and 2015 Paris Agreement, as well as decisions by bodies of the regime.

8 The decarbonisation of energy generation involves the entire energy system. Yet, the decarbonisation of the electricity sector is central to reducing carbon dioxide emissions in the course of overall energy generation. Thus, focusing on the electricity sector for the purpose of this chapter is warranted, as the path to decarbonisation of the energy system depends on the success of low-carbon measures in this sector. The decarbonisation of the electricity sector has already begun. Comprehensive approaches to other energy uses, such as heating and transport, still need to follow. Furthermore, strategic aspects of energy governance, such as investment by non-EU entities, which this chapter includes, solely concern the electricity sector.

9 *I. Maletić*, The Law and Policy of Harmonisation in Europe's Internal Market, 2013.

10 See for an overview of the evolution of EU environmental law and policy, *C. Hey*, EU Environmental Policies: A Short History of the Policy Strategies, in *S. Scheuer* (ed.) EU Environmental Policy Handbook: A Critical Analysis of EU Environmental Legislation: Making It Accessible to Environmentalists and Decision Makers, 2005, pp. 17 et seq.; *C. Knill & D. Lieferink*, The Establishment of EU Environmental Policy, in *A. Jordan & C. Adelle* (ed.) Environmental Policy in the EU: Actors, Institutions and Processes, 2013, pp. 13 et seq.

policy trajectories that respond to national circumstances. Eventually, the common goal is to work towards an integrated climate-neutral energy system, the contours of which are still evolving. Thus, *harmonised governance structures* to facilitate the energy transition can be understood as the outcome of policy convergence[11] in the EU legal context. To be clear, this chapter does not intend to provide a conclusive definition of the structures, but instead seeks to identify their basic tenets.

Accordingly, it investigates the impetus for striving for the harmonisation of governance structures that the EU energy and climate legislation creates. It centres on three issues: a) the approach of the legislative framework that governs the EU electricity sector; b) the inclusion of sustainability and energy justice; and c) the rules that deal with external systemic challenges.

Given the evolving nature of the future energy system and its links with the economy and society, it is vital that throughout the process of coordinating the EU energy transition, governments are able to adjust transition trajectories to local and national socio-economic circumstances and environmental requirements. In order to retain societal acceptance of the energy transition's implementation, oversight mechanisms need to take into account local socio-economic differences and varying environmental concerns, as well as diverging national security considerations. Thus, these mechanisms are the lynchpin of harmonised governance structures. They facilitate the further development of the common electricity market and the decarbonisation of the electricity sector, while incorporating a broader societal perspective.

For preserving the policy space in the various related fields of decision-making, the protection of the EU internal conversation about potential energy futures against external interference is particularly important. This line of thought is exemplified by State Grid's entry into the EU electricity market, as mentioned above. State Grid is a large, Chinese, state-owned electricity transmission company. Its presence in the EU electricity sector highlights an initially overlooked aspect of EU legislation to regulate the sector – namely, protection against an outside actor with deep pockets that advertises its own vision of a global energy transition.

It is not trivial that State Grid is headquartered in China. Under the country's current leadership, the EU considers China as a 'systemic rival' that promotes 'alternative models of governance'.[12] Moreover, in the global debate about climate

---

11 *K. Holzinger, C. Knill & T. Sommerer*, Environmental Policy Convergence: Harmonization, Transnational Communication, and Regulatory Competition, International Organization 2008 (62), pp. 553 et seq.

12 The European Commission coined this term in a document on the Union's relations with China in March 2019. See Communication from the Commission and the High Representative of the Union for Foreign Affairs and Security Policy, EU-China – A Strategic Outlook, JOIN (2019) 5 final, p. 1.

change mitigation and energy China has emerged as the 'elephant in the room.' This chapter, however, only examines the systemic challenge to the Union's energy transition that State Grid's activities bring about, mainly because assessing this company's involvement helps to draw attention to several substantive elements that are key to the conversation about a common EU energy future and the necessary oversight framework.

The next section of this chapter explores the governance structures that need to be harmonised in order to realise the low-carbon power transition in the EU. Section 3 shows the extent to which State Grid's investment and business strategies pose a systemic challenge to the EU low-carbon transition. The fourth section provides an overview of the EU oversight framework that is part of the Energy Union and pertains to the electricity sector. It discusses legislative acts that guide the low-carbon power transition, as well as legislation that aims to harmonise Member States' investment-screening mechanisms. The fifth section highlights the interaction between infrastructure and the mode of governance. It also shows how harmonised governance structures can facilitate the emergence of a common EU energy future that acknowledges the local nature of a just and sustainable energy system, while preventing objectionable external interference. The sixth section concludes.

2. GOVERNING THE EU LOW-CARBON POWER TRANSITION

The decarbonisation of the energy system is different from previous shifts from one fuel to another. For instance, unlike the transition from coal to oil in the shipping sector or the shift from coal to natural gas for heating purposes, the use of non-fossil fuels is not driven by these fuels' relative cost-effectiveness or more advantageous utilisation.[13] The fuel switch is instigated by concerns about global warming and the contribution of the energy sector to this global problem, rather than resulting from market developments. Therefore, government interference is necessary to incentivise energy producers and consumers to accomplish the transition, entailing the use of non-fossil fuels or technologies that help capture and store carbon dioxide. Furthermore, it will not be possible to decarbonise the entire energy system at once. Firstly, the low-carbon transition of the electricity sector has to proceed, and then much of the energy system will need to be electrified. Given the myriad processes and decisions that are involved in this long-term effort, a constant adjustment of policies and rulemaking at different

13 *R. Foquet*, The Slow Search for Solutions: Lessons from Historical Energy Transitions by Sector and Service, Energy Policy 2010 (38), pp. 6586, 6588 et seq.

levels of governance is necessary. Hence, decarbonising energy generation is a governed transition.[14]

In addition, the transition evolves in an institutional landscape that is embedded in the fossil economy. Since the shift to non-fossil fuels has far-reaching consequences for local and regional economies, policymakers need to take into account environmental impacts and socio-economic repercussions of low-carbon measures. The side effects of decarbonisation are mainly felt locally or regionally and require responses at these levels of governance, while the central level needs to coordinate long-term energy and climate policies. Hence, government plays a role in the planning and oversight of the low-carbon energy transition, and it is vital that the implementation of policies and laws is coordinated between different levels of governance.

This is particularly relevant in the case of the EU, as the leading role in policymaking regarding both climate and energy matters has incrementally been taken up by the Commission. Yet, as discussed, national governments of the Member States and subnational authorities also play an important role in ensuring the societal acceptance of the transformation.

Initially, the Commission's role was confined to market integration legislation for the electricity and gas sectors. The Commission introduced the first climate measures around the turn of the century.[15] However, it only began to dovetail its energy and climate policies from 2007 onwards.[16] Then, in 2011, the Commission, for the first time, introduced decarbonisation as a goal of energy and economic policymaking with the publication of the 2050 roadmap on the economy,[17] stipulating the objective of realising 'a competitive low carbon economy by 2050'.[18] The Energy Roadmap 2050 complemented this document by exploring routes towards decarbonising the energy system.[19] The creation of the Energy Union in 2015 gave fresh impetus for the evolution of governance structures that guide the low-carbon energy transition in the EU.

Oversight mechanisms are crucial to coordinate this transformation. The aim of the emerging oversight mechanisms is twofold. Firstly, they need to ensure

14 See on the implications of the need for government involvement in the energy transition, *F. Kern & K.S. Rogge*, The Pace of Governed Energy Transitions: Agency, International Dynamics and the Global Paris Agreement Accelerating Decarbonisation Processes?, Energy Research and Social Science 2016 (22), p. 13.

15 Legislation was enacted to establish the EU Emissions Trading System (ETS) and to promote the deployment of renewable energy sources. See European Parliament and Council Directive 2003/87/EC establishing a scheme for greenhouse gas emission allowance trading within the community, OJ 2003 L 275/32; European Parliament and Council Directive 2001/77/EC on the promotion of electricity produced from renewable energy sources in the internal electricity market, OJ 2001 L 283/33.

16 Communication from the Commission, An Energy Policy for Europe, COM (2007) 1 final.

17 Communication from the Commission, A Roadmap for Moving to a Competitive Low Carbon Economy in 2050, COM (2011) 112 final.

18 Ibid. at p. 3.

19 Communication from the Commission, Energy Roadmap 2050, COM (2011) 885 final, at p. 2.

that the energy transition is rules-based and fulfils the citizens' and economic actors' expectations regarding legal certainty and constitutionality. Secondly, the mechanisms enable a conversation that helps to arrive at a conceptualisation of the Union's energy future beyond the demand of further market integration. Thus, how the Commission and Member States' governments address environmental and social challenges in the course of the transformation shapes the EU brand of decarbonisation. Regard for sustainability and energy justice distinguishes the European project.

In the context of the low-carbon power transition, the concept of sustainability is relevant when considering the construction of new infrastructure, while energy justice concerns the affordability of and access to low-carbon electricity for vulnerable individuals and communities. Since market forces are unable to ensure an environmentally sustainable energy transition or prevent and alleviate energy poverty, government interference can help avoid aggravating the degradation of the environment or disadvantaging vulnerable people in their ability to access affordable electricity.

The low-carbon energy transition brings fundamental change to the structure of the socio-technical system of an economy.[20] Sustainable outcomes of this transformation primarily depend on governance processes that consider both the history of the existing electricity sector and responses of incumbent regime actors. Through these exchanges, a conversation develops that helps to incrementally re-imagine the future of the energy system, including its countless linkages with the economy and society. These exchanges inform government policies, and they take place in an environment where all participants are eager to voice demands and concerns. Governments need policy space when adopting measures that accompany the energy transition to consider various objectives. Frequent refinements of policy goals and amendments to legislation are almost unavoidable. As a result, the transition process is not linear and prone to setbacks.[21] It is even possible that one policy issue that requires government attention can be overlooked, as the next section shows.

3. STATE GRID AS THE BLACK SWAN OF THE EU LOW-CARBON POWER TRANSITION

State Grid entered the European energy sector when EU policymakers, business leaders and the public were preoccupied by the aftermath of the global financial

---

20 *C. Kuzemko, M. Lockwood, C. Mitchell & R. Hoggett*, Governing for Sustainable Energy System Change: Politics, Contexts, and Contingency, Energy Research and Social Science 2016 (12), pp. 96, 97.

21 Ibid. at p. 102.

and European debt crises (2007–12). The company began to buy stakes in electricity utilities in the EU, primarily in southern Member States.[22] Later, it also intended to make acquisitions in western Europe. However, the company failed to obtain shares in the Belgian distribution system operator Eandis[23] and the German transmission system operator 50Hertz.[24]

In fact, State Grid's actions in Belgium and Germany created further momentum for the adoption of an EU investment-screening regulation.[25] The notion of preventing investments in energy assets based on security concerns had become part of the debate about governing the electricity sector. This section explains what the stakes are in preventing a company like State Grid from participating in the construction of the EU energy future.

3.1. STANDARD SETTING AS A GLOBAL STRATEGY

State Grid's acquisitions in Europe are part of a greater scheme. They relate to China's Belt and Road Initiative,[26] and particularly to State Grid's involvement in global infrastructure interconnection and its strategic pursuit of global technology leadership. Thus, they are part of two major government projects. Firstly, with the Belt and Road Initiative, the Chinese government encourages companies to look for opportunities abroad and participate in the construction

---

22 State Grid International Development Ltd. acquired a 25% share in the Portuguese transmission system operator Redes Energéticas Nacionais (REN) in 2012. Two years later, the Cassa depositi e prestiti Spa (CDP) of Italy announced the sale of a 35% share in CDP Reti to State Grid Europe Ltd. CDP Reti holds 30% of SNAM Spa, a gas utility, and 29.851% of TERNA Spa, the majority owner of Italy's high-voltage and very high-voltage electricity national transmission system. In 2017, State Grid Europe Ltd bought a 24% share in the Greek Independent Power Transmission Operator (ADMIE).

23 *W. Lecluyse*, Hele Eandis-deal lijkt van de baan [Entire Eandis deal seems to have been stopped], *De Standaard*, 29 September 2016.

24 *D. Heide*, 'Brückenlösung' mit KfW vereitelt Einstieg der Chinesen bei 50Hertz ['Bridging operation' with KfW prevents Chinese entry into 50Hertz], *Handelsblatt*, 27 July 2018.

25 In both cases, national security concerns were raised during the public debate in order to argue against the transaction. Yet, in neither case was there a legal remedy to veto or otherwise prevent the investment. Politicians relied on ad-hoc decision-making. Prior to State Grid's attempts to acquire stakes in Belgian and Germany transmission system operator, France, Germany and Italy had sent a joint letter to the European Commission and asked for a reconsideration of EU rules on foreign investment. See *Y. Le Guernigou & L. Thomas*, France, Germany, Italy Urge Rethink of Foreign Investment in EU, *Reuters*, 14 February 2017; see also sub-section 3.2.

26 China's President Xi Jinping announced the commencement of the Belt and Road Initiative in 2013. It involves more than 60 states and has already allocated billions of US dollars in infrastructure spending, including the construction of power generation and transmission facilities. The policy scheme is primarily implemented by Chinese state-owned enterprises that obtain financing through state-owned banks.

of infrastructure, mainly transport and energy networks. The initiative seeks to interconnect Chinese state-owned enterprises' assets and services across the globe. The Chinese leadership has been pursuing this economic diplomacy scheme with gritty determination since mid-2013.

Secondly, and even more important, State Grid's incentive to get involved in electricity sectors abroad follows the Chinese government's requirement that, in the near future, the country's state-owned companies should become world leaders in technology standards in their respective economic sectors. Hence, companies – such as State Grid – plan their domestic and foreign activities against the political and economic backdrop of various party directives.

Generally, state-owned enterprises in core industries with high strategic value[27] are deeply embedded in the party-state hierarchy. This means that their executives are party members whose rank in the state bureaucracy equals that of ministers or deputy ministers. Furthermore, the party committees of the state-owned enterprises strongly influence the corporate activities, mainly because they have the power to set decision-making agendas.[28] Thus, party, state and corporate interests are interwoven.

In recent years, the focus of China's state-led corporate sector has shifted to the ability to control networks, standards and platforms that facilitate global movement, economic exchange and the dissemination of information. These vital components of the 21st-century global economy span economic sectors and territorial boundaries.[29] In the 1990s, the Chinese government began to call upon state-owned enterprises to expand abroad, capture systems of engagement and co-opt international standard-setting bodies. This policy intends to enable Chinese companies to acquire a decisive position regarding these components.[30] Infrastructure projects that state-owned companies conduct abroad form the link between technology-driven expansionist business strategies and international norms that govern exchanges through these networks and platforms. If the companies succeeded – and given the longevity of such systems and structures – the Chinese government would be able to exert influence on the nodes of modern-day exchange for decades to come.

State Grid's activities exemplify this strategic behaviour. Its position in the EU electricity sector needs to be assessed in the context of the company's systemic

---

27 Vital strategic industries include sectors such as defence, electricity, petroleum, telecommunication and transportation.

28 *W. Leutert*, State-owned Enterprises in Contemporary China, in *L. Bernier, M. Florio & P. Bance* (eds.) The Routledge Handbook of State-owned Enterprises, 2020, pp. 201 et seq.

29 *E. de la Bruyère & N. Picarsic*, China Standards 2035: Beijing's Platform Geopolitics and 'Standardization Work in 2020', *China Standard Series*, April 2020, https://www.horizonadvisory.org/china-standards-2035-first-report, p. 1.

30 *E. de la Bruyère*, The New Metrics for Building Geopolitical Power in a New World, *The National Interest*, 12 April 2020.

posture: State Grid's involvement in infrastructure-building in the Union and its periphery is flanked by the promotion of its ultrahigh-voltage (UHV) transmission lines and cross-continental interconnection plans, as well as ever closer links of current and former executives with international standard-setting organisations.

To be clear, the company's domestic business is the basis of State Grid's comprehensive international positioning. The company is powerful, both with respect to its financial means as well as its influence on Chinese policymaking. State Grid is peerless in its home market and the global electricity sector.[31] Xu Yi-chong reflects on the company's emergence as China's dominant transmission network operator[32] and describes it as 'a new type of state-owned "profit-driven" corporation'.[33]

Accordingly, in its dealings with domestic government agencies in China, State Grid generally relies on its vast size and knowledge of the power sector's functioning. As a result, it could obtain the central government's approval for testing and establishing UHV transmission lines that State Grid's 20,000 researchers had developed. Gaining government support for the implementation of this technology in several regions in China strengthened State Grid's overall capacity to realise large-scale construction projects.[34] From the outset, State Grid benefited from the weak regulatory environment that allowed it to further consolidate its dominant position in the Chinese power sector.[35] Its technological choices were not necessarily the best possible solutions, but the company's executives were in a position to 'market' them to high-ranking decision-makers.[36]

Operating in the international realm, State Grid's former executive Liu Zhenya has been proposing a 'global energy interconnection' scheme for years.[37] He was also instrumental in establishing the Global Energy Interconnection Development and Cooperation Organization (GEIDCO), whose headquarters are located in Beijing. Since its foundation in March 2016, GEIDCO has been used by Liu as a platform and vehicle to connect with international organisations

---

31 State Grid has about 913,000 employees and owns assets worth billions of U.S. dollars at home and abroad. In 2018, the company ranked second on the Fortunes Global 500 list. See, for more information, *Fortune*, Fortune Global 500: State Grid, https://fortune.com/global500/state-grid/.

32 *Y. Xu*, Sinews of Power: The Politics of the State Grid Corporation of China, 2017.

33 Ibid. at pp. 15–6.

34 Ibid. at p. 260.

35 *Y. Xu*, China's Giant State-owned Enterprises as Policy Advocates: The Case of the State Grid Corporation of China, The China Journal 2018 (79), pp. 21, 37.

36 In fact, State Grid's CEO Liu Zhenya took an enormous risk when in 2004 he started lobbying government officials for an approval of the first UHV project. See, ibid. at pp. 29, 31.

37 Liu Zhenya detailed his vision in books and other publications. See, for instance, *Z. Liu*, Global Energy Interconnection, 2015.

and regimes, such as the United Nations, UNFCCC and UNESCO, in order to promote his interconnection vision. Part of the plan is utilising wind power in the Arctic and solar power in equatorial regions of Africa and Asia, as well as hydropower in Russia and China to supply the global grid with renewable electricity. This grand global vision was readily supported by the Chinese leadership.[38]

State Grid managers are eager to further 'institutionalise' their interconnection plan not only by establishing GEIDCO, but also by attracting support from international organisations in the field of energy, such as the International Electrotechnical Commission (IEC) and International Renewable Energy Agency (IRENA). Numerous State Grid managers and researchers contributed to a 2016 white paper by the IEC.[39] This report details State Grid's grand vision and features UHV transmission lines when discussing the available technological choices.

In 2017, IRENA and State Grid signed a cooperation agreement to realise the global energy transition. During the signing ceremony, State Grid's CEO Shu Yinbiao emphasised that 'State Grid Corporation of China is dedicated to the interconnection of world power infrastructure to realize efficient, clean and sustainable development of global energy and contribute to the Belt and Road Initiative'.[40] In 2018, Shu Yinbiao was elected president of the IEC for a three-year term, effective from January 2020.[41] Summarising the incentive for State Grid to participate in the IEC, he emphasised that when 'a company's technical standards are accepted as IEC Standards, products will be more widely accepted on international markets'.[42]

Finally, during the Belt and Road Forum in April 2019, the Belt and Road Energy Partnership (BREP) was established.[43] At this occasion, representatives of GEIDCO presented plans for global energy interconnection for the periods

---

38 In China, independent regulatory bodies are either weak or were abolished after a brief period of market liberalisation that began in the 1990s. The State Electricity Regulatory Commission (SERC) only existed from 2003 to 2013. It was never able to act as an independent regulatory vis-à-vis State Grid. Ahead of a new wave of reform efforts in the power sector, SERC was integrated into the National Development and Reform Commission, which is part of the central government. See, *C. Tsai*, Regulating China's Power Sector: Creating an Independent Regulator without Autonomy, The China Quarterly 2014 (218), pp. 452, 468 et seq.

39 *International Electrotechnical Commission*, Global Energy Interconnection: White Paper, 2016.

40 *IRENA*, IRENA and State Grid of China to Cooperate on Accelerating Energy Transition, 8 June 2017.

41 *C. Marchand*, Council Elects Future IEC President: Dr Yinbiao Shu Will Take over Presidency in 2020, *IEC e-tech*, 15 June 2018.

42 *International Electronical Commission*, Interview: Sharing Know-how, Building Bigger Markets, June 2014, https://www.iec.ch/globalvisions/SGCC/.

43 The BREP was established and adopted a declaration on the partnership's principles on 25 April 2019.

until 2035 and 2050. These plans outline the construction of intercontinental transmission lines. The 'New Eurasian Land Bridge Channel'[44] intends to link China's electricity sector, including wind power generation areas in Xinjiang and Inner Mongolia as well as Yunnan Province's excess capacity in hydropower, with Kazakhstan and through Russia and Belarus with the EU electricity market.[45] The outbreak of the coronavirus pandemic might cast doubt over many facets of international economic exchange, but to assume that State Grid's grand interconnection plans have been shelved would be premature.

To sum up, State Grid is at the core of a multi-pronged strategy, backed by the Chinese leadership, to promote the idea of global energy interconnection, in particular with respect to the electricity sector. This strategy is driven by readily available capital of billions of U.S. dollars and a grand vision of Chinese party-state actors for the future of the global electricity sector. The mere existence of this policy scheme and State Grid's zeal to contribute to its implementation re-contextualise the EU's regulatory approaches to the low-carbon power transition. Compared with European utilities and their interaction with their regulatory environment, State Grid's ownership structure, its nearly unrestrained dominance of its home market and its allure to achieve a position of technological dominance abroad amount to a *systemic challenge*. By 2017, the EU felt the need to develop a well-thought-out response.

3.2. CONCEPTUALISING AND ADDRESSING THE CHALLENGE OF ROGUE STANDARDISING

The issue of standard setting needs to be central to the response to State Grid's activities. The EU approach is still evolving in this regard. In the late 2010s, some EU Member States, such as Belgium and Germany, primarily based their reaction to State Grid's attempts to acquire stakes in transmission companies on the ownership structure of the company – that is, its strategic embeddedness in the Chinese party-state. Broad public security concerns were the main reason for unease concerning the company's investments decisions. At that time, it was not further specified how the fact that State Grid is a state-owned enterprise

44 *GEIDCO*, Research Report on the Belt and Road Energy Interconnection, 2019, p. 3.

45 The European Commission tasked the Joint Research Centre with examining the potential for an electricity transmission link between China and the EU. The report only assessed whether the link would be feasible and concluded that it is technically possible. Yet, the authors suggested that a multi-terminal system would be more useful, as it would facilitate injecting or pulling electricity at other places than the two ends. However, this system would also be more complex (and more expensive) than the Chinese proposal. See, *M. Ardelean & P. Minnebo*, A China-EU Electricity Transmission Link: Assessment of Potential Connecting Countries and Routes, 2017, pp. 10 et seq., 83.

could translate into unwanted interference in the EU. The company's pursuit of global technological leadership, which essentially is the company's long-term vision, was not yet part of the conversation.

Arguably, the technological aspects of State Grid's activities concern the core of the EU energy transition. The systemic challenge of the company's involvement in the EU electricity sector involves a re-conceptualisation of *energy security* in the process of the low-carbon transition. In this regard, the case of State Grid provides three reasons for concern. The apprehension primarily relates to the policy space for future decision-making and specific technological aspects of the company's involvement in the transmission of electricity. In addition, there is a growing link between electricity supply and public security.

State Grid's ambition to create a global or, at least, Eurasian grid is a significant aspect when trying to preserve *policy space* for future decision-making in the EU. The company's plans have crucial geopolitical implications for EU Member States. Having an integrated grid at the Eurasian level would pose three risks to the EU. Firstly, energy security would be shared between the EU and China, and for that matter all transit states. Secondly, EU energy policies would have to adjust to China's policy priorities.[46] Thirdly, an official endorsement of the transmission link would impact the governance of the EU electricity sector. Teaming up with a powerful actor such as State Grid would have far-reaching consequences for the development of a common EU energy future.

This step would literally give the company's bosses a say in the debate about EU energy policies, while State Grid's plans to sell its UHV technology, in combination with its vision of electricity transmission via large-scale intercontinental infrastructure, does not match the evolving framework of EU climate and energy governance. The company's attitude to regulatory oversight and the rule of law at home is problematic. State Grid's global vision and the increasing institutionalisation of its plans in international forums are clearly aimed to shape and coordinate the global energy transition. These activities have already re-contextualised the energy security in the Union and the conversation about the construction of a common EU energy future. Hence, opting for closer ties with State Grid at this stage would considerably limit the set of choices for future policy decisions.

How does the involvement of State Grid in the EU electricity sector relate to the concept of energy security from the perspective of transmission technology? Two possible concerns arise. Firstly, the dependence on low-cost Chinese supplies and services could grow in the future, mainly because State Grid is able to outprice European companies in their home markets. The example of

46 *N. Mazzucchi*, China and European Electricity Networks, Strategy and Issues, *Note de la FRS*, no. 17, 2018, https://www.frstrategie.org/web/documents/publications/notes/2018/201817.pdf, p. 10.

Pinggao's involvement in Poland is a case in point.[47] In the long run, this might drive European companies out of business, while infrastructure service contracts are more frequently awarded to State Grid and its subsidiaries. Equipment would need to be imported from China on a regular basis. Secondly, with fewer European actors research and development in the Union will stall. European companies will lose the so-called standard wars, as State Grid's technological solutions are increasingly chosen when deploying new technologies. The functioning of the European electricity system would then become reliant on (licensed) Chinese technologies and imports, giving State Grid a leading role in the provision of services and technology in segments of the EU electricity sector without taking over assets in the EU. The fact that State Grid has already obtained stakes in European companies makes this turn of events even more likely. Thus, the technology challenge that relates to energy security concerns in the context of State Grid's actions in the EU has already materialised.

Considerations about public security relate to the fact that the low-carbon transition changes the resource and technological basis of the energy system. Maintaining the stability of electricity supply throughout the transition process is vital. The increasing reliance on wind and solar power requires an interconnection of regional networks in order to deal with variable electricity generation. Other changes are the establishment of smart grids and the digitalisation of the sector. The shift in the resource base and technological innovations to transmit and distribute electricity alter the conceptualisation of energy security, adding complexity and regional divergence. Hence, standards for a great variety of technological innovations that will be needed to realise the energy transition are at the core of the evolving notion of energy security in relation to the stability of the electricity system.

Both the growing electrification of the energy system and the increasing dependence on electric appliances in daily life, business processes, as well as the provision of public services emphasise the significance of a stable electricity supply for public security. In this sense, the quality and functioning of critical infrastructure components, such as transmission lines, interconnectors and relay stations, become vital for maintaining public security. Hence, energy security and public security concerns can be identified as the rationale for increasing scrutiny with regard to State Grid's involvement in the EU electricity sector.

Consequently, broader energy security considerations enter the policy field of market integration. The common market for electricity requires a

---

47 Pinggao is part of State Grid and mainly engages in construction and maintenance work. It was awarded a contract for a relay station near Warsaw by outbidding Polish companies and subsequently completing the project by subcontracting work to Polish companies. See *I. Sudak*, 'Chińskie firmy realizują strategiczne inwestycje w naszej energetyce. Polskimi podwykonawcami [Chinese companies realise strategic investments in our energy sector, through Polish sub-contractors], *wyborcza.pl*, 25 November 2018.

convergence of many policies. The challenge that third-party involvement poses to the conceptualisation of the EU energy transition highlights the need for coordinating the assessment of foreign investment. Thus, screening of non-EU actors that seek to invest in the electricity sector became a component of market integration and solidarity among EU Member States.

The rapid promulgation of the investment screening regulation, beginning in 2017, attests to the urgency that many Member States felt following State Grid's and other companies' increasing assertiveness in several EU Member States. During the period from 2013 to 2016, Chinese foreign direct investment grew rapidly and began to cause concern about the acquisition of vital technologies. Some governments chose to block proposed acquisitions by Chinese investors. In early 2017, the ministers of economic affairs of France, Italy and Germany sent a letter to Commissioner Cecilia Malmström pointing to a lack of 'effective instruments' to respond to takeovers of European companies for strategic reasons.[48] The Commission presented a proposal for an investment screening mechanism in September 2017.[49] The Member States agreed on the legislation in the first half of 2018. The regulation on investment screening[50] came into force in April 2019 and has been applicable in the Member States since October 2020.

External challenges, exemplified by State Grid's actions, and the Union's response to these actions show that the EU Member States have arrived at a crossroads where a comprehensive conversation about the continent's energy future is more urgent than ever. The next section evaluates the regulatory oversight framework that seeks to guide a just and sustainable low-carbon transition of the EU power sector, while avoiding undue interference by outside actors.

4. THE EMERGING OVERSIGHT FRAMEWORK

This section provides an overview of the legislative approach to the governance of the electricity sector in the EU, including the incorporation of sustainability and energy justice concerns, as well as the oversight mechanism to screen foreign direct investment in this sector.

---

48 *Bundesministerium für Wirtschaft und Energie, Ministère de l'Économie et des Finances, Ministero dello Sviluppo Economico*, Schreiben an die EU-Handelkommissarin Cecilia Malmström [Letter to the EU trade commissioner Cecilia Malmström, 21 February 2017], https://www.bmwi.de/Redaktion/DE/Downloads/S-T/schreiben-de-fr-it-an-malmstroem.pdf.

49 Communication from the Commission, Proposal for a Regulation of the European Parliament and of the Council establishing a framework for screening foreign direct investment into the European Union, COM (2017) 487 final.

50 European Parliament and Council Regulation (EU) No 2019/452 on establishing a framework for the screening of foreign direct investment into the Union, OJ 2019 L 79/1.

4.1. LEGISLATIVE APPROACH

The legislation that comprises the 'Clean energy for all Europeans' package was enacted from late 2018 through mid-2019 and constitutes the legislative response to both the Commission's communication on the creation of the Energy Union and the adoption of the 2015 Paris Agreement. For the purpose of this chapter's analysis, five legislative acts of this package are particularly relevant, as they, with an infrastructure perspective in mind, pertain to the decarbonisation of electricity generation. These concern recasts of the Electricity Regulation and Directive;[51] the recast of the regulation on the Agency for the Cooperation of Energy Regulators (ACER);[52] a renewables directive;[53] and the aforementioned Regulation 2018/1999 that guides the overall trajectory of EU energy and climate governance. Moreover, the investment-screening Regulation 2019/452[54] applies to the electricity sector, as pursuant to Article 4 (1) (a) energy is considered as 'critical infrastructure' in the context of assessing potential effects of foreign direct investment on security and public order. Taken together, these legislative acts establish a multi-faceted framework for governing the further integration and decarbonisation of the EU electricity sector.

Electricity Regulation 2019/943 and Electricity Directive 2019/944 concern the general rules of the common electricity market, including the generation, transmission, distribution, energy storage and supply of electricity. Article 28 of the Regulation 2019/943 states that the transmission system operators have to cooperate at a Union level through the European network of transmission system operators for electricity (ENTSO-E) to further promote the internal market for electricity, while ACER monitors the cooperation between these transmission system operators. ACER evaluates the fulfilment of their tasks and issues opinions on the union-wide network development plan, which ENTSO-E drafts.[55] To improve the cooperation between transmission system operators and distribution system operators (DSO), the EU DSO should be established.[56] Pursuant to Article 57 of Directive 2019/944, each member state designates a single, independent regulatory authority. The national authorities closely cooperate with regulators

---

51 European Parliament and Council Regulation (EU) No 2019/943 on the internal market for electricity (recast), OJ 2019 L 158/54; European Parliament and Council Directive (EU) No 2019/944 on common rules for the internal market for electricity and amending Directive 2012/27/EU (recast), OJ 2019 L 158/125.

52 European Parliament and Council Regulation (EU) No 2019/942 on establishing a European Union Agency for the Cooperation of Energy Regulators (recast), OJ 2019 L 158/22.

53 European Parliament and Council Directive (EU) No 2018/2001 on the promotion of the use of energy from renewable sources (recast), OJ 2018 L 328/82.

54 European Parliament and Council Regulation (EU) No 2019/452 on establishing a framework for the screening of foreign direct investment into the Union, OJ 2019 L 79/1.

55 Article 32 (1), (2).

56 Articles 52, 53.

of other Member States, the Commission and ACER in order to ensure the functioning of the common market for electricity.[57] Cooperation between regulatory authorities is particularly important with respect to cross-border issues.[58] Thus, with respect to market regulation and integration the legislative package extends and strengthens the rules and institutions that have been evolving since the adoption of the third energy package in 2009.

The Renewables Directive 2018/2001 sets a binding, collective target of reaching a share of 32 per cent from renewable energy sources in the Union's gross final energy consumption in 2030.[59] In order to integrate growing shares of renewable electricity, the construction of transmission infrastructure will be necessary. Article 3 (5) (c) of the directive states that the Commission has to support the development of transmission and distribution grid infrastructure, intelligent networks, storage facilities and interconnectors. Article 11 of the Renewables Directive allows Member States to cooperate with third countries to produce electricity from renewables and add this electricity to the renewables target of the Member State in question.[60]

Indeed, the construction of transmission lines to better integrate variable supplies of wind and solar power as well as the need to produce – and potentially import – renewable electricity provide various business opportunities in which companies from outside the EU might be interested. However, foreign investments in this segment of the electricity sector will most likely be subject to screening in host countries. The Investment-Screening Regulation 2019/452 introduces a common framework to assess foreign direct investment into the EU on the grounds of security or public order. It harmonises existing national screening legislation, as it sets minimum criteria for Member States that had already passed legislation to evaluate foreign direct investment. When the regulation was published, 14 Member States had a mechanism in place,[61] while some were preparing legislation.

Accordingly, the Investment-Screening Regulation 2019/452 introduces another form of EU oversight to the energy sector in the sense that the sector falls under 'critical infrastructure' in which foreign investments might affect security or public order[62] – a criterion that should be considered when determining whether a foreign direct investment is likely to affect security or public order concerns the direct or indirect control of the investing entity by the government of a third country, including through ownership structures or significant funding.[63]

---

57 Article 59.
58 Article 61.
59 Article 3 (1).
60 Article 11 (2).
61 Notable exceptions in western Europe were Ireland and Belgium.
62 Article 4 (1) (a).
63 Article 4 (2) (a).

The Member State where the screening takes place will take the final decision.[64] However, other Member States and the Commission can provide comments or give an opinion on the planned investment.[65] The Commission can give an opinion when an investment would affect projects or programmes of Union interests on grounds of security or public order.[66] The annex of the Investment-Screening Regulation mentions Trans-European Networks for Energy (TEN-E) as one project or programme to which this would be applicable.

To sum up, ACER's oversight capabilities regarding market integration have been bolstered, mirroring the broader approach of the 'Clean energy for all Europeans' package. Through its cooperation with national regulatory authorities, ACER forms an increasingly coherent oversight framework. In addition, the Commission established a loose consultative mechanism to screen foreign direct investments in the Member States' electricity sectors. Having an opportunity to scrutinise foreign investment constitutes a first step towards increasing union-wide vigilance in this regard.

4.2. ADDRESSING SUSTAINABILITY AND ENERGY JUSTICE

The Energy Union envisions an energy system that provides 'sustainable' and 'affordable' energy for households and businesses.[67] Obviously, energy infrastructure profoundly influences the environment and social fabric of the localities where they are situated or, in case of transmission lines, that they traverse. Constructing and adjusting energy infrastructure necessarily affects this interrelationship. Many communities, particularly in rural areas, currently deal with the consequences of being close to large wind and solar power installations or cross-regional transmission lines.

Governance Regulation 2018/1999 addresses these impacts and reiterates the goals of the Energy Union, stipulating that the 'fundamental transformation of Europe's energy system' must 'preserve, protect and improve the quality of the environment'.[68] It acknowledges that action is needed at Union, regional, national and local levels.[69] The governance mechanism that Regulation 2018/1999 establishes must 'ensure coherence and adequacy of policies and measures at Union and national level with regard to the transformation of the energy system towards a sustainable low-carbon economy'.[70]

64 Article 6 (9).
65 Article 6 (2), (3).
66 Articles 8 (1).
67 Communication from the Commission, *supra* note 1.
68 Recital 3.
69 Ibid.
70 Recital 23.

In addition, Recital 19 of the Governance Regulation 2018/1999 requires that public and private investment must be re-directed and urges that 'incentives across the entire policy spectrum' need to accomplish a 'socially acceptable and just transition to a sustainable low-carbon economy'. The Energy Union aims to offer 'a fair deal for energy consumers, including by addressing energy poverty and promoting fair competition in the internal market'.[71]

It goes without saying that energy installations and networks have to be built in accordance with international obligations and environmental laws – both EU and national legislation.[72] A balanced approached is advised. For instance, new interconnectors between the Member States' grids should only be built if the benefits outweigh socio-economic and environmental costs.[73] Environmental protection is one aspect that Member States have to take into account when designing procedures to authorise the construction of new electricity generation capacity.[74] The operators of the distribution and transmission systems have to manage and develop the systems 'with due regard for the environment'.[75] Relevant environmental legislation is also applicable to the work of ACER, the independent regulator at the EU level,[76] while the regulatory authorities of the Member States 'shall take all reasonable measures' to promote 'a competitive, flexible, secure and environmentally sustainable internal market for electricity within the Union'.[77] Finally, the Renewables Directive 2018/2001 stipulates that during assessment, planning and licensing procedures for renewables energy installations, coherence should be ensured between the objectives of the directive and EU environmental law.[78]

The implementation of the Energy Union also acknowledges the linkage between the energy transition and social issues, especially the just access to energy. As part of their ten-year integrated national energy and climate plans, Member States have to assess the number of households in energy poverty.[79] The issue of energy poverty is also a topic in the biennial progress reports that the Member States have to submit to the Commission.[80] The Member States are also required to consider, to the extent possible, the 'expected socio-economic effect of the decarbonisation measures' in their long-term strategies that cover 30 years.[81]

71 Recital 5.
72 Recitals 28, 38, 55.
73 Article 4 (d) (1) of Regulation 2018/1999.
74 Article 8 (2) (c) of Directive 2019/944.
75 Articles 31 (1) and 40 (1) (a) of Directive 2019/944, respectively.
76 Recital 33 of Regulation 2019/942.
77 Article 58 (1) (a) of Directive 2019/944.
78 Recital 45.
79 Article 3 (3) (d).
80 Article 24.
81 Article 15 (4) (d).

Electricity Directive 2019/944 acknowledges that energy services 'are fundamental to safeguarding the well-being of the Union citizens'. To ensure adequate supply with energy services, Member States are expected to 'collect the right information to monitor the number of households in energy poverty'.[82] The directive seeks to promote the adoption of national policies that support vulnerable and energy-poor customers.[83] Article 28 of the Electricity Directive specifically considers vulnerable customers – that is, people with low incomes, a high share of energy expenditure of their disposable income or a home with a low degree of energy efficiency.[84] Other vulnerable groups are people who are dependent on electrical equipment for health reasons or those who live in remote areas. To alleviate their situation, Member States are expected to implement measures under domestic social security systems or support energy efficiency improvements.[85] In order to identify vulnerable groups and the extent of energy poverty, the Commission assists the Member States by providing criteria that help them assess the domestic situation.[86] When reviewing the implementation of the Electricity Directive, the Commission pays special attention to the situation of electricity customers, especially those who are affected by energy poverty.[87]

To sum up, the EU legal framework clearly intends to mainstream environmental and social considerations into Member States' energy and climate policies. This is obvious from the provisions that relate to environmental effects of new technologies and installations and the concern for energy poverty. Regular reports, reviews and assessments are the basis for a frequent 'reality check,' both for the Commission and the Member States themselves. The next section explores how oversight mechanisms that are entailed in this framework can promote the evolution of a common energy future.

5. CONSTRUCTING ENERGY FUTURES IN HARMONISED GOVERNANCE STRUCTURES

The history of the EU electricity sector predetermines the choices that EU policymakers and Member States' governments can make when they implement the 'Clean energy for all Europeans' package to realise the goals of the Energy Union. Section 2 described the path to a governed energy transition that takes into account sustainability and energy justice considerations. The legislation examined in section 4 sets the parameters that are going to shape the conversation about the

82 Recital 59.
83 Recital 60.
84 Article 28 (1).
85 Article 28 (2).
86 Article 29.
87 Article 69.

design of future electricity generation and its provision to consumers and businesses, including oversight mechanisms that ensure the implementation of EU rules. This section explores the emergence of governance structures that deal with the challenges of the energy transition and facilitate the construction of a common EU energy future. Based on the evolving regulatory framework, this section focuses on the legacy of infrastructure from a governance perspective, the role of national plans to foster sustainability and energy justice and the response to State Grid's actions.

5.1. OBDURATE INFRASTRUCTURE AND THE LEGACY OF EU ELECTRICITY SECTOR GOVERNANCE

The integration of the EU electricity market commenced in the late 1990s. It was an effort framed by successive legislative packages, as summarised below. However, further interconnection of the Member States' power sectors and accomplishing a just and sustainable energy transition also depend on the physical infrastructure and the mode of governance that is embedded in this infrastructure. Governance legacies, together with the obduracy of physical links, influence Member States' choices when they implement regulatory frameworks to decarbonise power generation.

The history of electricity provision in Europe spans the entire 20th century. Transnational cooperation and interconnection became a force for both integration and division. It constituted a consequential socio-technological process that also reshaped the meaning of the term 'Europe', especially during the Cold War. The division of the continent during this period has been shaping the governance of the sector for decades.

Geographically and politically, the electricity sector was divided along the line of the Iron Curtain in post-war Europe; and this division was systemic in nature. In the west, a decentralised model of transnational organisation emerged that relied on the cooperation between the utilities to ensure economic benefits and the reliability of supply. In the east, the socialist states joined a centralised electricity system led by the Soviet Union whose control units were located in Moscow and Prague. This system relied on long-distance transmission lines. After the Cold War, former socialist states in central and eastern Europe sought to join the western European system. They began to cooperate with western partners in 1996.[88] Thus, the border between decentralised and centralised systems moved eastwards.

---

88 *V. Lagendijk & E. van der Vleuten*, Inventing Electrical Europe: Interdependencies, Borders, Vulnerabilities, in *P. Högselius, A. Hommels, A. Kaijser & E. van der Vleuten* (eds.) The Making of Europe's Critical Infrastructure: Common Connections and Shared Vulnerabilities, 2013, pp. 62, 79 et seq.

The systemic differences matter – mainly because infrastructure and society are closely linked. In fact, throughout the 20th century, the construction of transnational electricity networks was part of society-building efforts, as states shaped domestic and international relations through network building. The states sought to foster the political and social relations that these networks brought about and maintained.[89]

Inevitably, the process of building networks in Europe created winners and losers; and the road to success was littered with numerous failed projects. The network-building process left some regions at the periphery, while others emerged as centres of economic activity.[90] It goes without saying that the power sector closely interacts with other components of the economy – in particular, all forms of industry. Transmission lines emerged as essential parts of the continent's economic geography.

The legacy of previous infrastructure construction is an important point of departure when adjusting electricity networks to the needs of low-carbon power generation. It remains to be seen whether infrastructure planning in the course of the energy transition can avoid reinforcing the current notions of core and periphery of economic activity, while promoting economic development. Providing opportunities to regions that did not profit from the fossil economy or will be negatively affected by its demise is also vital in this process. These are crucial considerations at both national and regional levels when trying to prevent social disruptions. It is necessary to take into account the obduracy of network infrastructure – the ones that already exist and those that will enable the transition process.[91] In other words, generation facilities and transmission lines that will be built in the next few years will determine the infrastructure landscape in Europe for decades to come. Future generations will also have to deal with the embedded political and social relations that created them. Thus, the infrastructure of power supply forms a critical building block of the Union's future socio-economic fabric.

Considering the sector's regulatory framework, it is obvious that EU electricity sector legislation has gone a long way from being among those sectors where market integration seemed beneficial in the 1980s to its current position at the core of the continent's transition towards climate neutrality. In fact, the integration process started with the Single European Act[92] in the 1980s.

89 *E. van der Vleuten & A. Kaijser*, Networking Europe, History and Technology 2005 (21), pp. 21, 31 et seq.

90 Ibid. at pp. 31–4.

91 Corey Johnson examines energy infrastructure that spans long distances and describes its path dependency as obduracy of the system that complicates changes in the system. See *C. Johnson*, Mobile Energy and Obdurate Infrastructure: Distant Carbon and the Making of Modern Europe, in *S. Bouzarovski, M.J. Pasqualetti & V. Castán Broto* (eds.) The Routledge Research Companion to Energy Geographies, 2017, p. 99.

92 Single European Act, OJ 1987 L 169/1.

The expansion of the single market concept to network-bound sectors led to the decision to also liberalise the power sector and create a common market for electricity. This sequence of events greatly influenced the sector's governance. Legislation to implement the dual goal of liberalising and integrating national electricity sectors was passed in 1996,[93] 2003[94] and again in 2009.[95] The relatively brief periods between the passage of new legislation and repealing legislation point to the difficulties that the implementation of the legislative acts encountered. It attests to the contestation and far-reaching socio-economic considerations that have hampered the harmonisation of national legislation in this sector.

The first Electricity Directive 96/92/EC initiated a shift of policy- and law-making from the national to the EU level. This shift was the result of the dynamics of negotiations at the EU level, the emerging institutional context of European integration, including the attractiveness of the single market, and the interaction of these two factors with domestic political constituencies.[96] Following these initial steps, the liberalisation process gradually resulted in the establishment of an EU regulatory framework for the electricity sector. The 'Clean energy for all Europeans' package places the regulation of the electricity sector at the core of the energy transition.

In the context of overseeing the integration of the EU electricity market, ACER's role cannot be overstated. The recast of the ACER Regulation 2019/942 strengthens the role of this oversight body in coordinating national and regional entities. It also broadens the agency's responsibilities. It oversees the cooperation between transmission system operators and DSOs. Furthermore, its tasks include the participation in the development of network codes and guidelines and a facilitating role in the cooperation of national regulatory authorities. ACER also monitors the establishment of new interconnector capacity, the implementation of network development plans and the integrity and transparency of wholesale markets.[97] Above all, ACER's decision-making

---

93 Council Directive 96/92/EC concerning common rules for the internal market in electricity, OJ 1997 L 27/20.

94 European Parliament and Council Directive 2003/54/EC concerning common rules for the internal market in electricity, OJ 2003 L 176/37; European Parliament and Council Regulation (EC) No 1228/2003 on conditions for access to the network for cross-border exchanges in electricity, OJ 2003 L 176/1.

95 European Parliament and Council Directive 2009/71/EC concerning common rules for the internal market in electricity, OJ 2009 L 211/55; European Parliament and Council Directive 2009/72/EC concerning common rules for the internal market in electricity, OJ 2009 211/55; European Parliament and Council Regulation (EC) No 714/2009 on conditions for access to the network for cross-border exchanges in electricity, OJ 2009 211/15.

96 *R. Eising & N. Jabko*, Moving Targets: National Interests and Electricity Liberalization in the European Union, Comparative Political Studies 2001 (34), pp. 742, 745 et seq.

97 Articles 3 to 12 of Regulation 2019/942.

power with respect to cross-border issues has been strengthened, facilitating a union-wide conversation and enhancing regional cooperation.

The coordination of regional cooperation to establish the internal electricity market is particularly important. Given the complexity of the process of market integration, especially the physical interconnection of national grids, closer regional cooperation has become the first step towards a truly European electricity market. Ensuring the quality of regional cooperation and governance structures is essential for two reasons. Firstly, it acknowledges the legacy of how electricity generation and transmission developed in Europe in the past. Secondly, the reliability of regional and local power supply is vital for the legitimacy of EU electricity sector governance among electricity consumers.

The new Governance Regulation 2018/1999 emphasises the centrality of regional and local approaches. It refers to existing regional cooperation forums and suggests that Member States should deploy these forums to implement the regulation.[98] This is a significant endorsement and appreciation of regional approaches in the context of developing the common market for electricity.

The emerging common vision of the Union's energy future consists of a myriad of local stories in which communities re-imagine their energy futures in a decarbonising world. With the onset of the low-carbon energy transition, decentralised electricity generation plays a greater role than in the past. Therefore, it is the local level where the energy future of the continent is reimagined. DSOs are essential to realising this process. They form the lynchpin between large transmission grids and the consumer. National lawmakers need to acknowledge this shift[99] and allow DSOs sufficient flexibility to deal with ongoing technological and societal changes.[100] They have to be able to dispatch increasingly locally produced renewable electricity and take into account changing consumption patterns related to new forms of electricity uses. Hence, DSOs will be instrumental in transforming the EU electricity sector, in accordance with local circumstances. Electricity sector integration is a balancing act between large-scale projects and local developments.

The current regulatory framework of the EU power sector emphasises the importance of local developments and close regional cooperation to construct a common EU energy future. It facilitates the conversation between these levels of decision-making, reinforcing the decentralised development pattern of the power sector that emerged in western Europe during the Cold War period.

---

98 Recital 32.

99 *S.A.C.M. Lavrijssen*, Power to the Energy Consumers, European Energy and Environmental Law Review 2017 (26), pp. 172, 176 et seq.

100 *M.G. Edens & S.A.C.M. Lavrijssen*, Balancing Public Values during the Energy Transition: How Can German and Dutch DSOs Safeguard Sustainability?, Energy Policy 2019 (128), pp. 57, 64 et seq.

Decentralised decision-making is also preferable in the realm of environmental and social matters, as the next sub-section shows.

5.2. NATIONAL PLANS, SUSTAINABILITY AND JUST ELECTRICITY PROVISION

EU Member States have to take into account the five dimensions of the Energy Union when designing their future energy and climate policies. Regular updates and reporting is going to keep them engaged for years to come. In fact, the integrated national energy and climate plan on which Governance Regulation 2018/1999 centres has the potential to become a vital tool for Member States to reflect on their policies and share outcomes, challenges and best practices.

Article 3 of the Governance Regulation details the compulsory components of the national plans, including an assessment of the number of households in energy poverty. The Member States' first plan covers the period from 2021 to 2030. Pursuant to Article 3 (4), the national plans are publicly available.[101]

To streamline the process of delineating the national plans substantively, the Member States first send a draft to the Commission, which then assesses the national plans, issuing recommendations.[102] Pursuant to Article 9 (3) of the Governance Regulation, the Member States have to state a reason if they do not consider the recommendations of the Commission. Beginning in 2023, the Member States will have to submit draft update plans to their national plans, and thereafter every ten years. The Commission also assesses these plans and expects the final version of the update one year later.[103] Article 14 (4) of Governance Regulation 2018/1999 requires the Member States to include in the updates to the plans efforts to mitigate 'any adverse environmental impacts that become apparent' during the reporting activities.

In addition, every two years, the Member States have to submit progress reports on greenhouse gas measures and projections, adaptation action, renewable energy supply, energy efficiency objectives, the national energy security situation, the state of research, innovation and competitiveness, as well as the progress that they have made to contribute to the internal market (expressed in interconnection targets), and targets regarding the reduction of energy poverty.[104] Furthermore, the Commission issues its own assessments of the Union's energy and climate policies. Every year on October 31, the

---

[101] See, European Commission, National Energy and Climate Plans, https://ec.europa.eu/info/energy-climate-change-environment/implementation-eu-countries/energy-and-climate-governance-and-reporting/national-energy-and-climate-plans_en.

[102] Article 9 (2) of Regulation 2018/1999.

[103] Article 14 (1), (2) of Regulation 2018/1999.

[104] Articles 17 to 25 of Regulation 2018/1999.

Commission publishes its report on the 'State of the Energy Union', which includes information on the progress of the Member States' energy and climate policy implementation.[105]

Indeed, the governance mechanism that Regulation 2018/1999 creates amounts to a massive monitoring effort that takes into account all aspects of the energy transition, including sustainability and energy justice. The various reporting formats and the short frequency of reporting facilitate a dynamic and constant exchange between the Commission and the Member States and among the Member States, including through their regional forums. The European Environment Agency uses the data that the Member States provide regarding decarbonisation and energy efficiency to undertake further evaluation work in order to assist the Commission.[106] The energy poverty situation is assessed by the European Energy Poverty Observatory.[107] The reports by these agencies are regularly made public.

In addition, Article 11 of Governance Regulation 2018/1999 requires the Member States to establish a 'multilevel climate and energy dialogue' following national rules. These dialogues will enable local authorities, civil society organisations, business communities, investors and other stakeholders – as well as the general public – to participate in the discussion about different options for future energy and climate policies.

Ideally, these multilevel dialogues will inform the national energy and climate plans that the Member States submit to the Commission. The process of drafting and evaluating the national plans is the main tool to institutionalise the conversation about the direction of the energy transition, mainly because this process helps national governments to reflect on social and environmental aspects of the transformation and to share information about best practices with other Member States. Furthermore, valuable information is made public, providing essential input for societal debate and conveying a notion of transparency.

5.3. DEALING WITH THE TRANSMISSION LINK FROM CHINA

For years, State Grid and Chinese officials have been promoting the establishment of the China–EU electricity transmission link as part of the 'New Eurasian Land Bridge Channel'. Given the legacy of infrastructure development and market integration in the EU, the completion of this link by 2035, as is suggested in recent plans, would severely interfere with many domestic debates in EU Member States that are necessary to develop a shared understanding of a common EU

105 Article 35 of Regulation 2018/1999.

106 Article 42 of Regulation 2018/1999.

107 Article 24 of Regulation 2018/1999.

energy future. The cross-continental link would preclude the consideration of possible alternatives and create regional vulnerabilities as a result of a dominant infrastructure project for which the EU's internal debate is not prepared.

The persistence with which Chinese officials and former and current State Grid representatives lobby for the establishment of the global energy interconnection suggests that at least parts of the larger project might be realised soon. From an EU perspective, it would be irresponsible to disregard the project as megalomania or propaganda. Its promotion and partial realisation in other countries must be followed closely, in particular in potential transit states on the way to the EU market – that is, Kazakhstan, Russia and Belarus.

In addition, every new investment that State Grid wants to make in a member state, especially in eastern Europe and the Mediterranean region, increases the likelihood of establishing the transcontinental transmission link. Although State Grid is the main proponent of the GEI project, other Chinese utilities[108] that also have acquired assets in EU Member States could be interested in joining the effort. Hence, new investments by any Chinese utility must be scrutinised.[109]

Undoubtedly, a convincing case can be made against the investment effort that would finalise the physical link between the EU network and a (by then) Chinese-built UHV transmission line. The legal framework of EU energy governance supports (at least) three arguments against the China–EU transmission link. They relate to infrastructure construction, human rights and energy security.

Firstly, funding by State Grid for the 'final physical link' – such as a new interconnector – between the EU and Belarus or Ukraine or any other state can be screened because of its potential effect on national security or public order within the EU, as it is directed towards critical infrastructure (energy),[110] and the foreign investor is indirectly or directly controlled by the government of a third country.[111] Furthermore, pursuant to Article 8 (1) of the Investment-Screening

---

108 China Southern Power Grid, the country's second-largest transmission operator, has obtained a 25.48 per cent share in Encevo. This company has two main subsidiaries: Creos manages electricity and gas grids in Luxembourg, Enovos is engaged in energy trade in Luxembourg, Belgium, France and Germany.

109 This chapter shows that it is of particular importance to set limits to the involvement of Chinese state-owned enterprises in the electricity sector. At the end of 2020, the EU and China concluded a Comprehensive Agreement on Investment. The agreement was reached in principle and was still subject to a finalisation of the text and, after the signing by both sides, an extensive ratification procedure. It remains to be seen how investments in the energy sector will be treated. Energy is not mentioned among the sectors to which the agreement will not apply pursuant to Article 1 (2) of Section II (liberalisation and investment). Limitations, based on national reservations, are specified in an annex. See, for the Commission's statement, European Commission, EU-China Comprehensive Agreement on Investment: The Agreement in Principle, 30 December 2020; see for more information on the Agreement, European Commission, EU-China Comprehensive Agreement on Investment (CAI): List of Sections, 22 January 2021.

110 Article 4 (1) (a) of Regulation 2019/452.

111 Article 4 (2) (a) of Regulation 2019/452.

Regulation 2019/452, the Commission could issue an opinion to the member state in which the investment should be realised, mainly because the large-scale transmission link will definitely affect a project or programme of Union interest, such as the Trans-European Networks for Energy.

Secondly, the Chinese side promotes the transmission link as well as the entire global energy interconnection scheme by suggesting that it will help to transport renewable electricity from large-scale hydropower or wind and solar power facilities in remote places in China to the load centres. This is problematic for two reasons. It is impossible to control which kind of electricity is fed into the grid and then transported all the way to Europe. Is it possible to design a certification process with China? If an agreement can be reached to the extent that the EU customer can be assured that only renewable electricity is transmitted via this link, Article 11 (2) (d) of the Renewables Directive 2018/2001 requires that for imported renewable electricity to be consumed in the EU, the electricity must have 'been produced in accordance with international law, in a third country that is a signatory to the Council of Europe Convention for the Protection of Human Rights and Fundamental Freedoms, or other international conventions or treaties on human rights'. China has signed the International Convention on Civil and Political Rights, but has not yet ratified it. Human rights are frequently violated by government bodies and semi-officials in many places of the country, in particular in Xinjiang – a large production site of renewable electricity and the only viable transit region for export of renewable electricity from other parts of China to the west.[112]

Thirdly, the link would decrease rather than enhance the level of energy security within the EU. As one of the five dimensions of the Energy Union, energy security is a mandatory policy consideration that the Member States have to outline in their ten-year integrated national energy and climate plans pursuant to Article 4 (c) of Governance Regulation 2018/1999.

The China–EU transmission link does not contribute to EU energy security, mainly because its costs are unknown and the EU would become dependent on Chinese policies. The long-distance transmission of renewable electricity is not cost-effective.[113] The Chinese investors might initially subsidise the transmission

---

112 The human rights situation in Xinjiang has been deteriorating for years. It is estimated that state authorities have been incarcerating more than one million Uighurs, Kazakhs, and other members of ethnic or religious minorities. Many of them are forced to work for companies in Xinjiang or other parts of China. In early 2021, for the first time since the 1989 Tian'anmen massacre, the EU levied sanctions on Chinese officials and entities who are implicated in participating in the atrocities in Xinjiang. See Council of the European Union, EU Imposes Further Sanctions over Serious Violations of Human Rights around the World, 22 March 2021.

113 *B. Lin & W. Wu*, Cost of Long Distance Electricity Transmission in China, Energy Policy 2017 (109), pp. 132, 139.

of electricity to Europe in order to establish and secure their 'market position'.[114] Since it is uncertain for how long the Chinese side would subsidise the link, the cost factor will be unknown. In addition, the export of renewable electricity would be part of China's five-year plan. The EU will thus be forced to take into account China's energy policy. Finally, a transmission link via Russia will increase EU vulnerability with respect to its relations with Russia in the context of the Union's energy security. Hence, vital components of the transmission link with China violate EU energy law.

In all three cases, the overseeing body would be the Commission: it can issue an opinion pursuant to Article 8 (1) of Investment-Screening Regulation 2019/452. If a Member State wants to import renewable electricity and add it to its share of renewable energy use, it has to notify the Commission pursuant to Article 11 (4) and (5) of the Renewables Directive 2018/2001; and the Commission assesses the drafts of the integrated national energy and climate plans of the Member States in accordance with Article 9 (2) of Governance Regulation 2018/1999 and issues country-specific recommendations to the Member States. None of these oversight instruments allows the Commission to prohibit a certain activity. Yet, its written opinions and recommendations become part of the broader conversation about the energy future in the EU and help further crystallise a shared understanding of a common energy future among Member States.

The emergence of State Grid as an unexpected challenge to the evolving EU energy and climate governance framework contributed to the adoption of Investment-Screening Regulation 2019/452. This step completed the instruments that help to oversee the implementation of the low-carbon energy transition. It was a crucial extension in the process of harmonising governance structures in the context of the energy transition, mainly because State Grid's actions and grand plans truly constitute a systemic challenge to EU energy and climate governance. They put at risk the legacy of EU electricity sector integration and governance structures that ensure the consideration of sustainability and energy justice, as well as efforts to facilitate a just transition to a climate-neutral economy. The investment-screening mechanism, if used wisely, can prevent undue interference.

6. CONCLUSION

This chapter brought together three issues that shape the decarbonisation of the EU electricity sector – namely, the harmonisation of governance structures, infrastructure and a systemic challenge. This chapter sought to draw a picture in

[114] The same approach is pursued with the cargo train link from western China to train stations in Europe. Without Chinese subsidies, the transport service would be much more expensive.

which the interrelationship becomes clear: the harmonisation of the governance structures in the Member States can be achieved through oversight mechanisms that are included in recent legislation applicable to the power sector. Oversight is necessary to ensure that the decarbonisation of the power sector is conducted in an environmentally sustainable way, while the alleviation of energy poverty, energy security and the stability of the public order are also vital matters that the oversight mechanisms address. Thus, EU oversight ensures progress in harmonising governance structures and safeguards policy space at the national and subnational levels of decision-making.

The rigidity and approach of the oversight mechanisms differ, depending on the subject matter and nature of the policies that have to be harmonised – that is, market integration, sustainability, energy justice and security-induced investment screening. Yet, the goal of the regulatory effort is the emergence of a common energy future. If the Member States patiently adhere to the various forms of action and cooperation that these mechanisms require, harmonised governance structures to guide the decarbonisation of the EU energy system can emerge, advancing the imagination of a common energy future.

From a global perspective, the task of constructing a common EU energy future that is rules-based, constitutional and democratic is not trivial. This chapter described State Grid's involvement in the EU electricity sector as an instance of systemic rivalry. To label the relations with China as systemic rivalry, as the EU does, is one thing; to identify traces thereof in 'real life' is another. Studying State Grid's case helps to illustrate the ideational impact of an external actor on the governance of the EU energy transition. With China, the EU currently faces only one systemic rival. But this is no reason to sit back. If the system is challenged, we need harmonised governance structures across the Union and vigilant adherence to oversight.

EUROPEANISATION OF RENEWABLE ENERGY SUPPORT LAW

A Suspended Step Towards Harmonisation

Theodoros G. Iliopoulos*

1. INTRODUCTION

In ancient Greek mythology, the goddess Harmonia (Άρμονία), who personifies harmony,[1] was the daughter of Ares, god of war, and Aphrodite, goddess of beauty and love.[2] Extending the interpretation and the symbolism of the myth to the field of law, one could see harmonisation, that is, the action of bringing harmony between different legal systems,[3] as denoting the reconciliation outcome of a process of dispute and cooperation, of discordance and understanding. In the

* Postdoctoral researcher in Energy and Environmental Law at Hasselt University.

1 Also ἁρμονία in Greek.

2 Ἡσίοδος [Hesiodos], *Θεογονία* [*Theogonia*] (Papadimas Books 2007), lyrics 933–937.

3 See *K. Boele-Woelki*, Unifying and Harmonizing Substantive Law and the Role of Conflict of Laws, 2010, p. 35. Especially in the field of renewable energy support law, the term 'harmonisation' has been used in a broader context, denoting 'the top-down implementation of common, binding provisions concerning the support of RES-E throughout the European Union. Not more, but also not less'. See *J. Bergmann et al.*, Harmonisation of support schemes,

end, harmonisation reconciles 'the preoccupations and the interests of the various systems so as to avoid conflicts and clashes'.[4]

Of course, such processes do not always end up with the desired result. In many cases, conflicts between different parties cannot be bridged, and harmonisation plans collapse or simply fade over time. This seems to have been the case with the plan for supranational harmonisation of renewable energy support law and of support schemes for renewable energy sources (hereinafter 'RESSS'), which are instruments that Member States enact in order to promote renewable energy sources. But the recent enactment of the recast Renewable Energy Directive 2018/2001,[5] often cited as 'RED II', might change the picture.

Since the mid- and late-1990s, when the first seeds of supranational harmonisation of renewable energy support law were planted, there has been little progress. The two first generations of secondary renewable energy law in 2001[6] and 2009[7] did not bring about any harmonisation, as it proved impossible for Member States and the Commission to reach an understanding.[8] In response, in 2013 the Commission resorted to the term 'Europeanisation of support for renewables' and asked for more convergence in the field.[9] But more recently,

---

A European harmonised policy to promote RES-electricity – sharing costs and benefits, Work Package 3 of the project futures-e, 2008, Report D17, p. 7.

Of course, one should also have in mind that 'it is not easy to come up with something like a definition of 'harmonization' since the word is used in different ways and to cover legislative actions of different kinds. Usually it refers to a legislative process whereby various pieces of environmental legislation are either brought together in one new document, or are at least coordinated'. Furthermore, '[t]he notion of 'harmonization' is [...] particularly confusing since it refers both to the "harmonization" of various legislative acts within one legal system, as well as to the approximation of laws between different legal systems. It is obviously in the latter sense that the term is often used in the European legal context'. *M. Faure*, The Harmonization, Codification and Integration of Environmental Law: A Search for Definitions, EELR 2000 (6), p.174.

4 *M. Meulders-Klein*, Towards a European Civil Code in Family Law? Ends and Means in *K. Boele-Woelki* (ed.), Perspectives for the Unification and Harmonisation of Family Law in Europe, 2003, p. 106.

5 Directive (EU) 2018/2001 of the European Parliament and of the Council of 11 December 2018 on the promotion of the use of energy from renewable sources, OJ 2018 L 328/82.

6 Directive 2001/77/EC of the European Parliament and of the Council of 27 September 2001 on the promotion of electricity produced from renewable energy sources in the internal electricity market, OJ 2001 L 283/33.

7 Directive 2009/28/EC of the European Parliament and of the Council of 23 April 2009 on the promotion of the use of energy from renewable sources and amending and subsequently repealing Directives 2001/77/EC and 2003/30/EC, OJ 2009 L 140/16.

8 *D. Jacobs*, Designing Financing Mechanisms for Electricity from Renewable Energy Sources: The Role of the European Commission as an Agenda Shaper in *J. Tosun, S. Biesenbender* & *K. Schulze* (eds), Energy Policy Making in the EU, 2015.

9 *Commission*, Guidance for the design of renewables support schemes, SWD(2013) 439 final, Brussels, 5 November 2013, pp. 22–23.

in December 2018, Directive 2018/2001 brought about certain interesting developments. The directive set down an EU collective target of a 32 per cent share of energy from renewable sources to be reached by 2030. This target is only binding for the EU as a whole; it is not converted into national targets, as was the case under the previous directive.[10] Still, each Member State shall contribute to the attainment of the collective target, *inter alia* through the enactment and operation of RESSS. Moreover, Directive 2018/2001 for the first time introduced certain provisions regarding the design of RESSS, but there was no reference to an actual or future harmonisation plan. But there was no explicit or implicit rejection of the earlier harmonisation plans, either.

Within this framework, this chapter aims to examine the latest renewable energy support law developments under the light of 'Europeanisation' and harmonisation, and it intends to anticipate the effects of these developments on the national legal regimes. It concludes that Europeanisation and harmonisation are not poles apart.

In terms of structure, Part 1 contains the introduction. Part 2 adopts a historical approach to examine the rise and decline of the harmonisation plans. Part 3 presents the turn to Europeanisation, and Part 4 focuses on the renewable energy support law provisions brought about by Directive 2018/2001. Last, Part 5 puts forward certain concluding remarks.

2. THE EARLY YEARS OF EU RENEWABLE ENERGY SUPPORT LAW AND THE HARMONISATION PLANS

Renewable energy support law is manifestly linked with the policy target of promoting renewable energy sources, and it specifically deals with the design and enactment of RESSS. The concept of RESSS is defined by supranational law. It is a broad term that comprises:

> any instrument, scheme or mechanism applied by a Member State, or a group of Member States, that promotes the use of energy from renewable sources by reducing the cost of that energy, increasing the price at which it can be sold, or increasing, by means of a renewable energy obligation or otherwise, the volume of such energy purchased, including but not restricted to, investment aid, tax exemptions or reductions, tax refunds, renewable energy obligation support schemes including

[10] Directive 2009/28/EC set down a mandatory target of 'at least a 20% share of energy from renewable sources in the [EU]'s gross final consumption of energy in 2020'. This target was then translated into national mandatory targets, also determined at the EU level. See Article 3, Directive 2009/28/EC, *supra* note 7. See also *T. Iliopoulos*, Dilemmas on the Way to a New Renewable Energy Directive, EEELR 2018 (6), p. 210.

> those using green certificates, and direct price support schemes including feed-in tariffs and sliding or fixed premium payments.[11]

This definition also includes an indicative list of RESSS, which further proves the broad character of the term. The broad range of RESSS can be classified into two categories, namely, price instruments and quantity instruments.[12] Under price instruments, authorities set a price for energy from renewable sources, and the market responds by adapting energy generation accordingly. The price should be such to spur an increase in supply. Determining guaranteed prices for energy, like feed-in tariffs and premiums, are exemplary price instruments. On the other hand, quantity instruments – typically quotas and green certificates, but also auctions – set down the minimum amount of generation of energy from renewable sources. Price is then determined by market mechanisms, and it is expected to rise, given that demand is also increased because of the regulatory intervention.

Before the plethora of different RESSS, it comes as no surprise that there has been an interest in harmonisation at the supranational level. Accordingly, the harmonisation plans go back to the 1990s, before the enactment of the first Renewable Energy Directive.[13] The European Commission regarded the then – and still – existing variety of RESSS as causing imbalances in the functioning of the internal market and as putting at risk the project of the internal energy market. Member States apply different support schemes, and under different terms, which are subject to constant change, too. In response, the Commission put forward the enactment of one, uniformly applicable support scheme for every Member State. But it was not possible for Member States to reach an agreement on the nature of such a support scheme or how it should be designed.[14] In the end, recital 15 of Directive 2001/77 acknowledged that it was 'too early to decide on a [EU]-wide framework regarding support schemes, in view of the limited experience with national schemes'. This formulation implied that the harmonisation plan was not abandoned, but postponed for the future.

---

11 Article 2(5) of Directive 2018/2001, *supra* note 5. See also Article 2(k) of Directive 2009/28/EC, *supra* note 7. See also Article 4 of Directive 2001/77/EC, *supra* note 6.

12 *R. Hass et al.*, How to Promote Renewable Energy Systems Successfully and Effectively, Energy Policy 2004 (6), p. 833, 834; *P. Menanteau, D. Finon & M. Lamy*, Prices versus quantities: choosing policies for promoting the development of renewable energy, Energy Policy 2003 (8), p. 799.

13 *D. Jacobs*, *supra* note 8. See also *G. Resch et al.*, Coordination or Harmonisation? Feasible Pathways for a European RES Strategy Beyond 2020, Energy & Environment 2013, p. 147; *R. Hildingsson, J. Stripple* & *A. Jordan*, Governing Renewable Energy in the EU: Confronting a Governance Dilemma, Eur. Political Sci. 2012, p. 18; *V. Lauber* and *E. Schenner*, The struggle over support schemes for renewable electricity in the European Union: a discursive-institutionalist analysis, Environ. Politics 2011, p. 508; *I. Rowlands*, The European directive on renewable electricity: conflicts and compromises, Energy Policy 2005, p. 965.

14 Ibid.

But Directive 2009/28, which repealed the foregoing directive, did not bring about harmonisation either. This was expected, since in 2008 the Commission had already noted in soft law that 'the harmonisation of support schemes remain[s] a long-term goal on economic efficiency, single market and State aid grounds, but that harmonisation in the short term is not appropriate'.[15] For a second time, harmonisation was praised, but only as a future plan.

3. THE TURN TO 'EUROPEANISATION' OF RENEWABLE ENERGY SUPPORT LAW

Shortly after the enactment of Directive 2009/28, the problems associated with the lack of a supranational legal framework for RESSS were highlighted. Accordingly, a number of national support schemes, mostly feed-in tariffs, distorted energy markets and collapsed because of poor design.[16] Many Member States, like Czechia, Germany, Greece, Italy and Spain enacted very ambitious RESSS, guaranteeing a high fixed price for the whole amount of renewable energy produced – regardless of the market conditions. This resulted in over-investment and excessive production of energy from renewable sources, which in turn caused stability problems to the grid, as well as overcompensation for the producers. The Member States wound up unable to afford their own RESSS, and they imposed unilateral adjustments to contractual terms, like de-escalating tariffs, reductions in the contracts' duration and other measures. This resulted in a series of investor-state investment disputes, often before arbitration courts, which caused extra problems to the Member States and the European Union as a whole.[17] At the same time, electricity consumers were seeing their bills increasing, because the extra costs that the RESSS entailed were ultimately passed on them. Other design problems related to bureaucracy, with long and labyrinthine administrative procedures for projects causing significant delays,

---

15 *Commission*, The support of electricity from renewable energy sources, Staff Working Document, SEC(2008) 57.

16 *F. Montanaro*, 'Ain't No Sunshine': Photovoltaic Energy Policy in Europe at the Crossroads Between EU Law and Energy Charter Treaty Obligations in *G. Adinolfi et al.* (eds), International Economic Law, 2017; *A. Pyrgou, A. Kylili & P. Fokaides*, The Future of the Feed-In Tariff (FIT) Scheme in Europe: The Case of Photovoltaics, Energy Policy 2016 (95), p.94; *T. Iliopoulos*, Renewable Energy Regulation: Feed-in Tariff Schemes under Recession Conditions? ENLR 2016 (2), p. 110; *J. Prest*, The Future of Feed-In Tariffs: Capacity Caps, Scheme Closures and Looming Grid Parity, RELP 2012 (3), p. 25.

17 On this issue see, *inter alia*, *M. Fermeglia & A. Mistura*, The Fate of EU Environmental and Investment Law after the Achmea Decision, JEEPL 2020, p. 29; *A. López-Rodríguez*, The Sun Behind the Clouds? Enforcement of Renewable Energy Awards in the EU, TEL 2019, p. 279; *F. Montanaro, supra* note 16; *A. López-Rodríguez & P. Navarro*, Investment Arbitration and EU Law in the Aftermath of Renewable Energy Cuts in Spain, EEELR 2016 (1), p. 2.

increasing investors' risk and, finally, discouraging investments.[18] In addition, the support Member States granted has been almost always restricted to domestic generation, through so-called 'closed' support schemes.[19] Closed support schemes have been a significant advantage for domestically produced energy and have resulted in restricting trade. Such a restriction also entailed that each Member State kept working towards the promotion of renewable energy sources in isolation, while a properly functioning internal energy market could ensure the exploitation of the most productive renewable energy sources of each region for the needs of all Member States. Consequently, the benefits of economies of scale and scope could not be reaped.

Nevertheless, the European Union was lacking the legal instruments to prevent such phenomena. A supranational intervention in the national RESSS was only possible through primary law; worse, practically, only state aid law could impact on the national RESSS design. This is because the Court of Justice of the EU has held that closed RESSS can be in compliance with the law of the free movement of goods, because they serve the Member States' efforts for attaining the energy transition and they are linked with the protection of the environment.[20]

Faced with this situation, the Commission turned to soft law. In 2013, the 'Guidance for the design of renewables support schemes'[21] (hereinafter 'the Guidance') was published in order to steer national authorities in their efforts to reform their RESSS. And as harmonisation was seeming to be an unreachable utopia, the Commission employed the term 'Europeanisation of support for renewables'. The term 'Europeanisation' is rooted in political sciences, and it denotes a 'process of change affecting domestic institutions, politics and public policy'.[22] This process is not only one-way. The decisions

---

18 *P. Fokaides, A. Poullikkas & C. Christofides*, Lost in the National Labyrinths of Bureaucracy: The Case of Renewable Energy Governance in Cyprus in *E. Michalena & J. Hills* (eds), Renewable Energy Governance, 2013.

19 The cooperation between Sweden and Norway has been the only cooperation mechanism until 2015. More recently, more schemes have started to emerge, like the Baltic Energy Market Interconnection Plan (BEMIP). See *Commission*, Annex to the Third Report on the State of the Energy Union, Communication, Annex 2, COM(2017) 688 final, p. 5; *Commission*, Second Report on the State of the Energy Union, Communication, COM(2017) 53 final, p. 9; *Commission*, State of the Energy Union 2015, Communication, COM(2015) 572 final, p. 4.

20 Joined Cases C-204/12 to C-208/12 Essent Belgium [2014] published in the electronic Reports of Cases; Case C-573/12 Ålands Vindkraft [2014] published in the electronic Reports of Cases; Case C-379/98 PreussenElektra [2001] ECR I-2099.

21 *Commission*, SWD(2013) 439 final, *supra* note 9.

22 *C. Radaelli*, Europeanization: The Challenge of Establishing Causality in *T. Exadaktylos & C. Radaelli* (eds), Research Design in European Studies, 2012, p. 1. See also *R. Coman & A. Crespy*, Still in Search of Europeanization: From Limited to Structural Change? in *R. Coman, T. Kostera & L. Tomini* (eds), Europeanization and European Integration, 2014. According to another – similar – definition, Europeanisation refers to 'processes of (1) construction (2) diffusion and (3) institutionalisation of formal and informal rules, procedures, policy paradigms, styles, "ways of doing things" and shared beliefs and norms

taken and the choices made at the EU level impact on the national sphere, which is the top-down or 'downloading' expression of Europeanisation, but there is also an intertwined, bottom-up Europeanisation process, an 'uploading' equivalent: social, economic, political and legal contestation at the national level are also Europeanisation factors.[23] And the outcome of Europeanisation is not one-directional, either. It might lead to a more homogeneous or a more heterogeneous landscape.[24] The Europeanisation agenda put forward by the Guidance advanced the convergence of national support policies. It envisaged a process of increasing cooperation between Member States and convergence of support schemes towards the direction of their integration in an undistorted internal market.[25] The Guidance acknowledged the merits of regulatory competition, seen as the competition between different national regimes over the attractiveness of their support schemes for investors. Accordingly, allowing certain room for differences in national RESSS will reveal the strong and weak points of each model, as well as the investors' preferences, which will soon lead to 'a certain natural convergence'.[26] All Member States are expected to opt for the RESSS and the design features that have proven effective and efficient.

The next sections will examine how this plan of Europeanisation is being served by the newly enacted RED II and will prognosticate whether and how the new provisions also suit harmonisation plans.

4. THE NEW RENEWABLE ENERGY DIRECTIVE IN THE LIGHT OF EUROPEANISATION OF SUPPORT SCHEMES

It should be noted that Directive 2018/2001 does not contain any reference to Europeanisation. Nevertheless, since Europeanisation constitutes a policy

---

which are first defined and consolidated in the making of EU public policy and politics and then incorporated into the logic of domestic discourse, identities, political structures and public policies'. See *C. Radaelli*, Wither Europeanization? Concept stretching and substantive change, EIoP 2000 (8), p. 4. http://eiop.or.at/eiop/pdf/2000-008.pdf accessed 3 March 2021.

23 *C. Radaelli*, Europeanization: The Challenge of Establishing Causality in *supra* n 22, p. 2. See also *R. Ladrech*, Rethinking the Relationship between Europeanization and European Integration in *R. Coman, T. Kostera & L. Tomini* (eds), *supra* n 22; *I. Bache*, Europeanization and Multilevel Governance: Cohesion Policy in the European, 2008, ch 2.

24 *I. Solorio & H. Jörgens*, Contested energy transition? Europeanization and authority turns in EU renewable energy policy, J. Eur. Integr 2020, p. 77; *C. Radaelli & J. Salter*, Europeanization in reverse gear? in *S. Gänzle, B. Leruth & J. Trondal* (eds), Differentiated Integration and Disintegration in a Post-Brexit Era, 2019; *S. Strunz, E. Gawel & P. Lehmann*, Towards a general 'Europeanization' of EU Member States' energy policies? EEEP 2015 (2), p. 143.

25 *Commission*, SWD(2013) 439 final, *supra* note 9, pp. 22–23.

26 Ibid. at p. 22.

direction recently expressed by the Commission, it is useful to examine the relevant effects of the newly enacted renewable energy support law provisions. In doing so, this section is structured around four important issues of RESSS' design, which are covered by RED II, that is, RESSS design *stricto sensu*; RESSS openness; RESSS stability; and RESSS for renewables self-consumption.

4.1. SUPPORT SCHEMES' DESIGN *STRICTO SENSU*

While renewable energy support law generally relates to the selection, the formation and the implementation of RESSS, the term *stricto sensu* design is put forward to refer to the terms under which RESSS will operate, mostly the determination of the duration and the level of the support to be granted, as well as the technologies that can be covered by it.

Such issues are addressed by Article 4 of RED II. Paragraphs 2 and 3 of this article set down certain principles that should govern the enactment of all support schemes for electricity from renewable sources. In this regard, such support schemes shall be market-based and market-responsive.

More specifically, Article 4(2) states that these support schemes:

> shall provide incentives for the integration of electricity from renewable sources in the electricity market in a market-based and market-responsive way, while avoiding unnecessary distortions of electricity markets as well as taking into account possible system integration costs and grid stability.

The introduction of such principles in hard law is an important development and seems sufficient to prevent the enactment of too generous or inflexible RESSS that manifestly disregard market conditions. Nevertheless, the exact content of the obligation imposed on Member States is not clear. For instance, are national authorities required to prove *ex ante* the market-based and market-responsive nature of a RESSS that they enact, for example, through economic analyses and impact assessments? Alternatively, are they required to examine the economic effects of the selected RESSS against alternative schemes, by way of a proportionality analysis? On the basis of a teleological expansion, one could argue that Article 4(2) introduces a requirement for a minimum *ex ante* assessment of the RESSS to be enacted; but, in the absence of any such preconditions or criteria in the letter of the law, the wording of RED II ultimately seems to call attention to the effects of the RESSS once they are enacted and applied. This means that national authorities have a wide margin of discretion in evaluating a support scheme that they plan to implement against the indeterminate legal concepts introduced by RED II.

Article 4(2) is complemented by Article 4(3), which elaborates on the guiding principles that shall generally apply to all support schemes for electricity from renewable sources and assists in the interpretation of the paragraph 2 principles.[27] Accordingly, Article 4(3) states that support schemes 'shall be designed so as to maximise the integration of electricity from renewable sources in the electricity market and to ensure that renewable energy producers are responding to market price signals and maximise their market revenues'.

Next, Article 4(3) further specifies the implications that such principles have on the selection of the RESSS, by stating that 'with regard to direct price support schemes, support shall be granted in the form of a market premium'. In essence, this clause does not allow Member States to use feed-in tariffs and confirms the distrust of the EU legal order towards this type of RESSS. This is not only because such schemes collapsed in early 2010s, but also because feed-in tariffs by nature disregard market signals; thus, they relieve investors of risk and result in granting windfall profits to them.[28] By way of exemption, feed-in tariffs can be employed for the support of small-scale installations and demonstration projects, which might not be able to afford market exposure.[29] The foregoing provisions echo soft law, namely, the Guidance and the guidelines on state aid for environmental protection and energy;[30] indeed, the Commission had already stressed the need for market-responsive instruments and for a phase-out of feed-in tariffs.[31]

Article 4 also deals with the process through which support is granted. Accordingly, paragraph 4 requires that 'support for electricity from renewable sources is granted in an open, transparent, competitive, non-discriminatory and cost-effective manner'. Within this framework, Member States have a certain discretion in specifying the exact process of support allocation that they will follow; but it is also clear that Article 4 nudges or even pressures Member States to resort to technology-neutral 'tendering procedures', competitive bidding processes or auctions. These three terms can be used as synonyms, albeit they are slightly different.[32] It is noted that Article 4 only uses the first term. The merits of tendering procedures had already been highlighted by the 2013 Guidance.

---

27 See also *T. Iliopoulos*, Price Support Schemes in the Service of the EU's Low-Carbon Energy Transition in *T. Zachariadis et al.*, Economic Instruments for a Low-carbon Future, 2020, p. 2.

28 *T. Iliopoulos*, Finding the spearhead of the EU low-carbon energy transition in *M. Boeve et al.* (eds), Environmental Law for Transitions to Sustainability, 2021, p. 129; *A. Johnston* & *G. Block*, EU Energy Law, 2012.

29 Article 4(3), Directive 2018/2001, *supra* note 5. See also ibid. at recital 17.

30 *Commission* – Communication Guidelines on state aid for environmental protection and energy 2014–2020 [2014] OJ C200/1.

31 *Commission*, SWD(2013) 439 final, *supra* note 9, at p. 5 ff.

32 See *P. Crossley*, Renewable Energy Law: An International Assessment, 2019, pp 227–228; *P. del Río et al.*, Overview of Design Elements for RES-E Auctions, Report D2.2 (a), AURES – EU Horizon 2020, October 2015.

Through auctions, investors compete for a contract with the authority, and thus the bids they make reveal the real costs of a project. The best offer is awarded with the contract. This ensures the support granted does not exceed what is actually necessary.[33]

One can hardly doubt that auctions have by nature a strongly procedural character that is capable of ensuring the requirements of openness, transparency, competitiveness, non-discrimination and cost-effectiveness. Although Member States are not explicitly required to resort to auctions, the fact that Article 4(4) allows small-scale installations and demonstration projects to be exempted from tendering procedures can lead, via an *argumentum a contrario*, to the conclusion that support allocation through auctions shall be the rule for most installations and projects. In a similar vein, Article 4(5) sets down certain conditions that exceptionally allow technology-specific tendering procedures. Again, in an *argumentum a contrario* one can conclude that auctions shall in principle cover all technologies. Next, Article 4(6) and (8) contain special rules for ensuring a post-auction high realisation rate and rules for reporting on the auctions' effects respectively. Of course, it should be also accepted, on the basis of a reasonable interpretation, that Member States are allowed to not use auctions, if auctions provenly cannot lead to an outcome in line with the requirements of Article 4 of RED II. But the EU legislature should include clear exception rules and criteria.

Given the above, it can be argued that RED II has brought about a minimum harmonisation of RESSS, in the sense that it has introduced certain principles and rules with which national choices have to conform. But the actual outcome of Europeanisation over the *stricto sensu* RESSS design issues will be dependent on the common understanding of the indeterminate legal concepts that function as guiding principles. Directive 2018/2001 shows an apparent preference for technology-neutral auctions and an explicit mistrust of feed-in tariffs. On the other hand, Member States retain a wide margin of discretion in selecting the type of RESSS they prefer and in deciding about the design details. Europeanisation is thus expected to lead to a landscape of convergence in diversity, with auctions and feed-in premiums prevailing, but under different terms in each Member State, and without totally excluding the enactment of other RESSS, like special schemes for renewables self-consumers, or quotas and green certificates, or even straightforward feed-in tariff regimes for small-scale and demonstration projects.

---

33 Ibid. See also *R. Hass et al.*, A Historical Review of Promotion Strategies for Electricity from Renewable Energy Sources in EU countries, RSER 2011 (15), p. 1003.

4.2. SUPPORT SCHEMES' OPENNESS

Article 5 deals with the opening of national support schemes to generators located in other Member States. The introduction of this article follows the controversial CJEU case law, which has accepted that closed RESSS restrict trade, but are exceptionally legal under Article 36 TFEU or under the mandatory requirements doctrine that *inter alia* includes the protection of the environment.[34] This is because through closed RESSS, Member States attain their energy and environmental protection policy objectives.[35] This case law has been criticised as adopting an ambiguous interpretation of primary EU law in order to make closed RESSS fit in the European Union legal order.[36]

In response to the lack of strictness of primary law, the enactment of explicit secondary law obligations for open RESSS has been put forward as the instrument to legally impel Member States to proceed with the opening of their RESSS.[37] However, what ultimately passed in Directive 2018/2001 was a lengthy and knotty article with no obligations for Member States. Thus, Article 5 of RED II does not force, but only encourages Member States to open their RESSS. At the same time, by way of a warning, it lays the foundation for the introduction of an openness requirement in the future. Accordingly, Article 5(1) uses non-coercive language and provides that Member States shall have the right to decide 'to which extent they support electricity from renewable sources which is produced in another Member State' and that they 'may open participation in support schemes for electricity from renewable sources to producers located in other Member States'. The same paragraph also provides that Member States may opt to only partially open their support schemes.

Interestingly, the rest of Article 5 instead pertains to the imposition of an obligation. More specifically, Article 5(1) adds indicative shares that the opening of newly supported capacity may reach: at least 5 per cent from 2023 to 2026; and at least 10 per cent from 2027 to 2030. But determining minimum

---

34 Consolidated version of the Treaty on the Functioning of the European Union, OJ 2016 C-202/47.

35 See Joined Cases C-204/12 to C-208/12 *supra* note 20; Case C-573/12, *supra* note 20; Case C-379/98, *supra* note 20.

36 *K. Talus*, Float Like a Butterfly, Sting Like a Bee: Judicial Challenges to Renewable-Energy Support Schemes in Europe, Climate Law 2016, p. 250; *A. Steinbach & R. Brückmann*, Renewable Energy and the Free Movement of Goods, Journal of Environmental Law 2015 (1), p. 1; *M. Szydło*, How to reconcile national support for renewable energy with internal market obligations? The task for the EU legislature after Ålands Vindkraft and Essent, CMLR 2015 (2), p. 489.

37 Article 5, *Commission*, Proposal for a Directive of the European Parliament and of the Council on the promotion of the use of energy from renewable sources (recast), COM(2016) 767 final/2, 23 February 2017.

targets is mostly appropriate to accompany the introduction of an obligation. Next, Article 5(2) holds that 'Member States may limit participation in their support schemes to producers located in Member States with which there is a direct connection via interconnectors'. Again, introducing a reason justifying a possible refusal of a Member State to enact cross-border support schemes would better fit a legal framework requiring – and not just encouraging – the opening of RESSS.

Paragraphs 3 and 4 of Article 5 deal with more procedural issues. In this regard, it is provided that the opening of RESSS shall be based on an agreement between Member States and that the Commission will have the role of assisting Member States throughout the negotiation process.

Lastly, paragraph 5 states that by 2023 the Commission shall evaluate the implementation of Article 5 in order to assess the need to introduce a clear obligation for the enactment of open support schemes, with a view to actually reaching the aforementioned indicative targets. This latter provision might prove crucial for Article 5's coercive power; Member States might enact cross-border support schemes, fearing that they will be obliged to do so if they stick to their current practice. However, the exact meaning of this paragraph is unclear. More specifically, it is unclear what the consequences will be after a possible conclusion that an obligation should be introduced. It is argued that a revision of Directive 2018/2001 will be necessary, under the ordinary legislative procedure. This means that eventually, Member States in the Council, as well as the European Parliament, will evaluate the Commission's evaluation.

Within this context, the effects of Europeanisation in the opening of support schemes constitute a matter that depends to a large extent on the Member States' willingness to enact cross-border support schemes. No harmonisation has been attained, in the sense that the law does not set down any explicit obligation and national authorities retain the right to limit the support they grant to domestic generation of energy. Nevertheless, the Commission's evaluation to come in 2023 might incentivise Member States to open their support schemes, at least partly, in accordance with the indicative targets set, and thus avoid the initiation of a procedure that might end up in the introduction of an obligation and the delimitation of their discretion. This will lead to a convergence stemming from provisions assimilating to nudges or soft law – the more so, if Member States also follow the procedural paragraphs of Article 5 and conclude agreements with the Commission playing an assisting role. This is because such agreements might lead to national regimes sharing more and more common features.

4.3. SUPPORT SCHEMES' STABILITY

Article 6 of RED II is entitled 'Stability of financial support' and aims to deal with the phenomenon of sudden changes in the support framework. As mentioned previously, the unilateral imposition of such adjustments was a common situation in the early 2010s, when numerous national RESSS proved non-viable under their original versions. After the lessons learned from this negative experience, the EU legislature now aims to prevent the imposition of such abrupt changes in the future – and also to offer an alternative and thus avoid the problematic energy arbitration dispute settlements.[38] Accordingly, Article 6(1) provides that:

> [w]ithout prejudice to adaptations necessary to comply with Articles 107 and 108 TFEU, Member States shall ensure that the level of, and the conditions attached to, the support granted to renewable energy projects are not revised in a way that negatively affects the rights conferred thereunder and undermines the economic viability of projects that already benefit from support.

This contains the core rule and establishes a concrete obligation for Member States. However, this is not an absolute obligation. According to Article 6(2), Member States may still adjust the level of support; but for this to happen, they shall first determine objective criteria, in accordance with which the adjustments will be made. Moreover, a reform that is *prima facie* in breach of Article 6 of RED II can be justified on the basis of overriding considerations of public interest, such as the security of supply, the resilience of the grid or the sustainability of the support regime. Consequently, it seems that Member States still have the right to revise the enacted support regimes, even if this entails negative ramifications for renewable energy projects, as long as the reforms are in accordance with predetermined criteria. Of course, this provision should apply in line with the principle of proportionality and should be interpreted in light of the principle of legitimate expectations.[39]

In addition, Article 6(3) requires Member States to 'publish a long-term schedule anticipating the expected allocation of support, covering, as a reference, at least the following five years, or, in the case of budgetary planning constraints, the following three years'. Moreover, this schedule 'shall be updated on an annual basis or, where necessary, to reflect recent market developments or expected allocation of support'. Lastly, the same paragraph also determines the minimum content of such schedules. Accordingly, they shall include 'the indicative timing, the frequency of tendering procedures where appropriate,

---

[38] On this issue see, *inter alia*, *M. Fermeglia & A. Mistura*, *supra* note 17; *A. López-Rodríguez*, *supra* note 17; *F. Montanaro*, *supra* note 16; *A. López-Rodríguez & P. Navarro*, *supra* note 17. See also *M. Fanou*, Intra-European Union investor–State arbitration post-Achmea: RIP?, MJECL 2019, p. 316; *J. Kokott & C. Sobotta*, Investment Arbitration and EU Law, CYELS 2018, p. 3.

[39] For more about these principles see *P. Craig*, EU Administrative Law, 2012, p. 607 ff., p. 687 ff.

the expected capacity and budget or maximum unitary support expected to be allocated, and the expected eligible technologies, if applicable'.

Article 6(4) sets down an evaluation requirement. At least every five years, Member States shall:

> assess the effectiveness of their support schemes for electricity from renewable sources and their major distributive effects on different consumer groups, and on investments. That assessment shall take into account the effect of possible changes to the support schemes. The indicative long-term planning governing the decisions of the support and design of new support shall take into account the results of that assessment.

Article 6 contributes to a Europeanisation of renewable energy support law. It imposes an unconditional and sufficiently precise obligation on Member States that is expected to bring convergence in the terms of stability of RESSS and in the terms under which a revision is possible. Moreover, it might lead to a more diligent selection and design of RESSS, so that no need for reforms occur during the implementation stage.

4.4. SUPPORT SCHEMES FOR RENEWABLES SELF-CONSUMPTION

Articles 21 and 22 require Member States to ensure that citizens are entitled to become 'renewables self-consumers' and to participate in 'renewable energy communities', respectively. Renewables self-consumers generate renewable electricity for their own consumption and may store or sell part of it, provided that this does not constitute their primary commercial or professional activity.[40] Renewable energy communities allow self-consumers to come together and coordinate their actions.[41] They are entities that own and collectively develop and manage renewable energy projects. The shareholders of a renewable energy

---

[40] Article 2(14), Directive 2018/2001, *supra* note 5. See also the definition of the similar concept of 'active customers' in Article 2(8), Directive (EU) 2019/944 of the European Parliament and of the Council of 5 June 2019 on common rules for the internal market for electricity and amending Directive 2012/27/EU, OJ 2019 L 158/125. For an interpretation of these two concepts see *T. Iliopoulos*, The promotion of renewable energy communities in the European Union in *D. Borge-Diez & E, Rosales-Asensio* (eds), Energy Services Fundamentals and Financing, 2020; *T. Iliopoulos*, Regulating Smart Distributed Generation Electricity Systems in the European Union in *L. Reins* (ed.), Regulating New Technologies in Uncertain Times, 2019. For an analysis of the issues stemming from the rise of prosumers see *S. Lavrijssen*, The right to participation for consumers in the energy transition, EEELR 2016 (5), p. 152.

[41] Article 2(16), Directive 2018/2001, *supra* note 5. See also the definition of the similar concept of 'citizen energy community' in Article 2(11), Directive 2019/944, *supra* note 40.

community have a share from the benefits deriving from the electricity that the community generates.[42]

The rise of renewables self-consumers and renewable energy communities is becoming more affordable thanks to new technologies and it renders energy consumers active actors in the efforts for an energy transition. Thus, Member States should enact support schemes that specifically address their needs. This is clearly acknowledged by RED II.

Article 21(2)(d) requires Member States to ensure that renewables self-consumers are entitled to:

> receive remuneration, including, where applicable, through support schemes, for the self-generated renewable electricity that they feed into the grid, which reflects the market value of that electricity and which may take into account its long-term value to the grid, the environment and society.

In addition, Article 21(6)(e) also provides that 'Member States shall put in place an enabling framework to promote and facilitate the development of renewables self-consumption'. This framework shall *inter alia* 'grant renewables self-consumers, for self-generated renewable electricity that they feed into the grid, non-discriminatory access to relevant existing support schemes'. Similarly, Article 22(7) holds that 'Member States shall take into account specificities of renewable energy communities when designing support schemes in order to allow them to compete for support on an equal footing with other market participants'.

On the other hand, Member States may apply – under certain conditions – non-discriminatory and proportionate charges and may apply fees to renewables self-consumers and transparent, cost-reflective charges, levies and taxes, to renewable energy communities.[43]

The introduction of Articles 21 and 22 is expected to increase convergence because Member States are now required to create a legislative framework that will enable and facilitate the involvement in renewables self-consumption and the participation in renewable energy communities. Moreover, the fact that a right to remuneration is explicitly conferred on self-consumers can further boost convergence. It can spur interest in self-consumption, which means that those willing to be involved in such initiatives and projects are expected to pressurise and coerce Member States to legislate accordingly. The rise of self-consumption might thus become a driver of Europeanisation. But these provisions might also lead to divergence. Member States have a wide margin of discretion in deciding not only about the support, but also about the charges,

---

42 Ibid.

43 See Article 21(3) and Article 22(4)(d), (e), Directive 2018/2001, *supra* note 5.

fees or levies they will apply to self-consumers. This discretion might lead to completely different landscapes of treating and promoting self-consumption and energy communities.

5. CONCLUSION

The enactment of Directive 2018/2001 came at a time when the plan for a harmonisation of RESSS had apparently reached a dead-end. It should be noted that RED II did not make any reference to an actual or future harmonisation plan. Nevertheless, it did introduce for the first time certain provisions that specifically deal with the national support schemes. This undoubtedly increases the impact of the European Union on national legal orders. In light of the concept of Europeanisation, this chapter examined the nature and the intensity of the expected effects of the supranational renewable energy support law provisions. These effects are found to be bidirectional. Although in general, Directive 2018/2001 leads to more convergence between the national legal orders, it also legitimises a certain degree of diversity and regulatory competition. But in spite of the anticipated differences, the design and operation of national support schemes will now be under a stricter EU control. And in any event, the lessons that will be learned from such diversity are expected to lead to more convergence in the future. Of course, the actual extent of convergence and divergence will depend on how the law will apply in practice, that is, on the choices that Member States will make and on the way that the Commission will exercise its powers.[44]

It should be noted that Europeanisation of renewable energy support law and harmonisation plans are not poles apart. Indeed, a Europeanisation process led to the enactment of RED II, which introduced broad, top-down rules that are mandatory for Member States, in line with what can be characterised as a 'minimum' harmonisation. European Union law set down certain rules for the RESSS that are enacted by Member States, while Member States retain a relatively wide discretion to decide about the design elements and support

44 More powers are conferred on the Commission by the Energy Governance Regulation. But it lies beyond the scope of this chapter to also examine the content of this legal act. See Regulation (EU) 2018/1999 of the European Parliament and of the Council of 11 December 2018 on the Governance of the Energy Union and Climate Action, amending Regulations (EC) No 663/2009 and (EC) No 715/2009 of the European Parliament and of the Council, Directives 94/22/EC, 98/70/EC, 2009/31/EC, 2009/73/EC, 2010/31/EU, 2012/27/EU and 2013/30/EU of the European Parliament and of the Council, Council Directives 2009/119/EC and (EU) 2015/652 and repealing Regulation (EU) No 525/2013 of the European Parliament and of the Council [2018] OJ L328/1.

levels that they deem best.[45] RED II clearly favours premiums and auctions that are technology-neutral and open to cross-border participation, but it does not set down strict or detailed design requirements.

Given the above, the legal framework that has been instituted after the Europeanisation process thus far has elements of harmonisation and, more importantly, can be seen as a harbinger of harmonisation. The newly enacted renewable energy support law introduces a new stage of interrelationship between the supranational and the national legal orders that might alleviate the reservations about further harmonisation in the field. What's more, the process of Europeanisation does not stop – and the next stages, already under way by the EU Green Deal and the relevant policy documents[46] – might pave the way for an explicit harmonisation in the future.

45 *G. Resch at al.*, Design and impact of a harmonised policy for renewable electricity in Europe, Final report of the beyond2020 project: approaches for a harmonisation of RES(-E) support in Europe, 2014, D7.4, pp. 6–7; *P. del Rio et al.*, Key policy approaches for a harmonisation of RES (-E) support in Europe – Main options and design elements, Design and impact of a harmonised policy for renewable electricity in Europe, 2012, Report D2.1, pp. 9–10.

46 *Commission*, The European Green Deal, COM(2019) 640 final, Brussels, 11 December 2019. See also *Commission*, Stepping up Europe's 2030 climate ambition Investing in a climate-neutral future for the benefit of our people, SWD(2020) 176 final, Brussels, 17 September 2020.

BLIND SPOTS IN THE HARMONISATION FOR AN H_2-CCS CHAIN

Daniel BENRATH*

1. INTRODUCTION

The energy economy is changing fast. New policies and technologies have shifted and are shifting the way power is generated and distributed in Europe.

---

* Postdoctoral Assistant in Energy Law at the Ruhr University Bochum, Germany. This chapter reflects research and results within the German Case Study of the ELEGANCY Project. ACT ELEGANCY, Project No 271498, has received funding from DETEC (CH), BMWi (DE), RVO (NL), Gassnova (NO), BEIS (UK), Gassco, Equinor and Total, and is co-funded by the European Commission under the Horizon 2020 programme, ACT Grant Agreement No 691712.

The market structure is evolving, with changing roles for the existing stakeholders and new players. New business cases have emerged and are developing. Even more so, the progressing climate change demands rapid and unprecedented actions[1] and adjustments on all levels of the economy and the energy economy in particular. The massive changes that can be observed and foreseen may easily overburden the legislators. Law lags behind when the legislative process does not keep up with the pace of transition or the legislator has blind spots in regard to a new situation, especially new technologies.

Law can be an enabler and a coordinator. It is the major tool to transmit policy choices and to shape the economy. If law lags behind, governance is weakened. Within a legal blind spot, the legal impulses do not fit the actual needs. This is particularly relevant for the area of infrastructure and energy: this area is governed by a plethora of conflicting interests and intricate interactions among different levels of actors, which have to be coordinated and demand a strong regulatory framework. Additionally, lagging law can create frictions between the actual and the legal status quo, which can provoke unwanted distortions, lead to unnecessary costs and hinder further developments. The consequences of a law that does not keep up with actual developments go beyond mere legal problems.

EU law is particularly vulnerable to blind spots and lagging. It is fragmented and punctual by nature. The legislative process is rather lengthy and needs a broad support among different institutions. In actuality, it tends towards unanimity even more than required by the treaties. At the same time, EU harmonisation measures are specifically aimed at coordinating different interests and regimes and enabling new approaches to common challenges, especially in cross-border constellations. A lack of adequate regulation questions the purpose of EU harmonisation law itself.

This chapter discusses the EU law for H_2-CCS chains – a set of technologies and business cases associated with 'blue hydrogen' – as an example of the problem of legal timeliness and blind spots in the time of climate change.

1.1. BLUE HYDROGEN AND H_2-CCS CHAINS

Before the approach of this analysis is further outlined, the concepts of H_2-CCS chains and 'blue hydrogen' are described for clarification.

1 e.g. *IPCC*, Global Warming of 1.5°C: An IPCC Special Report on the impacts of global warming of 1.5°C above pre-industrial levels and related greenhouse gas emission pathways, in the context of strengthening the global response to the threat of climate change, sustainable development, and efforts to eradicate poverty, 2018, pp. 15 et seq., 129 et seq., 313 et seq.

Hydrogen as an energy carrier is discussed as a key element of a future economy with net zero emissions. The production, storage, transport and usage of hydrogen may be able to tackle some major challenges of a net-zero economy dominated by renewable energy, especially in regard to industrial applications and energy storage.[2] The hydrogen used in this context has to have a low carbon intensity, while traditionally hydrogen is predominantly produced from fossils ('grey hydrogen'), especially natural gas, also producing CO_2.[3] One way to produce low-carbon hydrogen is electrolysis based on renewable energy. This hydrogen is considered 'green' and can be carbon-neutral in the long run.[4] Alternatively, 'blue hydrogen' is discussed, especially for a bridging period.[5] Blue hydrogen is produced from fossils, like grey hydrogen, but the produced CO_2 is captured and permanently removed from the atmosphere by CCS. Although not all of the CO_2 produced can be removed in this way, CCS can substantially reduce the carbon footprint of the hydrogen.[6] Blue hydrogen is in particular discussed as a more climate friendly alternative to the (direct) use of natural gas.

The notion of an H_2-CCS chain highlights the fact that the production of blue hydrogen is integrated into different chains of production, transport and usage. The fossil raw material has to be exploited and transported to the site of hydrogen production. The hydrogen has to be transported and can be used in different settings. The CO_2 has to be captured and transported, it may be used along the chain and, ultimately, it is geologically stored. These chains can drastically differ, depending on where the hydrogen is actually produced (closer to the use of hydrogen, closer to the fossil raw material or closer to the site of CCS) and how the different materials are used and transported. The overall design of the H_2-CCS chains is determined by a complex set of parameters, including legal issues.

---

2 *C. Buchmüller et al.*, Der Rechtsrahmen für die Vermarktung von grünem Wasserstoff, Zeitschrift für Neues Energierecht 2019 (23), pp. 194, 194 et seq.; *IEA*, The Future of Hydrogen: Seizing today's opportunities (Report prepared by the IEA for the G20, Japan), 2019; *J. Michalski et al.*, Wasserstoffstudie Nordrhein-Westfalen: Eine Expertise für das Ministerium für Wirtschaft, Innovation, Digitalisierung und Energie des Landes Nordrhein-Westfalen, 2019.

3 *R. Fleming & J. Fershee*, The 'Hydrogen Economy' in the United States and the European Union: Regulating Innovation to Combat Climate Change, in *D. Zillman, M. Roggenkamp, L. Paddock & L. Godden* (eds), Innovation in Energy Law and Technology: Dynamic Solutions for Energy Transitions, 2018, pp. 137, 139.

4 Cp. *Buchmüller et al., supra*, note 2 at pp. 194 et seq.

5 e.g. *L. van Cappellen, H. Croezen & F. Rooijers*, Feasibility study into blue hydrogen: Technical, economic & sustainability analysis, 2018; IEA, *supra*, note 2 at pp. 39 et seq.

6 IEA, *supra*, note 2 at pp. 39 et seq.

For H_2-CCS chains, there are manifold cross-border issues. The raw material for the hydrogen production, CO_2 and hydrogen – as well as the products or, respectively, the power produced from hydrogen – can all be traded and transported across the border in an H_2-CCS chain. These potential cross-border transactions can interact with each other and with other aspects of the common market. Therefore, H_2-CCS chains can easily touch areas of EU law or call for further harmonisation.

1.2. GOALS, SCOPE AND PROCEDURE OF ANALYSIS

The goal of this contribution is to analyse the legal blind spots in EU harmonisation and to discuss potentials for a development in regard to selected areas that are connected to H_2-CCS chains. The first area is the cross-border transport of CO_2 for CCS. The second area of the analysis is the transport of hydrogen in pipeline networks. Thirdly, the integration of H_2-CCS chains into the existing harmonised regimes for guarantees of origin, on the one hand, and of the EU Emission Trading System (EU ETS), on the other hand, is investigated.

The first step of the analysis for each of the selected areas is a short presentation of the existing EU law that is relevant for H_2-CCS chains in the respective fields.

Based on this, relevant legal blind spots are identified and analysed: which parts of the H_2-CCS chain are not covered by EU harmonisation? How do these blind spots relate to legislative history and the overall systematic background? And how relevant are the legal blind spots actually? Since harmonisation measures in EU secondary law are sector-specific and fragmented by nature, not every legal blind spot in EU law is necessarily a lacuna that demands further legislative action.

The analyses for the respective areas are wrapped up by a discussion on some options to react to the blind spots. This discussion on options for further development does not aim at an in-depth evaluation of all legislative possibilities.[7] Rather, it is a rough sketch of policy options based on the respective existing systematic lines of EU law on climate change, the probable needs of future investors and on-going policy discussions to contribute to the general discussion on climate change policy from the perspective of H_2-CCS chains.

The conclusions summarise key findings of the analysis in regard to the legal status quo, its deficiencies and potential further legal developments.

---

7 For a broader discussion on legislative options in the German context, see *D. Benrath et al.*, CO_2 and H_2 Infrastructure in Germany: Final Report of the German Case Study (Elegancy D.5.5.3), 2020, esp. pp. 83 et seq., 91 et seq., 105 et seq., 107 et seq.

Furthermore, these findings are discussed in the overarching contexts of H_2-CCS chains and of the challenges of climate change and energy transition for EU law in general.

2. HARMONISATION FOR THE CROSS-BORDER TRANSPORT OF CO_2 FOR CARBON CAPTURE AND STORAGE

2.1. STATUS QUO

The central legal tool for harmonisation in regard to CCS is the CCS directive.[8] Relevant stipulations in the context of cross-border CO_2 transport are: the overall purpose of the CCS directive (Article 1); criteria for the CO_2 stream (Article 12); and non-discriminatory third party access to CO_2 transport networks (Article 21). The directive aims at a legal framework for the permanent containment of CO_2 to contribute to the fight against climate change while limiting negative effects and risks to the environment and human health. In regard to the composition of the CO_2 stream, impurities are restricted and the integrity of the transport infrastructure has to be safeguarded. Based on this stipulation, the commission has adopted guidelines for the CO_2 stream composition, which present challenges and technical requirements in regard incidental substances.[9] In regard to third-party access, the directive stipulates the aspects that the detailed national legislation on CCS may refer to for exceptions. These aspects include a wider range of different policy aspects and are applicable to transport networks and to storage sites (capacity, national strategy for CCS, technical incompatibility, other duly substantiated needs in the context of the storage site and the transport network). Additionally, a special settlement regime for third-party access is foreseen (Article 22). Especially for transport, the harmonisation by the CCS directive is rather broad and leaves a wide margin for political decisions of the Member States: for example, what aspects for the rejection of third party access are considered and further details on the non-discriminatory access regime, if transport is even allowed.

CCS and CO_2 transport, especially by pipelines, are also covered by other acts of EU law. The EU ETS directive[10] also covers CCS and CO_2 transport and

8 Directive 2009/31/EC on the geological storage of carbon dioxide, OJ 2009 L 140/114.

9 European Commission, Implementation of Directive 2009/31/EC on the Geological Storage of Carbon Dioxide: Guidance Document 2: Characterisation of the Storage Complex, CO_2 Stream Composition, Monitoring and Corrective Measures, 2011, pp. 58 et seq.

10 Directive 2003/87/EC establishing a scheme for greenhouse gas emission allowance trading within the Community, OJ 2003 L 275/32.

will be discussed later on. Notably, CO_2 transport for CCS is covered by the recent TEN-E regulation[11] and the environmental impact assessment directive.[12] The TEN-E regulation foresees the possibility to have facilities for cross-border CO_2 transport identified as projects of common interests. The environmental impact assessment directive foresees environmental impact assessments for large pipelines of CO_2 for CCS.

2.2. BLIND SPOTS

The EU legislature was well aware of different ways to apply CCS, including offshore storage and CO_2 pipeline transport, and thus the regulatory coverage is – albeit guarded – mostly complete. The major blind spots in regard to cross-border and especially the CCS directive are subtler: the EU harmonisation measures are shaped by a perspective which does not match the recent trends and challenges in respect of CCS and CO_2 cross-border transport. The CCS directive focused on a prototypical point-to-point situation where CO_2 from a single source (especially coal plants) is permanently stored at a single site, which is onshore and may be even on-site. Onshore (and even more so on-site) CCS has a merely marginal need for cross-border transport,[13] let alone transport networks, and can provoke trans-border conflicts primarily in respect of possible environmental impacts. Whereas today, onshore CCS faces public resistance,[14] and it is considered more feasible to collect the CO_2 from different sources and transport it to the storage sites.[15] Thus, CCS concepts today have a much stronger emphasis on transport networks with multiple sources and cross-border transport than foreseen by the CCS Directive.[16] Additionally, the free movement of CO_2 within the common market becomes a major aspect of CCS regulation.

---

11 Regulation (EU) No 347/2013 on guidelines for trans-European energy infrastructure, OJ 2013 L 115/39. The proposal for the new TEN-E Regulation, COM(2020) 824 final, still covers cross-border carbon dioxide networks.

12 Directive 2011/92/EU on the assessment of the effects of certain public and private projects on the environment, OJ 2012 L 26/1.

13 Cp. European Commission, accompanying document to the proposal for a directive of the European Parliament and of the Council on the geological storage of carbon dioxide: Impact Assessment (Commission Staff Working Document COM(2008) XXX), 2008, p. 86.

14 e.g. Bundesregierung, Evaluierungsbericht der Bunderegierung über die Anwendung des Kohlendioxid-Speicherungsgesetzes sowie die Erfahrungen zur CCS-Technologie: Unterrichtung der Bundesregierung (BT-Drs 19/6891), 2018, p. 6.; Triple, Ricardo-AEA & TNO, Study to support the review and evaluation of Directive 2009, 2015, pp. 22 et seq., 27.

15 e.g. *M. Ros et al.*, Start of a CO_2 hub in Rotterdam: connecting CCS and CCU, Energy Procedia 2014, p. 2691; *D. Sadler et al.*, H21 North of England: H21 NoE Report/2018, 2018, pp. 334 et seq. See *H. Mahgerefteh et al.*, A Trans-European CO_2 Transportation Infrastructure for CCUS: Opportunities & Challenges, 2020.

16 Cp. *D.E. Henriksen & I. Ombudstvedt*, Cross-Border Transportation: A key to Unlock Full-Scale CCS, Energy Procedia 2017, pp. 7443, 7444.

To integrate the transport of CO_2 into an international exercise to collect CO_2 for CCS and to enable the free movement of CO_2, a cross-border coordination regime for CO_2 streams from multiple sources is essential.[17] Impurities of CO_2 streams from different sources create specific technical challenges (and even may interact and create new hazards).[18] The design and operation of respective pipelines have to consider this. But the relevant harmonisation provided by the CCS directive on CO_2 stream composition (Article 12 (1)) is limited to a safety requirement in regard to dangers for the respective transport network or storage site, without reference to any coordination. Even the commission guidelines that discuss the hazards of impurities in the CO_2 stream and the differences between different sources say little on coordinating CO_2 streams from multiple sources. This is consistent since the guidelines are to address CO_2 stream criteria only in regard to safety issues and not for additional coordination within networks (Article 12 (2) of the CCS Directive). Coordination has to be done by the CCS stakeholders (e.g., operators of storage sites, transport systems and CO_2 sources) without legal tools or a regulatory framework on the matter. But the coordination by the stakeholders is impeded by the third-party access regime of the CCS Directive since the operators cannot freely refuse the injection of CO_2 streams that are not in line with the coordination. In regard to third-party access and the rejection of CO_2 streams, the CCS Directive allows the Member States to take into account technical incompatibilities and other reasonable needs. But it is questionable whether this can suffice to establish an operational coordination framework, and it does not provide for cross-border coordination. Although the lack of coordination mechanisms and therefore functional coordination may create distortions, actual consequences on the free movement of CO_2 or the operation of CCS networks cannot be observed at this point; in actuality, there is no CO_2 infrastructure and there will not be such an infrastructure for a while. For the time being, the main problem connected to this legal blind spot is rather the technical harmonisation, which may already be relevant for long-term planning, but does not necessarily need sovereign intervention.

Interestingly, this blind spot in regard to the specific challenges of cross-border transport networks in case of the CCS Directive cannot be observed for the TEN-E Regulation, which addresses the issues of cross-border transport and international CCS networks.[19] Yet, the stark contrast between the foreseen role of the potential and actually identified CCS

---

17 Cp. Triple, Ricardo-AEA & TNO, *supra*, note 14 at p. 48.

18 *Mahgerefteh et al.*, *supra*, note 15 esp. at pp. 33 et seq.; *H. Rütters et al.*, Towards an optimisation of the CO_2 stream composition – A whole-chain approach, International Journal of Greenhouse Gas Control 2016 (54), p. 682.

19 Cp. *Henriksen & Ombudstvedt*, *supra*, note 16 at p. 7444.

projects of common interest,[20] on the one hand, and the boundaries of the existing legal environment for CO_2 cross-border transport, on the other, only highlight the blind spots of the overall EU CO_2 transport regime.

2.3. OPTIONS

In regard to the lack of coordination, an immediate legislative reaction in the context of the CCS Directive is not necessary. In respect of third-party access, neither the market structure and the actual distortions nor the appropriate tools to reconcile coordination and market failures can be foreseen at this point. Aspects of technical harmonisation can be discussed by the potential stakeholders on a private level without legislative action of the EU. Premature new EU law could even be harmful and create new uncertainties.[21] Yet, the guidelines on CO_2 stream composition can and should be amended with a stronger focus on multiple CO_2 streams from different sources within a common network. This would create a common ground for the further technical discussion and a visible (though low-profile) political signal that the EU is still determined to promote cross-border cooperation on CCS and the free movement of CO_2 for CCS.

In the long term, the need for better coordination in a cross-border CCS network will have to be addressed by the EU legislature. A strong legal coordination mechanism on the EU level for CO_2 stream composition in a network (and perhaps other technical issues like pipeline design) would probably match the challenges of a CCS network best while ensuring the free movement of CO_2. At the very least, the third-party access regime of the CCS Directive has to be amended and clarified to allow an effective coordination by the stakeholders without surrendering the objectives of fair and open access.

3. HARMONISATION FOR HYDROGEN IN NETWORKS

3.1. STATUS QUO

Whereas there is no specific EU law on hydrogen networks, there is extensive regulation on natural gas networks, especially in the

20 See No. 12.1–12.4 in the list in Annex VII to the amended TEN-E Regulation.

21 Cp. Triple, Ricardo-AEA & TNO, *supra*, note 14 at p. 132.

Natural Gas Directive[22] and the Natural Gas Transmission Network Regulation.[23] The natural gas regime is also applicable to hydrogen: the Natural Gas Directive explicitly provides that it is applicable to all gases that can safely be injected into and transported through the natural gas grid (Article 1 (2)), which also includes hydrogen.[24] The Natural Gas Transmission Network Regulation does not have such a stipulation, but given that the Natural Gas Directive and the Natural Gas Transmission Network Regulation are considered to be interlocking parts of a uniform regulatory background for the natural gas market, it can be assumed that the scope of application is concurrent to the Natural Gas Directive in this regard. However, the scope of the application to hydrogen is not clear from the wording alone: while the wording refers to any gas that can be injected and transported, which implies the application to all hydrogen in networks,[25] the context shows that these pieces of legislation are aimed at natural gas networks and are only applicable to other gases, as long as these are connected to natural gas networks. Thus, hydrogen in natural gas networks is covered by EU law on natural gas, whereas hydrogen in dedicated hydrogen networks is not covered at all.[26]

In particular, the harmonisation in regard to gas quality also refers to the admixture of hydrogen in natural gas networks. As differences of gas quality may disrupt the interoperability of networks and thus the free movement of natural gas, EU law provides a range of tools to promote interoperability. These tools do not harmonise natural gas quality as such, but rather, they create mechanisms of cooperation and coordination between the different actors, such as the establishment of the Agency for the Cooperation of Energy Regulators (ACER) and of the European Network of Transmission System Operators for Gas (ENTSO-G), as well as the network codes – namely, the network code on interoperability and data exchange rules.[27]

---

22 Directive 2009/73/EC concerning common rules for the internal market in natural gas, OJ 2009 L 211/94.

23 Regulation (EC) No 715/2009 on conditions for access to the natural gas transmission networks, OJ 2009 L 211/36.

24 *D. Benrath*, Applicable law to hydrogen pipelines for energy purposes in Germany, Journal of Energy & Natural Resources Law 2020 (38), pp. 65, 68 et seq.; *R. Fleming*, Regulating Power-to-Gas in the Energy Union, OGEL 2018 (4)16, pp. 7 et seq.; *R. Fleming & G. Kreeft*, Power-to-Gas and Hydrogen for Energy Storage under EU Energy Law, in *M. Roggenkamp & C. Banet* (eds), European Energy Law Report XIII, 2020, p. 101 at 4.2.1; *U. Ronnacker*, Rechtliche Herausforderungen bei der Umstellung von Gasbezugsquellen und Gasarten, Recht der Energiewirtschaft 2020, pp. 178, 181. Cp. *Fleming & Fershee, supra*, note 3 at p. 148.

25 Cp. *Fleming & Fershee, supra*, note 3 at p. 151; *Ronnacker, supra*, note 24 at p. 181.

26 *Benrath, supra*, note 24 at pp. 69 et seq. Cp. *Fleming & Kreeft, supra*, note 24 at 4.2.2.

27 Commission Regulation (EU) 2015/703 establishing a network code on interoperability and data exchange rules, OJ 2015 L 113/13.

3.2. BLIND SPOTS

The most obvious and blunt blind spot in regard to hydrogen in networks is the absence of any specific EU harmonisation for dedicated hydrogen networks.

Much more intricately, the blind spot on hydrogen networks also extends to the demarcation between dedicated hydrogen networks and natural gas networks. As the regulatory background between the densely harmonised natural gas networks and the non-harmonised hydrogen networks vastly differ, a clear demarcation is needed to produce legal certainty for any investments in hydrogen networks.[28] Yet, as dedicated hydrogen networks were not considered by the legislature, there are no criteria or hints to answer the question at what point a natural gas network with admixed hydrogen turns into a hydrogen network with admixed natural gas. Even more so, if there are punctual interconnections between a hydrogen and a natural gas network, what determines the independence of the dedicated hydrogen network and how to handle the interconnecting facilities remain unclear.

For admixed hydrogen in natural gas networks, there is no notable blind spot. The natural gas regulation is well aware of the issue of admixtures and gas quality and provides respective legal mechanisms. However, the coordination mechanisms of the natural gas regime are aimed at rather technical issues, and it is questionable whether they are a suitable arrangement to coordinate substantially rising amounts of hydrogen, which will create many conflicts and tensions.

3.3. OPTIONS

In regard to the missing demarcation between natural gas networks and dedicated hydrogen networks, action of the EU legislature is needed to produce legal certainty for investments into hydrogen (or other gas) networks.[29] As such a demarcation should work for different scenarios, it should start from the natural gas network and refer to functional aspects rather than technical thresholds. For example, the Natural Gas Directive (and following it the Natural Gas Transmission Network Regulation) can be amended to limit its scope to all facilities predominantly integrated into the transport and supply of natural gas; and if a facility has more than one dominant function, the regulatory framework for natural gas is only applicable as far as the natural gas network is directly affected. Thus, the existing regulation cannot be circumvented by

---

[28] Cp. *Benrath, supra*, note 24 at pp. 69 et seq. Cp. *Fleming & Kreeft, supra*, note 24 at 4.2.2.

[29] *Benrath et al., supra*, note 7 at pp. 92 et seq., 106.

actors of the natural gas market, while independent networks can be put in place without falling under the natural gas regime. The amount of hydrogen or natural gas should have no impact on the demarcation. As long as end-users of natural gas rely on the network, it should be considered to be a natural gas network. Yet, the applicability of the natural gas regime is not to be extended to a dedicated hydrogen network supplying hydrogen to end-users (behind possible interconnection points). In this context, the rules on unbundling would only apply to the operation of those parts of the hydrogen network that (also) directly serve the supply of hydrogen as an admixture to the natural gas networks. Of course, for some constellations, this approach would demand further technical details or even corrections.

In regard to the lack of substantial harmonisation for dedicated hydrogen networks, there is no immediate need for EU harmonisation measures. At this point, the coordination of cross-border hydrogen networks can be carried out by the respective stakeholders (system operators, hydrogen producers, hydrogen customers, national governments and authorities). Since there is no relevant hydrogen network economy, there are neither existing market barriers nor distortions in the common market, which have to be addressed by the EU legislature.[30] Potential conflicts can be addressed by the general EU competition law. In particular, it is not recommendable to merely extend the natural gas regime to hydrogen networks. The natural gas regime was created and further shaped as a reaction to the actual market situation of natural gas networks (and its reaction to the previous regime)[31] with mature economies and powerful economic actors, as well as structural rigidities.[32] The regulatory tools of this regime do not fit an emerging market such as a hydrogen network economy with the need for large scale and high-risk investments and for intensive coordination between different actors in the chain. In fact, in Article 36 of the Natural Gas Directive, the natural gas regime foresees exemptions for certain situations of new investments, which have great similarities to the situation for hydrogen networks as a whole.[33] Therefore, the extension of the natural gas regime would just create new frictions, barriers and blind spots. At this point, it seems more recommendable to let the national legislators compete for practicable solutions in regard to dedicated hydrogen networks and learn from their experiences, before

---

30 For similar reasons, the natural gas regime was not extended to CO_2 networks; cp. European Commission, *supra*, note 13 at p. 45.

31 Cp. recitals 5–8, 25 of the Natural Gas Directive. See also *H. Vedder, M. Roggenkamp & I. del Guayo*, EU Energy Law, in *M. Roggenkamp, C. Redgwell, A. Rønne & I. del Guayo* (eds), Energy Law in Europe: National, EU and International Regulation, 3rd ed., 2016, p. 187, paras. 4.201 et seq.

32 Cp. recitals 36–37 of the Natural Gas Directive. Cp. also *Vedder, Roggenkamp & del Guayo*, *supra*, note 31 at paras. 4.192, 4.197 et seq.

33 Cp. recital 35 of the Natural Gas Directive.

engaging in EU harmonisation measures. Nevertheless, on a more restrained level, the EU legislature can contribute to facilitating international cooperation on cross-border hydrogen networks, especially by promoting the consideration of hydrogen and other gases in the network development plans and including hydrogen projects as potential projects of common interest pursuant to the TEN-E Regulation.[34]

However, in the long run, due to the nature of energy infrastructure, the need for cross-border energy transport and the special dangers of natural monopolies, as well as the need for further harmonisation and regulatory interventions, will probably arise. In particular, the growing number of stakeholders in a rising hydrogen economy and the danger that incompatible networks develop may engender the need for new instruments of coordination. And at some point, a regulatory framework suitable for a more mature hydrogen network and its specific problems will be necessary. To avoid unnecessary adaption costs and stranded investments, the EU should engage in the discussion on dedicated hydrogen networks at an early stage and steer, for example, with soft law instruments, the development with clear indications of the overarching policy aims relevant for the hydrogen economy.

In regard to the admixture of hydrogen in natural gas networks, a close coordination on the EU level is needed to substantially increase the amount of hydrogen in the strongly interconnected European transmission systems.[35] Due to the legitimate expectations of transport customers and the plethora of possible conflicts, this will probably need a more political approach than the existing rather technical coordination mechanisms on EU level. Finally, this calls for an intervention of the EU legislature to create an appropriate framework if this path is being followed.

4. INTEGRATION OF H_2-CCS CHAINS INTO EXISTING EU CLIMATE PROTECTION SCHEMES

4.1. STATUS QUO

The EU ETS directive demands allowances for the emission of CO_2 by certain activities. These activities are singled out in Annex I. The emissions by

34 The proposal for the new TEN-E Regulation, COM(2020) 824 final, actually endorses hydrogen networks and also introduces hydrogen into the Union-wide development plan pursuant to Article 8 (10) of the Natural Gas Transmission Network Regulation.

35 *Benrath et al., supra*, note 7 at pp. 88, 91; *K. Petrov et al.*, Study on the Future Role of Gas from a Regulatory Perspective, 2018, p. 49; *J. Wachsmuth et al.*, Roadmap Gas für die Energiewende, 2019, p. 199.

other activities are covered by other regimes on EU level that do not refer to single emissions, but rather, to collective goals and regulatory measures. For example, heating is not an activity covered by the EU ETS scheme, but it is considered for the goals in regard to renewable energy, Article 3, 7 (1) lit. b of the new Renewable Energy Directive,[36] and in regard to energy efficiency, Article 3, 7, 2 no. 1 of the Energy Efficiency Directive,[37] and it is addressed by specific regulatory measures, especially the Energy Performance in Buildings Directive.[38] The recent EU ETS Directive covers the large scale (more than 25 tonnes per day) production of (blue and grey) hydrogen from fossil raw material by reforming or partial oxidation, the capture of CO_2 (and other greenhouse gases), the transport of CO_2 for CCS in pipelines and the final geological storage, whereas any emission mitigated by CCS pursuant to the CCS directive demands no allowances, Article 12 (3a) of the EU ETS directive.

Guarantees of origin allow for trading of renewable energy within the European context. They legally link the production of renewable energy to the use of energy, although there is no discrete connection between the production and the use of energy within an energy network. The uniform guarantees of origin can be used to effect legal consequences in connection to the state support of renewable energies and to transparency for the final customers. The new Renewable Energy Directive extends the guarantees of origin scheme to gases including hydrogen produced with renewable energy.[39]

Thus, the whole H_2-CCS chain in regard to hydrogen and CO_2 is covered by the existing schemes of EU ETS and guarantees of origin.

4.2. BLIND SPOTS

The recent inclusion of hydrogen into the guarantees of origin scheme created some new legal challenges. In particular, it leaves a broad margin in respect of the requirements in regard to the power used for the production of the hydrogen (use of guarantees of origin for renewable energy, physical use of renewable energy and use of excess renewable energy),[40] an issue which was not relevant for the scheme before. This potential lack of harmonisation may lead to tensions when trading hydrogen between Member States and demands further development.[41] Yet, in regard to blue hydrogen in

---

36 Directive (EU) 2018/2001 on the promotion of the use of energy from renewable sources, OJ 2018 L 328/82.

37 Directive 2012/27/EU on energy efficiency, OJ 2012 L 315/1.

38 Directive 2010/31/EU on the energy performance of buildings, OJ 2010 L 153/13.

39 *Buchmüller et al., supra*, note 2 at pp. 198 et seq.

40 Ibid. at p. 199.

41 Ibid. at p. 204.

H_2-CCS chains, the new scheme is quite clear: it is not covered by the extension to solely green hydrogen. And this is not a blind spot, but a consistent policy: in the current system of EU law, measures to mitigate the emission of CO_2 by CCS are addressed by the EU ETS. For blue hydrogen, only private initiatives like CertifHy[42] can address the origin of the hydrogen, without prompting any legal effect.

In regard to the EU ETS, the EU legislation focuses on the transport by pipeline and has a blind spot in regard to the transport of CO_2 with individual vessels, especially ships and lorries. This is reflected in the Annex I of the EU ETS Directive, which only covers the pipeline transport, and in the reference to CCS pursuant to the CCS Directive, which does not address the transport by ship. Therefore, it is legally uncertain if allowances can be saved in the case that the CO_2 is transported by ship or how emissions during the transport by ship can be taken into account.[43] At the connecting points between those parts of the CCS chain that are covered by the allowances system and the transport by individual vessels, the attribution of emissions – and therefore the need for allowances – is especially unclear.

Additionally, the EU ETS Directive only applies to CO_2 transport for CCS, not for usage. Thus, it remains unclear how emissions in pipelines that transport CO_2 for CCS as well as for usage have to be handled. Although large-scale transport of CO_2 will be dominated by CCS, this uncertainty may affect the whole chain, especially if the use of captured CO_2 gains momentum.

Furthermore, the current EU ETS has some bizarre and unwanted effects in regard to blue hydrogen in H_2-CCS chains, especially in comparison to natural gas. The large-scale production of blue hydrogen (and the subsequent CCS) needs allowances, whereas users of hydrogen do not produce CO_2 emissions and do not need allowances. In contrast, the production of natural gas does not need allowances, whereas only some usages of natural gas demand allowances. Thus, for usages that are not covered by the EU ETS – such as heating – blue hydrogen needs allowances for the (mitigated) emissions, while natural gas needs no allowances for the (non-mitigated) emissions. Therefore, the EU ETS actually creates costs for mitigation measures instead of rewarding them. The consequences are even more contradictory when the blue hydrogen is injected into a natural gas network. Since the use of hydrogen does not create CO_2 emissions, a higher amount of hydrogen in

42 See https://www.certifhy.eu/.

43 *R. Boekholt*, Regulation of liability and safety in ship transport of CO2: a comparative analysis (CATO2-WP4.1-D11), 2013, p. 50; *N. Rydberg & D. Langlet*, CCS in the Baltic Sea Region – Bastor 2: Work Package 4 – Legal and Fiscal Aspects (Elforsk report 14:48), 2015, pp. 30 et seq. This issue is actually acknowledged by the recent proposal of the EU ETS Directive, COM(2021) 551 final, recital 41 and Annex lit. c vi.

the natural gas networks will reduce the need for allowances. And because all customers of the network use the same mixture, all customers directly profit from this reduction, no matter where they purchased the gas. Pursuant to the current system, the mitigation measures at the site of the production of the blue hydrogen cannot be attributed to the actual reduction of the need for allowances on the use side. Despite its purpose, the EU ETS does not give any tradable incentive to mitigate the emission of greenhouse gases. These effects are closely connected to the contribution of hydrogen to sector integration and point to its intricate challenges.

4.3. OPTIONS

Despite the substantial blind spots in the existing schemes in regard to H_2-CCS chains, the options to develop the existing systems are rather limited. The extension of the guarantees of origin scheme for renewable energy to blue hydrogen would introduce an alien aspect to the renewable energy regime. And to create pinpoint solutions in the EU ETS for the specific issues of H_2-CCS would necessarily be overcomplicated, and thus prone to new blind spots, and introduce new structures, which might destabilise the policy tool as a whole. In particular, any measure to allow a customer of blue hydrogen in a natural gas network to specifically link its emissions to the mitigation measures would need a legal correction of the actual emission, either by adding fictional emissions to the free riders or by assuming an overall emission that is lower than the actual one.

Only single aspects can be corrected within the existing system: a clarification can easily be inserted in regard to single vessels for CO_2 transport.[44] Further clarification can settle the issue in regard to other uses of CO_2.

Beyond the existing systems, there are more options for development. Especially in respect of the discussion around reforming the EU emission pricing scheme, the blind spots for H_2-CCS chains highlight the deficiencies of the existing system and the advantages of a system that focuses rather on the production or import of fossil raw materials than on the emitting activity. The recent proposal on the EU ETS Directive[45] actually aims at a corresponding reform in respect of road transport and housing. Such a reform should then take the H_2-CCS chains into account and address the blind spots and their consequences. Additionally, if there is an according political will, a line for

44 *Boekholt, supra*, note 43 at pp. 52 et seq.; *Rydberg & Langlet, supra*, note 43 at p. 32.; Triple, Ricardo-AEA & TNO, *supra*, note 14 at p. 128.

45 COM(2021) 551 final.

the facilitation of CCS comparable to the renewable energy regime could be developed. Such a regime could easily encompass its own guarantees of origin scheme.

Additionally, national measures might mitigate the consequences of the blind spots. A national pricing mechanism for CO_2 outside of the EU ETS system would reduce the relative disadvantage of blue hydrogen against natural gas, but could also create new issues and barriers.[46] A fixed quota of hydrogen in comparison with natural gas (either for transport or for supply) would remove this disadvantage completely, but would also create intense frictions with the current gas system.

5. CONCLUSION

In regard to the cross-border transport of CO_2, the focus of the legal status quo does not match the actual challenges in respect of the recent discussion on the deployment of CCS. In particular, there are blind spots in the harmonisation on the free movement of CO_2 and in the coordination of different streams in (cross-border) CCS networks. At this point, immediate EU legislation is not necessarily the best option. Rather, the technical guidelines of the commission should be amended. Yet, in the long term, the EU legislature will have to tackle the coordination issue to enable the operation of workable cross-border CCS networks.

In regard to hydrogen in networks, there are no EU harmonisation measures on dedicated hydrogen pipelines. Also, the demarcation between hydrogen and natural gas networks is not addressed. While immediate legislative action to clarify the demarcation line is desirable, a substantial harmonisation for dedicated hydrogen networks does not seem to be recommendable now. Rather, the EU legislature should wait and learn from actual developments and the experiences of Member States, while the overall process should be accompanied by EU soft law and coordination instruments. In contrast, a substantial increase of admixed hydrogen in the interconnected European natural gas transmission systems will need strong coordination on the EU level and probably some legislative action for crucial political decisions connected to such a shift.

The EU ETS scheme has blind spots in regard to the transport of CO_2 with individual vessels and produces unwanted consequences in regard to the production and usage of blue hydrogen by actually penalising mitigation measures. While clarifications or amendments of the EU ETS Directive can handle the CO_2 transport by vessels, there is no easy way to address the blue

46 Cp. *Benrath et al.*, *supra*, note 7 at p. 90.

hydrogen issues within the existing system. Rather, these issues should be taken into account by a general reform.

While H_2-CCS chains as a concept are not addressed by EU law, the provisions in the analysed areas do cover the chains in large parts. There are, however, substantial blind spots, which lead to distortions, unwanted results and unnecessary barriers – and therefore challenge technology neutrality. The blind spots are pretty diverse, and even more diverse are the potential remedies with their respective advantages and drawbacks. While the analysis underlines the need to evolve the existing harmonisation in the light of new developments, there is no uniform way to address all these developments. This analysis can only vaguely highlight both the need for clear demarcation lines and a more general legislation that refers to actual results or overarching principles to allow technology neutrality and keep pace with the recent developments. The right response to the blind spots has to navigate between the need to find specific solutions for specific problems and the advantages of a more general regulation and faces different challenges in this conflictual field. For some aspects, immediate technical EU legislation seems to be appropriate, while for other aspects, harmonisation can wait – or has to be integrated into broader legislative projects. Moreover, the EU is not the right level to address the issues in all cases.

Further inquiries into the challenges for law and lawmakers by new technologies, new developments and new concepts under the sign of the great speed of changes in the time of climate change may discover further structures and foci. They may lay the foundation for more specific conclusions in regard to certain aspects or for well-founded and more general recommendations for policy development.

CONCLUSION

Matteo FERMEGLIA*

The tortuous path towards harmonisation in EU environmental and energy law constitutes a far-reaching effort, which shall be supported by far-reaching knowledge. The 2019 conference on 'Harmonisation in environmental and energy law' held at Hasselt University – and this book – have provided a one-stop-shop to gauge the notion of harmonisation and appraise its inherent meaning in the European Union (EU). According to Oxford's Dictionary of Law, harmonisation of laws refers to the process whereby 'member states of the EU make changes in their national laws, in accordance with Community legislation, to produce uniformity, particularly relating to commercial matters of common interest'. Thus, harmonisation per se ought not pursue any further aim than mere approximation between legal regimes.[1] As is well known, however, this concept acquires a rather different meaning when put in the broader context of the EU's environmental, energy (and climate) policies. Crucially, harmonisation here serves as a means to specific EU ends, namely: a) to achieve a high level of protection and improvement of the quality of the environment (art. 3(3) TEU, art. 37 of the EU Charter of Fundamental Rights); b) to achieve a general standard of environmental and climate protection while taking into account context-specific differences across Member States (art. 191(2) TFEU); and c) to ensure the functioning of the energy market while fostering a low-carbon economy (art. 194 TFEU). Thus, harmonisation essentially results in a choice for the EU as to how to ensure the attainment of its environmental and energy policy objectives.[2]

* Assistant Professor of International and European Environmental Law, University of Hasselt, Belgium.

1 *A. Mads & C. Andersen*, Theory and Practice of Harmonisation, 2012, p. 309.

2 *L. Squintani*, Beyond Minimum Harmonisation: Gold-Plating and Green-Plating of European Environmental Law, 2019, p. 5 (paraphrasing *S. Weatherill*, The Internal Market as a Legal Concept, 2017, 153).

Against this backdrop, this book – as well as the 2019 conference from which it stems – aims to address the following fundamental question: has harmonisation in the EU delivered on the (increasingly urgent) needs to render mainstream and enhance the effectiveness of environmental and energy law?

The book has tried to answer this question by addressing the core substantial and methodological issues entailed in achieving a fully-fledged harmonised EU regime on environmental and energy matters. Furthermore, it has emphasised the heavy-lifting role of critical thinking, while progress on the implementation of the existing regime of EU law at the Member State level remains largely undermined by several political and, significantly, legal factors. In this respect, three main threads of original thought stand out from the contributions comprised in this collection, as unpacked in the following sub-sections.

1. HARMONISATION TOOLS AND TECHNIQUES

Let us first address the issue as to *how* to pursue proper harmonisation in the EU. The EU is already resorting to manifold approaches to ensure consistency across Member States' legislation, both through hard law instruments (direct regulation and standards) and soft law instruments (e.g. by incorporating World Health Organisation and other international guidelines or providing them itself, also in the form of codes of good practices, in close collaboration with local governments). Both categories of such approaches have been appraised throughout this book. The preliminary choice as to the relevant legal basis for harmonisation, however, is crucial here. In fact, the subsidiarity and proportionality principles lie at the foundation of the delicate equilibrium between sovereign Member States and the EU. In this regard, Nicolas de Sadeleer analyses the dichotomy between Articles 114, 191 and 192 TFEU. Moreover, he stresses the potential pivotal role – as-of-yet probably not fully explored and deployed – of art. 11 TFEU as a driver to both fully embed environmental considerations in all EU policies, including those related to energy issues, and to ultimately enshrine the prevalence of environmental protection over the internal market and other considerations.

As to the actual use and design of harmonisation tools in the EU, the long-standing and contentious issue of codification has been addressed. Quoting Anna Vanhellemont, 'harmonising for the sake of harmonising should be avoided'. And, rephrasing Michael Faure, it seems clear that to resort to a static, rigid 'bible' of environmental law would entail more economic, legal and political caveats than benefits. While an EU environmental code would possibly reduce transaction costs by streamlining the existing complex body of EU legislation, it would not lead beyond the current state of harmonisation of EU policies. Therefore, a more comprehensive and more effective EU regime is advocated instead. Such a regime should flip the current one, whereby the EU's body of environmental law provides a minimum level of protection and Member States ought to do the rest by adopting stricter measures. It is acknowledged that when Member States' actions dare to go beyond the EU's environmental standards (albeit based on an accurate cost-benefit analysis), this has mutually improved both Member States' and the EU's environmental legislation.[3] However, this is not happening at the scale or pace required by the urgency of the environmental and climate threats faced by the EU. In other words, the EU should aim for strengthening the level of protection and reducing the leeway for Member States, instead of relying on Member States' goodwill to step up action locally. Of course, proportionality, subsidiarity, sincere cooperation and solidarity should go hand-in-hand when developing EU environmental and energy law – because, as noted by Nicolas de Sadeleer, 'the gap between the rules and the problems which the law is supposed to regulate has never been so marked'.

Against this context, the European Green Deal launched by the European Commission in 2019 signals a remarkable paradigm shift. The very underlying concept of mainstreaming sustainability in EU policies and overcoming silo-thinking towards integrated and binding long-term targets (net-zero emissions and net-zero pollution by 2050) strengthens the role of sustainable development across all EU policies, and of course primarily on EU environmental and energy policies. As such, the European Green Deal concomitantly recognises the urgency for a strong and more coordinated action across Member States and champions the principle of integration as a steppingstone to strengthen the EU's action on the protection of the environment and the fight against climate change. As Ludwig Krämer noted recently elsewhere, whether to such far-reaching aims will correspond a feasible and concrete action on the ground has yet to be seen.[4] Yet it is doubtless that the change sparked by the European Green Deal will mark a point of no return in the EU's approach to sustainability in its future action.

2. MATERIAL SCOPE OF HARMONISATION

The second main aspect unfolding in the contributions relates to the actual degree to which harmonisation should be pursued. The EU's environmental and energy law still entail major blind spots stemming from poor coordination across different policies or utter lacunae of regulation. In particular, different authors have analysed such blind spots in the fields of soil protection; animal welfare and natural species protection; civil liability for environmental damage; support to renewable energy generation; and breakthrough low-carbon technologies.

3 *Squintani*, supra n 2, at p. 202.
4 *L. Krämer*, Planning for Climate and the Environment: The EU Green Deal, JEEPL 2020 (17), pp. 267, 268.

These pitfalls are well known to the EU legislature, as well. Hence, unsurprisingly, most of the issues addressed in the book constitute what – at the time of the harmonisation conference – could barely be conjectured as the future conceptual and material setup of the European Green Deal. For example, the issue of soil and wildlife protection has been strongly embedded in both the EU Biodiversity Strategy to 2030 and the EU Farm-to-Fork strategy, thus filling the loopholes existing among existing EU environmental and agricultural policies. An updated EU Soil Thematic Strategy and a Zero Pollution Action Plan for air, water and soil are expected to be put forward by the European Commission in 2021, which should set the stage for a more comprehensive approach to environmental pressures and foster further coordination among existing legislation. Moreover, the 2020 EU Hydrogen Strategy has been adopted in order to devise an EU framework specifically devoted to hydrogen networks, with a view to demarcating them from gas networks, as recommended in Daniel Benrath's contribution. Progress at the EU level is more difficult to expect on the more complex issue, analysed by Georgios Kalogerakis, of recognising a generally established duty of care to protect the environment. Yet a clear path of convergence can be seen at the Member State level, in particular with regard to the importance given to the European Convention of Human Rights (Articles 2 and 8) in establishing liability of public authorities for their action vis-à-vis their citizens. Civil law could thus indeed serve as a tried-and-tested tool to achieve implementation of EU law and deserves further attention by environmental lawyers. Lastly, it is clear that the European Commission is pursuing enhanced governance mechanisms for harmonisation in the fields of renewable energy generation, energy security and justice, as advocated by Theodoros Iliopoulos and Susann Handke. The system established under the EU Energy Union Governance Regulation, operating through integrated national climate and energy plans, provides for an innovative system of checks and balances that should result in a stronger oversight and control by the same European Commission over Member States' actions.

3. TO HARMONISE OR NOT TO HARMONISE?

Thirdly, and perhaps more importantly, is the issue of the case for a stronger degree of harmonisation of environmental and energy law in the first place. In general terms, the responses provided by each legal system are based on an underlying normative assumption about what a good environment would look like, as informed by historical, natural, cultural and political conditions. These conditions inherently vary widely among countries. In other words, the decisions about and approaches towards environmental and energy issues normatively reflect people's thinking about how they want to shape the environment in which they live (and in which they will live) in the future. While a major obstacle to ensuring proper harmonisation in the EU lies in the excessive leeway left to the Member States, one has to bear in mind that the EU consists of a tangled heap of (now) 27 legal traditions. As outlined by Valentina Jacometti with regard to the key definition of EU Emission Allowances under the EU Emission Trading System, this reflects on the continuous endeavour to reach compromise, in order to ensure a minimum harmonisation, whereby the very terms and definitions ultimately enshrine different political tensions and – often – legal cultures.

Furthermore, this book underscores how EU environmental and energy law can hardly achieve their objectives without effective regimes in place to achieve full functioning on the ground. Harmonisation, therefore, does not only entail rule-shaping and approximation of laws, but also administrative and judicial implementation and enforcement. As expressly mentioned by Michael Faure and repeatedly stressed throughout this book, however, very little knowledge is available on the action taken by EU Member States when it comes to implementing and enforcing the EU's *acquis* on the ground. One might therefore agree with Ludwig Krämer's view that as far as public participation, access to justice and access to information – as well as reporting requirements – are concerned, a strong case for EU-driven, top-down harmonisation should be pursued. The European Commission can hardly be operating as the one and only watchdog over each Member State's conduct against the thriving proliferation of EU environmental and energy legislation. The very limited effectiveness of the same European Commission's infringement procedures in the field of air quality is striking evidence in this regard. In addition, the enforcement setup in the EU is undermined by a general lack of accountability and transparency, as denoted by Costanza Di Francesco Maesa. And, as pointed out by Allison Hough, the current system falls short of ensuring access to justice against decisions taken by EU institutions in line with the UNECE Aarhus Convention. This is a 'legitimacy wound' that the EU should take into due consideration and try to fix if it is indeed to purport an inclusive, widespread system of enforcement of its legislation locally. Against this context, a prominent institutional solution could be to attribute extensive implementation and enforcement powers to an EU agency. The thought in this connection goes straight to the US context, where from the outset of the enactment of federal pivotal environmental statutes (such as the Clean Air Act and the Clean Water Act), the EPA has played a prominent role in terms of standard-setting, monitoring and enforcement. By contrast, EU agencies (such as the European Environmental Agency) are generally operating as a scientific component of the majestic technical apparatus supporting the European Commission's law-making process. The establishment of an independent EU body with no legislative powers, yet operating void of any political and institutional influence and embodying coercive and enforceable powers with regard to the full implementation of EU law, could constitute the missing link in the current multi-level EU governance scheme which has been established on paper, albeit not fully functioning in practice.

The critical analysis above reveals how, while striving to pursue harmonisation as an endeavour towards approximation among 27 domestic legal regimes, EU law is facing compelling problems of juxtapositions, poor coordination and, ultimately, implementation. In fact, the capability of the EU to deliver an adequate response in terms of redistribution of environmental impacts and uptake of action at the domestic level is relatively small. Member States in the EU are still allowed to externalise environmental harm to other Member States, thus ultimately undermining both European citizens' health and the integrity of the European environment. Such a system, as stressed here by Michael Faure, would be neither desirable, nor tolerable.

In fact, a seminal 2018 report of the European Environmental Agency shows a pattern of inequality, with discrimination targeting specific social and economic groups – namely, persons with lower socio-economic status, especially in urban areas – and geographical areas, such as eastern and south-western Member States.[5]

What therefore seems to be the missing piece in the current EU approach to environmental and energy issues is an adequate set of mechanisms, in order to avoid the (concrete) risk that efforts made by the most ambitious Member States would easily be frustrated by passivity of the others. In this regard, the stances taken by the Court of Justice of the EU's General Court in *Poland v. Commission* and Advocate General Campos Sánchez-Bordona in *Germany v. Poland* with regard to the spirit and principle of solidarity on energy matters (art. 80 and 194 TFEU) are thought-provoking in terms of the need to address transboundary externalities and avoid a race to the bottom among Member States. Both the General Court and the AG have recognised that 'the principle of solidarity entails rights and obligations both for the European Union and for the Member States'.[6] These rights and obligations should operate among Member States, institutions, peoples and generations; between Member States and third countries; and among the European Union and its Member States.[7] Importantly, such an obligation should also bind Member States with regard to the common interest of the European Union and the policies it pursues.[8] If eventually upheld

5 *European Environmental Agency*, Unequal exposure and unequal impacts: social vulnerability to air pollution, noise and extreme temperatures in Europe, EEA Report no. 22/2018, 2018.

6 Opinion of Advocate General Campos Sanchez Bordona in Case C-848/19 P Germany v. Poland [2021] ECLI:EU:C:2021:218, para. 95.

7 Opinion of Advocate General Campos Sanchez Bordona (supra note 6), para. 60.

8 Case T-883/16 Poland v. European Commission [2019] ECLI:EU:T:2019:567, para. 70. With specific regard to the energy policy of the European Union, that policy requires the European Union and the Member States to endeavour, in the exercise of their powers in the field of energy policy, to avoid adopting measures liable to affect the interests of the European Union and the other Member States, as regards security of supply, its economic and political viability, the diversification of supply or of sources of supply, and to do so in order to take account of their interdependence and de facto solidarity (Ibid. para. 73).

by the CJEU, such a dimension of solidarity as a legal principle entailing binding force upon Member States and between Member States and the European Commission could provide a meaningful tool for institutional stewardship among a more coherent application of EU energy policies.

Therefore, arguably, the most promising response to the staggering gap between the deterioration of our only common home and the ambitious legal response to this predicament is not more harmonised EU law, but more EU.

INDEX

ABOUT THE EDITORS

Bernard Vanheusden is Professor of Environmental and Energy Law at Hasselt University. In 2020, he was elected as Rector of Hasselt University. He is Associate Editor of the Journal for European Environmental & Planning Law (JEEPL) and a member of the World Commission on Environmental Law (WCEL) of the International Union for Conservation of Nature (IUCN).

Theodoros Iliopoulos is a postdoctoral researcher in energy and environmental law at Hasselt University. He is also a lawyer (Athens Bar Association) and he has previously worked as a graduate teaching assistant at the National and Kapodistrian University of Athens. He received the GCET21 'Young Researcher' Award for 2020.

Anna Vanhellemont is a doctoral researcher in environmental law at Hasselt University. Her main research topics are harmonisation and codification of EU environmental law.

www.ingramcontent.com/pod-product-compliance
Ingram Content Group UK Ltd.
Pitfield, Milton Keynes, MK11 3LW, UK
UKHW051921100926
8556IPUK00021B/1297